Understanding Public Opinion

Understanding Public Opinion

Second Edition

Edited by

Barbara Norrander
University of Arizona

Clyde Wilcox
Georgetown University

CQ PRESS

A Division of Congressional Quarterly Inc.
Washington, D.C.

CQ Press
A Division of Congressional Quarterly Inc.
1255 22nd Street, N.W., Suite 400
Washington, D.C. 20037

(202) 822-1475; (800) 638-1710

www.cqpress.com

♾ The paper used in this publication meets the minimum requirements of the American National Standard for Information Sciences—Permanence of Paper for Printed Library Materials, ANSI Z39.48-1992.

Printed and bound in the United States of America

05 04 03 02 01   5 4 3 2 1

Typeset and designed by G&S Typesetters, Austin, Texas.
Cover designed by Gary Gore

Library of Congress Cataloging-in-Publication Data

(*in process*)

ISBN: 1–56802–625–0

Contents

Tables and Figures

FIGURES

Contributors

Alan I. Abramowitz is Alben W. Barkley Professor of Political Science at Emory University. His articles on elections, public opinion, and voting behavior in the United States have been published in the *American Political Science Review, American Journal of Political Science, Journal of Politics,* and other scholarly journals. His most recent book, *Senate Elections,* was cowritten with Jeffrey Segal.

Henry E. Brady is professor of political science and public policy at the University of California, Berkeley, where he is also director of the Survey Research Center. He has written on elections in Canada, the United States, and Eastern Europe; political participation in the United States, Estonia, and Russia; and statistical methods and political methodology. He is the co-author of *Letting the People Decide: Dynamics of a Canadian Election* and *Voice and Equality: Civic Voluntarism in American Politics.*

Paul R. Brewer is assistant professor of political science at George Washington University. He has written on public opinion, political psychology, and the mass media. His most recent research appears in *Political Psychology* and *Press/Politics.*

Allison Calhoun-Brown is associate professor of political science at Georgia State University. Her research interests include public opinion, religion and politics, and African American politics. Her research appears in scholarly journals including the *Journal of Politics, American Politics Quarterly,* and *Journal for the Scientific Study of Religion.*

Edward G. Carmines is Rudy Professor and Warner O. Chapman Professor of Political Science at Indiana University at Bloomington. His research, which focuses on American politics, political behavior, and public opinion, has been published in a variety of journals including the *American Political Science Review, American Journal of Political Science,* and *Journal of Politics.* His most recent book is *Reaching Beyond Race,* cowritten with Paul Sniderman.

Laurel Elms is a doctoral candidate in political science at the University of California, Berkeley. Her dissertation focuses on measuring and explaining short-term changes in public opinion.

F. Chris Garcia is professor of political science at the University of New Mexico. He has taught and written extensively in the areas of Latino politics, public opinion, campaigns and elections, and political socialization. He is the coauthor of *Latino Voices: Mexican, Puerto Rican and Cuban Perspectives on American Politics* and editor of *Pursuing Power: Latinos and the Political System.*

John R. Hibbing is Foundation Regents Professor of Political Science at the University of Nebraska-Lincoln, where he specializes in Congress and American public opinion. His book *Congress as Public Enemy,* cowritten with Elizabeth Theiss-Morse, received the American Political Science Association's Fenno Prize in 1996. He and Theiss-Morse have recently completed *Stealth Democracy: Americans' Beliefs about How Government Should Work.* His current research interests revolve around experimental studies of retributive behavior.

Shanto Iyengar is professor of political science and communication at Stanford University. His research focuses on political campaigns. His recent books include *Going Negative: How Political Advertisements Shrink and Polarize the Electorate, Do the Media Govern?,* and *Explorations in Political Psychology.*

William G. Jacoby is a professor in the department of government and international studies at the University of South Carolina. He is currently the editor of the *Journal of Politics.* His areas of specialization include mass political behavior and quantitative methodology.

Kathleen M. McGraw is professor of political science at Ohio State University. Her research focuses on political judgment and cognitive processes, accountability, and the implications of the interplay between elites and the mass public for understanding the dynamics of public opinion. She has published widely in political science and psychology journals.

William Mishler is professor and head of the department of political science at the University of Arizona. A specialist in democratic theory, he has written extensively on public opinion, political representation, and the dynamics of popular support for democratic parties, leaders, and regimes. His most recent book is *Democracy and Its Alternatives: Understanding Post-Communist Societies,* cowritten with Richard Rose and Christian Haerpfer.

John Mueller is professor of political science and Woody Hayes Chair of National Security Studies, Mershon Center, at Ohio State University. Among his books are *Capitalism, Democ-*

racy, and *Ralph's Pretty Good Grocery; Policy and Opinion in the Gulf War; Retreat from Doomsday: The Obsolescence of Major War;* and *War, Presidents and Public Opinion.*

Barbara Norrander is professor of political science at the University of Arizona. Her research, which focuses on presidential nomination politics, gender politics, and state public opinion, is published in the *American Journal of Political Science, Journal of Politics,* and *Public Opinion Quarterly.* She is the coauthor, with Michael Corbett, of *American Government: Using MicroCase ExplorIt,* seventh edition.

Markus Prior is a doctoral candidate in the department of communication at Stanford University. His dissertation examines the impact of changes in the media environment on levels and distribution of political knowledge and participation.

Wendy M. Rahn is associate professor in the department of political science and adjunct associate professor of psychology at the University of Minnesota. She serves on the Board of Overseers of the National Election Studies and is coeditor of *Political Psychology,* the official scientific journal for the International Society of Political Psychology. Her research interests include the role of emotions in political thinking and behavior, citizen participation in politics, the origins and consequences of political and social trust, and American national identity. Her articles appear in such publications as the *American Political Science Review, American Journal of Political Science, Public Opinion Quarterly,* and *Political Communication.*

Richard Rose is director of the Centre for the Study of Public Policy at the University of Strathclyde in Glasgow, Scotland. He is the author or editor of more than thirty books in comparative politics and public policy, most recently *The International Encyclopedia of Elections* and *Democracy and Its Alternatives: Understanding Post-Communist Societies.* Rose has given seminars and lectures in more than three dozen countries, and his writings have been published in seventeen languages.

Thomas J. Rudolph is assistant professor of political science at the University of Illinois. His research focuses on public opinion, political psychology, and campaign finance. His work has been published in the *Journal of Politics, Public Opinion Quarterly, Social Science Quarterly,* and several edited volumes.

Virginia Sapiro is the Sophonisba P. Breckinridge Professor of Political Science and Women's Studies at the University of Wisconsin-Madison. She is former principal investigator of the American National Elections Studies. She has written widely in the areas of political psychology, political behavior, and gender politics. Among her books are *Women in American Society: An Introduction to Women's Studies,* fourth edition; *A Vindication of Political Virtue: The Political Theory of Mary Wollstonecraft;* and *The Political Integration of Women: Roles, Socialization, and Politics.*

Kyle L. Saunders is assistant professor of political science at Northern Illinois University. His research interests include public opinion, voting behavior and elections, and political parties. Currently, he is writing a book with Alan I. Abramowitz on voting behavior and elections. He and Abramowitz recently published their research on ideological realignment in the *Journal of Politics.*

Kay Lehman Schlozman is professor of political science at Boston College, where she teaches and writes about various aspects of citizen politics in America. She is the coauthor, most recently, of *Voice and Equality* and *The Private Roots of Public Action.*

Paul M. Sniderman is professor of political science at Stanford University. A fellow of the American Academy of Arts and Sciences, he is the author, along with Periangelo Peri, Rui de Figueiredo, and Thomas Piazza, of *The Outsider,* among many other books.

Carole Jean Uhlaner is associate professor of political science at the University of California, Irvine. Much of her research focuses on political participation, partisan choice, and ethnic politics in the United States, especially Latino politics. Her research is published in the *American Journal of Political Science, Political Behavior, Public Choice,* and *Journal of Politics.*

Sidney Verba is professor of government at Harvard University. He has written a number of books on comparative and American politics and many on issues of citizen participation. He is the coauthor of two recent books on the subject: *Voice and Equality* and *The Private Roots of Public Action.*

Clyde Wilcox is professor of government at Georgetown University. He has written extensively on religion and politics, gender politics, and campaign finance. His most recent books include *Onward Christian Soldiers: The Christian Right in American Politics,* second edition; *Campaigns and Elections: Contemporary Case Studies;* and *Religion and Politics in Comparative Perspective: The One, the Few, and the Many.*

Preface

Having taught courses in public opinion and political behavior for many years, we have become increasingly frustrated by the difficulty of introducing students to real political science research. Most journal articles on public opinion contain statistical analyses that are far too complex for undergraduates—and often for beginning graduate students. Textbooks generally summarize the results of research but fail to show students anything about the process by which the results were obtained. Clearly, a need existed for a book that would expose students to the substance of public opinion and include a bit of the process of that research.

We designed this collection of essays to meet that need. After developing a broad outline of the main topics covered in courses in public opinion and political behavior, we selected specific topics in these areas on which there has been ongoing, interesting research. We approached scholars who had conducted some of that research and asked them to contribute an original research essay to this collection. Each author was asked to meet three requirements. First, the chapter should be both comprehensible and interesting to upper-division undergraduates yet rich enough to sustain the attention of graduate students. Second, the chapter should pose an interesting question or questions about American public opinion and use appropriate data to find answers. Third, the chapter should shed light on public opinion as the twentieth century ended and the twenty-first century began.

The book that emerged has met our goals, and we have each of the contributors to thank for this. Teachers of courses in public opinion and political behavior at both the undergraduate and graduate levels will find this text helpful as they present topics and approaches in the field. With these essays instructors can show how scholars approach a question, what their research looks like, and how their conclusions are derived. In addition to students enrolled in political science courses, those studying journalism, sociology, and communications will find much of interest in this book.

The second edition of *Understanding Public Opinion* contains fifteen new essays written by twenty-five leading scholars. This edition is organized into five parts. The first considers some key factors that influence individuals' opinions—gender, ethnicity, the intersection between race and religion, and the media. The second part explores the content of public opinion on racial, social, and foreign policy issues. How opinion is organized through core values and partisanship is the third section of the book. The roles of public opinion in elections and political participation are examined in the fourth part. The final part addresses questions of public trust and attempts by the political elite to mold public opinion.

Many of the authors relied on familiar national surveys such as the National Election Studies and the General Social Survey. Both data sources are available to the academic community through the Inter-University Consortium for Political and Social Research. Polls of specialized groups, polls originally conducted for the media, and cross-national surveys also are used in these chapters. Finally, some authors have collected data from experiments and focus groups.

We thank the people who helped us through the process of putting this book together. At CQ Press, Michelle Tupper was closely involved throughout the project. She helped us develop our outline, read the chapters, made helpful suggestions, and helped coordinate the project. Brenda Carter offered guidance on the second edition, as she had done for the first. Nola Healy Lynch was our copy editor, and Ann O'Malley shepherded the book through the various stages of production.

Understanding Public Opinion

Introduction:
The Diverse Paths to Understanding Public Opinion

Clyde Wilcox and Barbara Norrander

If you are reading this sentence in the daytime or early evening, it is likely that somewhere in the United States a small group of citizens is sitting around a table sharing their political opinions with focus group moderators. If you are reading this at night, it is likely that various political polls are being conducted—polls commissioned by candidates to assess their popularity and understand how they might win the election, polls commissioned by newspapers or television stations to gauge public sentiments on some topic in the news, and polls conducted for interest groups to help them understand how to attract and keep members or how to frame a particular political issue to their best advantage. It is also likely that an academic survey is being administered in the field, and it is possible that a scholar is conducting a long, in-depth interview with a citizen or an activist.

In many cases, the data gathered from these studies will be made available to the academic community—to scholars and students who want to understand the causes and consequences of public opinion. In fact, as you are reading this sentence, it is likely that several political scientists, sociologists, psychologists, and students are performing statistical analyses on surveys and polls that others have previously collected. More academics, journalists, and political professionals are engaged in the study of public opinion now than ever before.

Approaches to Public Opinion

Scholars, journalists, and pollsters do not all agree on how we should study public opinion. Professional associations such as the American Association for Public Opinion Research allow professional pollsters, journalists, and academics an opportunity to meet and share their views; such organizations also publish journals to help those in the field air their differences and improve their techniques. Perhaps more important, those who study public opinion do not agree on what questions are interesting, what theories and approaches are best, what methods are the most appropriate, or even what the nature of public opinion is. The increase of academic, journalistic, and political interest in public opinion has led to a flowering of diversity in the field.

Consider, for example, the question of equal treatment of and opportunity for all citizens. This is an important political and social issue that public opinion scholars approach from a variety of perspectives. Some researchers look at egalitarianism as a core value which can structure opinions toward more specific issues. In their studies, survey respondents are asked whether they agree with statements such as those used by the National Election Study in its 1996 survey: "Our society should do whatever is necessary to make sure that everyone has an equal opportunity to succeed," and "It is not really that big a problem if some people have more of a chance in life than others." Some scholars are concerned with validating the existence of such a core value as egalitarianism (Feldman 1988), while others examine the conflict between egalitarianism and other core values such as individualism (Alvarez and Brehm 1997; Kinder and Sanders 1996).

Other researchers look at more specific issues linked to equality, such as attitudes toward the civil rights of minorities and women. Within this vein of research, some scholars look at changing attitudes toward racial issues over time (Schuman et al. 1997). While only one-third of Americans supported school desegregation in the 1940s, more than 90 percent of Americans in the 1990s believed that blacks and whites should attend the same schools. Today Americans hold complex attitudes on racial equality. For example, white Americans favor desegregation but oppose affirmative action programs.

Various research techniques are used to explore attitudes toward equality. Many scholars investigate the vast number of survey questions asked about equality and racial issues by both scholarly and commercial polls (for instance, Gallup). Others have used new technology to investigate how changes in questions or question wording affect the public's perception of equality (Kinder and Sanders 1990, 1996; Kuklinski et al. 1997). Using CATI (computer aided telephone interviewing), researchers can easily ask random subsamples of respondents different questions. Still other researchers (Hochschild 1981) have conducted extended interviews with a smaller number of people to uncover the complexity of thinking that underlies an individual's evaluations of issues involving equality.

Public opinion is therefore a field characterized by diversity: diversity of concepts and theories, diversity of questions, and diversity of methods. In this book we have sought to capture some of this diversity while adopting a common focus on the changing sources, content, and implications of public opinion.

The first part of the book investigates many of the important sources of public opinion—both individual traits (sex, ethnicity) and the influence of various institutions (churches, the media). The second part explores the content of opinion on racial, social, and international issues. The third part discusses the broad political dispositions that help structure political attitudes and cognition, and the fourth investigates the way attitudes influence political behavior. The final part examines public opinion about local and national governments in the United States and public opinion toward government in the emerging democracies of Eastern Europe and the former Soviet Union.

Diversity of Conceptions and Theories

In political science, the central concept of most public opinion research remains the attitude. There are countless definitions of attitudes, each emphasizing different characteristics. In 1935, Gordon Allport reviewed many different definitions, then suggested that an attitude is "a mental or neural state of readiness, organized through experience, exerting a directive or dynamic influence upon the individual's response to all objects and situations with which it is related" (p. 810). Some forty years later, Martin Fishbein and Icek Ajzen suggested that a consensus had been reached that an attitude is "a learned predisposition to respond in a consistently favorable or unfavorable manner with regard to a given object" (1975, 6). Although the two definitions differ in defining attitudes as mental states or response tendencies, respectively, they both emphasize consistent responses to objects. Moreover, Allport (1935) stated that attitudes are learned. Thus, theorists agree that attitudes are learned and involve consistent responses to objects and situations.

Attitudes have three main components: a cognitive element that links the object to information, an affective element that links the object to an evaluation or emotional reaction, and a conative element, that is, an element that may link the object to actual behavior. Consider, for example, one hypothetical attitude toward President George W. Bush's tax-cut proposal in 2001. A cognitive element of an attitude toward the tax cut might be the perception that "the largest tax cuts will go to the wealthy." This belief may or may not be an accurate reflection of the effect of Bush's tax cut, but it reflects what an individual believes to be true and is therefore a cognitive aspect of public opinion. An affective element would be the feeling behind the statement, "I'm angry that the tax cut benefits the rich." A conative element would be the behavioral intention, "I will write my senator urging her to oppose the tax cut."

Not all attitudes have such consistent elements. A citizen's cognitive element might be a belief that the tax cut will be fairly distributed across all Americans, yet his affective response may be fear that the loss of revenue could jeopardize needed government programs for the disadvantaged. Attitude researchers have frequently explored such conflicting attitude elements, but they have reached no consensus on precisely how the three attitude elements affect one another.

Perhaps more important, no consensus exists on just how attitudes relate to other concepts, such as values, beliefs, opinions, habits, and identifications (that is, aspects of personal identity). Most political scientists would consider values to be a more general concept, linking many related attitudes (for instance, equality values involve attitudes on gender, race, sexual preference, and disability), and that beliefs and opinions are specific cognitive elements of attitudes (for instance, opinions on equal pay for equal work). Yet the meaning of these terms and the relations between them remain imprecise, primarily because these are words from our ordinary language and therefore carry many meanings. The chapters of this book contain various combinations of these terms, and their usages are typical of the way public opinion scholars use the terms today.

There is no single attitude theory; rather, there are many different theories (Fishbein and Ajzen 1975). Some theories focus on how attitudes are learned, others on how various attitudes relate to one another, still others on how attitudes influence behavior. Probably the most frequently used attitude theory in political science has been cognitive dissonance theory. Leon Festinger theorized that inconsistent attitudes or beliefs should cause some psychological discomfort and thus "motivate the person to try to reduce the dissonance and achieve consonance" (1957, 3). Much as dissonant chords in music evoke in the listener a "need for resolution into a consonant interval" (Piston 1978, 6), so should inconsistent beliefs evoke in the citizen a desire to resolve the dissonance.

This formulation of cognitive dissonance suggests that people are aware when their beliefs appear contradictory and then seek to resolve the problem. Yet research has shown that Americans often hold inconsistent beliefs. Doris Graber (1984) reports that many respondents in her experimental study of information processing did not perceive the inconsistencies in the attitudes they were expressing. Jennifer Hochschild (1981) finds that the men and women whom she interviewed at length about their attitudes toward equality held conflicting, ambivalent feelings stemming from commitment to opposing values. Many were well aware of the contradictions among their values and beliefs, and some were bitter about their inability to resolve the inconsistencies. John Zaller summarizes the results of a great deal of scholarly research when he writes that "most people are relatively uncritical of the ideas they internalize. . . . they fill up their minds with large stores of only partially consistent ideas, arguments, and considerations" (1992, 119).

Recent research, in an attempt to account for seemingly contradictory opinions among the American public, often focuses on the way political information is transmitted or survey questions are asked. Issue framing by the media and by politicians and question framing by pollsters alter people's perception of political issues. Framing is defined as "the process by which a communication source constructs and defines a social or political issue for its audience" (Nelson, Oxley, and Clawson 1997, 221). Every individual holds a variety of beliefs which can be called upon in influencing a stated opinion on a specific issue. If the issue of welfare is framed as helping poor people, especially poor children in a time of need, public support for welfare is higher. If welfare is framed as providing government benefits to those unwilling to work, public support declines. The framing of the welfare issue leads the public to focus either on sympathy for those in need or tenets of individualism that stress individual responsibility. Frames provide the public with "stories" through which to interpret political issues.

While some researchers focus on framing effects, others investigate the related concept of priming. With priming, events or the content of media stories lead people to focus on certain aspects when evaluating a candidate or issue (Iyengar and Kinder 1987; Krosnick and Kinder 1990). Priming brings to the top of one's head certain pieces of information that then shape one's opinion on a specific issue. In a classic example, the extensive coverage of the Gulf War in 1991 affected how the American public evaluated President George Bush on his foreign policy expertise: his overall approval ratings soared to 90 percent. A few months later, as a slow economy became the focus of much attention, Bush's approval ratings dropped because the public had been primed to evaluate the president on his economic performance. Some disagreement exists within the field of public opinion on the distinctions between framing and priming. Some authors argue that one is a form of the other, while others assert a theoretical and empirical difference between the two (Nelson and Oxley 1999). Nevertheless, the two concepts are similar in suggesting that the beliefs the public brings to the evaluation of a specific issue are a consequence in part of recent events, media coverage, and politicians' statements.

Politicians attempt to frame public events to their advantage. After each presidential debate, each candidate's supporters place their own spin on the outcome. The news media also are frequently studied for the way they frame issues. Whether the media cover racial issues as questions of egalitarianism or individualism may make the public appear liberal or conservative on questions such as civil rights and government aid to minorities (Kellstedt 2000). The manner in which the media cover issues also may lessen the American public's ability to understand the complexities of political issues. The tendency of television news to discuss political issues as isolated events—one person being homeless or another being a crime victim—rather than as broader societal questions of poverty and crime rates, hampers viewers' ability to understand the complex relationships between economic conditions, government actions, and societal outcomes (Iyengar 1991). In addition, the media may contribute to low levels of political knowledge by using frames that the public finds confusing, irrelevant, or boring (Graber 1994).

In survey settings, question wording, question ordering, and recent political events can alter the answers given by respondents. Because people process a number of beliefs and attitudes in responding to survey questions (Zaller and Feldman 1992), any factor that highlights one belief more than another will shape respondents' answers. Yet in a different setting or time period, respondents may give different answers to the same survey question, as events or media frames focus attention on a different belief. Inconsistency between answers about similar or related government programs also may arise from the way survey questions are framed. The apparent inconsistency between high public support for most budget items and more conservative responses to questions about desired levels of government services arises as the former leads respondents to focus on the beneficiaries of such programs, such as the poor, while the latter links individuals' responses to their more generalized evaluations of the government (Jacoby 2000).

Diversity of Questions

Analysts who study public opinion seek to answer many kinds of questions, as the following chapters demonstrate. First, scholars ask where attitudes and opinions come from. One way to investigate the sources of opinion is to see just how attitudes differ among demographic groups. The differences in men's and women's attitudes, generally called the gender gap, have been the source of a great deal of research (Andersen 1997; Cook and Wilcox 1991; Norrander 1999; Shapiro and Mahajan 1986). Studies have not only investigated the differences in the attitudes of men and women, but have also explored differences in how men and women reason about politics (Gilligan 1982). Most political scientists assume that gender differences in attitudes arise out of different life circumstances, even between men and women from similar backgrounds. From birth, parents, friends, and strangers respond differently to boys and girls, and children quickly learn the roles they are expected to play. Some scholars, however, have argued that essential differences between men and women lead them to different positions on some kinds of issues (Ruddick 1980). In Chapter 1, Virginia Sapiro analyzes how the influences of gender on public opinion might be understood in three ways: (1) aggregate differences between men and women, which form gender gaps in partisanship, voting, and issue positions; (2) the influence of gender identities; and (3) public issues that have a gender basis to them, whether they are overtly gender issues such as women's rights or less obviously gender issues but involve government programs used more frequently by women than by men.

Most Americans learn about politics directly from television and newspapers and indirectly by talking to others who have learned from those sources. Controversy exists on precisely how much influence the media have on public thinking, but the general consensus is that the media can increase the salience of issues in the public mind and "prime" citizens to focus on certain aspects of public problems (Zaller 1992). Yet not all citizens are equally influenced by mass media—some resist media news accounts, while others have too little information to fully process news stories (Graber 1984). Nevertheless, the media are the main outlets through which politicians speak to the American public. During campaigns, the public learns about candidates from both media coverage and commercials produced by the candidates. Shanto Iyengar and Markus Prior in Chapter 2 ask whether the public transfers relatively negative opinions about candidate advertisements to product advertisements shown in the same commercial break.

Since the 1970s, scholars have examined closely the impact of race on public opinion. Racial differences in political attitudes and behavior are often large, and scholars have devoted considerable attention to explaining these differences. Blacks and whites disagree on a host of public opinion issues, from civil rights to social welfare policy (Tuch and Sigelman 1997).

Race and religion can intersect to influence public opinion. Religion may influence people's political attitudes by shaping their core values and influencing opinion on specific issues (Jelen 1997). Yet the influence may flow in both directions. Some individuals may have their political views influenced by habitually watching televangelists who stake out very conservative positions on social and other issues. Other people attend churches where the pastor preaches politics in the pulpit, distributes campaign materials in the church, and even endorses candidates. Still others interact frequently with members of their church and take cues from the most politically astute congregants (see Leege and Kellstedt 1993 for an extended discussion). Black churches have often played a central role in the civil rights movement. In Chapter 3, Allison Calhoun-Brown illustrates the continuing role churches have had in molding the political attitudes of African Americans.

As of the 2000 census, Latinos have been identified as the largest minority group in the United States, yet Latino public opinion has only recently been the focus of public opinion research. In Chapter 4, Carole Jean Uhlaner and F. Chris Garcia discuss some of the barriers to surveying Latino public opinion. They depict Latino public opinion on specific issues, such as bilingual education, and on more general attitudes, such as ideology and partisanship.

Another type of research asks about the content of public opinion. Some scholars have focused on the substance of opinion in a particular domain (Cook, Jelen, and Wilcox 1992; Jacoby 1997; Mueller 1994), while others have examined changes over time in the direction of opinion in a particular area. In this book we include chapters that focus on attitudes toward racial issues by Edward G. Carmines and Paul M. Sniderman, social issues (abortion and gay rights) by Clyde Wilcox and Barbara Norrander, and foreign policy issues by John Mueller.

A third set of questions frequently asked by scholars concerns the organization of public opinion. Although attitude theorists in the 1950s had focused on cognitive pressures that people might feel to make their opinions internally consistent, Phillip Converse in 1964 found little evidence of attitude consistency in the general public. Converse argued that as they adopted positions people might be constrained in two ways. First, they might reason deductively from an ideological position—for example, a libertarian should be constrained against adopting a position in favor of laws regulating sex acts, since they inhibit personal liberty. Second, they might adopt packages of ideas that have been assembled by elites or social groups—for example, fundamentalist Christians might oppose abortion and gay rights because their church teaches that the associated activities are sinful. Yet Converse found that the attitudes of most Americans were not constrained in these ways and that Americans in general understood little of the ideological language used in campaigns. Converse's findings sparked a raging debate about the sophistication of the American electorate that continues today (Knight and Erikson 1997).

Ideology may be more meaningful today than it was in the 1950s, but public opinion scholars also are searching for alternative beliefs and values that may structure and influence public opinion. Much recent scholarship focuses on core values—broader-based views on desired goals for the nation, rights and obligations of citizens, and functions of the government. Previously we mentioned that egalitarianism has been studied as a core value. William Jacoby in Chapter 8 explores the interrelationships and influences of four core values: economic security, social order, freedom, and equality.

While the ideological sophistication of the electorate was suspect, given early results such as those reported by Converse, partisanship was found to be a strong, stable attitude that shaped voting decisions and colored citizens' views of the political world by acting as a "perceptual screen" (Campbell et al. 1960). Yet beginning in the 1960s, levels of partisanship began to decline as more Americans called themselves political independents. Among those remaining attached to the two political parties, partisanship was less often linked to voting choices as split-ticket voting increased among the American electorate. Many scholars in the 1970s began to write about the decline in party identification. Yet predictions of the demise of partisanship may have been premature. Partisanship was slowly changing in the 1970s and 1980s, in large part as southern conservatives began to move away from their traditional support for the Democratic Party (a tradition that dated back to the Civil War). Southerners, and others across the nation, were adopting new partisan preferences that more closely matched their ideological preferences. In Chapter 9, Alan I. Abramowitz and Kyle L. Saunders show how this ideological realignment has affected congressional elections.

The most common area of investigation is the impact of opinions on electoral participation and vote choice. Scholars study the impact of political attitudes on vote choice and seek to determine the relative importance of attitudes toward parties, candidates, and issues. Other studies examine the impact of a particular issue such as abortion on vote choice (Abramowitz 1995, 1997; Cook, Jelen, and Wilcox 1995). Economic status and economic opinions are often linked to voting choices. Americans today do not vote as often as their predecessors did, and some scholars are concerned that participation in civic and social groups also has declined (Putman 2000). Henry E. Brady, Kay Lehman Schlozman, Sidney Verba, and Laurel Elms in Chapter 10, however, show that there has been consistency in the importance of socioeconomic status in determining who participates in American politics. In Chapter 11, Paul R. Brewer demonstrates the importance of economic evaluations in influencing voters' choices among presidential candidates.

Scholars are also often interested in the intersection between public opinion and government institutions. In a democracy we expect the government to respond to public opinion, but we also expect our elected officials to lead. In their role as leaders, government officials may try to shape public opinion. When President George W. Bush speaks on behalf of his tax-cut plan, he is trying to shape public opinion. When a member of Congress justifies a vote that was unpopular in the district by appealing to the needs of the nation as a whole, he or she is trying to influence public opinion. In Chapter 12, Kathleen M. McGraw delineates the ways in which government officials attempt to influence public opinion.

Wendy M. Rahn and Thomas J. Rudolph in Chapter 13 investigate public trust in local government, a level of government that is less often studied than the national level. Although the public is slightly more trusting of the local governments, considerable distrust also exists at that level. Furthermore, individuals' levels of trust in their local government are shaped not only by their own attitudes and traits but also by the characteristics of the local community. Americans' low level of trust in their government is often bemoaned. John R. Hibbing, in Chapter 14, carefully traces trends in public trust in America's national government and finds the source of increasing distrust to be the public's belief that politicians act more for the benefit of themselves and special interest groups that support them than for the benefit of the general public.

Public trust in government is not only a vital question for studying American democracy, it is an even more important question for the new democracies. The 1990s saw the collapse of Communist regimes in the Soviet Union and Eastern Europe. How has the public in these countries reacted to their new "democratizing" governments, especially in the face of major economic upheaval? William Mishler and Richard Rose ponder the question of political trust in countries transitioning to democratic governments in Chapter 15.

Diversity of Methods

With this diversity of conceptualizations, theories, and research questions, it should come as no surprise that there is a diversity of research methods as well. There is variety both in the kinds of data that are collected to answer research questions and in the statistical techniques that are used to manipulate those data. By far the most common source of public opinion data are polls and surveys. These two terms are often used interchangeably, although some scholars use *polls* to describe data gathered for candidates, newspapers, or political groups and *surveys* to describe longer interviews designed to test social science theories. In any event, a poll or survey consists of interviews from a sample of individuals who represent a larger population, designed to measure their preferences, opinions, attitudes, values, or behavior.

Methodologies

Types of Polls and Surveys

There are many kinds of polls and surveys. Academic surveys consist of long interviews designed to gather information to explain attitudes or behavior, often after the fact. For example, every two years the Survey Research Center at the University of Michigan conducts the National Election Study (NES), which includes a postelection interview with a sample of American citizens. These data are used by scholars to answer questions such as who voted and what kinds of voters supported each candidate. Scholars may write books or articles based on these surveys, sometimes many years after the election.

To help scholars answer their questions, academic surveys include many questions designed to measure concepts that can help explain attitudes and behavior. For example, NES surveys include a long battery of items on religion to help measure denomination, doctrine, practice, experience, and identity. Scholars have found that each of these aspects of religion is relevant in explaining political thinking and behavior (Leege and Kellstedt 1993). Over time the NES Board has experimented with questions to better measure feminism, group consciousness, feelings toward parties, and other concepts that have become important in theories of political thinking and behavior. Similarly, the General Social Survey (GSS) included a large set of special religion questions in 1989. The NES and GSS surveys are used in several of the chapters in this book.

Media polls, in contrast, generally seek more to report opinion than to explain it. Although leading national newspapers such as the *Washington Post* and the *New York Times* do feature detailed postelection analyses, a majority of the polls they conduct are used to describe opinion—how many Americans approve of the president's performance in office, whom does the American public blame for high prices and shortages of energy, or which government programs would the public like to see increased or decreased. Media polls usually do not include many questions that would help explain opinions—they may have a single religion question, for example, if they have any. However, the abundance of media polls means that such polls may more frequently survey specialized populations, such as the media surveys of Latino attitudes used by Carole Jean Uhlaner and F. Chris Garcia in Chapter 4. At other times, media polls may ask a wider variety of questions on a specific topic, such as the *Los Angeles Times* poll questions on abortion and gay rights used by Clyde Wilcox and Barbara Norrander in Chapter 6.

Strategic polls seek to help consultants achieve a goal—electing a candidate, enacting a policy, enabling a political group to grow, helping a company to better market its products more effectively. Strategic polls therefore may not seek to determine precisely why some individuals strongly oppose or favor a candidate, but they do focus extensively on how to convince uncommitted voters to support their candidate. Frequently a candidate's polls test potential arguments for or against the candidate and evaluate voters' assessments of the candidate's characteristics. Strategic polls are generally coordinated with a client's advertising campaigns to help determine whether particular ads are moving public opinion in the desired direction.

Finally, advocacy polls are surveys done to present a distorted picture of public opinion.

Scholars and survey research experts know that subtle changes in question wording can produce shifts in public opinion, and not-so-subtle changes can produce large shifts. For example, consider the following two possible survey questions:

1. Millionaire Steve Forbes has proposed a flat income tax that would result in rich Americans paying the same tax rate as those who work for wages. Do you support Forbes's plan?
2. Some Americans favor a flat tax, which would eliminate most deductions and tax all citizens at the same rate. Others support a progressive tax, in which those with higher incomes pay a higher rate. Which do you support?

The first question is obviously biased, for it provides cues that the person proposing the plan is himself rich and would benefit from the policy, and it contrasts rich Americans with those who work for wages. The second question provides two positions with no bias in favor of either and allows the respondent to choose. A few polling firms are willing to write questions to provide misleading results, but their reputation quickly suffers and few analysts take their results seriously.

In early 1996, Republican officials admitted that polls conducted by Frank Luntz and used by GOP leaders to document support for the Contract with America (the Republican platform used to win the 1994 congressional elections) were quite similar to advocacy polls. Luntz's questions did not directly measure support for the Republican contract but instead tested various arguments that might be used to increase support. For example, the survey asked respondents whether "we should stop excessive legal claims, frivolous lawsuits, and overzealous lawyers," and counted those who agreed as supporting the Republican plan for tort reform. Such obviously biasing words as *excessive, frivolous,* and *overzealous* created artificially high levels of agreement with the question, making responses worthless as a measure of genuine political support. Republican officials distanced themselves from the poll and privately complained that they had not been aware of the precise wording of the questions.

Types of Interviews

Those who conduct surveys can gather responses in three ways. First, they can send the interviewer into the respondent's home to ask questions in person. This technique has the advantage of allowing the interviewer to carry cue cards and visual materials. In addition, in-person interviews are generally of the highest quality because the interviewer and the respondent both work harder at the survey. But in-person interviews are expensive, for they involve increased training costs and salaries as well as extensive travel costs. Moreover, in-person interviews must be scheduled in advance, and it often takes several weeks to complete a survey that uses this technique. Some academic surveys continue to be conducted in person, because academics value the quality of the data and generally do not worry about speed. However, many researchers cannot afford the high costs of this method.

Phone surveys have the advantage of speed. A large company can interview several hundred respondents in an evening, providing a quick estimate of public opinion. For this reason, political campaigns rely heavily on phone polls, often performing a small number of interviews every night to track opinion change. Phone surveys present their own problems, however. Most important is the difficulty in reaching a truly random sample of citizens: not everyone has a phone; young people are often out in the evenings and difficult to reach by phone; busy professionals use answering machines or caller identification to screen their calls and do not pick up when interviewers call; and couples with young children are not available to answer political questions while their babies are crying.

Finally, mail surveys have the advantage of low cost—for the price of two first-class stamps (the second for the return envelope) you can send a survey to a respondent. Mail surveys are frequently used to obtain information from political elites such as campaign contributors and party activists (Brown, Powell, and Wilcox 1995; Rozell and Wilcox 1996). Yet mail surveys also have problems. Many Americans routinely throw away surveys instead of answering them, and typically half or more of those sampled never respond to a mail survey despite repeated mailings. Mail surveys are of course slow. Finally, there is no way to know whether the addressee actually filled out the survey—a spouse, child, nanny, or friend might have done so instead.

Although each of these techniques has limitations, polling experts have developed ways of minimizing the problems and increasing the reliability of the data. Today more surveys and polls are conducted than ever before. Political scientists have available a wealth of information on public opinion and behavior. The vast majority of public opinion studies in political science use survey data to test their hypotheses, and the chapters in this book rely heavily on survey research as well.

Nonsurvey Techniques

Although surveys are by far the most important source of data for scholars who study public opinion, there are many other techniques for measuring public opinion. Professional pollsters now conduct about as many focus groups as surveys for corporate and political clients. For a focus group a small number of individuals generally sit around a table, and a moderator directs the discussion. Because this small number of participants is not representative of the large American public, political scientists have until recently seldom used focus groups. But focus groups have the advantage of allowing citizens to talk about politics in their own words and to make and respond to arguments. At its best, focus group research allows scholars to see just how individuals express and defend their opinions and how they process opposing arguments (Conover, Crewe, and Searling 1991; Hibbing and Theiss-Morse 1995, 1997; Jelen and Wilcox 1995). In this book, John R. Hibbing (Chapter 13) combines focus groups and survey data to explore the public's trust in the national government.

Professional pollsters use other techniques that are less frequently used by academics, including electronic devices that allow individuals to register a continuous range of positive or negative evaluations at all times during political speeches or commercials. These pulse-meters enable public opinion specialists to determine who reacts positively to precisely what parts of a speech or advertisement. Some polling firms have equipment that enables them to determine precisely what portion of an advertisement the subject's eyes are focusing on when he or she responds, enabling the advertising firm to fine-tune the message.

Political scientists also occasionally use techniques, such as experiments or participant observation, that are not used by professional pollsters. Experiments allow more precise control of conditions, enabling researchers to pinpoint the exact source of a response. The chapters by McGraw and by Iyengar and Prior both use experiments to test the public's reactions to politicians' explanations and campaign commercials. Participant observation can allow scholars to observe the effects of social interaction in settings that may not be otherwise accessible, especially in small groups.

Finally, both scholars and public opinion professionals often rely on in-depth interviews to inform them of how individuals think about politics. These interviews, which may last several hours, help us better understand the worldview of particular groups of Americans. In one such study, Jennifer Hochschild interviewed a number of citizens with varying incomes and education about equality and justice (Hochschild 1981). In another, Kristin Luker interviewed activists in pro-life and pro-choice groups and compared their worldviews (Luker 1984). Both studies show the rich insights that can be gained from this technique. Public opinion professionals often use structured in-depth interviews to develop maps of values and opinions.

Statistical Manipulation of Data

When social scientists examine survey data, they use statistics as tools to better understand the content, sources, and consequences of attitudes. The appendix to this book is a primer in which we describe in greater detail some of the statistics used by the contributors. The appendix provides a brief overview of the kinds of statistics used and why we use them.

Some statistics are simple and descriptive: they might report what percentage of Americans believes that abortion should never be allowed, or what proportion rates Bush's job performance as excellent. Other simple descriptive statistics report a central tendency of public opinion. The *mean* is the arithmetic average of a variable: for example, we might find that our survey data give President Bush an average approval rating 5.5 on a 1–10 scale. The *median* is the middle score in a distribution; this statistic is often used when there are some extreme scores on a variable. For example, a very small number of Americans have very high incomes, so it is common to report median incomes rather than means.[1] The mode, which is the most frequent score, is often used in a general way to describe opinion. On most issues, opinion is unimodal, with the largest number of Americans in the moderate position. On a few issues, however, opinion may be bimodal, with roughly equal numbers of conservatives and liberals.

Although many of the chapters in this book report some of these simple descriptive statistics, social scientists are usually interested in understanding the relationship between two or more variables. For example, we might want to know just how closely related two seemingly similar opinions are—for example, support for gay rights and support for abortion rights. We usually measure the strength of that association with some kind of correlation coefficient. If most Americans who support gay rights also support abortion rights, and if most of those who oppose gay rights oppose legal abortion, then there will be a strong positive correlation between the two variables, and the value of the correlation coefficient will approach 1. If most Americans who support gay rights oppose abortion rights (a very unlikely result), then there will be a strong negative correlation, because high scores on one variable are associated with low scores on another. If there is no relationship between these two attitudes—if knowing someone's position on gay rights would tell us nothing about his or her position on abortion, then the correlation will be very close to 0. We can examine the correlations between several different opinions, and if they are all high we can build a scale to measure a more general attitude. For example, if there are high correlations between opinions on abortion, gay rights, school prayer, and the role of women in society, then we can build a scale to measure attitudes on these social and moral issues.

Usually we are interested in the relationships between more than one independent variable and a dependent variable that we think may be influenced by them. Consider, for example, the relationship between race and support for legal abortion. Most surveys in the 1980s reported that blacks were less likely to support legal abortion than whites. Yet we might suspect that it is not race that is the source of this difference but rather other characteristics that are associated with race. We know that blacks in America for a variety of reasons are less likely to complete college than whites, and we also know that blacks attend church more often and hold more conservative religious views. Both education and religion are associated with attitudes toward legal abortion. So we might ask whether blacks are less supportive of abortion because of their differences from whites in education and religion, or whether there are racial differences beyond those caused by these other factors.

To answer this question we *control* for education and religion, then examine the relationship between race and attitudes toward legal abortion. What we seek to do in this process is compare blacks and whites who are similar with regard to education and religion. For example, we compare whites and blacks with high school educations who attend church weekly, and we also compare separately whites and blacks with college degrees who attend church only occasionally. To make these comparisons physically would be quite cumbersome, for there are many possible combinations of religion and education. Moreover, we might suspect that other differences between blacks and whites might also affect this relationship—the average age of blacks is lower than that of whites, they are more likely to live in the South, more likely to live in urban areas, and so on. Thus the possible combinations of factors on which to compare is very large.

We can statistically hold constant a number of variables simultaneously, using techniques such as multiple regression, logistic regression, and probit. Many of the chapters in this book use these techniques to assess the independent impact of one variable on the dependent variable once all others are held constant. For example, we might include a variety of variables in an attempt to explain abortion attitudes: religion, region, race, age, sex, education, income, attitudes on women's roles, attitudes on the sanctity of life, attitudes on sexual morality, partisanship, and ideology. When we estimate these relationships using regression, we learn that blacks are actually more supportive of legal abortion than whites if all of these other factors are held constant. In other words, blacks are more liberal on abortion than whites who are similar in their socioeconomic characteristics and have similar attitudes. A closer look reveals that black women are far more liberal than white women on abortion and that black men are slightly more conservative than white men (Cook, Jelen, and Wilcox 1992).

This example illustrates the way in which statistical research can answer one question and raise others. If we looked only at the simple percentage of blacks and whites who favor legal abortion, we learn that blacks are less supportive than whites. Yet we can entirely explain that difference by racial differences in region, religion, education, and attitudes. Once we have estimated a complete statistical model, a new question emerges: Why are black women more liberal than white women who have similar demographic characteristics and attitudes, while black men are slightly more conservative than comparable white men?

The process of answering one question while raising another may sound a bit like Sisyphus rolling the stone up the mountain—there are always new questions to be answered and so the work of a public opinion scholar is never done. Yet for those who study public thinking, this process can be fun. Herbert Kritzer writes that if we could always answer our questions quickly and thoroughly, our task would be boring, but that instead it is fun because "data occasionally tell us things we did not know; they often confuse and confound us . . ." (1996, 26). James Stimson writes that the pleasures of analysis are "what sensible people experience when they read or watch detective thrillers" (1984, 76).

Although public opinion specialists try to apply scientific methods to their analysis, their work also involves creativity and can be thought of as part art and part science. C. Wright

Mills (1959) described a "sociological imagination" as the ability to connect broad trends in society, politics, and technology with individual biographies. There are many forms of imagination in public opinion scholarship, and the joy of public opinion research is the opportunity to investigate interesting questions, solve puzzles, and use that imagination. For most scholars, a puzzling result is like a mosquito bite—it has to be scratched, investigated, and thought about. Some of the anomalies we are left with can be explained with better theory, some can be resolved with better data, and some resist explanation for a time.

The chapters in this book show the variety that characterizes the study of public opinion, the creativity of the investigation, and the joy of the enterprise.

Note

1. Means are distorted by extreme cases, while medians are less distorted. To see how, imagine that we surveyed five Americans and asked their income. Four had identical incomes of $35,000; the fifth had an income of $35,000,000. The median, or middle, score is $35,000. The mean, or average, score is $7,028,000.

Part 1   The Causes of Public Attitudes

During his first months in office, President George W. Bush promoted a number of policies, and the public evaluated his performance based in part on the content of these proposals. Some of Bush's programs focused on longstanding issues in American politics, where opinions are well established. His tax cut was popular with conservative Republicans, but many liberal Democrats thought it benefited mainly rich Americans. His executive orders on abortion were popular with antiabortion activists, but generated anger among prochoice citizens. On both of these issues, most Americans have relatively stable attitudes that they often share with their parents and peers.

Yet Bush also grappled with issues such as whether the government should provide funding for stem-cell research, using cells from fertilized embryos. This issue was new to the political agenda and involved technical questions, and thus at least some Americans were forced to develop their own position on the issue. Even antiabortion leaders were not united on the issue. Without clear cues from political elites, it is more difficult for Americans to decide their position on new issues (Zaller 1992).

Where do political opinions and attitudes come from? How do Americans come to hold longstanding positions such as those on abortion or form new attitudes such as those on stem-cell research? The earliest studies in political science focused on how children acquire their attitudes from their parents. Ample reasons existed to believe that children would share their parents' political opinions—most children and parents lived in the same communities, were members of the same social class and race, and attended the same churches. Yet M. Kent Jennings and Richard Niemi (1974) found little relationship between the attitudes of high school students and their parents, except on issues that involve religious, moral, or lifestyle concerns. Children also appear to learn more general approaches to politics from their parents, such as partisanship (Chaffee 1975). Yet adults can change their minds on these issues and must form their own opinions on new issues.

More recently, researchers have focused on how social group membership, identity, mobilization, and leaders affect attitudes (Conover and Sapiro 1993; Cook and Wilcox 1991; Jelen 1991; Wilcox 2001; Rimmerman 2002). Social movements have transformed American politics in important ways. Civil rights, feminist, gay and lesbian, and Christian rights groups work hard to mold a consensus on policy issues among group members and sympathizers (Klein 1978; McAdams 1982). Even those who are not members of social movement organizations may have their attitudes molded by common experiences based on their social characteristics: black and Latino college students see security guards touch their guns when they enter jewelry stores, women find their views ignored in corporate headquarters, and conservative Christians see their values and lifestyles caricatured in popular media.

In addition, the mass media shape public opinion, although the effects are neither straightforward nor simple. Media effects can come from news coverage or from paid advertisements. News reports shape public perception of issues by highlighting some aspects while downplaying others. New coverage is becoming more pervasive, with television and the Internet providing instant information and 24/7 coverage (Graber 1997). Candidates and interest groups develop their own paid media campaigns: President Bill Clinton's health care plan was attacked by the insurance industry with a series of advertisements featuring actors portraying average citizens talking about their fears (West 2000).

In this section, we begin with a chapter by Virginia Sapiro on gender differences in public opinion. Sapiro shows that the relationship between gender and public opinion is far more complicated than portrayed by the media. Men and women do hold different opinions on some issues (the "gender gap"), but men and women agree on most issues. Gender also influences public opinion through gender-based identities. Gender roles, gender identities such as feminism, and gender stereotyping can affect the attitudes people hold about political issues and candidates. Finally, some political issues have a gender basis to them, such as sexual harassment, women's role in society and politics, women in the military, and so on.

Political attitudes are shaped by the information that the public receives from the media. Newspapers, television, radio, and the Internet provide the public with information about the world, and the ways in which new organizations choose to frame the news influences the types of information the public receives. Politicians use media outlets to communicate directly with the public by purchasing advertising time, but the largely negative political advertisements are not popular with the public. How do candidates' ads affect perceptions of advertisements for commercial products? Shanto Iyengar and Markus Prior's chapter lends some empirical support to product advertisers' fears of a negative spillover effect from candidate to product commercials.

Religion can influence political attitudes by shaping core values or by influencing attitudes toward specific issues. Some churches take unambiguous stands on political issues, such as the Roman Catholic Church's opposition to abortion and the death penalty, though parishioners do not always adopt these same views. Churches also have played a vital role in social movements, such as the civil rights movement. In her chapter, Allison Calhoun-Brown focuses on the contemporary role of black churches in influencing the attitudes of

African Americans toward the two major parties, various political leaders, and several political issues.

Racial and ethnic identities shape individuals' personal, social, economic, and political lives. In their chapter, Carole Jean Uhlaner and F. Chris Garcia provide a picture of Latino public opinion. They note important divisions within the Latino community, as Mexican Americans, Puerto Ricans, and Cuban Americans differ in their partisanship and political attitudes. Generations, citizenship, and length of residency in the United States also matter in shaping the opinions of Latinos. Nevertheless, recent public opinion polls reveal that Latinos are patriotic, perhaps more trusting of the government than Anglos, and support bilingual education but want their children to learn English. In many areas, Latinos share the same concerns and hopes as other Americans.

1 It's the Context, Situation, and Question, Stupid: The Gender Basis of Public Opinion

Virginia Sapiro

Do women and men think about politics *as* women and men? That is, does gender affect the political values or attitudes people hold? Does it make them disagree with each other about current issues or candidates? Conventional wisdom certainly says gender makes a difference. During every electoral campaign season, journalists and other commentators focus on the "gender gap" between men and women voters. Many people still believe that because women and men are distinctly designed by nature, certainly in terms of their reproductive capacities and roles, they must surely hold different attitudes toward politics and policy. Feminist leaders seem quite sure that gender makes a difference in political orientation; otherwise, why would they worry about how many women play a role in elections and policymaking?[1] Feminists are not alone in this belief that the presence of women makes a political difference; antifeminist social conservatives also believe that men and women have different orientations to politics.

One difficulty with analyzing the relationship between gender and public opinion is that conventional wisdom, and even some academic discussion, is often entwined with stereotypes. Some commonly held views are simply implausible when subjected to basic logical and empirical analysis. Moreover, debates on the subject are often emotionally charged. This chapter therefore will emphasize basic problems in theorizing about the gender basis of public opinion—the relationship between gender and public opinion—illustrated with results of survey-based research and public opinion poll findings. We begin with a definition of the basic conceptual framework. Next, we turn to alternative approaches to explaining why there might be a gender basis to public opinion. We conclude with an extended review of the research literature on gender differences in partisanship and electoral choice.

Defining the Gender Basis of Public Opinion

Our task is to define and explain the gender basis of public opinion. There are three different forms that this relationship may take. Each is introduced briefly in this section and then discussed and explained more fully in the next. First, and probably most obvious, the gender basis of public opinion may refer to aggregate gender differences between men's and women's political attitudes, beliefs, perceptions, or identities. When the *New York Times* reports that 53 percent of male voters voted for George W. Bush in 2000, while 54 percent of female voters voted for Al Gore, they are reporting on an aggregate gender difference in men's and women's voting (Connelly 2000). In research on gender differences, gender (defined simply as whether a person is male or female) is the independent variable of interest, and it is used to predict a wide range of dependent variables, such as party identification, evaluation of particular candidates, or attitudes toward specific issues.

Most discussions of gender and public opinion focus on gender differences of this sort. The scholarly research on gender and public opinion also is aimed at discovering what gender differences exist and why. A survey of the relevant research literature shows that articles on gender and public opinion usually begin by reciting a litany of some aggregate gender differences that have appeared in one study or another. Very often these lists are drawn from the same source: an article published in 1986 by Robert Y. Shapiro and Harpreet Mahajan in *Public Opinion Quarterly.* The article listed results from public opinion polls conducted in the United States between the 1960s and the 1980s. Shapiro and Mahajan established that gender differences are most pronounced on use-of-force issues (for example, war and capital punishment), followed by regulation and public safety issues (for example, consumer protection and environmental regulation), and then by compassion issues (for example, benefits for the poor and funding for public education).

A second way to think about the gender basis of public opinion is to consider the impact of gender identity, attitudes, and roles on women's and men's political thinking. As most scholars who think about these things argue, gender is defined not just by biology (that is, chromosomal, hormonal, or other physiological structures), but also by culture and social expectations that tell us what it means to be female or male and how to act appropriately male or female. Some people have traditional conceptions of how men and women ought to act, while others de-emphasize gender as a way of thinking about human behavior. Some men and women hold jobs or engage in other day-to-day activities that culturally are closely associated with their own sex (for example, female nurses and male truck drivers); others hold jobs that are more often associated with the other sex (male nurses and female truck drivers); and still others hold jobs that are not particularly associated with one or the other sex (real estate agents). Different cultures have varying ideas about masculinity and femininity and the kinds of activities and characteristics that are appropriate for men and women.

Thus, researchers interested in the gender basis of public opinion can expand beyond biological divisions and consider gender identity, norms, and roles as independent variables to help understand and explain political attitudes and behavior. For example, do homemakers and employed women have the same level of interest in politics or the same attitudes toward policy issues? How does motherhood and fatherhood affect political attitudes? In what ways are feminist women's political attitudes different from those of other women? Do those who hold traditional ideas about men's and women's roles think in particular ways about other aspects of politics and policy? These are the kinds of questions we might ask in this second framework for research on the gender basis of public opinion.

A third way to think about the gender basis of public opinion is to recognize that many important questions about politics and policy are themselves at least partly about gender or have specific gendered effects. We can analyze how the gendered aspects of the issues affect people's thinking about them and their responses to the issues. This third way of thinking about the gender basis of public opinion emphasizes not whether people's gender or gender orientation influences the way they think about politics but how political issues are constructed in gendered terms.

How might policy issues incorporate gender to the extent that it might influence the way people think about these issues? Consider three possibilities:

- First, some politics and policy questions are manifestly about gender; their subjects are women as women and/or men as men. Examples include questions of women's rights, whether women should serve in combat roles in the military, and whether men should be able to exclude women from their clubs.
- Second, politics and policy questions can be gendered in the sense that they relate to situations in life in which men and women tend to play different roles; have different experiences, needs, or problems; or are often treated differently. Thus, it is difficult to think about these issues without paying attention to gender questions. Because women generally are held responsible for caring for their children, and women are more likely than men to be left to care for children on their own, child care and parental leave issues have a different relationship to men's and women's lives. Women are more likely than men to be victims of sexual violence, and they are more likely to suffer injury from domestic violence. It also is difficult to ignore gender in such issues as whether insurance companies that cover Viagra should also cover the birth control pill.
- Third, policies and political arrangements, even those designed without gender in mind, can have quite different effects on men and women because of their different life situations. Controlling the size of government by cutting social services has gendered effects because women are more likely than men to use many of those services. Women also are more likely to have to take up the slack with their own labor when government services disappear. Compared with other advanced industrial democracies, the United States has an unusually large population that has little or no health insurance or other assistance with health care costs. Although health care policy affects both women and men, women's particular health care needs during their reproductive years mean that

the apparently gender-neutral problem of health care costs in fact affects men and women differently.

Not everyone sees the gender basis of particular issues and policy problems in the same way. In the case of abortion, for example, some people think about abortion as "a woman's right to choose," and others think abortion should be banned as a matter of "protecting the life of a child."

To take another example, the public opinion dynamics surrounding the confirmation hearings for Clarence Thomas's appointment to the U.S. Supreme Court show that the degree to which people understand particular issues to be about gender can vary. During these 1991 hearings, Anita Hill, a lawyer who had worked under Thomas's supervision in both the Department of Education and the Equal Employment Opportunity Commission, stepped forward to say that Thomas had sexually harassed her during that time. Thomas and Hill were both African American lawyers. He was a conservative nominated by a Republican president, while she was strongly supported by Democrats, liberals, and feminists. The Senate panel considering the case was composed of white male senators. Thomas fought back, eventually accusing his attackers of staging a "high-tech lynching." The country was riveted by this spectacle for days, so much so that many people predicted that this controversy would play a role in the 1992 reelection attempt of President George Bush.

As later public opinion research shows (Sapiro and Soss 1999), one reason these hearings were so controversial was that the public disagreed not only about whether Hill's charges were true but also about the real subject of the debate. For some people, the whole spectacle was about gender and related issues, such as sexual harassment of women. For other people, gender was much less relevant than race, political ideology, or party.

Explaining the Gender Basis of Public Opinion

We have seen that there are three distinct gender bases in public opinion—gender differences in opinions and behavior, gender roles that can influence opinion, and gendered understandings of political issues. A crucial task in understanding the gender basis of public opinion is to ask why gender is linked to public opinion. In what circumstances should we expect to see gender as an element of public opinion? Let us now review the three different varieties in detail.

Gender Differences

We begin with that most commonly discussed aspect of the gender basis of public opinion: gender differences. Why and in what circumstances would we expect to see gender differences in public opinion? A traditional view is that women and men are constructed differently in terms of biology or in some other nearly universally different way that leads them to have divergent views of politics. If this were true, we would expect to see dramatic differences between women and men, and these differences would be constant across time and culture. But such is not the case. Even where the differences are at their largest, women's and men's opinions overlap more than they diverge. This point is both important enough and overlooked enough that it is worth dwelling on at some length.

All reviews of gender differences in public opinion suggest that the areas of greatest difference focus on the use of violence: defense issues, capital punishment, and gun control, for example. Many people believe that these divergences in public opinion either must have some biological basis or must stem from women's involvement in nurturing children. Let us look over time at these cases of greatest gender difference to see what the magnitude of difference is.

The General Social Survey (GSS) has asked questions about gun control and capital punishment almost annually since the early 1970s. Figures 1-1 and 1-2 show gender differences in attitudes toward gun control and capital punishment, respectively, in each available year.[2] As we would expect, women are generally more favorable than are men toward gun control and less favorable toward capital punishment. But, in fact, the majority of both women and men support basic gun control legislation, and the majority of both women and men are in favor of capital punishment. Gender differences on gun control never exceed 20 percentage points and on capital punishment, 13 percentage points. On these attitudes, those on which gender differences are greatest, the overlap between women and men's attitudes is much greater than the difference. Note also that the magnitude of the gender differences varies over time; such fluctuation would not be expected if the source of gender differences were biological.

Consider the related example of gender differences in attitudes toward war and militarism. Pamela Johnston Conover and Virginia Sapiro's (1993) study of public opinion about the time of the 1991 Persian Gulf War shows that the degree of gender differences in attitudes toward defense and foreign policy depends on what aspect of these attitudes is under investigation. When questioned right before the war began, women were more fearful of war and more isolationist than men, but they did not express less militaristic attitudes than men. Part of the explanation may be that the items in the study related to the military asked about particular actions for particular purposes, rather than trying to gauge broad-based attitudes toward the military in general. When questioned after the war had occurred, men and women did not differ in how much attention they had paid to the war, but women had more negative evaluations and were more distressed by it. We cannot make blanket generalizations about women, war, and the military. Rather, we have to consider more carefully what the questions and circumstances are.

Figure 1-1 Gender Differences in Support of Gun Control, 1972–1996

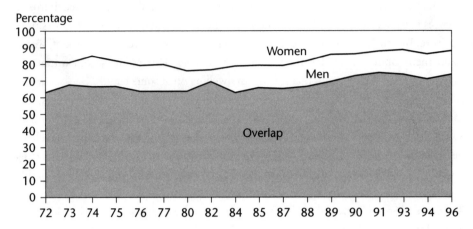

Source: General Social Survey.

Note: The graph shows support of gun control among women and men as well as the overlap (gray) for each year. The question was "Would you favor or oppose a law which would require a person to obtain a police permit before he or she could buy a gun?"

Men and women are often thought to regard different issues as more important. Women, for example, are thought to care more about social service and safety net issues because they stereotypically are believed to be more concerned with "compassion" issues. Men are often assumed to focus more on "economic" issues such as employment and taxes. (This labeling is itself a problem; social service and safety net issues *are* economic issues, especially to those who depend on government assistance to meet their basic needs.) Although considerable data are available that allow us to investigate how and why men's and women's attitudes may differ, it is more difficult to find data that help us figure out what issues are more important to men and women. We can gain some insight, however, from a question that appears regularly in the American National Election Studies (NES): "What do you think are the most important problems facing this country?" The NES codes up to three or four answers. Although the open-ended question allows for many answers, people's answers tend to cluster around a few categories. Among these are economic problems such as the general state of the economy, taxes, prices, and employment; social policies such as poverty relief and the provision of social services; law-and-order matters including crime enforcement and gun control; defense and foreign policy; education; and the environment and natural resources. Analysis of data from the 1992, 1994, 1996, and 1998 studies shows consistently modest but statistically significant gender differences in two areas: men were somewhat more likely to name economic issues, while women were more likely to cite social

Figure 1-2   Gender Differences in Support of Capital Punishment, 1974–1996

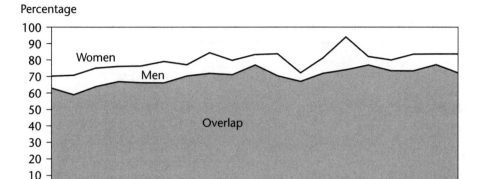

Percentage

Source: General Social Survey.

Note: The graph shows support of capital punishment among women and men as well as the overlap (gray) for each year. The question was "Do you favor or oppose the death penalty for persons convicted of murder?"

policies. Virtually no significant gender differences occurred in any of the other issue clusters. For the most part, men and women named the same sorts of problems as the major ones facing the country.

Let us probe a little further to explore these gender differences in naming economic and social policy as the most important issues. Table 1-1 shows the percentage of men and women who (1) named only economic issues, (2) named only social issues, or (3) named both or neither. Looking across the columns, we see that in each year, women appear less likely than men to mention only economic issues and more likely to mention only social issues. The differences, once again, are not huge. Another aspect of this table is equally important. How people frame their "most important problem" varies from year to year, as we should expect. In 1996 most people saw both economic and social issues as the nation's most important problems. In 1994 and 1998 the public seemed especially likely to think about social issues. Were there gender differences in how people defined the most important problem? In 1994, 1996, and 1998 women named social issues much more often than they named purely economic issues, as conventional wisdom would expect. But this is certainly not true in 1992. Conversely, we would conclude from the 1992 data that men are more purely concerned with economic issues than social issues, just as stereotypes would lead us to believe. But there is no evidence of this supposedly traditional pattern in the other years.

Table 1-1 Economic and Social Policy as the "Most Important Problem," 1992–1998

	Men	Women	Difference: Women − Men
1992			
Economic issues only	37.3	24.7	−12.6
Both/neither	50.1	52.9	2.8
Social issues only	12.6	22.4	9.8
Total	100.0	100.0	r = .16*
1994			
Economic issues only	20.3	10.5	−9.8
Both/neither	44.4	39.7	−4.7
Social issues only	35.3	49.7	14.4
Total	100.0	99.9	r = .17*
1996			
Economic issues only	10.5	4.4	−6.5
Both/neither	75.1	72.5	−2.6
Social issues only	14.3	23.0	8.7
Total	99.9	99.9	r = .15*
1998			
Economic issues only	19.0	10.8	−8.2
Both/neither	46.1	44.2	−1.9
Social issues only	35.0	45.0	10.0
Total	100.1	100.0	r = .13*

Source: National Election Studies.

Note: Entries are percentages except where noted. Percentages may not equal 100 because of rounding.

*p < .05.

In two years (1994 and 1998) social issues seemed especially important to men, and in one year (1996) social and economic concerns were of equal importance.

We can explore a wide range of issues and surveys and find gender differences in some issue attitudes at some times, but not at other times, and gender differences in some countries, but not in others. Even where we find gender differences that fit conventional wisdom, these differences tend to be rather small, even when statistically significant. Consider the evidence in Figures 1-3 and 1-4. These show the pattern of gender differences on all of the policy budget questions included in the 2000 NES survey. Figure 1-3 shows the percentage of

Figure 1-3 Gender Differences in Support of Decreasing Public Spending

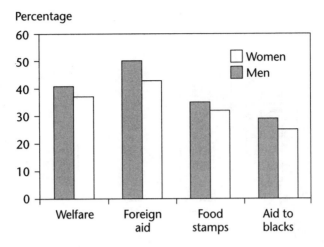

Percentage

Source: 2000 National Election Study.

Note: Bars show the percentage of men and women who support decreasing the federal budget allocation in each of these policy areas.

men and women who favor decreasing the federal budget for welfare programs, foreign aid, food stamps, and government aid to blacks. Although the difference between men's and women's preferences for decreasing spending on these programs is statistically significant in the case of welfare and foreign aid, the actual degree to which men are more in favor of decreasing spending is quite small. The gender differences with respect to food stamps and government aid to blacks are not statistically significant.

Figure 1-4 shows the percentage of men and women who favored increases in federal spending on AIDS research, aid to poor people, Social Security, environmental protection, public schools, fighting crime, child care, and tightening border security to prevent illegal immigration. In all but the cases of environmental protection and border security, gender differences are statistically significant. In four cases the differences are as large as 10 percentage points: aiding the poor, Social Security, fighting crime, and child care. On the remaining two issues, the gender gap is less than 10 percentage points.

Other gender differences are documented in the 2000 NES survey as well. Women were at least 10 percentage points more likely than men to believe that homosexuals should be allowed to serve in the military and to adopt children. Women were also more likely to be in favor of making it more difficult for people to buy guns and to be opposed to the death penalty. Indeed, as groups women and men responded somewhat differently to basic ques-

Figure 1-4   Gender Differences in Support of Increasing Public Spending

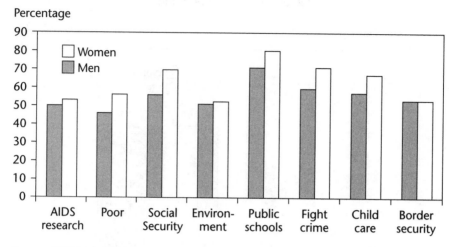

Source: 2000 National Election Study.

Note: Bars show the percentage of men and women who support increasing the federal budget allocation in each of these policy areas.

tions about the nature of government. People were asked whether they thought "we need a strong government to handle today's complex economic problems" or whether "the free market can handle these problems without government being involved." Forty-four percent of the men and 58 percent of women supported strong government. Yet again, the overlap is bigger than the difference.

When it comes to issues that are concerned specifically with people's rights and roles as men and women, we might expect significant gender differences. Even here, though, the differences are not stark. In Figure 1-4 we saw that women in 2000 were somewhat more in favor of increased funding for child care than were men, but a majority of men were also in favor. In fact, remarkably little evidence exists of gender differences in attitudes toward policies such as parental leave, day care, and women in the military (Conover and Sapiro 1992). Historically, the gender differences in attitudes toward abortion have been minute and inconsistent (Alvarez and Brehm 1995). On the other hand, some surveys show that women are somewhat more concerned with the issue of sexual harassment and want more to be done about it. The 1992 NES survey showed that while 25 percent of men thought that sexual harassment was a very serious problem, 38 percent of women thought so. About 50 percent of men and 60 percent of women thought more should be done to "protect women from being sexually harassed in the workplace." And many men and women indicated they were personally familiar with the problem; about 32 percent of men and 41 percent of women said they knew someone who had been subjected to sexual harassment in the workplace.

Certainly there are aggregate gender differences on a number of contemporary political and policy questions. But the degree and pattern of the differences and similarities strongly weigh against the general conclusion that biology or personality differences alone drive apart men's and women's public opinion. Developing and testing propositions about a connection between biological sex differences and political viewpoints are difficult tasks. But if universal gender differences shaped our political viewpoints, surely we would find more, and more consistent, political distinctions between men and women. Gender difference is clearly a variable phenomenon; therefore, any explanation must take into account the variation as well as the gender differences themselves. Thus, we have to turn to more complex and nuanced explanations.

A variety of other explanations exist for gender differences in public opinion, each of which has some merit, at least in certain situations. Evidence suggests that girls and boys may be socialized to different norms and expectations. Although socialization effects are far from uniform or universal, they can affect the way people think about issues. To hypothesize about the impact of socialized gender norms on public opinion, we would have to think specifically about what kinds of socialized norms would have an effect on what aspects of public opinion. In searching for an explanation of some of the differences in attitudes on defense policy and militarism, for example, Conover and Sapiro point to studies of early childhood development that suggest that girls and boys develop different strategies for dealing with threat and different orientations toward the use of violence. As these authors note, "The point is *not* that girls learn early in life never to engage in conflict or use violence, but rather that they learn to put off the use of violence until later in the course of a conflict than men do, to escalate its use more slowly, and to be more upset by it" (1993, 1096).

A very important set of hypotheses about the sources of gender differences refers to the impact of differences in women's and men's education, as well as that of other aspects of their roles and social situations. Until the last quarter of the twentieth century, women's and men's education in the United States was different, and their daily roles and responsibilities were different in the family and in work settings. Thus, we might consider a variety of hypotheses. Because women are much more responsible for the day-to-day care of children and other dependents, women might be more aware of and interested in issues that seem to relate to these roles. As caregivers, women also might be more favorable toward policies that help children and their families. Women are concentrated into certain kinds of jobs—they are employed disproportionately in the service sector, for example, while men are more heavily employed in blue-collar jobs—which in turn will shape their political attitudes. Women are disproportionately impoverished and therefore will have different views on economics and social service issues. With these hypotheses, however, we have turned away from gender differences per se and are focusing instead on the impact of gender roles, activities, norms, and so forth. This is the second major category of understanding the gender basis of public opinion, to which we will now turn.

The Impact of Gender Identity, Attitudes, and Roles

There are many reasons why people's gender identities, attitudes, and roles might shape the way they think about politics. Let us consider some of the hypotheses found in the research literature about the effects of (1) gender-differentiated roles; (2) gender identity, schemas, and consciousness; and (3) feminism. Much of the early discussion of gender differences in public opinion centered on assumptions about the impact of women's "special" roles as wives and mothers on their political activity. It makes more sense to look directly at the impact of such things as parenthood, marital status, and work roles than merely to make assumptions about it. A majority of adult women are mothers at some point in their lives, a majority of men are fathers, and a majority of both men and women are in the work force. The question, then, is, What is the effect of variations in social roles on public opinion? Much research has pursued this kind of question. We will touch on only a few examples here.

Many have suggested that women who are homemakers or mothers might hold different views of the political world than do women who are employed or who have no children, or even men who have children. Such social roles have different effects on the way people spend their time, on their relationships with others, on the kinds of information they receive, and on their interactions with the social and economic worlds. Some, but not all, research suggests that women with small children can be especially isolated from politics because of other demands on their attention. Therefore, mothers of small children may be less involved in politics and even less confident about their relationship to politics. However, empirical evidence finds that these familial roles have little impact on substantive political attitudes once education and age are taken into account. It is not even clear that motherhood has an impact on women's attitudes toward war and military matters (Conover and Sapiro 1993). In recent elections some observers have noticed a "marriage gap," in which both married men and women are more supportive than their unmarried counterparts of the more conservative, Republican candidate (Weisberg 1987). This pattern has held up in presidential elections from 1984 through 2000 (Connelly 2000).

Perhaps it is not the gender-linked roles but rather people's subjective interpretations of gender and gender roles that help shape their political views (Sapiro 1983). Women with a traditional notion of what it means to be a woman, especially those who believe that a woman's place is in the home, are indeed likely to be less involved in politics (Sapiro 1983). Yet even women with traditional views of femininity tend to believe not that women should withdraw from politics but rather that they should be active on behalf of certain conservative issues. More study is needed to fully establish the linkages between different forms of gender ideology and political attitudes.

A long stream of research shows evidence that gender stereotyping plays an important role in the way people assess electoral candidates. Stereotypes are sets of beliefs about particular groups of people that serve as automatic frameworks for perceiving and understanding individuals within that group. Gender stereotypes are drawn from cultural beliefs about the nature of men and women, and they vary somewhat across cultures and historical eras. Evidence clearly shows that people make assumptions about the kinds of personality traits women and men possess. These stereotypes, in turn, lead people to assume that particular female or male candidates will be more competent at dealing with particular matters, such as military or social welfare issues (Huddy and Terkildsen 1993; Koch 2000).

Of course, not everyone holds the same stereotypes to the same degree. Psychologists use the concept of gender schemas to investigate the degree to which people use concepts of male and female to organize their understanding of the world (Payne, Connor, and Colleti 1987). Some people are highly gender schematic; that is, they tend to have a more inclusive and rigid understanding of gender. Those who are less gender schematic do not tend to see the world in such male–female terms. For people in this second group, gender is less likely to play a role in their reaction to political candidates or issues. Some research finds that men tend, on average, to be more gender schematic than women and are more negative toward people who violate conventional gender norms (LaMar and Kite 1998). Because attitudes toward sexual orientation are partly driven by gender schemas and stereotypes, this research also applies to perceptions of and attitudes toward gays and lesbians (LaMar and Kite 1998). The stereotypes people have learned, including those relating to gender and sexuality, are often activated automatically. People apply stereotypes nonconsciously in their evaluations of candidates and issues. An interesting line of research, however, shows that people's use of stereotypes can be brought under control by a little thought (Payne, Connor, and Colleti 1987; Blair and Banaji 1996). That is, people can learn to override stereotypes they have learned but do not like.

In some cases, gender identity (how one identifies as male or female) and related understandings of gender take on a distinctly political dimension and develop into gender consciousness, a sense that people of one's own sex have particular political interests and should engage in collective action to pursue these interests (Tolleson and Rinehart 1992; Cook 1989; Wilcox 1997). The most familiar form of gender consciousness since the 1970s has been feminist consciousness, defined as an awareness of a woman's identity not just as an individual woman but as part of women as a group. Feminist consciousness leads to the belief that women have faced unfair limitations due to gender inequality and a commitment that women should work together to right these wrongs (Conover and Sapiro 1993). Feminism appears to have important effects on the way women think (Conover 1988).[3] Certainly, although most women and men understand full well what gender category they are in, some, in addition, develop a politicized sense of their gender; in which case they would be more likely to use gender-oriented interest groups and social movements as reference groups for thinking about politics.

One way that feminism might influence women in particular is through the impact of particular social movements and organizations. Men and women do not just drift naturally toward their political opinions and attitudes but are persuaded and mobilized through the actions and appeals of political organizations. These groups aim messages at men and women in particular ways to stimulate support. Certainly, this is how social movements, such as the women's movement, work. As we will see shortly, political parties can do the same, with wide-ranging effects.

In summary, people's gender identity, attitudes, and roles may have an impact on public opinion for many reasons. These factors can focus people's attention selectively on certain types of information or shape their interpretation of political information. Gender attitudes and identities can lead people to associate with some people and groups rather than with others, which in turn shapes how people see and respond to political problems. Finally, gender-based attitudes can influence the subjective connections people make between themselves and the political world. Many aspects of these connections have not been studied enough for researchers to understand fully the ways gender identities influence the wider range of public opinion attitudes.

The Evolution of Gender-Based Issues

The question of whether and in what circumstances policy questions will themselves be understood as gendered problems is both a cultural and a sociological issue. Gender equality has periodically been a topic of political discussion—and thus a public issue relevant to gender. In the United States the saliency of gender equality issues depends partly, but not entirely, on whether an active women's movement exists. An equal rights amendment to the U.S. Constitution (the ERA) was proposed to Congress in 1922 and in every Congress after that until the 1970s. The two major parties even began to endorse the amendment in their platforms beginning in the 1940s (although the Republicans withdrew support in 1980). The ERA, however, was not actively on the public agenda, in the sense of mattering to much of the mass public, until the 1970s, when the amendment was passed by Congress. After swift approval by a number of states, the ERA became bogged down in other states until 1982, when the time allowed by Congress for ratification ran out.

Sexual harassment was not a public issue until the 1980s in the United States (and not until later in most countries). The term was not even invented until the late 1970s. Of course, women had faced inappropriate demands for sexual activity well before that period.

A number of things changed, however, that made sexual harassment a political issue and therefore a subject of public opinion. First, cultural attitudes about the equality of women and men were changing. Second, since World War II the number of women in the labor force had been increasing. By 1980 half of all adult women were in the labor force, and by the end of the decade, half of all women with one-year-old children were in the labor force. In other words, it was no longer unusual for women to be employed, and most women in the labor force knew plenty of other employed women. Furthermore, many women were becoming supervisors and bosses and therefore had become less likely to be "fair game" for sexual predators than women had been in the past. Third, some activists in the women's movement, including some legal specialists, began arguing not only that women should demand more respectful treatment but also that the law should make harassment illegal as a form of sex discrimination.

With cultural change in attitudes toward women, changes in women's employment, the backing of the women's movement, and the increasing support of women who were tired of being hassled on the job, sexual harassment became a subject for public debate and therefore a subject for public opinion. This process of change is an example of what Edward Carmines and James Stimson (1989) call *issue evolution*. We do not have public opinion polls about sexual harassment before the late 1980s because pollsters do not ask about matters that have not yet become questions culturally. Still, we can be sure that at one time most people would have assumed that if men treated women as sex objects on the job, nothing much could or should be done about it; there was no legal recourse. Data from the 1992 National Election Study show that at that time, 32 percent of Americans thought that sexual harassment was a "very serious" problem in the workplace, 47 percent thought it was "somewhat serious," and 22 percent thought it was "not too serious." Only a few years after the term was invented, sexual harassment was on Americans' radar screen, but most people did not think it was a serious problem.

Many issues that incorporate gender as a subject of political and policy debate can be explored to gain better understanding of the gender basis of public opinion. General attitudes toward women's and men's relationship to politics has changed to some degree over the past generation or two. The General Social Survey asked Americans at least sixteen times between 1974 and 1998 whether they thought women should "take care of running their homes and leave running the country up to men." In the 1970s between 32 percent and 38 percent of Americans are recorded as agreeing that women should concentrate on family life. In 1982 about 28 percent agreed, and by 1989 the figure was down to 20 percent. By 1998 only 15 percent held this position. Similarly, in the 1972 GSS about 26 percent of Americans said they did not think that they would vote for a woman for president even if she were qualified and nominated by their own party. By 1998 that figure had declined to 6 percent. At the same time, we have seen increasing discussion and debate about issues that have direct bearing on men's and women's roles—sexual harassment, child care, parental leave, women in the military, abortion, single-sex schools, and women's athletics, as well as a host of issues relating to policy regarding sexuality. These will no doubt continue to be important.

Summary

Research on gender and public opinion typically incorporates a subtle bias in favor of finding gender differences, partly because culturally we tend to expect gender differences to occur. The main impact of this expectation is not that researchers alter data or find differences where they do not really exist but rather that investigators tend to stress the instances of gender differences they find and de-emphasize the data in which they are not found. Writers typically do this by data summaries that begin, "Gender differences have been found in. . . ." Such summaries do not give us a good idea of how often or in what conditions gender differences appear.

One thing is certain: To explain differences between men and women as groups, we have to focus on explanations that incorporate gender as relevant to both men and women. All too often, explanations for gender differences appear to take men as the norm and seek to explain why women are different. If there is a gender basis to public opinion—that is, if our lives as men and women shape our view of politics—an adequate explanation must incorporate the meaning and impact of gender for both men and women.

Public opinion—the way people think about, feel about, and respond to political phenomena—is fascinating, complex, and often subtle. As long ago as 1922 the journalist, writer, and philosopher Walter Lippmann had it right when he discussed public opinion as a matter of the "pictures in our heads" about topics that were too big and often too distant from our day-to-day lives to be experienced and grasped directly. Thus, the forces that shape these pictures are many, and different circumstances can alter the way people think about politics. An adequate explanation of the gender basis of public opinion must take account of what aspect of public opinion we are discussing and the circumstances in which women and men might be thinking about politics.

The Gender Gap in Elections

In recent years, much of the discussion of the gender basis of public opinion has centered on the gender gap, or the differences between men and women in support of the Democratic and Republican Parties and their candidates, especially at the presidential level. Since the 1970s, women have tended to be more supportive of Democratic candidates than men have, although the press and the public took little notice of this phenomenon before 1980. Although the gender gap in voting has appeared regularly since 1980, its size has varied

Figure 1-5 Gender, Party, and Vote, 1948–2000

Female – Male

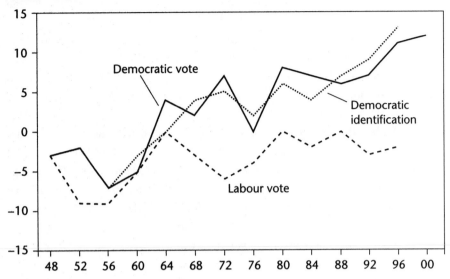

Sources: 2000 National Election Study.

Note: Each line shows the "female advantage" among the specified party's identifiers or voters. "Democratic vote" shows the percentage of women who voted Democratic minus the percentage of men who voted Democratic. "Democratic identification" shows the percentage of women who identified with the Democratic Party minus the percentage of men who identified with the Democratic Party. "Labour vote" shows the percentage of women who voted for the Labour Party minus the percentage of men who voted for the Labour Party. British election years as shown are approximate. The actual years are 1950, 1951, 1955, 1959, 1964, 1966, 1970, 1974 (figures for the two elections of that year are averaged), 1979, 1983, 1987, 1992, and 1997.

across elections. The existence of the gender gap raises a number of important questions. First, what causes the gender differences in voting? Second, when and why did the gender gap emerge? Third, why does the gender gap vary across elections? Finally, how can we develop an adequate explanation of gender differences in electoral behavior that takes account of the variation in the size of the gap?

Presidential Elections

The record of gender difference in electoral behavior and partisan support over time and cross-nationally reinforces the point that any adequate explanation of gender differences must be able to take account of change. The recent advantage that the Democrats have among women is well known. Figure 1-5 shows gender differences in presidential support and party identification since 1948, expressing the difference as the percent advantage Democrats hold among women, calculated simply by subtracting the Democratic vote or partisan identity of men from that of women. As a point of comparison, Figure 1-5 also includes the advantage obtained by the Labour Party among women in each British general election since 1950.[4]

Clearly, gender differences in partisanship are a historical phenomenon. The Democratic Party held a slight advantage among men in the 1950s. By the 1970s the tables were turning, and since 1980 — and even more since the middle of the 1990s — Democrats have held a distinct advantage among women and a disadvantage among men. At the same time, the British Labour Party never gained such an advantage among women (or disadvantage among men). Rather, the Labour Party held a distinct advantage among men in the earlier period, but today gender is not related to party support in Great Britain. The pattern of gender differences in partisan support in the United States is even more variable than Figure 1-5 suggests. In a single election year the size of gender difference in the presidential vote varies from state to state. The magnitude of partisan gender differences in congressional elections varies substantially from one congressional district to another and from one election to the next. How, then, do scholars explain these gender differences?

Explaining the Variable "Gender Gap"

Although many scholars have investigated partisan gender differences, research published in the 1990s raised the theoretical and empirical level of the field by paying specific attention to variation over time, competition among different hypotheses, and the importance of understanding the role of both men's and women's preferences and their sources in understanding the gender basis of the vote (Plutzer and Zipp 1996; Norrander 1997, 1999; Sapiro with Conover 1997; Chaney, Alvarez, and Nagler 1998; Mattei and Mattei 1998; Kaufmann and Petrocik 1999). Some of these studies focus mostly on congressional elections and others on presidential elections; they vary in which factors they consider, how they measure them, and exactly what conclusions they find. Together, they lead us to the following general conclusions.

The pattern of gender differences in party and electoral support we see at any given time is determined by some aspects of women's and men's lives as women and men, as well as other things that affect the nature of parties, campaigns, and contemporary politics. Many features of the American political economy and social system — such as race politics or the economic crises of the 1970s — affected the political parties and the nature of political institutions, office holding, and campaigns in the past fifty years. The responses that institutions and leaders made sometimes had different effects on women and men.

The Democratic Party, which had become the dominant American political party in the 1930s, started losing support in the post–World War II period, especially in the South, as white people began to abandon the party because of race politics. The economic and international crises of the 1970s further weakened the Democratic Party. These events led the Republican Party to reinstate its historic resistance to domestic expenditure in social programs, emphasize budget containment, sharpen its attacks on regulation, and highlight its strong stand on defense. The Republican messages found particular favor among white men, especially younger white men.

At the same time, the women's movement and women's interest groups were rising in importance and placed social policies and programs aimed at women, children, and families high on their priority list. Women who had developed an affinity for the women's movement would have heard these messages. In addition, a large percentage of the leaders of the women's movement and women's interest groups were Democratic activists. Thus, we have a recipe that kept women relatively sympathetic to the Democratic Party. In the 1970s and 1980s a key group of men abandoned the Democratic Party, while women were more buffered from the forces that influenced the men, thus creating the gender gap. The policy approaches and appeals of the Clinton years reinforced the difference.[5]

The emerging differences in partisanship are crucial for understanding differences in the voting records of men and women. Despite increases in the percentage of Americans who call themselves independents, partisanship remains as important as it ever was in determining people's voting choices (Bartels 2000). In their study of the changing voting patterns of men and women, Karen Kaufmann and John Petrocik (1999) find that partisanship has become more important over the years in explaining the gap in men's and women's voting.

Partisan differences are important, but researchers also have focused on the gender basis of issue positions as another potential explanation of gender difference in the vote. As several scholars have pointed out, there are two different ways that issue stands or partisanship might lead women and men to vote differently (Sapiro with Conover 1997; Chaney, Alvarez, and Nagler 1998; Kaufmann and Petrocik 1999). One group of researchers explain it this way:

First, the gap could be explained by different preferences of men and women on different political issues. For instance, a majority of women might feel that the government should increase social welfare spending, whereas a majority of men might feel that the government should decrease social welfare spending. Given candidates representing different views on this issue, we would expect to see a gender gap in vote choice. Second, men and women might have the same preferences (ideal issue positions) on issues but attach different levels of salience to different issues. For instance, women and men might favor legalizing abortion in roughly the same proportions; but women might view this as an important issue that could determine their vote, whereas men might view this as a relatively unimportant issue. (Chaney, Alvarez, and Nagler 1998, 312)

Research reveals both bases for gender differences in the vote, although the balance changes somewhat from year to year. Men and women take somewhat different positions on a number of issues, including in the 1990s social welfare issues and defense and use-of-force issues. How much influence gender differences on issues have on any one election depends on what issues are important in the campaign. Kaufmann and Petrocik (1999) show evidence that in some years women and men place different weights on particular issues (remember our discussion of "social" versus "economic" issues), and if any of these issues are stressed in the campaigns, the two sexes' different weighting factors can affect the vote.

Other aspects of elections can enter into creating gender differences in the vote. Contrary to the common stereotype, little evidence supports the notion that one or the other sex is more likely to make judgments on the basis of candidates' personality. Nevertheless, women and men sometimes interpret the personalities of candidates differently. In 2000, for example, women and men assessed the character and skills of George W. Bush and Al Gore very differently. Men were far more likely than were women to see Gore as a bland, unexciting candidate: when asked in a focus group which car each candidate might like to be, men likened Gore to a Chevy station wagon and Bush to a Maserati or a Mustang convertible (Purdum 2000).

Moreover, we cannot generalize across all women and men when we talk about the gender basis of public opinion because the effects we are discussing vary across different demographic and social groups, such as region (Norrander 1999) or racial or ethnic group (Lien 1998). Thus, any complete explanation of gender differences would also take account of these factors.

Finally, campaigns themselves may vary in the degree to which they make specific gender appeals. In the 2000 election, both presidential candidates worked hard to capture women's votes, but Gore was much more successful than Bush. The mere presence of women candidates on the ballot may have an effect on the gender basis of the vote. A study of the 1992 elections compared the presidential voting choices of people who lived in two different kinds of political environments. In one setting at least one female candidate was running for high political office (U.S. House, Senate, or governor). In the other cases, no woman was running for high office in the respondents' political environment. Also, in 1992, many women running for office were emphasizing the importance of having more women participate in government. Perhaps as a result, in those cases where a woman was running for high office, a larger gender gap occurred in presidential voting. In addition, certain gender-related attitudes played a larger role in presidential voting in those areas with a woman running for major office. In other words, the gender of the candidates had an effect not just on voting in those particular races, but on the gender-related considerations people had in mind when they thought about other races as well (Sapiro with Conover 1997).

Conclusion

Gender plays important roles in shaping public opinion. Indeed, gender appears to have played an increasingly important role since the 1970s. However, saying that gender is important does not mean that men and women are neatly divided into different camps when it comes to public opinion. Most important, our theories and explanations of the gender basis of public opinion must take into account the fact that gender differences vary in size depending on the subject, specific questions, historical time, and country studied.

A full explanation of gender-based public opinion would have to consider the various elements we have covered here. Women and men may still be socialized to think about politics somewhat differently, or at least some groups of women and men are. The two sexes play different kinds of roles in society and family life and thus have different kinds of experiences. Women and men are mobilized by somewhat different interest groups and social movements, and political actors make a variety of appeals that can have varying gendered content. The context in which people think about politics and make their choices matters in determining the gender basis of public opinion. The differences often lie mostly at the margins. But at times—as in close elections—the margins count for a lot.

Notes

1. Group composition might make a difference because of the differences of opinion among the people included. The composition of a group might also affect group dynamics.

2. All analysis of General Social Survey and National Election Study data was done by the author unless otherwise specified.

3. Men can be feminists and have feminist attitudes, and these too tend to be related to other political attitudes, especially liberal attitudes. But feminist consciousness is a form of group consciousness, which is defined by most scholars in this area as a form of politicized identity, not just a set of attitudes.

4. Throughout this period, the British electoral system could best be considered a two-and-a-half party system. The two main parties were the Conservatives on the right and Labour on the left. There was also a series of important third parties. On gender and British elections, see Norris 1998.

5. For a discussion of President Clinton and gender politics, see Sapiro and Canon 1999.

2 Giving Advertising a Bad Name? The Effect of Political Ads on Commercial Advertising

Shanto Iyengar and Markus Prior

Commercial advertising has always been central to American culture. As encountered in the mass media, advertising is pervasive and inescapable. Most Americans take for granted the "rules" of commercial advertising, even though they may not be aware that any formal guidelines exist and may have little or no idea what the legal effect of such guidelines might be. Commercial advertising is usually accepted as fair and legitimate marketing (Shavitt, Lowrey, and Haefner 1998).

Contrast the world of political advertising. In recent years, political advertising has become essential to campaign strategy (at least in major campaigns), and many regard it as far more intrusive than routine commercial advertising. But the world of political advertising is very different from the world of commercial advertising. There really are no "rules" when it comes to the content and form of political advertising. Political advertisers are not accountable to any regulatory body, voluntary or otherwise, for the accuracy of their claims. They readily engage in so-called comparative advertising. They blatantly criticize their competitors. They complain incessantly about the fairness of the comments made about them, while their opponents do the same. There is no acknowledged forum for the review of these claims and counterclaims. The press attempts to provide some sporadic checks on political advertisers by running "ad watch" reports, but these reports provide even more air time for the negative exchanges and may well increase public cynicism. Considerable evidence suggests that the negativity associated with contemporary political campaigns has created an "avoidance" mentality that is serving to shrink the electorate and the level of political participation generally (see Ansolabehere and Iyengar 1995; Ansolabehere, Iyengar, and Simon 1999).

Political advertising is not a welcome addition to the world of commercial advertising. Major advertising firms and professional associations have widely deplored the lack of accountability of political advertisers and their unwillingness to adhere to a code of ethics (see *Advertising Age,* April 29, 1996; *New York Times,* April 29, 1996; *Washington Post,* July 30, 1996). What exactly are commercial advertisers concerned about? Perhaps they fear that the apathy—and all too frequently, aversion—induced by political advertising campaigns may damage the credibility, and ultimately the persuasiveness, of more traditional forms of advertising. As Alex Kroll, former chairman of the American Association of Advertising Agencies (AAAA), put it: "We must stop politicians from ruining our reputation" (*Advertising Age,* April 29, 1991). Kroll's was not a solitary voice. In 1984, John O'Toole, then chairman of AAAA, claimed that political ads were "giving advertising a bad name" (*Advertising Age,* June 24, 1996); in 1996, Burt Manning, another former chairman, went so far as to assert that the "smear and scare" tactics of political advertisers meant that "today, the issue is survival of brand advertising" (*Advertising Age,* June 24, 1996). Our goal in this chapter is to provide some evidence on the issue of whether political advertising does, in fact, taint the image of commercial advertising. We compare people's reactions to commercial advertising in the absence of any political ads to their reactions when the commercial break contains one or two political ads. Do they like commercial ads better or worse when they also watch a political ad? We test two rival hypotheses, an assimilation effect and a contrast effect.

An assimilation effect occurs when people perceive political and commercial advertising as similar, so that their evaluations of product ads move in the same direction as their evaluations of political ads. For example, their evaluations of product ads become more positive when they also watch a political ad they like (compared to the situation where they only watch the product ads). The assimilation hypothesis is consistent with advertisers' fears: exposure to disliked political ads will drag down viewers' appreciation of product ads.

A contrast effect is the opposite. People perceive political and product ads as clearly different categories, so that the evaluation of the political ads influences product ad evaluations in the opposite direction. For example, people evaluate product ads more positively when they also watch a political ad that they dislike (again compared to watching only the product ads, but no political ad). According to the contrast hypothesis, all the nasty political ads make commercial advertising appear more appealing, because in comparison product ads look better.

In the sections that follow, we will first provide some background on the scope and extent of commercial and political advertising and the regulatory environment in which advertisers operate. Next, we describe recent scholarly research into the content and effects of political advertising. We then provide the theoretical basis for our expectation that the evaluation of product ads depends on the advertising context—defined in our case as whether people are also exposed to political ads. Next, we describe our experimental methodology and the findings. Finally, we consider the implications of our evidence.

Comparing Commercial and Political Advertising

Even though the use of political advertising has spread exponentially, in terms of both the frequency of exposure and the increased length of political campaigns, political advertising still constitutes only a tiny percentage of all advertising. The total cost of the 1996 election (all races combined) amounted to approximately $2.5 billion (Center for Responsive Politics 1997). This figure is less than the *annual advertising* budget for major U.S. corporations. During the height of the 1996 campaign, the research firm CMR found that fewer than 1 percent of all televised advertisements (750,000 out of 93,000,000) in the top seventy-five media markets were sponsored by political candidates or organizations (Goldstein 1998). Clearly, the public's distaste for these advertisements is based on factors other than frequency alone.

The most distinctive feature of contemporary political campaign advertisements is the negativity of their content and tone. Political advertisers frequently engage in comparative advertising in which the opposing candidate's program and performance are criticized and even ridiculed. Highlighting the opponent's liabilities and weaknesses usually takes precedence over identifying the sponsor's program and strengths. In the most comprehensive tracking of campaign advertising to date, scholars at the Annenberg School of Communication have found that such negative advertising makes up approximately one-third of all campaign ads used in presidential campaigns (Jamieson, Waldman, and Sherr 1998). The level of negativity is actually significantly greater when one considers frequency-weighted indicators of content (Prior 2001). In 1996, for instance, while fewer than one-half of the ads produced by the major candidates featured negative appeals, these appeals accounted for some 70 percent of the candidates' ad buys (Goldstein 1998). While we do not have comparable data for any commercial advertising campaign, we have observed that the comparative element is unlikely to be so prominent; compared with commercial ads, political ads are much more negative in content.

Not only is the content of political ads more likely to be negative, political advertisers are also less accountable for their claims. All commercial advertisers voluntarily subscribe to a code of advertising ethics administered by the Advertising Division of the Better Business Bureau. This code includes provisions for dealing with complaints of false or misleading information. Complaints directed at specific ads are reviewed and arbitrated by a panel appointed by the National Advertising Review Board. After reviewing the evidence from both sides, the panel may find the complaint to be valid and require that the ad in question be modified or discontinued. The panel may also refer the complaint to the appropriate governmental agency. If the advertiser fails to comply with a request for modification or termination, the panel may issue a "notice of noncompliance" identifying the advertiser in question.

Unlike commercial advertisers, political advertisers do not adhere to any codes or procedures intended to protect the public from inaccurate and unsubstantiated claims (see, for example, Tinkham and Weaver-Lariscy 1994). First Amendment protections make it virtually impossible to impose involuntary restraints on the content of political advertising. The American Association of Political Consultants has shown no inclination to encourage any form of self-restraint. The result is a free-for-all environment in which candidates repeatedly attack and counterattack the claims of their competitors. The only accountability is provided by the press, in the form of sporadic ad-watch news reports that scrutinize specific ads for their accuracy (for a review of research into the effects of these reports, see Pew Commission 1998).[1] The very nature of ad-watch journalism, however, is bound to exacerbate public cynicism about the fairness and credibility of political advertising.

The Effects of Political Advertising

The harsh tone of political advertising, the often controversial techniques employed by political advertisers, and the fact that the competing claims made in campaign ads are beyond review have raised questions about the goals of political advertisers. Many critics have suggested that political advertisers seek votes at any cost, even including a degraded sense of public regard for the candidates and the electoral process. Perhaps the amount of negativity featured in political campaigns is designed to shrink the market rather than increase the sponsor's relative share: discouraging people from voting is much more feasible than persuading supporters of one candidate to vote for the opponent. It is well known that most Americans hold fast to their partisan attachments. The act of voting generally serves expressive, as opposed to instrumental, needs. People do not vote because they expect material benefits from voting, but in order to express their political opinions, their support for the political system, or their sense of civic duty (for a review of research on political participation, see Rosenstone and Hansen 1993). Since people acquire their affiliation with the Democratic or Republican Parties early in life, the probability that they will cross party lines in response to an advertising campaign is slight. And since the motivation to vote is typically symbolic or psychological (in the sense that one's vote is unlikely to be pivotal in determining the outcome of the election), increasing the level of controversy and conflict in ad campaigns is bound to discourage voters from making a choice and casting a vote. In effect, negative campaigns create an avoidance mindset within the electorate (see Houston and Roskos-Ewoldsen 1998; Houston, Dean, and Roskos-Ewoldsen 1999).

Although the scholarly evidence is mixed, experimental studies substantiate these claims. Carefully controlled manipulations of advertising tone demonstrate that exposure to negative (rather than positive) campaign advertising heightens political cynicism and diminishes voter turnout (see Ansolabehere and Iyengar 1995; Ansolabehere, Iyengar, and Simon 1999; Houston and Roskos-Ewoldsen 1998; Houston, Dean, and Roskos-Ewoldsen 1999). It is hardly coincidental that the public's views of elections and the importance of voting have soured as political advertising campaigns have become increasingly reliant on negative appeals. In 1960, for example, only one in four Americans endorsed the statement that "public officials don't care much about what people like me think." By 1990, the cynical response was given by six of ten Americans (see Rosenstone and Hansen 1993; Patterson 2000).

Exposure to political campaigns has extracted a similar toll on the public's views of political advertising. There is ample survey data showing that the public dislikes media-based political campaigns. According to the most recent surveys by the Pew Center, a majority of the electorate (some 60 percent) felt that campaign commercials were *not* useful in helping them choose a candidate during the 1998 elections, and more than two-thirds (68 percent) judged the campaign as nasty (Pew Commission 1998). And in a recent survey of voters in Virginia, some three-fourths of the sample indicated that negative campaigns were likely to discourage people from voting (Freedman and Lawton 2000).

Theoretical Framework: Political Advertising as a Context for Product Advertising

We consider two rival context effects, both of which rest on the assumption that commercial advertising is evaluated more favorably than political advertising. The assimilation hypothesis suggests that exposure to political advertising encourages people to equate their feelings about other, nonpolitical advertising with their feelings about political ads. The essence of this concept is that negative reactions to political ads will lower evaluations of product ads. The competing possibility is that product and political ads are perceived sufficiently distinctly to bring about a contrast effect. According to this view, the negative response to political advertising should make commercial advertising appear more appealing during political campaigns. By accentuating the negative attributes of political advertisements, political campaigns strengthen the standing of commercial advertisers.

Two theoretical perspectives provide the basis for these alternative hypotheses, each focusing on a different element of political attitudes. Social judgment theory focuses on the cognitive element of political attitudes—that portion that involves beliefs about what is factually true. Theories of mood transfer and priming, in contrast, focus on the affective component of attitudes—evaluations and emotion.

The Cognitive Perspective: Social Judgment Theory

According to social judgment theory (introduced by Sherif and Hovland 1961; see Petty and Cacioppo 1986), someone evaluating an object compares it with some reference point or anchor. If the object and the anchor are seen as close and related, then an existing negative evaluation of the anchor will lead to a more negative judgment about the object. Equivalently, an existing positive evaluation of the anchor improves evaluations of the object. This is called an assimilation effect because evaluations of anchor and object become more similar than they would be if both were evaluated in isolation.

The opposite phenomenon is labeled a contrast effect. If anchor and object are perceived as unrelated and distant, the difference in evaluations between the target object and the anchor is exaggerated. If you like the anchor, and the anchor is clearly different from the object, then you will not like the object as much as you would like it in isolation.

It follows that an identical object is judged differently depending on whether a person focuses on its similarities to or differences from a reference point. In both situations, the objects are evaluated differently than they would be in the absence of any reference point. In Richard E. Petty and John T. Cacioppo's words, "Judgments about physical as well as social stimuli are thought to be subject to two judgmental distortions—contrast and assimilation" (1986, 99).

The application of social judgment theory to evaluations of political and product advertising effects is straightforward. Product ads are the target object and political ads the anchor. How do people evaluate a product ad when they have just seen a political ad they disliked? Depending on whether political ads are seen as similar or dissimilar to product ads, we expect either an assimilation or a contrast effect on evaluations of product ads. If people regard political ads as categorically similar to product ads, social judgment theory predicts an assimilation effect—dislike of a political ad will result in reduced evaluations of the product ads. If political ads are seen as a distinct form of advertising, however, the theory predicts a contrast effect—dislike of a political ad leads to improved evaluations of the product ads.

The Affective Perspective: Mood as a Basis for Assimilation or Contrast

Social judgment theory explains context effects in cognitive terms. Assimilation or contrast effects occur depending on whether we see two things as similar or not. A second theoretical basis for predicting assimilation or contrast effects deals with the feelings or moods elicited by the viewing context.

Our mood state influences how well we like televised commercials. Our mood, in turn, can be influenced by other commercials (advertising context) or by the program in which the commercial appears (program context). Some studies show that we like all product ads better when they appear within "happy" programs (Goldberg and Gorn 1987; Mattenklott 1998). Other studies suggest that we like happy ads better in happy programs, but sad ads better in sad programs (Kamins, Marks, and Skinner 1991). In other words, ads induced more favorable thoughts when they appeared in programs with a similar emotional tone.

Lynda Lee Kaid, Mike Chanslor, and Mark Hovind (1992) observe a similar effect for political ads. Negative ads were found to be most effective when placed in the context of local newscasts (which usually contain a fair amount of negative news). Image ads were found to be most effective when placed in a sitcom context. Apparently, program–context consistency operates both at the level of affective consistency (happy context, happy ad) and cognitive or content consistency (negative news, negative ads). With respect to our study, these results suggest an assimilation effect: political ads put people in a negative mood; this leads them to evaluate product ads more negatively, too.

But is there an equivalent effect of the closeness between target and anchor to that we saw in social judgment theory? People's evaluations of a product commercial are influenced by the mood that is made salient by whatever they saw just before the commercial (see, for example, Goldberg and Gorn 1987; Sanbonmatsu and Fazio 1991). This effect is also referred to as affective priming (Murphy and Zajonc 1993). The literature on mood priming emphasizes that the content of the anchor must be relevant to the target to achieve the intended priming effect. When the primed consideration is not relevant, priming can have a reduced or even reverse effect (see, for example, Higgins, Rholes, and Jones 1977; Fiske and Taylor 1991, 258–261). For our study, this evidence leads to the prediction that the affective prime (the political ad) produces either a contrast or an assimilation with the commercial advertisement, depending on whether subjects perceive the prime as applicable or not. The political ad works as an applicable affective prime only when subjects ignore or discount the generic difference between product and political ads. In that case, the literature predicts a mood-induced assimilation effect. Conversely, if people perceive differences between political and product ads, we expect a contrast effect.

In sum, both cognitive and affective explanations suggest that the direction of the context effect depends on the difference between anchor and target. In our study, the objective difference between the political ads and the product ads remains constant because we show the same ads to all participants. Is it possible that some people perceive the difference to be larger than do others?

Victor C. Ottati and Lynda M. Isbell (1996) have argued that the efficiency with which people process information matters in whether mood consistency affects subsequent judgments. They argue that people who are efficient processors realize that mood is not a helpful basis for evaluations of unrelated stimuli and therefore mentally correct for the mood bias. In fact, they overcorrect, which means that their positive mood states have a negative impact on the evaluation of the target (contrast effect). Inefficient processors, on the other hand, failing to grasp the mismatch between mood and stimulus, do not attempt to correct; they treat positive mood as a relevant factor in favor of the stimulus, thus leading to an assimilation effect. In sum, based on Ottati and Isbell's (1996) analysis, we expect that the direction of the context effect in our study may depend on how efficiently people process political information.

Method

To assess the effects of political ads on evaluations of product ads, we conducted experiments during the 1996 election campaign.[2] The advantages and disadvantages of experimentation are well known. Unlike surveys, experiments provide accurate measures of exposure and hence yield precise causal inferences about the effects of campaign advertising. Of course, experiments have their own liabilities. Most are administered upon captive populations—college students who must serve as guinea pigs in order to gain course credit. A further weakness of the typical experiment is the somewhat sterile, laboratory-like environment which bears little resemblance to the cacophony and confusion of election campaigns.

To avoid these weaknesses we enhanced the realism and generalizability of our experiments in several ways. Each was administered during a political campaign (1996) and featured real candidates (presidential candidates Bob Dole and Bill Clinton) or statewide ballot propositions (Proposition 209 or Proposition 211) as the sponsors. Proposition 209 (the California Civil Rights Initiative) prohibits preferential treatment based on race or gender in public employment or education. The proposition essentially banned affirmative action in hiring and in college admission, and it passed with 54 percent of the vote. Proposition 211 (the Securities Fraud–Lawsuits Initiative) was designed to make it easier to file lawsuits against companies for deceptive conduct. It was defeated.

The experiments were conducted at three separate sites in the greater Los Angeles area. One was located in predominantly Democratic West Los Angeles, in a popular shopping mall. The second was based in a small shopping area in Moorpark, a conservative northern suburb of Los Angeles. The third was located in Manhattan Beach, a coastal city southwest of Los Angeles. This variety of locations helped to ensure a large and diverse subject pool.[3] Subjects, who were recruited by the use of flyers, announcements in newsletters, and personal contact in shopping malls and who were offered payment of fifteen dollars for participation in "media research," were reasonably representative of the Southern California voting-age population. A total of 1,553 subjects participated in the study.

The experimental "laboratory" consisted of a two-room office suite located in or near a retail shopping area. One of the rooms was used as a viewing room and the other for filling out questionnaires. The viewing rooms resembled, as closely as possible, the normal conditions in which a person views political advertisements. Comfortable couches and chairs were arranged in front of a television set, with houseplants and wall hangings placed around the room. Respondents were offered coffee, cookies, and soft drinks to enjoy during the viewing sessions. In most cases, family members or friends took part in the experiment at the same time, so that respondents did not find themselves sitting next to a stranger while viewing the political advertisements.[4]

Experimental Stimuli and Procedure

On their arrival, subjects read the instruction sheet that described the research (in general terms) as a study of consumer reactions to advertising. They then completed a brief pretest questionnaire concerning their personal background, media habits, and recent purchasing behavior. They were shown into the viewing room, where they watched a videotape containing nine advertisements. In the control conditions all nine ads were sponsored by nonpolitical organizations. In the "treatment" conditions, the tape included one or two political spots replacing one or two of the product ads. In the one-ad treatment conditions, the political ad appeared in the fifth position. In the two-ad treatment condition, the political ads were placed in the third and fifth slots.

There were three different treatment conditions. In the presidential ad condition, subjects saw one presidential ad among the product commercials. A total of 710 subjects were assigned to this condition. In the proposition ad condition, the ad collection included one ad for or against a proposition on the California ballot (321 subjects). Finally, in the two-ad condition, subjects saw two political ads, one presidential ad and one proposition ad (366 subjects). In the control condition 156 subjects saw all nine nonpolitical ads.

The political ads used in the experiment were real ads that appeared during the 1996 campaigns. The presidential ads corresponded to those being aired in southern California by Bill Clinton and Bob Dole. They covered a variety of issues, including illegal immigration, drug abuse, federal spending on social programs, and cutting taxes.[5] In other conditions, we substituted ads for and against Proposition 209 and Proposition 211. Both positive and negative political ads were used as experimental stimuli. Following the presentation, subjects completed an extensive posttest questionnaire that included a series of questions about product and political advertising. Finally, they were debriefed and paid.

Indicators

The consumer behavior literature distinguishes among several concepts implicated in viewers' responses to advertising messages. Since we did not have strong prior expectations of which of these concepts would be most affected by the advertising context, we constructed a variety of different measures of response to product advertising. We want to measure the spillover effects of political advertising onto commercial advertising, and therefore we need to measure emotional and cognitive evaluations of the companies and products advertised. We can then compare the evaluations of those who saw and those who did not see political commercials.

Our first measure captures feeling toward business in general, using the "feeling thermometer" format. In this format, people are asked to rate objects on a scale from 0 to 100. The values between 50 and 100 are described in the question as increasingly "favorable and warm," whereas 0 to 50 represents "cold" and less favorable ratings. Our measure of feeling toward business in general is calculated by taking the average rating for four major U.S. companies (IBM, AT&T, Dodge, American Express). Statistical analysis confirms that the average of these four ratings reliably measures people's feelings toward business in general.[6]

Our second indicator focuses more specifically on the ads included on the videotape. Subjects were asked to think back to two product commercials presented on the tape, an American Airlines ad (placed second in all conditions), and a pain reliever ad (either Advil or Aleve, placed third in all conditions)[7] and indicate whether each of these ads elicited the following six feelings: anger, hope, sadness, happiness, pride, disgust. We use separate positive and negative feeling indicators.[8]

Since the consumer behavior literature has found differences with respect to affective and cognitive responses to advertising, we created a third indicator designed to capture cognitive processing of the product ad. An open-ended item was used to record subjects' thoughts and reactions to the American Airlines and pain reliever ads. While completing these items, people had the chance to look at brief descriptions of the respective ads. As many as three comments per ad were possible. In total, 4,927 comments were coded. Eighty-three percent of all comments were about the specific ad, rather than about advertising in general or the product or product category. The percentage of subjects with at least one comment was very high (97 percent for American Airlines, 95.9 percent for the pain reliever). To have a measure comparable to the affective response scales, we summed the number of positive comments and the number of negative comments across the two ads and use them as separate indicators.[9]

We have shown earlier in the chapter that efficiency of political information processing is an important mediating factor in subjects' reactions to political and product ads. Vincent Price and John Zaller (1993) have demonstrated that education is a good proxy for political expertise (defined in terms of level of factual political information).[10] Consequently, we use education as a control for processing ability in our analysis. We dichotomized our education measure by distinguishing between people who had graduated from college ($N = 794$) from those who had not ($N = 753$).

A common analytical tool for experimental data is analysis of variance, or ANOVA. ANOVA tests the statistical significance of differences between average, or mean, scores on the dependent variable for different experimental groups. It measures the difference in means between experimental groups, and also the variance in means within an experimental group. When the difference within groups is small but the difference between groups is large, we conclude that the experimental condition had an important effect. When the difference within groups is larger than the difference between groups, we conclude that the experiment had little effect.

The statistical significance of the comparison between the across group and within group variation is given by the F statistic, which has associated degrees of freedom accounting for the number of variables examined and the number of people in the experiment. The value of the F statistic along with the degrees of freedom can be used to attain a level of statistical significance. Since experiments often involve smaller numbers of participants, an acceptable level of statistical significance may be expanded to 0.10, meaning a 10 percent chance that the outcome could have occurred by chance alone. In our study we expect that both the experimental condition (viewing a political advertisement) and level of education will interact to influence the amount of spillover effect of political advertisements on product advertisements. Thus, the F statistics that we present test for differences in mean values both across the experimental groups and across education levels. Finally, an indication of the amount of variation explained by the experimental condition and education levels is provided by the eta (η^2) statistic. This is simply interpreted as the amount of variation explained, with .00 indicating no variation explained and 1.00 indicating that all the variation occurs across the group means and no variation remains within each group.

Results

As predicted, the interaction between exposure to a political ad and education is a significant determinant of evaluations of product advertising. Table 2-1 shows the results for presidential advertisements. The table lists the mean scores on the five dependent variables by experimental condition and education. As the means in the table demonstrate, the effect was consistent for all five measures: exposure to a political ad produced assimilation among better educated people but contrast among less educated viewers. This effect is in the opposite direction from what we originally had expected, a finding we will explore more fully later. (See the appendix to this book for guidance in understanding statistical techniques.)

For now, let's examine some of the specific outcomes. The second set of numbers in Table 2-1 indicates that better educated respondents expressed, on average, 1.70 positive comments about product advertising when the ads were unaccompanied by a political ad, but only 1.41 comments when a political ad was present. By contrast, the number of positive comments increased from 1.31 to 1.52 with the presence of a political ad among the less educated. There is only a 5 percent chance that the difference in mean number of positive comments between the two experimental groups at the different levels of education could

Table 2-1 Effects of Watching a Presidential Ad on Responses to Product Commercials, by Level of Education

	Education		
	Low	High	Average
Feeling toward business in general			
No political ad	51.5	57.9	54.7
Political ad	58.9	57.7	58.3
	$F[1, 853] = 6.10, p = .014, \eta^2 = .007$		
Number of positive comments			
No political ad	1.31	1.70	1.51
Political ad	1.52	1.41	1.46
	$F[1, 858] = 3.68, p = .055, \eta^2 = .004$		
Number of negative comments			
No political ad	1.07	1.03	1.05
Political ad	1.00	1.46	1.23
	$F[1, 858] = 4.35, p = .037, \eta^2 = .005$		
Positive feeling toward product ad			
No political ad	−.098	.056	−.021
Political ad	.128	−.002	.062
	$F[1, 857] = 2.46, p = .117, \eta^2 = .003$		
Negative feeling toward product ad			
No political ad	.347	.013	.180
Political ad	.008	.06	.034
	$F[1, 857] = 3.99, p = .046, \eta^2 = .005$		

Note: Cell entries are mean scores. *P* values are for interaction terms in two-by-two ANOVA with education and experimental conditions as factors.

have occurred by chance. The other differences in number of responses are statistically significant at the .05 level, with the exception of the level of positive feelings, which has a slightly higher .12 level of significance.[11]

Do these findings generalize to political ads other than those for presidential candidates? To replicate the results with proposition ads, we again ran 2 × 2 ANOVAs with the experimental condition and education as factors. These results are presented in Table 2-2. We find additional support for conditional context effects with respect to feelings toward business

Table 2-2 Effects of Watching a Proposition Ad on Responses to Product Commercials, by Level of Education

	Education		
	Low	High	Average
Feeling toward business in general			
No political ad	51.5	57.9	54.7
Political ad	58.0	58.1	58.0
	$F[1, 466] = 2.79, p = .096, \eta^2 = .006$		
Number of positive comments			
No political ad	1.31	1.70	1.51
Political ad	1.04	1.20	1.12
	$F[1, 464] = .92, p = .338, \eta^2 = .002$		
Number of negative comments			
No political ad	1.07	1.03	1.05
Political ad	0.84	1.22	1.03
	$F[1, 464] = 3.21, p = .074, \eta^2 = .007$		
Positive feeling toward product ad			
No political ad	−.098	.056	−.021
Political ad	.112	−.206	−.159
	$F[1, 462] = 1.49, p = .221, \eta^2 = .003$		
Negative feeling toward product ad			
No political ad	.347	.013	.180
Political ad	−.009	−.152	−.080
	$F[1, 462] = .99, p = .321, \eta^2 = .002$		

Note: Cell entries are mean scores. *P* values are for interaction terms in two-by-two ANOVA with education and experimental conditions as factors.

in general ($p = .096$) and the number of negative comments about product ads ($p = .074$). As was the case in Table 2-1, positive comments and feelings decreased after exposure to a proposition ad among better educated subjects. Similarly, the less educated had more positive and less negative feelings after exposure to the proposition ad. These results are parallel to the conditional context effect obtained for presidential ads. However, the level of significance for interaction terms is weaker for the proposition ads ($p > .05$ but $< .10$); hence, the evidence of conditional context effects is weak only in the case of exposure to

Table 2-3 Effects of Watching Two Political Ads on Responses to Product Commercials, by Level of Education

	Education		
	Low	High	Average
Feeling toward business in general			
No political ad	51.5	57.9	54.7
Two political ads	57.4	57.1	57.3
	$F[1, 509] = 4.18, p = .041, \eta^2 = .008$		
Number of positive comments			
No political ad	1.31	1.70	1.51
Two political ads	1.23	1.48	1.35
	$F[1, 510] = 0.28, p = .600, \eta^2 = .001$		
Number of negative comments			
No political ad	1.07	1.03	1.05
Two political ads	1.17	1.34	1.26
	$F[1, 510] = .64, p = .426, \eta^2 = .001$		
Positive feeling toward product ad			
No political ad	−.098	.056	−.021
Two political ads	.022	.034	.028
	$F[1, 509] = 0.48, p = .489, \eta^2 = .001$		
Negative feeling toward product ad			
No political ad	.347	.013	.180
Two political ads	−.075	−.031	−.053
	$F[1, 509] = 3.52, p = .061, \eta^2 = .007$		

Note: Cell entries are mean scores. *P* values are for interaction terms in two-by-two ANOVA with education and experimental conditions as factors.

proposition ads. The interaction terms are in the predicted direction but not statistically significant for the other three measures.

Having found traces of support for the proposition that the conditional context effects generalize across different types of political ads, we now address the question whether a double dose of political ads increases the effect (see Table 2-3). Experimental design considerations led us to use only negative ads in the two-ad condition. The test is thus between the control group and subjects who saw the product ads accompanied by two negative political ads. The interaction effects for negative feelings toward product ads ($p = .061$) and for feelings toward business in general (.041) were in the same direction as seen on the other two tables, indicating an assimilation effect among better educated subjects and a contrast effect among the less educated.

The remaining three interaction terms failed to attain significance. As Table 2-3 shows, after exposure to two political ads, subjects had fewer and more negative comments about product ads, *independent of their education*.[12] In other words, what is distinct about the two-ad data is the behavior of the less educated subjects. As a comparison of the mean number of comments in Tables 2-1 through 2-3 reveals, better educated subjects offered consistently more negative and fewer positive comments after exposure to political ads, no matter how many political ads they watched. The number of comments by the less educated, however, changed with the number of political ads; after exposure to only one political ad, they had fewer negative and more positive comments than control subjects. But after exposure to a double dose of political ads, the tone of their comments began to resemble those of the better educated subjects.[13] They also had more negative and fewer positive comments to offer after seeing two negative political ads. More research is clearly needed on this point, but our results suggest that the contrast effect among the less educated might hold only for moderate to high doses of political ads. When the difference between political and product ads is more clearly apparent (that is, when two rather than one out of the nine ads were political), even the less educated become more negative in their evaluation of product ads. Because a two-to-nine ratio of political to product ads is within the normal range during the last stages of election campaigns, the threat of an assimilation effect, even among the less educated, should be taken seriously by product advertisers.

Conclusion

In this chapter, we have attempted to synthesize two areas of study that have previously been kept apart. Product advertising has been studied mostly in the fields of consumer behavior and marketing. Political advertising is the focus of research in political science and political communication. During election campaigns people watch product ads in close proximity to political ads. It seems plausible that the presence of political ads can influence responses to product ads, and that both fields of study might benefit from an approach that considers the interaction between the two forms of advertising. We have taken a small first step in this direction by examining the effects of political commercials on evaluations of product commercials that appeared in the same ad break.

We find evidence for an assimilation effect among better educated subjects and for a contrast effect among the less educated. After watching political ads that they perceive as less favorable, less educated subjects come to realize that product ads, relatively speaking, are not so bad. Among better educated subjects, on the other hand, product commercials suffer from their proximity to political ads; negative feelings about political ads rub off on product ads. Results from the two-ad design suggest that this interaction with education disappears when the number of political ads increases. After exposure to two political ads, the comments of our less educated subjects resembled those of the better educated in tone. The interaction effect was still present for feelings toward product ads and business in general, however. In sum, we find an interaction effect with education, but that might depend on the number of political messages in the context. Results suggest the possibility that greater exposure to political ads for the less educated leads them to exhibit the same assimilation effect displayed by better educated subjects. Only future research can clarify this point.

Why does the occurrence of a contrast or assimilation effect depend on education? We surmise that the explanation concerns the similarity between product and political advertising. Consider again the study by Ottati and Isbell (1996). Seemingly, their results run exactly counter to our findings. They found a contrast effect among efficient processors and an assimilation effect among inefficient processors. Their explanation focuses on the correction for the biasing influence of mood. Efficient processors "understand" that mood is most likely not a helpful basis for evaluations of unrelated stimuli. Consequently, they correct—ultimately, overcorrect—for the mood bias. As a result, positive mood has a negative impact on the evaluation of the target (contrast effect). Inefficient processors, on the other hand, failing to realize the mismatch between mood and stimulus, do not attempt to correct, thereby treating positive mood as a relevant factor in favor of the object and thus experience an assimilation effect.

Whereas Ottati and Isbell unobtrusively induced a mood that was unrelated to the information to be evaluated, our study design involved exactly the opposite situation. We used the presence of a stimulus resembling the target (a political commercial) to induce negative mood toward the target and then measured evaluations of the target. Because of the similarity between the political and product ads, the better educated might more quickly perceive product ads and political ads as belonging to the same category. A mood state induced by a political ad is an appropriate basis for evaluations of product ads, and consequently well-educated subjects might not attempt to correct for the mood bias. The less educated, on the other hand, may place political and product ads in different mental categories, and thus attempt to correct for the irrelevant influence of mood induced by the unrelated political ad. In other words, Ottati and Isbell created a situation where mood was irrelevant and correcting necessary. Our study, however, presents subjects with a situation where mood is relevant. To the extent that people regard political advertising as just another manipulative attempt to influence their behavior, the tone of political advertising is relevant to product ad evaluations and correcting therefore is unlikely to occur among well-educated subjects.

Much of the last paragraph reads like a cognitive explanation along the lines suggested by social judgment theory. Social judgment theory predicts an assimilation effect when people regard political ads as categorically similar to product ads, as the better educated might well do. It postulates a contrast effect if political ads are seen as a generically different type of advertising, a view plausibly held by less educated people. Hence, although our research design does not allow us to distinguish affective and cognitive explanations for our findings, we are convinced that a crucial role in conditioning context effects is played by the connection people see (or do not see) between political and product advertising.

Our study was motivated by advertising executives' gut reactions to what they perceive as the threat of political advertising. An association with "dirty" political ads, so they reasoned, would harm their "clean" product advertisements. Our results substantiate their intuition. Among better educated people, political ads pollute the advertising airwaves. To the extent that businesses care about the enhanced purchasing power of well-educated customers, our findings should alarm the advertising industry and their clients. Moreover, we find suggestive evidence that political advertising even inflicts harm on product advertising among less sophisticated consumers when they encounter higher doses of political messages that are not unusual in major campaigns.

Notes

1. Some states (such as Minnesota and Maine) have formulated voluntary campaign guidelines that include an "in person" rule which requires candidates to appear in their negative ads. To date, however, few major candidates have agreed to be bound by these guidelines.

2. This research was supported by grants from the John and Mary R. Markle Foundation and the University of California, Los Angeles.

3. The demographic characteristics of the participants are as follows: median age, 37; 51 percent with college degree; party identification distributed as 31 percent Republican, 14 percent independent, and 41 percent Democrat; race, 3 percent Asian, 10 percent black, 8 percent Hispanic, and 76 percent white.

4. While participants were free to converse with each other during the viewing sessions, they completed their responses to the questionnaires individually.

5. Most of Clinton's ads focused on social welfare issues. Typically, Clinton's negative ads depicted Sen. Bob Dole and Speaker Newt Gingrich as advocates of cuts in social security, Medicare, student loans, child care, and other benefit programs. Clinton's positive ads focused on the president's steadfastness in resisting congressional Republicans' efforts to slash government programs and agencies. Dole's ads on social welfare programs tended to focus on "wasteful" government spending (for example, funding of "midnight basketball" in the inner cities) and on labeling President Clinton as a big spender. Senator Dole's ads on the subject of taxes contrasted his 15 percent tax cut plan with the tax increases supported by President Clinton. Clinton's ads in the taxes category either attacked Dole's tax cut plan ("risky" and a threat to the health of the economy) or depicted Dole and Gingrich as supporters of tax increases themselves ("taxmen for the welfare state").

In the case of illegal immigration, Dole used a series of attack ads concerning the administration's failure to curb the flow of illegal immigrants. Clinton used a rebuttal ad in which he claimed credit for strengthening border patrols and protecting American workers from illegal immigrants.

In the general category of crime, Dole's ad campaign concentrated on teenage drug abuse. We included a pair of Dole ads that featured footage from the infamous 1992 MTV interview in which Clinton admitted to having used marijuana while a college student. The Clinton crime ad focused on the successful passage of the Brady bill.

6. Exploratory factor analysis using principal component extraction generated a one-factor solution (explaining 52 percent of the variance) with very similar factor loadings. For simplicity, we use the average of the four thermometer ratings as our dependent measure. The reliability of this index is 0.7 (Cronbach's alpha).

7. Two different pain reliever ads were randomly varied to protect against idiosyncratic results caused by specific ads.

8. We used exploratory factor analysis with principal component extraction to examine the underlying structure of responses to these six items. For both ads, a two-factor solution (corresponding to positive and negative feelings) was obtained, where the second factor added roughly 20 percent to the explained variance. We computed factor scores on the two factors after varimax rotation as our measures of positive and negative feelings toward product ads.

9. The Pearson correlation between the positive and negative indicators is $-.32$.

10. Ottati and Isbell (1996) use recall of information and political knowledge to operationalize processing efficiency.

11. We carried out an identical analysis with respect to the tone of the political ad, but found that effects were similar for positive and negative political ads. Moreover, neither controlling for education nor analyzing the effects of Republican and Democratic ads separately revealed any systematic differences in subjects' responses to product ads that could be attributed to the tone of the adjacent political ad.

12. Statistical significance of these effects is marginal for positive ($F[1,515] = 2.18$, $p = .140$, $\eta^2 = .004$) and negative comments ($F[1,515] = 2.86$, $p = .092$, $\eta^2 = .006$).

13. The number of positive and negative comments is not significantly different between the one-ad (presidential and proposition ads pooled) and two-ad conditions among the better educated ($t[698] = .31$, $p = .75$ for negative comments; $t[698] = -1.25$, $p = .21$. for positive comments). Conversely, less educated subjects had significantly more negative comments after two ads ($t[691] = -2.14$, $p = .03$), and marginally fewer positive comments ($t[691] = 1.41$, $p = .16$).

3 This Side of Jordan:
Black Churches and Partisan Political Attitudes

Allison Calhoun-Brown

Since the 1980s, many political scientists and sociologists have researched the relationship between religion and politics.[1] Their research has focused on how personal religiosity, religious group identification, and theological beliefs influence political opinions and behaviors. Often motivated by the rise of the Christian right in the 1980s and 1990s, the researchers clearly demonstrated the important effects of individual religious attributes on political mobilization. However, most of this research has been focused on white Christians only, because African Americans are thought to be sufficiently different in their religious, cultural, and political traditions to warrant separate study.

The interplay of religion and politics in the black community has been well studied, particularly questions of how communal or church-based forms of religion influence political mobilization and electoral choice. This is obviously an important area of research in which significant results have been documented (Harris 1999; Tate 1993). Yet the focus on elections has meant relative neglect of the question of whether personal religiosity and attendance and participation in church also influence the political attitudes of African Americans. It might seem that such an inquiry is hardly needed, since the vast majority of blacks consistently vote Democratic. This fact might imply that if black churches influence public opinion, they would be likely to foster liberal perspectives.

However, there are reasons to investigate the impact of religiosity on political attitudes. First, it is possible that the black church does not promote consistently liberal political attitudes. Black churches are overwhelmingly evangelical, and evangelicalism is consistently a strong predictor of conservative positions on moral and cultural issues, in particular among whites (Calhoun-Brown 1997; Leege and Kellstedt 1993; Wilcox 1992). Some scholars have characterized black churches as very conservative institutions (Reed 1986). Thus, while attending black churches may lead to pro-Democratic political mobilization, it is not safe to assume that attending such churches is associated with the development of liberal opinions on all policy issues.

A second reason to assess the relationship between black churches and public opinion is that even though the majority of blacks identify themselves as Democrats, it is possible to maintain identification with a party and yet manifest differing levels of satisfaction with the party's behavior, candidates, or issue positions. African American churches may play a role in this dynamic because they act as one of the primary socialization agents in the African American community (Walton 1985).

Finally, although much research has been conducted into the effects of the media on public opinion, less attention has been given to the impact of other important sources of information in people's lives. Churches are uniquely positioned to influence attitude formation because they often express a consistent theological perspective; have moral authority; constitute a genuine community; have regular interaction; share a common set of beliefs, values, and traditions; and receive legitimacy from God (Wald, Owen, and Hill 1988). Considering the historical importance of African American churches to the black community, the churches might be expected to affect the evaluation and assessment of a broad range of political matters.

Black Churches and Politics

Historically, black churches have been the largest and most resource-rich institutions in the African American community. Many scholars have observed that because of the lack of access to the broader society that slavery, and later segregation, mandated, black churches once constituted the entire civil society for the black community (Lincoln and Mamiya 1990; Wilmore 1983; Raboteau 1978; Lincoln 1974; DuBois [1903] 1965). Benjamin Mays and Joseph Nicholson contended that "it is not too much to say that if the Negro had experienced a wide range of freedom in the social and economic spheres, there would have been fewer Negro churches" (1933, 11). But opportunities for African Americans were severely constricted, and black churches became the arena of their political and social activities. The churches had to play a role in ameliorating the social, economic, and political conditions that impinged on the lives of parishioners. W. E. B. DuBois concluded that black Christianity and struggles for equality and freedom were uniquely interwoven: "The Negro religion transformed itself and identified with the dream of abolition, until that which was a radical fad in the white North and an anarchistic plot in the white South had become a religion to the black world" ([1903] 1965, 148).

The centrality of churches to the black community gave them the capacity to speak for a people ubiquitously oppressed on the basis of race. The lack of other institutions gave them a mandate to do so. The political importance of black churches is most clearly exemplified by the mobilizing role they played during the civil rights movement. Scholars highlight the communication network, money, facilities, and audience that churches provided (Morris 1984; McAdam 1982). They suggest that without the mobilization of these resources, the movement would have been impossible.

In part because of the importance of churches in the politics of the civil rights movement, contemporary theories of the political role of African American churches have focused on mobilization. These theories emphasize the role of organizational resources in fostering all types of collective action. According to this kind of analysis, the civil rights movement was not primarily a manifestation of an oppressed minority but the result of the urbanization of the southern black population, the increase in the number of middle class blacks, and the organizational expansion of black churches (Piven and Cloward 1977; McAdam 1982). These theories underscore how institutions are able to marshal participants for specific events and strategies, garner support from potential allies, and sustain action even in the face of failure (Fireman and Gamson 1979; Tilly 1979). From this perspective, mobilization is the

process by which a group secures collective control over the resources needed for collective action. The major issues therefore are the resources controlled by the group prior to mobilization efforts, and the processes by which the group pools resources and direct these toward social change (Jenkins 1983, 552–553).

Because black churches are the most resource-rich institutions in the black community, churches are central to this dynamic.

Black churches mobilize their members to take part in electoral politics as well. Michael Preston, Lenneal Henderson, and Paul Puryear (1982) suggest that voting itself is a type of collective action aimed at increasing the power of the group. As William Nelson observed, "The new black politics constitutes an immensely serious effort to build bases of electoral strength in the black community and to organize black political interests around the power to vote" (1982). The costs entailed in registering and voting are eased by the work of organizations directed at getting out the vote. Thus, organizational involvement can become an important determinant of political participation.

Several studies have shown that churches can provide this organizational involvement. For instance, in their analysis of Jesse Jackson's 1984 presidential campaign, Patricia Gurin, Shirley Hatchett, and James Jackson (1989) identify churches as important political resources. In examining the 1984 and 1988 presidential election campaigns, Katherine Tate (1991) establishes that politically active churches can encourage electoral activity. Clyde Wilcox (1990) reports similar findings concerning political activity and participation. Ronald Brown and Monica Wolford (1994) explain that African American church culture encourages members to engage in political action, even when the government is perceived as being unresponsive to the political concerns of African Americans. Research has shown that activist churches have a consistent impact on political behavior. Activist churches are ones in which parishioners hear overt political messages and are encouraged and even assisted by the church with the process of electoral and political participation. Activist churches may issue pastoral endorsements, organize voter registration drives, make political announcements, give political candidates opportunities to speak from the pulpit, distribute voting slates, make financial contributions to candidates or give opportunities for congregants to do so. Activist churches may not engage in all of these activities, but it is clear that such churches provide an environment in which politicization can take place.

These kinds of churches also enhance the psychological resources associated with individual political participation. Many believe that African American religiosity most significantly influences participation and public opinion indirectly through its contribution to the development of racial group-based attitudes and beliefs. Richard Allen, Michael Dawson, and Ronald Brown found religiosity to be a major influence on how African Americans use racial constructs to process, store, and organize information about the social environment. Although they operationalized religiosity in terms of personal indicators such as reading religious books, praying, and watching religious programming, they concluded that the main source of religion's influence was communal in nature. For example, they posited that "those who have strong religious commitments will be integrated into social networks in the black community." They conceptualized a religious community as having members who share a common set of religious beliefs, values, and traditions and who engage in regular social interaction (1989, 425). Although Allen, Dawson, and Brown included no organizational or communal measures in their study, other research utilizing such measures has confirmed their results. In these studies, respondents who went to activist churches were found to have more intense feelings of racial identity, group consciousness, system blame, political efficacy, and political interest (Calhoun-Brown 1996; Harris 1994). Their research, along with that of Laura Reese and Ronald Brown (1995), clearly establish that attending activist churches in which political messages are communicated can increase participation as well as the psychological resources associated with it. Psychological resources promote political action (Verba and Nie 1972; Conway 2000). In the case of minorities, psychological resources such as racial identity and consciousness, political interest, and political efficacy have been used to explain why blacks participate in politics at higher rates than their social, economic, or educational backgrounds alone would suggest (Verba, Ashmed, and Bhatt 1971; Verba and Nie 1972). If attending activist churches can increase political participation indirectly through the enhancement of these psychological resources, then these churches might also directly influence the evaluation and assessments of other aspects of politics.

Research has consistently shown religion to be an important source of political values (Leege and Kellstedt 1997). Indeed, some have argued that religion and the values associated with it have helped to provide the basis for a new partisan alignment in which the economic issues central to American politics since the Depression have been replaced by cleavages based on cultural issues and matters of personal morality (Jelen 1997; Kellstedt et al. 1994; Hunter 1991). To be sure, African Americans have not participated in any partisan realignment; but considering the centrality of African American churches to the black political experience, it would be strange to conclude that attending African American churches can motivate participation and increase the psychological resources associated with participation without influencing the political attitudes that often provide a rationale and purpose to the mobilization effort. Yet there has been little research to date to examine the impact of black churches on political attitudes.

This chapter examines public opinions and attitudes important to the electoral environment. Because other research has clearly shown the impact of attending African American churches on individual voter turnout, this study examines whether such churches direct turnout in particular ways by facilitating more positive assessments of certain political leaders, parties, and issues. Thus, this study evaluates the assumption that respondents who attend African American churches will have more positive assessments of the Democratic Party, Democratic political figures, and Democrats' ability to handle national political issues.

Data and Methods

To examine the impact of religion on political attitudes in the African American community, this chapter uses the 1996 National Black Election Study (NBES). The NBES is a national cross-sectional survey that in 1996 yielded a sample of 1,216 African American adult respondents. In most national election studies, there are too few black respondents to closely examine African American partisanship. The NBES is based upon a large, representative national sample of African Americans, however, and thus it permits more subtle statistical analysis.

The dependent variables in this analysis are attitudes toward political parties, political leaders, and candidates. Although it is commonly assumed that black churches foster strong partisan feelings and liberal issue orientations, little research has been devoted explicitly to this topic. As Hanes Walton observed, "Volumes have been written about partisan identification and partisan realignments, yet African American partisan behavior remains a virtual enigma" (1997, 208). Because the majority of African Americans are nominal Democrats, it is important to examine variations in the strength of the psychological attachment to the party, which can reveal dissatisfaction with the party. Attitudes toward parties are operationally defined as affect toward the parties and beliefs about which party would better handle various issues facing the country.

Respondents in the NBES were asked to rate both the Democratic and the Republican Parties on "feeling thermometers," which measure affect toward parties. Feeling thermometers range from the coolest rating of 0 to the highest rating of 100 degrees, with higher scores indicating warmer (and thus more favorable) evaluations. Respondents were also asked which party would better handle health care and welfare, and whether the Democrats or the Republicans cared about issues facing black Americans.

In addition, this analysis examined affect toward key electoral figures such as Bill Clinton and Bob Dole, as well as other highly symbolic political figures including Jesse Jackson, Newt Gingrich, and Louis Farrakhan—again measured by feeling thermometers. All feeling thermometers were corrected for positivity bias.[2] Respondents were also asked which presidential candidate, Clinton or Dole, they believed would do a better job handling a range of particular issues, including foreign affairs, health care, race relations, poverty, the budget deficit, and welfare reform.

The independent variables that are the central focus of this inquiry are attendance at a political church and frequency of church attendance. Past research on the political roles of African American churches has distinguished between political churches, in which church members are exposed to church-based political information from the pastor or other members of the congregation, and nonpolitical churches where this kind of political information is not communicated (Tate 1991; Reese and Brown 1995). "Political churches can be differentiated from other churches in that they provide an environment in which politicization can take place" (Calhoun-Brown 1996, 941). In such churches electoral participation is the communicated norm, and political activity is often facilitated by the institution itself.

There were two questions that determined whether a respondent attended a political church in the 1996 NBES. The first question asked respondents whether or not they had heard political announcements at their church. The second asked them whether or not their church had encouraged members to vote in the election. The data reconfirm that not all African American churches are political churches. Although just over 60 percent of the respondents worshiped where they were encouraged to vote, only 36 percent reported attending churches in which political announcements were made. These two items have been combined to form a single indicator of the political nature of the church the respondent attended.[3]

Although much research concludes that African American churches stimulate political participation, a number of scholars have contended that black churches are a negative influence on political mobilization (Powdermaker 1939; Myrdal 1944; Marx 1967; Frazier 1976; Reed 1986). These scholars assert that black churches are inherently noninterventionist and may actually discourage the political empowerment of blacks. From this perspective black churches are seen to foster conservative attitudes and not to promote liberal political activity—especially among working class and poor blacks.

It may be that attending nonpolitical churches will have a different impact on evaluations of parties and policymakers than attending a church with high levels of political discussion. Thus, frequency of church attendance is entered into the model separately from the political church variable. In the 1996 NBES frequency of church attendance could be operationalized by responses to a question about how often respondents went to church. Responses ranged from once a week or more to never.[4] No interesting interaction effects were found between the frequency of church attendance and political church variables.

Churches are not the only source of attitudes toward political objects. The analysis that follows holds constant a number of control variables to see whether religion matters even when the effects of these other variables have been controlled.

Several studies indicate that attending African American churches increases a sense of racial identification and that racial identification can influence political attitudes and behaviors (Tate 1993; Allen, Dawson, and Brown 1989). Thus, racial identification is entered as a control variable. Four racial identification questions were combined to create a composite measure of this indicator. The four questions include two indicators of whether respondents think that what happens to black people will have something to do with what happens in their lives, as well as an indicator of how often they think about what they have in common with other blacks, and an indicator of the degree to which they believe being black determines how people are treated.[5]

Respondents were asked whether or not they belonged to an organization working to improve the status of black people. These organizations, like the churches, may be important sources of political socialization and information. Although extensive research has not been done on black organizations and the formation of public opinion, in general organizational membership is regarded as an important predictor of political participation because such organizations can disseminate and frame political information in ways that influence political attitudes (Tate 1993; Tarrow 1992; Verba and Nie 1972).

The responsibility of the government to regulate the economy and provide social welfare benefits underlies the major divisions between the two political parties as well as between major electoral figures (Flanigan and Zingale 1994, chap. 6). Thus, this analysis includes a question about whether the respondent feels the government should make a special effort to help blacks or whether blacks should help themselves; these attitudes are potential determinants of electoral assessments.

Because socioeconomic factors are important determinants of the evaluations of parties, candidates, and issues, controls are entered for region, education, family income, gender, age, and home ownership. This analysis also includes a control for level of political knowledge. Respondents were evaluated according to whether they could correctly identify the name and party of their national senators and representative. One point was given for each correct response. Respondents who knew the name and party of both their senators and their representative received a 6, one point for each correct name and one for each correct party. If they could correctly identify nothing they received a 0. Accordingly, this scale ranges from 0 to 6. Finally, respondents were asked about their basic partisan identification.

Basic partisan identification is included in the analysis because it naturally is an important determinant of the evaluation of political parties, electoral figures, and their ability to handle important national issues. Respondents identified themselves as Democrats, Republicans, or independents. In this analysis, a dichotomous variable is created and Democrats are coded 1.

In the analysis that follows, the two independent variables—attending a political church and frequency of church attendance—are regressed on a series of attitudes toward political objects. The control variables are also included in the models, to see whether religion has an independent impact on attitudes.

Results

Table 3-1 presents the data on the impact of religion on assessment of the political parties. The data show that African Americans who attended a political church in 1996 rated the Republican Party significantly more coolly than did other blacks who shared the same partisanship and attitudes. Frequent church attenders, however, were significantly cooler toward the Democratic Party and warmer toward the Republicans. This does not mean that African Americans who attend church regularly prefer the Republican Party—they prefer the Democratic Party by a large margin. Instead it means that frequent attenders are less likely to have strongly polarized partisan evaluations than are less frequent attenders.

The data in Table 3-2 show a similar pattern. Those who attended political churches were more likely to believe that Democrats would do a better job on health care, but they were not significantly more likely to believe that Democrats would do a better job on welfare, perhaps because Democratic president Bill Clinton had signed a welfare reform bill before the 1996 election that significantly limited the length of time that citizens could collect welfare benefits. In contrast, those who attended churches regularly were significantly less likely than other respondents to believe that the Democrats were better on these issues.

The data in the last four columns of this table show that those who attended political churches were more likely to believe that Democrats were best on black issues, whereas those who frequently attended church were more likely to choose the Republicans. Once again, attending a black church heightened pro-Democratic sentiments, whereas church attendance dampens partisan sentiments once the effects of political churches are held constant.[6]

The data in Table 3-3 show the impact of religion on evaluations of key political figures. The first six columns of the table present evaluations of three prominent white politicians: Democratic president Bill Clinton, Republican presidential candidate Bob Dole, and Republican Speaker of the House Newt Gingrich. Clinton and Dole would have been mentioned by name in political churches during the 1996 campaign, but Gingrich would

Table 3-1 Indicators of Affect Toward Parties, 1996

	Affect Toward Democrats		Affect Toward Republicans	
	B	SE	B	SE
Attendance of politically active church	1.95	1.40	−3.40*	1.61
Frequency of church attendance	−1.85*	.60	2.23*	.69
Age	.10	.05	.02	.06
Education	−1.40*	.49	1.57**	.56
Family income	.04	.30	−.19	.36
Gender (female)	2.77	1.47	−2.27	1.70
Region (South)	1.01	1.38	.19	1.59
Special government help for blacks	.36	.32	−1.28**	.37
Level of racial identification	.11	.70	−1.10	.80
Democratic identification	13.17***	1.50	−11.82***	1.72
Level of political knowledge	.76	.42	.28	.49
Home ownership	−.17	1.47	−1.13	1.70
Membership in black organization	.21	1.54	−3.84*	1.76
Constant	13.17***	3.67	−11.44*	4.27
Adjusted R²	.14		.13	

Source: National Black Election Study, 1996.

Note: Entries are regression coefficients. Racial identification and government role are coded toward the liberal perspective.

*p < .05, **p < .005, ***p < .0005
B = Unstandardized beta coefficient
SE = Standard error

probably not have been mentioned. Neither attending a political church nor frequency of church attendance had any impact on evaluations of Bill Clinton. Feelings for Clinton were best predicted by basic partisanship and by age and gender. Those who attended a political church were significantly cooler toward Bob Dole, however, and those who attended church frequently were significantly warmer toward Dole. Involvement in a political church also led to more negative evaluations of Newt Gingrich, but church attendance had no effect. In addition, those who knew the most about American politics were the coolest toward Gingrich.

The last four columns of this table report the results for affect toward two key black political figures, both of whom are also religious leaders. If African American churches have a significant influence on political evaluations, it is likely that they will have an especially strong effect on evaluations of black leaders. Those who attended political churches were

Table 3-2 Indicators of Partisan Ability to Handle Issues, 1996

	Health Care		Welfare		Democrats and Black Issues		Republicans and Black Issues	
	B	SE	B	SE	B	SE	B	SE
Attendance of politically active church	0.70*	0.22	0.30	0.18	0.55*	0.24	0.22	0.28
Frequency of church attendance	−0.31**	0.09	−0.29**	0.08	0.20*	0.10	0.42***	0.12
Age	−0.00	0.01	0.00	0.01	−0.00	0.01	0.02	0.01
Education	−0.06	0.07	−0.03	0.06	−0.16*	0.08	−0.23*	0.10
Family income	0.00	0.04	−0.02	0.04	0.03	0.05	−0.01	0.05
Gender (female)	−0.21	0.23	−0.16	0.19	0.42	0.25	−0.61*	0.29
Region (South)	−0.06	0.21	0.25	0.17	0.18	0.23	−0.12	0.28
Special government help for blacks	0.06	0.05	0.00	0.04	−0.07	0.06	−0.17**	0.06
Level of racial identification	0.18	0.10	0.08	0.09	−0.18	0.12	−0.26	0.13
Democratic identification	1.05***	0.21	1.04***	0.18	0.75**	0.24	−0.43	0.29
Level of political knowledge	0.18*	0.07	−0.02	0.05	0.23***	0.07	−0.05	0.09
Home ownership	−0.12	0.22	−0.07	0.19	−0.35	0.24	−0.14	0.29
Membership in black organization	0.20	0.23	0.27	0.19	−0.71**	0.25	−0.41	0.32
Constant	1.13	0.55	0.47	0.47	−0.60	0.62	−0.96	0.76
−2 log likelihood	640.3		846.1		518.9		379.4	
Percentage of cases predicted correctly	79		68		77		84	

Source: National Black Election Study, 1996.

Note: Entries are logistic regression coefficients. Racial identification and government role are coded toward the liberal perspective.

*p < .05, **p < .005, ***p < .0005
B = Unstandardized beta coefficient
SE = Standard error

Table 3-3 Indicators of Affect Toward Political Figures, 1996

	Clinton		Dole		Gingrich		Jackson		Farrakhan	
	B	SE	B	SE	B	SE	B	SE	B	SE
Attendance of politically active church	1.90	1.43	−5.48***	1.53	−3.47*	1.62	5.94***	1.46	2.66	1.92
Frequency of church attendance	−0.69	0.61	2.64***	0.65	0.14	0.69	−.06	.61	−3.22***	.82
Age	0.28***	0.05	0.00	0.06	−0.06	0.06	−.19**	.06	−.26**	.07
Education	−0.71	0.50	1.41	0.54	−0.40	0.56	.05	.50	−.12	.66
Family income	0.41	0.31	−0.03	0.33	−0.02	0.35	−.51	.31	−.02	.41
Gender (female)	4.40**	1.50	−3.09*	1.60	−3.68*	1.68	1.74	1.52	−1.82	2.02
Region (South)	0.92	1.41	0.43	1.50	0.18	1.62	.69	1.43	−3.04	1.89
Special government help for blacks	0.80	0.33	−1.63***	0.34	−0.10	0.54	.40	.33	1.56*	.45
Level of racial identification	0.48	0.71	−1.23	0.76	−1.45	0.82	1.76*	.73	2.48*	.95
Democratic identification	8.80***	1.52	−11.65***	1.62	−8.80**	1.76	9.95***	1.50	−1.30	2.04
Level of political knowledge	1.90*	0.44	−0.43	0.46	−1.90***	0.48	.35	.44	.46	.58
Home ownership	−2.59	1.51	−0.09	1.61	1.15	1.72	−.45	1.54	5.28*	2.02
Membership in black organization	2.87	1.57	−4.17**	1.67	−1.91*	1.76	−.68	1.60	8.36***	2.10
Constant	−3.62	3.76*	−9.50	4.03	−8.12*	4.32	12.10**	3.84	5.35	5.09
Adjusted R²	0.16		0.16		0.20		0.10		0.11	

Source: National Black Election Study, 1996.

Note: Entries are regression coefficients. Racial identification and government role are coded toward the liberal perspective.

*p < .05, **p < .005, ***p < .0005

B = Unstandardized beta coefficient

SE = Standard error

significantly warmer toward the Protestant minister Jesse Jackson, but not toward the Black Muslim leader Louis Farrakhan. The impact of attending a political church on evaluations of Jackson is strong, even after controls for levels of racial identification and partisanship are taken into account.

Interestingly, frequency of church attendance does not increase positive affect for Jackson, despite his close relationship with black churches. Frequent church attenders were substantially more negative toward Farrakhan, however. This finding reinforces the importance of the messages that are communicated in politicized contexts. Black Muslims represent a considerable challenge to the hegemony of black Christian churches in the arena of sociopolitical activity. Furthermore, their theology is not consistent with that of most Christians. For these reasons, churches that do not frame Farrakhan's activities as beneficial to the African American community may encourage much cooler feelings toward him.

The data in Table 3-4 reinforce the idea that without overt political framing, churches in the African American community can have a significant moderating effect on respondents who attend them frequently. This table reports the impact of political churches and church attendance on beliefs that Clinton was better able than Dole to handle race relations and Social Security benefits. In no instance did attending a political church increase the belief that Clinton was best able to handle the nation's problems, once partisanship, racial identity, and political information were held constant. However, frequent church attendance decreased the belief that Clinton could best improve race relations. Amazingly, the more often respondents went to church, the more likely they were to believe that Clinton would cut Social Security benefits. On each of these issues, church attendance was one of the few variables that reduced support for Clinton. These results are unanticipated, and they strongly suggest that it is important to examine separately the impact of political churches and of church attendance.

Discussion

Overall, the data presented in this chapter reveal several important findings about the relationship between black churches and the formation of attitudes toward politics. First, this research indicates that defining a political church is not as straightforward as it might seem. Previous research suggested that political churches are those in which members are exposed to church-based political messages. In that study, only political churches impacted group consciousness, interest in politics, political efficacy, or political participation. Frequency of church attendance, by itself, had no impact (Calhoun-Brown 1996).

However, the data analyzed for the present chapter demonstrate that both frequency of church attendance and attending political churches can have important, and often quite dif-

Table 3-4 Indicators of Clinton's Ability to Handle Issues, 1996

	Better Able to Improve Race Relations		More Likely to Cut Social Security Benefits	
	B	SE	B	SE
Attendance of politically active church	0.39	0.22	−0.23	0.35
Frequency of church attendance	−0.20*	0.09	0.47**	0.14
Age	0.01	0.01	−0.03*	0.01
Education	−0.19*	0.08	0.08	0.13
Family income	0.11*	0.05	−0.08	0.07
Gender (female)	0.09	0.23	−0.32	0.36
Region (South)	0.02	0.21	−0.15	0.33
Special government help for blacks	0.08	0.05	−0.07	0.08
Level of racial identification	0.07	0.11	−0.21	0.16
Democratic identification	0.84***	0.22	−0.76*	0. 33
Level of political knowledge	0.31***	0.08	−0.38**	0.14
Home ownership	−0.36	0.23	0.36	0.35
Membership in black organization	0.14	0.24	−0.70	0.42
Constant	0.32	0.56	−0.97	0.88
−2 log likelihood	601.5		282.6	
Percentage of cases predicted correctly	81		92	

Source: National Black Election Study, 1996.

Note: Entries are regression coefficients. Racial identification and government role are coded toward the liberal perspective.

*p < .05, **p < .005, ***p < .0005
B = Unstandardized beta coefficient
SE = Standard error

ferent, effects on the formation of attitudes and opinions about political objects. In most studies of the political roles of African American churches, frequency of church attendance has not been a key indicator. However, the data analyzed here show that churches are uniquely positioned to impact attitude formation and that attendance matters.

Second, this research emphasizes that what is often referred to as the black church is in fact a collection of heterogeneous institutions. Important variations exist between churches with high levels of political discussion and those that do not stress politics. Indeed, in this analysis, the effects of attending a political church increased pro-Democratic sentiments overall, but frequent church attendance had the opposite effect. This finding was unanticipated because black churches are considered to be a cornerstone of Democratic politics. However, these data indicate that even in the black community—absent blatantly political messages—attending church can promote conservative political attitudes.

It is important to put the results in context, however. The data do not suggest that attending black churches makes blacks identify as Republicans or vote for GOP candidates. Blacks are overwhelmingly Democrats and have much warmer feelings toward the Democratic Party and Democratic candidates. Still, this study may offer some support for those who have contended that black churches are inherently conservative institutions. Outcomes such as feeling positive toward Dole are hardly radical; but finding that attendance at nonpolitical black churches actually works against pro-Democratic opinions—the notion that the Democratic Party and Democratic candidates are best able to handle important national issues—speaks to the level of conservatism that may exist in some of these "nonpolitical" institutions.

Third, the analysis suggests that the dynamics of attitude formation are different from those of political mobilization and that the two processes may not be naturally linked. Previous research has found that political churches impact voter turnout and electoral participation. However, the data presented here do not support the conclusion that frequent church attendance leads automatically to a liberal evaluation of political parties and their candidates or the ability of these entities to do a good job with issues. In fact, without overt political messages the converse seems to be true. Moreover, although attending churches had a significant impact on pro-Democratic affect, the relationship of attendance with beliefs that the Democrats or President Clinton could best handle the specified problems was far weaker.

Finally, this research reconfirms the centrality of black churches to politics in the African American community. Both attending political churches and frequency of church attendance had considerable impact on evaluations of parties and electoral figures and of their ability to handle national issues. Although black churches no longer constitute most of civil society for black people, the data indicate that these institutions continue to have substantial influence on the attitudes of the people sitting in the pews. The fact that the political church variable and the frequency of church attendance variable did not have similar impacts highlights the need for continuing research into the nature of churches as political environments as well as into how attitudes and public opinion, not just political participation, are shaped by these contexts.

Notes

1. See, for example, Leege and Kellstedt 1993; Wilcox 1992; Wald 1992; Jelen 1991; and Bruce 1988.
2. Positivity bias refers to individual differences in the use of feeling thermometers. Some respon-

dents use a wider range of the temperature scale than other respondents. Feeling thermometers were corrected for positivity bias by subtracting the mean score on all the preelection feeling thermometers from the score for the party or political figure in question (Wilcox, Sigelman, and Cook 1989).

3. Both variables loaded equally on the factor. The factor loading was 0.85.

4. Those who reported never attending church were not asked questions about the political nature of the church that they attended, since there could be no answer. However, only 5 percent of respondents reported never attending.

5. The factor loadings for each of the variables were black fate (0.74), black-linked fate (0.78), blacks similar treatment (0.64), and things in common with blacks (0.49).

6. It is important to note that Table 3-2 reports only issues on which the religious variables had significant impact. In the 1996 NBES, questions were asked about which party was better able to handle the nation's economy, foreign affairs, poverty, the budget deficit, Social Security, race relations, and taxes. On none of these issues were the religious variables important factors. Further research is required into why attending African American churches affects the evaluation of a party's ability to handle some issues and not others.

4 Latino Public Opinion

Carole Jean Uhlaner and F. Chris Garcia

A full chapter on Latino public opinion could not have been written before 1990. Only since the 1980s has much attention been paid to the opinions of Latino or Hispanic American publics. Recent burgeoning numbers of Latinos in the United States have led to considerable interest by social scientists and others in various aspects of the Latino experience, including the attitudes, beliefs, and values of this population. Some of the attention has been driven by the perception that Latinos constitute a very significant voting bloc. Some comes from the curiosity of marketers, eyeing Latinos' estimated $350 billion of buying power. Today Latinos' opinions and attitudes are closely monitored for these and other reasons. However, because this attention is recent, our knowledge of the dynamics of opinion among Latinos is somewhat limited. We have isolated snapshots of Latino public opinion. Nevertheless, we do know that one must be cautious even in using the very expression "Latino public opinion." On many dimensions, notably political ideology, party preference, and some issue positions, Latinos differ among themselves, especially by national origin and citizenship status.

Scholars face tremendous difficulty in accumulating data about Latino public opinion. Since until the 1990s Latinos made up less than 10 percent of the United States population, typical national samples yielded too few Latino respondents for reliable analyses. One solution to this problem is to oversample, that is, to include in a national sample more respondents from a particular subpopulation than their percentage of the population would normally produce. The overall sample can then be reweighted so that population figures are accurate, and yet enough persons from the subpopulation are polled to allow for reliable analyses of their preferences.

Another solution to the problem of studying a rare population, or a population of a relatively small incidence within the general population, is to conduct a study focused exclusively on them; in these cases, interpretations are limited by the absence of a control sample of the general population. Minority population surveys are methodologically tricky and usually quite expensive. They are most feasible when the rare population is heavily concentrated in a small number of geographic areas, as historically has been the case for African Americans. Partially for these reasons, and partially because of a relative lack of interest in the attitudes of Latinos, until recently virtually no comprehensive, nationally representative opinion studies existed that oversampled Latinos or that focused exclusively on the Latino population in the United States. Thus, we have a very shallow pool of information about the opinions of Hispanic Americans in the United States.

The few early (pre-1980s) surveys of Latino public opinion either tended to focus on only one component of the Latino population or were conducted in only a few states or localities (see Valdez 1987 and Forsyth and Melgoza 1987 for summaries).[1] Of all the early studies, arguably the most comprehensive was the National Chicano Survey conducted by the Survey Research Center and the University of Michigan (1979).[2] This survey drew a representative sample of persons of Mexican American ancestry throughout the southwestern United States and in the Chicago area. The National Chicano Survey provided invaluable new information. Nonetheless, it was restricted to two geographic regions and to one national origin group (albeit one making up some two-thirds of the Latino population).

Events in the late 1960s and early 1970s produced more interest in the attitudes and behaviors of Latinos. This was a time of considerable civil unrest and radical politics, including the civil rights movement and the anti–Vietnam War protests. During this period, the Chicano movement also came to the attention of much of the nation, as Latinos (primarily of Mexican ancestry but including some Puerto Ricans and Filipinos) made their needs known to the general public through participation in protest demonstrations, boycotts, sit-ins, and other types of unconventional politics. Perhaps the best known of these was the farm worker-led boycott against grapes, headed by César Chávez.

In part as a consequence of these movements, Latinos (defined as Hispanic-surnamed persons) were added as one of the protected groups in the 1975 extension of the Voting Rights Act. Political, judicial, and scholarly attention increased once the Voting Rights Act covered Latinos. Parallel to these developments, the number of Latino social scientists earning advanced degrees began to increase markedly. The Latino population also had grown, both in absolute numbers and as a percentage of the U.S. population. Latinos continued to make their voices heard, and interest increased in clearly hearing and understanding these voices. Even so, few systematic studies of Latino public opinion nationwide were conduced until the late 1980s. The absence of information had consequences. As Rodolfo de la Garza stated, "By not having their views regularly reported in polls, Latinos are effectively excluded from influencing [candidates and issues]" (1987, 4).[3] The lack of information about Latino public opinion changed substantially with the undertaking of the Latino National Political Survey.

The Latino National Political Survey

Although social scientists had become more interested in the politics of Latinos by the mid-1980s, the absence of empirical information left standing much mistaken conventional wisdom. Shortly before the 1984 presidential election, four Latino political scientists (Rodolfo de la Garza, Angelo Falcon, F. Chris Garcia, and John A. Garcia), disturbed by unsupported beliefs and the lack of empirical data on Latino attitudes, decided to encourage major polling organizations to include in their pre-1984 election surveys several additional questions of particular relevance to Latinos and/or to expand their small Latino samples to allow for reliable data analysis. These attempts met with very little success. The four social scientists decided they would conduct a national survey research study that focused on the Latino population. It took a considerable amount of planning plus substantial backing by four major philanthropic organizations before the Latino National Political Survey (LNPS), as the study became known, could be conducted. The study had three objectives. First, the researchers wanted to find out as much about Latino orientations as could possibly be covered in one survey. Second, they wanted to establish a foundation of baseline knowledge for later studies. Third, and underlying all of the rest, these researchers wanted to lay an empirical foundation for establishing whether a national community of Latinos existed.

Design and operational challenges were tremendous, since investigators were entering an area largely unexplored in terms of either survey methodology or content. How could one find an adequate sample of this rare (9 percent) and scattered population? What size sample would be sufficient for reliable estimates and yet be economically feasible? How would respondents be identified, since the boundaries of the Latino or Hispanic ethnic group are sometimes quite ambiguous? What modes of interviewing would be best employed? The pervasive, and less expensive, mode of telephone interviewing might be inappropriate for people whose culture was believed to value personal contact. What language and linguistic difficulties might be encountered? Inevitably, some unknown proportion of the interviews would have to be conducted in Spanish, with respondents who spoke different dialects. How could one ensure that questions that appeared to be equivalent when translated really meant the same thing? What questions would be of most significance and relevance in such a study, not only to the social scientist investigators but also to the people who would be participating in the survey? There was little data available and even less experience to help investigators design this project.

Details on the resolution of the methodological considerations are recounted elsewhere (de la Garza et al. 1992). Here we will elaborate on how the study handled sampling. Early on, it became clear that the population could not simply be "Latinos." First, Latinos include persons from two dozen countries. Since investigators suspected that national origin would be a very significant variable, they were forced to decide to sample only the three largest Latino groups—Mexican Americans, Puerto Ricans, and Cuban Americans. These groups comprised about 80 percent of all the Latinos residing in the mainland United States. Second, because researchers decided to conduct in-person interviews, a sample from all land areas of the United States was not possible. However, investigators realized that to sample simply from areas with a high density of Latinos would introduce a major bias into the results. Therefore, the sampling design included areas of high-, medium-, and low-density Latino populations. All areas of the country with generally a 3 percent or greater Latino population were included in the sampling frame. Forty standard metropolitan statistical areas throughout the United States were included as primary sampling units. In-household, personal interviews were completed with 2,817 Mexican Americans, Puerto Ricans, and Cuban Americans. To increase the analysts' ability to make comparative statements, 456 Anglo American (non-Hispanic white) respondents were interviewed in the same geographic areas.

The LNPS went into the field in the fall of 1989 and was completed in early 1990. This survey became the first major study of a nationally representative sample of the three largest Latino groups in the United States. It has provided an empirical basis for assessing previously unproved ideas and sometimes challenging conventional wisdom. Most important, the LNPS has served to provide useful comparative, baseline data.

No subsequent project has yet matched the scope and breadth of the LNPS. However, since 1990, the study of Latino opinion has expanded. Some (but not all) of the national polling organizations and some academic studies now oversample Latinos. In addition, a few studies have been directed specifically at the Latino population, though most used telephone interviewing and were not national samples. Typically, these surveys are drawn from one or more of the metropolitan areas with the largest Latino populations—Los Angeles, San Antonio, Miami, New York City, or Chicago—or cover states with large Latino populations—California, Texas, Florida, and sometimes New York or Illinois. Finally Latinos have begun to be targeted in election studies, including many media surveys and some exit polling. Most notable among these are surveys by the *Washington Post*/Henry J. Kaiser Family Foundation/Harvard University National Survey on Latinos in America polls (1995, 1999) and the Knight Ridder/*San Jose Mercury*/*Miami Herald*/*Fort Worth Star-Telegram* National Latino Voter Poll (2000). These studies and the LNPS provide much of the substantive information of this chapter (see Table 4-1).

Is There a Hispanic Political Community?

One of the basic questions that must be answered when examining Latino public opinion is whether or not a Latino political community actually exists. Is there a group of people who share enough characteristics or who have enough of a feeling of identification with one another that they can truly be classified as a distinctive community, in short, a "public"?

By comparison, American public opinion can easily be defined by geographical boundaries. It is less clear that African Americans can be spoken of as a single public, but because of shared historical experience and contemporary discrimination, that community is

Table 4-1 Polls of Latino Public Opinion

Sponsor or Poll Name	Details
Knight Ridder/*San Jose Mercury News*/*Miami Herald, Fort Worth Star-Telegram,* 2000	National Latino Voter Poll. Telephone survey of 2,721 registered Hispanic voters in twelve states. June 7–13, 2000, by International Communications Research.
Latino National Political Survey, 1989–1990	In-household interviews of 1,546 Mexican Americans, 589 Puerto Ricans, 682 Cuban Americans, and 499 non-Latinos. Data available from Inter-university Consortium for Political and Social Research (ICPSR No. 6841).
Los Angeles Times, 1995	Poll no. 356. National telephone survey of 1,285 respondents. March 15–19, 1995. Report available from *http://www.latimes.com/news/custom/timespoll/la-statsheetindex.htmlstory*
Los Angeles Times, 2001	Poll no. 454. Poll of 1,570 Los Angeles residents. February 24–March 1, 2001. Report available from *http://www.latimes.com/news/custom/timespoll/la-statsheetindex.htmlstory*
Newsweek, 1999	Poll of 505 Hispanics nationwide. June 25–30, 1999. Conducted by Princeton Survey Research Associates.
Public Agenda, 2000	Telephone interviews of 801 parents of public school students, including 203 Hispanic parents. September 3–16, 1998. Report available from *http://www.publicagenda.org/issues/nation_divided.cfm?issue_type=education&list=6*
Shorenstein Center on the Press, Politics and Public Policy, 2000	Vanishing Voter Project. Nationwide telephone surveys of approximately 1,000 adults. November 14, 1999–May 14, 2000. See May 18, 2000, report, "Hispanic Americans Less Involved in Campaign, but Also Less Cynical." *http://www.vanishingvoter.org/releases/05-18-00.shtml*
Southwest Voter Registration Education Project and University of Texas, Austin, Center for Mexican American Studies, 1983–1985	The Mexican American Electorate Series. Various surveys conducted from 1983 through 1985.
Southwest Voter Research Institute, 1996	National Latino Opinion Poll. Poll of 2,420 Latinos in Texas, California, New York, Florida, Illinois, Arizona, Colorado, and New Mexico. May 3–26 and June 13–July 6, 1996.

(table continues)

Table 4-1 *(Continued)*

Sponsor or Poll Name	Details
Tomas Rivera Policy Institute, 1995	Survey of 1,621 Latinos in four states. November 20–December 5, 1995. "U.S. Hispanic Perspectives Poll: A Four State Survey of Latino Attitudes Towards Four Current Policy Issues: Affirmative Action, Crime, Immigration, and Welfare Reform." Rodolfo de la Garza, Harry P. Pachon, and Dennis Falcon. Claremont, Calif.: Tomas Rivera Policy Institute, 1996.
Univision poll, 1998	Survey of 750 Hispanic respondents in seven U.S. major media markets. April 5–18, 1998. Conducted by Penn, Schoen & Berland Associates and Edelman Public Relations Worldwide. Report available from *http://www.lulac.org/Issues/Voter/UnivPres.html*
William C. Velasquez Institute, 2000	Latino Issues Survey. Poll of 560 Latino registered voters in California. September 27–October 4, 2000.
Washington Post/ Henry J. Kaiser Family Foundation/Harvard University, 1995	Four Americas Survey. Survey of 1,970 adults including 252 Latinos. August–September 1995.
Washington Post/ Henry J. Kaiser Family Foundation/Harvard University, 1999	National Survey of Latinos in America. Nationwide telephone survey of 4,614 adults including 2,417 Latinos. June 30–August 20, 1999. Conducted by International Communications Research.
Yankelovich Hispanic Monitor, 2000	In-home surveys of 1,206 Hispanics in Los Angeles, New York, Miami, San Francisco/San Jose, Chicago, Houston, and San Antonio. March–May 2000. Reported in *http://secure.yankelovich.com/about_us/hispanic_release.asp*

arguably cohesive and identifiable. More difficulties arise in defining a Latino political community, a Latino opinion public. This challenge is particularly difficult if survey researchers themselves attempt to define the community a priori, before undertaking the survey. One way that this challenge may be approached is to define Latinos or Hispanics as those residents in the United States whose ancestors come from the twenty-two to twenty-four countries greatly influenced by the Spanish culture. These origins would entail almost all the countries in the Western Hemisphere, including some in the Caribbean, and may or may not include Spain, the Philippines, or Brazil.

One could simply ask the national origin of the respondents. More typically, in ethnic/cultural studies, qualifications for participating are met by respondents' own identification of their ethnic group. In this case, respondents were asked whether they consider themselves Latino, that is, whether they "self-identify" as members of the Latino community. Making this determination is more difficult than it may seem and certainly is more difficult than self-identification of African Americans or Native Americans, for example. The problem stems from the fact that Latinos are arguably the most heterogeneous ethnic grouping in the United States. Not only do they originate in almost two dozen countries, but each of the national origin groups has had a very different historical experience in the United States. The Mexican American group, one of the largest national origin categories, includes persons descended from settlers who came in the 1500s and recent immigrants. Researchers are challenged by 400 years of varying historical experiences.

One approach to these problems, the one used by the LNPS, is first to ask persons about their national ancestry and which generation (on both sides) first came to the United States, then later to ask respondents about their self-identification both in the terms they spontaneously apply to themselves and in their reaction to such terms as *Latino* or *Hispanic.* Identity can then be assessed from the data instead of being imposed by the researcher. Research has shown that Latinos or Hispanics tend to have a preferred identity which relates to their country of national origin, that is Mexican American, Cuban American, Puerto Ricans, and the like—or in some cases, just as Americans. The umbrella terms such as Latino or Hispanic often are a secondary or tertiary identification. Among the umbrella terms, Hispanic is preferred over Latino by survey respondents (Jones-Correa and Leal 1996).

Nonetheless, some basis exists for using such panethnic identity terms as *Latino.* Members of this loosely defined group appear to identify some commonalities with one another. These typically revolve around culture, primarily the Spanish language and shared ancestry. Such *cultural* commonality is much more widely perceived than is any kind of common *political* interest (de la Garza et al. 1992; *Washington Post*/Kaiser/Harvard 1999; Knight Ridder/*Mercury News* 2000). Shared political values or goals, which could serve as a basis for a cohesive political community, are less obvious. In particular, as noted later in the chapter, in various areas significant variation occurs between national origin groups. Moreover, in some arenas opinions vary by generational status. That is, the foreign-born differ from the native-born. The native-born whose parents or grandparents were themselves born in the United States differ on some issues from those whose parents are immigrants.

Basic or Fundamental Values

One previously widespread notion is that Latinos are somehow less American than other groups, holding a loyalty at least as great to their homelands, such as Mexico, as to the United States. In fact, studies of the perceptions of Hispanics by non-Hispanic whites reveal that one of the most common stereotypical characteristics attributed to Hispanics by other Americans is that they are unpatriotic (Smith 1990). However, in the seminal LNPS investigation, Latinos—or at least those of Mexican, Cuban, and Puerto Rican ancestry—were in reality extremely patriotic to the United States, at least as much so as non-Hispanic whites (de la Garza, Falcon, and Garcia 1996).

Latinos from all three of these national origin groups professed a great love for the United States and stated outwardly that they were extremely patriotic. When asked about what country's history it was most important to learn about in schools, the majority of Latinos favor U.S. history rather than the history of their homelands. Latinos also expressed a very great desire to learn the English language, although this was accompanied by a concurrent strong desire to maintain the Spanish language, or at least a great reverence for the symbolism of that language as a manifestation of the Hispanic culture.

Support for civil liberties such as freedom of speech and tolerance also has been investigated. Latinos appear to be somewhat less tolerant than non-Hispanic white Americans toward those groups they most dislike and especially intolerant of some groups such as homosexuals. Latinos who are less acculturated to U.S. culture, that is, those who are foreign-born and/or still Spanish speaking, are more likely than more English-acculturated Latinos to be intolerant of homosexuality (LNPS, *Washington Post*/Kaiser/Harvard 1999). Cubans differ from Mexicans and Puerto Ricans in whom they most dislike, with almost half of the Cuban Americans naming Communists (compared with a fifth in the other two groups). The last two groups are more likely to name the Ku Klux Klan (about 38 percent versus one quarter of the Cuban Americans) (de la Garza et al. 1992, 82).

Latinos also appear more collectivist or communalist in orientation than non-Latinos, that is, they tend to place greater emphasis on their groups' advancement or common good than on individual advancement. Much of this is related to Latinos' relatively strong beliefs in the importance of the family. For example, Latinos (82 percent) are more likely than Anglos (57 percent) to agree that relatives are more important than friends (*Washington Post*/Kaiser/Harvard 1999). Still, considerable support exists among Latinos for individual advancement, particularly through perseverance, hard work, and education.

Latinos consistently differ from Anglos, and resemble each other, in holding optimistic and trusting attitudes. Latinos are very optimistic in general and with regard to the way things are progressing in their lives, in government, and in the economy. The Shorenstein Center survey of March 2000 reported that 74 percent of non-Hispanics, but 60 percent of Hispanics, felt that "politics in America is pretty disgusting." While 57 percent of non-Hispanics felt that politicians were "not worthy of respect," only 39 percent of Hispanics shared this feeling. (However, the same survey did find that in general Hispanics were more detached from, and less attentive to, politics.) The Public Policy Institute of California (Andres Martinez 2000) and a 2001 *Los Angeles Times* poll have both called Latinos the most consistently optimistic of all demographic groups (McDonnell 2001; Moore 2001). The *Washington Post*/Kaiser/Harvard survey reported that first-, second-, and third-generation Latinos were more optimistic about the future of their children than were Anglos. However, this confidence does fade significantly in each succeeding generation (Knight Ridder/*Mercury News* 2000).

In addition, Latinos trust government significantly more and are less cynical about politics than are white and black Americans. The LNPS found all three Latino groups had a higher degree of trust in government officials doing what is right than did Anglos. The Latino groups also were more likely to feel that government was run for the benefit of all than did Anglos. Cuban Americans were the most trustful (de la Garza et al. 1992, 81). Once again, immigrants are the most idealistic and trusting. With each passing generation in the United States, Latino cynicism increases and mirrors that of Anglo Americans (*Washington Post*/Kaiser/Harvard 1999).

Latino Policy Positions: Priorities and the Latino Agenda

Often it is asked: "What do Latinos want?" This is a very difficult question to answer for this extremely heterogeneous group, bearing in mind that it subsumes people of different national origins whose families came to the United States at different times across a span of 400 years. Furthermore, the socioeconomic conditions of Latinos vary widely. Thus, the simplest answer is that Latinos' political agenda is very surprisingly similar to that of non-Latino whites.

Since the 1990s most surveys—which simply ask Latinos in an open-ended way to identify "the most important problem facing this country" or "your community"—produce a list very similar to that generated by non-Hispanic whites. While the Latino public agenda is virtually the same as that of non-Hispanics, some notable exceptions exist. Latinos often place education, crime, and the economy at the top of the list. Education is an even higher priority for Latinos than for the general American public. For Mexican Americans, education is most often the top priority even when it is a second or third priority for the non-Hispanic population (Knight Ridder/*Mercury News* 2000; LNPS). The William C. Velasquez Institute survey of Latinos in California in the fall of 2000 found that public education was the number one priority issue for Latinos, as did the bipartisan Battleground 2000 National Poll (Martin 2000).

Two other differences, although they are slight, reflect Latinos' demographic circumstances. Because of the generally lower economic status of Latinos, the economy, particularly low wages and a greater opportunity for jobs, receives a slightly higher priority ranking than found for non-Hispanic whites in general. As expected, controls for socioeconomic status reduce this difference. Also, because Hispanics are a very urban people, perhaps the most urban ethnic group in the United States, matters dealing with crime often rank a notch or two higher among Hispanics than among non-Hispanic whites, but usually not quite as high as among African Americans. In spite of these differences, the most accurate generalization that can be made about the domestic policy agendas of Latinos is that their priorities are (probably surprisingly to some) very similar to those of non-Hispanic whites.

Latinos favor strong, active governments that provide for the collective social good (LNPS, Knight Ridder/*Mercury News* 2000; *Washington Post*/Kaiser/Harvard 1999; Andres Martinez 2000). Again, variation exists among the national origin groups. On issues such as minimum guaranteed income, employment opportunities, and public support of housing, Puerto Ricans are generally the most in favor of a strong welfare state and Cuban Americans least so, but still more so than non-Latino whites (de la Garza et al. 1992, 85–86).

On issues on which white Americans and African Americans take very different positions, it is quite common to find Latino opinions in between those two groups. In terms of specific policies, Latinos tend to be more liberal. They support an activist government that protects minority civil rights and enhances the economic and material well-being of individual citizens and minority groups. However, Latinos also hold some issue preferences that are associated with the more conservative end of the political spectrum. For example, they tend to be more in favor of the death penalty than are whites or African Americans. Latinos also are slightly more opposed to abortion than are Anglo Americans.

However, one must be very careful about these generalizations because again considerable variation occurs among national origin groups as well as along generational lines. In addition, socioeconomic status often makes a difference. As among whites and African Americans, the higher a Latino's socioeconomic status, the less he or she favors government involvement in social welfare activities and the more he or she favors greater protection for business interests and support of the business community. Thus, some of the apparently distinctive Latino policy preferences reflect the social and economic circumstances in which many Latinos find themselves.

Cultural Issues

Cultural issues with an ethnic component are one arena in which Latino opinions often differ significantly from those of Anglo Americans and African Americans. Once one moves from more general policy issues to those with cultural or ethnic components, more variation occurs between Latinos and other ethnic groups as well as among and within the Latino groups. In general, Latinos are very protective of their culture and its manifestations, such as the Spanish language. For example, a 1998 survey by Spanish-language television network Univision found that more than 90 percent of Hispanics placed importance on sustaining the Spanish language and preserving Spanish heritage and traditions. The Yankelovich Hispanic Monitor 2000 survey reported that an increasing percentage (69 percent) of Hispanics say the Spanish language is more important to them now than it was five years ago (63 percent). Yet even on these cultural issues, where conventional wisdom holds that Latinos are very cohesive and unified in their positions on such ethnic-related issues as immigration, affirmative action, and bilingual education, empirical studies show that the picture is much more complex.

Language Policy/Bilingual Education

Language policy is the area that usually exhibits the highest level of consensus among Latinos and often reveals significant differences between them and other racial/ethnic groupings. Latinos are unified by their support for the protection of the Spanish language (as a symbol of their cultural heritage) and for bilingual education. Their position contrasts markedly with that usually taken by Anglo Americans and African Americans, who tend to oppose bilingual education. The LNPS revealed that 80 percent of Mexican Americans, 87 percent of Puerto Ricans, and 89 percent of Cuban Americans support bilingual education; large majorities of each group would be willing to pay more taxes for it. Univision's 1998 survey of seven major media found that 83 percent of Hispanics supported bilingual education programs. A Texas poll taken by the Southwest Voter Research Institute in 1996 found that 84 percent would not support a measure eliminating bilingual education.

This overwhelming support for bilingual education is in marked contrast to the position of whites. The *Washington Post*/Kaiser/Harvard survey of 1999 found that 59 percent of Hispanics nationwide favored providing immigrants in public schools with courses in their native language, while 40 percent of them preferred English instruction. The percentages were reversed for the total sample, including non-Hispanics. In California in 1984, 79 percent of Mexican Americans born in Mexico and 73 percent of those born in the United States supported bilingual education, versus only 46 percent of Anglos (Uhlaner 1991a, 362). Interestingly, almost as many African Americans in California at that time (71 percent) supported bilingual education as did Mexican Americans, with U.S.-born Asian Americans scarcely more supportive than Anglos (49 percent); Asian American immigrants were in between (with 61 percent supporting it). After the 1998 passage of Proposition 227, which in principle abolished bilingual education in California, 65 percent of Latinos, compared with 56 percent of whites, thought local school districts should be able to decide whether to keep their bilingual education programs (Hajnal and Baldassare 2001).

However, some studies indicate differences among Latinos. Further analysis of the 1984 California data showed that citizenship status made a large difference in the attitudes of immigrants. Noncitizens were substantially more supportive of bilingual education, among both Mexican Americans and Asian Americans. Support also was stronger from Mexican Americans who perceived that they had fewer opportunities than other people did (Uhlaner

1991a, 366–367). The LNPS data show some variations along lines of national origin, place of nativity, and citizenship, but even two-thirds of the least favorable group, the foreign-born Mexican American citizens, supported bilingual education.

Although they support bilingual education, Latinos also exhibit a strong desire for themselves and their children to learn English as quickly as possible (Public Agenda 2000). In fact, the LNPS found that 70 percent of Mexican Americans, 74 percent of Puerto Ricans, and 77 percent of Cuban Americans agreed that the objective of bilingual education is to learn two languages (not just to learn English or to maintain Spanish language and culture) (de la Garza et al. 1992, 99). More than 90 percent of each group agreed or strongly agreed that U.S. citizens and residents should learn English. Agreement with this statement was equally strong among noncitizens (de la Garza et al. 1992, 177). More generally, people have very different definitions of bilingual education. Responses to specific questions can thus vary substantially, depending upon the context and the exact wording. Nonetheless, it seems clear that the vast majority of Latinos would like their children to learn English and also to have facility in Spanish.

Immigration

Although Latino "leaders" and "spokespersons" often have spoken in favor of either a very liberal immigration policy or even something approaching open borders, several studies of Latino mass opinion show that support for a more relaxed immigration policy is mixed at best. In fact, considerable opposition exists to relaxing restrictions on immigration. The LNPS caused quite a stir and elicited several attacks from Latino politicians, academics, and activists when it reported in the early 1990s that 75 percent of Mexican Americans, 79 percent of Puerto Ricans, and 70 percent of Cuban Americans agreed with the statement that there are too many immigrants coming to the United States. Still, less than 1 percent of persons within each of the three Latino groups rated immigration as the most important national problem.

Several subsequent objective surveys have validated (as well as elaborated upon) the findings from the LNPS. Knight Ridder found that Latinos nationwide ranked immigration policy among their lowest priorities—eleventh among a list of twelve issues facing the nation. So immigration appears on the Latino political agenda, but items that are common to all Americans have a higher priority. The *Washington Post*/Kaiser/Harvard survey reported that 67 percent of Latinos felt that the number of new immigrants allowed into the United States each year should be kept the same or decreased. A National Latino Opinion Poll conducted by Southwest Voter Research Institute in the summer of 1996 discovered that 50 percent of Latinos wanted to cut legal immigration back greatly while 44 percent opposed cutting legal immigration. The *Mercury News* reported that 43 percent of all Latinos nationwide think the government is not doing enough to stop illegal immigration (Anne Martinez 2000). A *Los Angeles Times* poll in the early spring of 2001 asked whether "the growing immigrant population in Los Angeles is a good or a bad thing for the city, or does it have no effect either way." Thirty-five percent of Latinos thought a growing immigrant population was a good thing, as did 31 percent of whites and 24 percent of blacks. However, 39 percent of Latinos thought it was a bad thing for Los Angeles, as did 40 percent of whites and 54 percent of blacks.

Generational differences appear on immigration issues: earlier generations favor a more restrictive policy than more recent arrivals. The Knight Ridder/*Mercury News* survey showed support for curbing illegal immigration increases from 37 percent among the foreign-born to 45 percent of first-generation U.S.-born to 50 percent of second-generation Latinos. National origin differences also are evident. Cuban Americans are the most concerned with illegal immigration. Mexican Americans are twice as likely as Cubans to feel that the government is doing too much to stop illegal immigration. Language and income levels also differentiate among Latinos on this issue. Spanish speakers are the most likely to say that fair immigration policy is important. Only one-third of them think tighter immigration policies are needed, compared with half of the English-speaking Latinos. Similarly, Latinos who were in the lowest income levels were twice as likely as those earning more than $50,000 to assign a high priority to a fair and more open immigration policy (Anne Martinez 2000).

Differences in Latino opinion on immigration are also evident from state to state. In 1996, the Tomas Rivera Policy Institute (TRPI) surveyed Latinos in four states. When presented with a survey item proposing that Congress significantly reduce the number of legal immigrants, a majority of Texas Latinos agreed (53 percent), pluralities of New York Latinos (48 percent) and Florida Latinos (47 percent) agreed, and only in California did a plurality (47 percent) disagree. TRPI also found that in California noncitizens more often than citizens tended to oppose such restrictive legislation; but in the other three states, a majority of citizens supported such a law while the noncitizens were more likely to disagree. In California, differences among racial/ethnic groupings are evident. Statewide surveys of 20,000 adults over a period of two years revealed that when it comes to illegal immigration from Mexico, 67 percent of Latinos consider it a problem, compared with 80 percent of Asians, 86 percent of blacks, and 91 percent of whites (Hajnal and Baldassare 2001).

Since Latinos are largely in the lower socioeconomic brackets of society and hence more likely to be impacted by competition for jobs with immigrants, Latinos tend to be more concerned about the often harmful economic impact on them that unlimited immigration into the United States could have (Miller, Polinard, and Wrinkle 1984; Polinard, Wrinkle, and de la Garza 1984). Yet some of these studies also show that many Hispanics or

Latinos, many of whom are immigrants or first-generation descendants of immigrants, have a positive and supportive attitude toward the treatment of recent immigrants into the United States (de la Garza et al. 1991).

Even though many Latinos seem to have reservations about increased immigration, they are not anti-immigrant—a very important distinction. Thus, the picture on Latino attitudes toward immigrants and immigration is very complex, confounded by many demographic, attitudinal, and situational variables (Binder, Polinard, and Wrinkle 1997; Wrinkle 1991). Once we pay attention to the national origin differences among Latinos, differences in legal status further complicate attitudes toward immigration. Most of the Cuban Americans born abroad entered the United States as refugees, whose legal status differs in many ways from that of immigrants. Puerto Ricans who migrate to the mainland are already American citizens, not immigrants. In contrast, Mexican Americans who were born outside the United States generally enter as immigrants without refugee status and must naturalize to become citizens.

Affirmative Action

Latinos also resemble each other in the priority they give to other ethnically related issues such as discrimination, the protection of minority groups, and affirmative action. These issues rank low or are absent from the policy priorities of non-Hispanic white groups but almost always appear among the issue priorities of Latino groups. However, discrimination and affirmative action issues often appear lower in the rankings of Latinos than might be expected. Latino leaders and spokespersons tend to be very strong proponents of affirmative action programs, yet careful analysis of Latino responses to various kinds of survey questions on affirmative action show that again the picture is very complex, with support for, or opposition to, affirmative action being largely dependent upon the exact wording of the question (F. C. Garcia 1997). Simply worded questions, usually those that include the phrase "affirmative action," elicit the most support.

The Tomas Rivera Policy Institute surveys of 1995 asked Latinos in four states: "Do you favor continuing affirmative action programs or do you favor abolishing them?" Answers were uniformly in favor of affirmative action across the states (California, 71 percent; Florida, 72 percent; New York, 77 percent; and Texas, 71 percent) and across national origin groups (Mexican Americans, 71 percent; Cuban Americans, 68 percent; Puerto Ricans, 73 percent; "other Latinos," 73 percent) and between citizens and noncitizens. The Knight Ridder national survey of Latinos in 2000 found that 47 percent of Latinos thought that the government should continue affirmative action programs to aid women and minorities, 39 percent thought these programs should be expanded, and only 11 percent thought the programs should be reduced.

African Americans are usually the strongest supporters of affirmative action. Non-

Hispanic whites sometimes favor and sometimes oppose it. Latinos again exhibit the pattern of being in between black and white opinions—usually supportive of the programs but not as strongly as blacks. A series of California surveys conducted between 1998 and 2000, a period in which affirmative action was highly salient on that state's policy agenda, shows a similar pattern by ethnic group of opinions on the continuation of affirmative action programs. Twenty-seven percent of whites favored continuation, compared with 66 percent of Latinos and 78 percent of blacks (Hajnal and Baldassare 2001).

In 1995 the *Los Angeles Times* conducted a very detailed national survey on attitudes toward affirmative action. These results agree with the ones already mentioned. One question asked whether affirmative action needed to be continued because of continuing discrimination or if such programs were no longer needed. Seventy-five percent of blacks thought that affirmative action programs needed to be continued; 64 percent of Latinos took the same position; 45 percent of white women and 32 percent of white men agreed (*Los Angeles Times* poll 1995).

However, when variations in question wording are used, a much more complex picture emerges. One finds that among Latinos in some cases there is support for some forms of affirmative action, and in other cases there is opposition. Latinos tend to be supportive when either the general term or positive words such as *equal opportunity* are used, and less supportive when words such as *preferences* are used instead. An example of the powerful effect of question wording comes from a 1996 survey in Texas conducted by the Southwest Voter Research Institute. Respondents were asked to strongly agree, agree, disagree, or strongly disagree with three statements concerning affirmative action. One item requested respondents' level of agreement with a benevolently worded statement: "Affirmative Action programs provide needed opportunities and access for minorities and women who historically do not have fair access in the areas of education and employment." More than 70 percent of Latinos seem to support affirmative action—31 percent strongly agree, 40 percent agree, 13 percent disagree, and 5 percent strongly disagree. Another question combines affirmative action with a statement about the abilities of minorities and women: respondents were asked how much they agreed that "Affirmative Action is unnecessary, minorities and women can achieve their goals on their own merit without any help from the government." Now only a slight plurality of Latinos supports affirmative action, with 30 percent disagreeing with the statement, and 17 percent strongly disagreeing (versus 15 percent who strongly agree and 27 percent who agree).

Moreover, even on the same question, significant variations on opinion occur depending upon the national origin or socioeconomic status of the respondent. Puerto Ricans tend to support affirmative action more strongly than Mexican Americans. Cuban Americans, on the other hand, oppose affirmative action programs more than either of these other groups of Latinos and about as much as Anglo Americans. For example, one of the most common "specific" items on affirmative action asks about the use of race or ethnicity as a criterion for admission to colleges and universities or in employment. The LNPS asked its Latino and white respondents to take positions on a 5-point scale ranging from favoring the use of quotas to favoring strict merit in college admissions and job hiring. By eliminating the middle position and collapsing both ends of the scale we can compare those who favor the merit position with those who favor quotas. Slightly more than half of Puerto Ricans favor quotas (51 percent). The Mexican American position tips toward favoring merit (53 percent) but is very close to that of Puerto Ricans. Large majorities in the other two groups favor the merit position—almost three-quarters of Cuban Americans (73 percent) and more than 90 percent of Anglos (91 percent) (F. C. Garcia 1997, 392–393). Better-educated respondents and those with greater income were more likely to support the merit position instead of quotas, although the socioeconomic differences were slight among Cuban Americans (F. C. Garcia 1997, 393). It is worth noting that the more recent 1999 *Washington Post*/Kaiser/Harvard poll found almost as many Latinos (75 percent) as people in the overall population (82 percent) support selecting "students without considering their racial or ethnic backgrounds." In all cases opinions on affirmative action depend heavily upon the specific wording of the question and its placement in the questionnaire.

Discrimination

The opinion of Latinos with regard to prejudice and discrimination also follows an interesting pattern. African Americans tend to be very distinct from white Americans in that they feel that considerable prejudice and discrimination still exist in the United States. In addition, African Americans are even more distinctive in their opinions about whether the government needs to continue programs to assist minorities or whether enough already has been done. In contrast, white Americans tend to believe that minorities have been discriminated against in the past but that enough programs and policies already have been put in place to combat the legacy of past discrimination. This pattern was exemplified in a 1995 study that reported that 68 percent of African Americans thought racism is a "big problem" in this society. Forty-six percent of Latinos thought this was so, while only 38 percent of whites agreed this was the case (*Washington Post*/Kaiser/Harvard 1995). Again the picture for Latinos is much more complex, and again their positions are typically between those of blacks and those of whites.

A relatively low percentage of Latinos say that they themselves have been discriminated against personally, with Cubans being the least (18 percent) and Mexican Americans the most (39 percent) likely to say so (LNPS). Yet when asked whether there is still considerable discrimination against members of their groups in general, as well as against other groups such as African Americans, Native Americans, and women, Latinos tend to believe that rather high levels of discrimination still exist (LNPS). Persons who perceive structural disadvantage for one group tend to perceive it for others as well. For example, in a 1984 study in California, over half of Mexican American respondents who believed that Latinos had fewer opportunities than other people also believed that African Americans were disadvantaged. In contrast, among those who did not see Latinos as disadvantaged, less than 10 percent believed that African Americans had fewer opportunities (Uhlaner 1991a, 355).

The LNPS found some differences between Cuban Americans and other Latinos. Eighty percent of Mexican Americans feel their group is discriminated against; 74 percent of Puerto Ricans perceive discrimination against Puerto Ricans. About 70 percent of Anglos believe these groups (in addition to Cuban Americans) are subject to discrimination. But only 47 percent of Cubans themselves perceive discrimination against their group. National origin differences were again found in a 1995 study. The TRPI found 71 percent of Central American Latinos think that U.S. society discriminates against Latinos, with over half of Mexican Americans sharing that view and only 42 percent of Cuban Americans agreeing.

The *Washington Post*/Kaiser/Harvard 1999 survey revealed a continuation of the same patterns of Latinos' perceptions of discrimination, with one major change. Compared with whites, a much larger proportion (82 percent) of Latinos thought that discrimination against Latinos was a societal problem, with 55 percent of those believing discrimination to be a big problem. This proportion was even larger than the number of non-Latino blacks perceiving this problem (69 percent). Part of this increase may result from the inclusion of Central and South Americans in the Latino sample. This group is distinctive in perceiving the highest level of discrimination (90 percent). Again, when asked if they themselves personally have experienced discrimination in the last five years, the proportions for most Latino groups are halved. The exception is Puerto Ricans, two-thirds of whom state that they personally have experienced discrimination. The Knight Ridder/*Mercury News* poll in the summer of 2000 found that only 18 percent of Latino likely voters had experienced discrimination in the past five years; 80 percent said they had not.

There are significant differences in the perceptions of types of discrimination among the foreign-born, the native-born with immigrant parents, and the native-born whose families have been in the United States longer. For instance, about one-third of Mexican Americans in California reported personally experiencing discrimination (in a 1984 study), and the numbers were about the same for each generation. However, almost half of the immigrants who report that they experienced discrimination said it occurred on the job and about a quarter had been discriminated against in social situations, while almost half of the native-born reported experiencing discrimination in social situations and only a quarter on the job (Uhlaner 1991b, 150).

We have already seen that Latinos in general (with the particular exception of the Cubans) feel that in the domestic sphere government ought to be very active and involved, working on behalf of the masses of the people to advance their collective welfare. The data also show that although there has been great suspicion about the patriotism of Latinos, Latinos' attitudes and behaviors evidence very strong support, loyalty, and patriotism to the United States (de la Garza, Falcon, and Garcia 1996).

The point is reinforced by Latinos' positions on foreign policy issues. Latinos show relatively little interest in the political activities or policies of their home countries nor much concern about U.S. policies toward their home countries. In fact, the preponderance of data does not indicate the existence of a "Latino diaspora" in the United States, nor is there a strong Latino lobby pushing for favorable foreign policy toward their homelands (de la Garza and Pachon 2000). There does seem to be a close bond between immigrants and other U.S. residents from their homelands, but this bond does not necessarily result in close ties between immigrants and the governments of their countries of origin. Contrary to the general pattern, there is a very strong Cuban American lobby for the overthrow of the Castro regime. However, even this interest seems to be diminishing with subsequent generations of Cuban Americans. Nonetheless, as we will see below, there is some effect of opinions about politics abroad on U.S. party choices for those Cuban Americans and Puerto Ricans who do closely follow politics in Cuba and Puerto Rico, respectively.

Political Partisanship and Ideology

Political parties are arguably the most important of the political organizations in the United States, and a strong party identification is associated with many political activities, including participating in campaigns and, of course, voting. Partisan identification is an arena in which the Latino national origin groups differ most visibly from each other. While overall, Latinos are more likely to identify with the Democratic than with the Republican Party and are more likely to identify as Democrats than are Anglos, this generalization masks the enormous exception of Cuban Americans' affinity for the Republican Party. Latinos resemble African Americans, and differ from Anglos, in supporting one dominant party identification within each national origin group.

These patterns appear quite consistently across many data sets. We illustrate with data from the LNPS. Table 4-2 reports party choice for citizens. Two sets of numbers are given: a full scale, which designates both the direction (Democrat, independent, Republican) as well as intensity (weak or strong), and a collapsed scale, which lists only the direction of affiliation. Note that the "Anglos" in these tables reside in the sampling areas covered by the LNPS. An extraordinary two-thirds of Cuban Americans (63 percent in the collapsed scale) identify with the Republican Party. On the other side of the partisan spectrum, Puerto Ri-

Table 4-2 Political Party Identification of Latino and Anglo Citizens, by National Origin (in percent)

Party Identification	Mexican American		Puerto Rican		Cuban American		Anglo	
	Full	Collapsed	Full	Collapsed	Full	Collapsed	Full	Collapsed
Strong Democrat	29	56	35	60	14	19	18	44
Weak Democrat	27		25		5		26	
Independent	28	28	26	26	17	17	28	28
Weak Republican	11	15	7	13	16	63	13	28
Strong Republican	4		6		47		15	
Number of cases	865		570		306		434	
Chi-square (significance)	Full scale: 509.5 (.00) Collapsed scale: 384.9 (.00)							

Source: Latino National Political Survey.

Note: Percentages may not equal 100 because of rounding.

cans identify strongly with the Democratic Party, approaching (but not reaching) the well-known high levels at which African Americans identify with the Democrats (82 percent in the 1988 National Election Study). Mexican Americans (at 56 percent) are only slightly less likely to be Democrats than are Puerto Ricans, but still significantly more so than Anglos and vastly more so than Cuban Americans. (The statistical significance of the chi square value in Table 4-2 tells us that the differences in partisanship patterns found in this survey are strong enough that we are virtually certain that such differences exist in the U.S. population.)

Moreover, Latino partisans tend to strongly identify with their party, at least when it is the dominant party for their national origin group. Three-quarters of the Cuban American citizens who identify as Republican (47 percent divided by 63 percent) call themselves strong Republicans. By comparison, strong identifiers make up only slightly more than half of Anglo Republicans. Among Democrats, about 40 percent of the Anglos call themselves strong identifiers. In contrast, 52 percent of the Mexican American Democrats characterize themselves as strong partisans, as do an even greater proportion (57 percent) of Puerto Rican Democrats. Citizenship patterns (not shown) have a slight effect on the party preferences of Mexican Americans: citizens are more likely to identify with the Democrats (56 percent) than are noncitizens (42 percent). Citizen and noncitizen Cuban Americans equally strongly support the Republican Party.

More recent studies continue to find strong attachment to the Democratic Party overall among Latinos. For Latinos who were likely voters in the 2000 election, 59 percent identified themselves as Democrats, 28 percent as independents, and 20 percent as Republicans (Knight Ridder/*Mercury News* 2000). A *Newsweek* survey (June 1999) found a similar split among all Latino adults: 55 percent Democratic, 24 percent independent, and 19 percent Republican. The *Washington Post*/Kaiser/Harvard 1999 survey shows Puerto Ricans to be the most Democratic of the subgroups, with Mexican Americans somewhat less so because more of them were independents. Cuban Americans in this survey favored the Republican Party, although somewhat less overwhelmingly than in the earlier LNPS data.

In general, Mexican Americans and Puerto Ricans are strong Democratic partisans and Cuban Americans are strong Republicans. Yet, there are exceptions, as we have seen, as some people do identify with the other party and some are independent. Standard socioeconomic predictors of partisanship, where greater education and income are associated with Republican partisanship, work differently for Latinos. Income is not related to Latino partisanship, and for Mexican Americans greater education increases the likelihood of a Democratic Party affiliation. One of the more powerful demographic predictors of partisanship among all three Latino groups is experience with U.S. politics. Thus people of all three national origins are more likely to identify as Democrats if they are older, if they were born in the United States, or if, as immigrants, they have been in the United States longer. This effect may reflect greater knowledge of the U.S. party system.

Another powerful demographic predictor of partisanship is an individual's degree of cultural integration with the ethnic group, as indicated by religion, language, and social interaction with group members as contrasted with Anglos. Latinos who speak English, who are not Catholic, or who socialize predominantly with Anglos are also the ones more likely to identify with the minority party. Persons who are less integrated with the group are more likely to be Republican Mexican Americans or Puerto Ricans or Democratic Cuban Americans than are people who speak Spanish, are Catholic, and socialize within the national origin group. The causality may go in both directions. People who identify with the minority party might feel more comfortable socializing with others outside their ethnic group, and people who are less socially integrated into the group might be more exposed to alternative political views (Uhlaner and Garcia 1998, 2001).

Often political ideology, stated on a liberal–conservative or left–right scale, is used to categorize political opinions, including those of Latinos. Yet various scholars have suggested that these scales are not very useful in understanding the political thinking of most Ameri-

Table 4-3 Ideology of Latino and Anglo Citizens, by National Origin (in percent)

Ideology	Mexican American		Puerto Rican		Cuban American		Anglo	
	Full	Collapsed	Full	Collapsed	Full	Collapsed	Full	Collapsed
Very liberal	4	29	7	28	4	25	4	26
Liberal	13		12		15		9	
Slightly liberal	12		9		6		13	
Moderate	32	32	25	25	23	23	35	35
Slightly conservative	17	40	16	47	15	52	17	39
Conservative	17		23		30		17	
Very conservative	6		8		7		5	
Number of cases	1,513		574		666		441	
Chi-square (significance)	Full scale: 129.9 (.00) Collapsed Scale: 54.5 (.00)							

Source: Latino National Political Survey.

Note: Percentages may not equal 100 because of rounding.

cans, particularly those who are not in the political elite or who belong to a minority group. If measures of mass ideology are really meaningful, they will relate to something else of interest, notably party identification and issue positions. Analysis of LNPS data shows that among Latinos, self-identified ideology connects more weakly to party preference than it does among Anglos. Nonetheless, a connection is there, and a connection to issue positions as well, in the usual ways. Thus, it is worth giving ideology some attention.

As with partisanship, substantial variation occurs across national origin lines. Table 4-3 reports respondents' self-report of their ideology along a standard 7-point scale from very liberal to very conservative, with moderates in the middle. A second column for each ethnic group collapses the 7-point scale into the broader categories of liberal, moderate, and conservative. The table includes both citizens and noncitizens. Mexican Americans label themselves very similarly to Anglos. Puerto Ricans are more likely to call themselves conservatives than are Mexican Americans or Anglos, but Cuban Americans are even more likely to label themselves as conservatives. Cuban Americans and Puerto Ricans appear to be the most polarized groups, having fewer moderates (about one in four) than are found

Table 4-4 Ideology and Party Identification, by National Origin (in percent)

Party Identification	Mexican American			Puerto Rican			Cuban American			Anglo		
	L	M	C	L	M	C	L	M	C	L	M	C
Democrat	58	56	42	65	68	55	26	20	14	57	52	24
Independent	24	26	35	25	22	27	19	17	13	35	32	21
Republican	18	18	24	10	10	18	55	64	72	8	16	54
Number of cases	374	400	512	168	127	265	144	136	335	104	150	174
Chi-square (significance)	13.8 (.01)			1.71 (.79)			17.15 (.00)			75.3 (.00)		

Source: Latino National Political Survey.

Note: Percentages may not equal 100 because of rounding.

L = Liberal, M = Moderate, C = Conservative.

among Mexican Americans or Anglos (about one in three). Not shown in the table are differences within each Latino group. Puerto Ricans and Cuban Americans born in the mainland United States are more liberal than those born on the respective islands. By a smaller margin, Mexican American immigrants are, similarly, more conservative than the U.S.-born.

As already noted, ideology is a weaker predictor of party preference among Latinos than it is among Anglos. Table 4-4 uses the collapsed three-category scales for ideology and partisanship. For each ideological group the table presents the percentage of respondents who identify with the Democrats, who identify with the Republicans, or who call themselves independent. In all cases liberals are more likely to be Democrats and conservatives are more likely to be Republicans. But there are many more conservative Democrats among Mexican Americans and Puerto Ricans and many more liberal Republicans among Cuban Americans than among Anglos. In fact, the relationship between party and ideology is so weak among Puerto Ricans as to be statistically insignificant.

Findings such as these have led some scholars to discount the meaning of ideology for Latinos, but such a conclusion would be premature. There is a relationship. Even in a full model that estimates the effect of ideology on partisanship, controlling for demographic variables, ideology matters. Conservatives are significantly more likely to be Republican than Democrat (Uhlaner, Gray, and Garcia 2000). Conservative ideology raises the probability of being Republican by about 20 percentage points. Of course, it raises the same probability by about 70 percentage points for Anglos. Thus it is fair to conclude that ideology has weaker effects on partisanship for Latinos.

One possibility is that Latinos interpret ideology differently from Anglos. However, we find that ideological positions relate to issue preferences in ways that are quite similar in the Latino population and the rest of the public, and the same is true for various subpopulations of Latinos. Part of the explanation lies in two issues that significantly impact some Latinos' party choice but that matter for few other Americans and that do not enter into the standard ideological scales. Puerto Ricans who care about island politics and support Puerto Rican statehood are substantially more likely to be Republicans than are other Puerto Ricans. Mexican Americans and Cuban Americans who care about politics in their countries of ancestry and who want to limit U.S. relations with Cuba are, similarly, more likely to be Republicans than are their co-ethnics. Thus, the standard thinking on ideology is not wrong. It is useful in understanding Latino opinions. It is just incomplete.

Summary and Concluding Comments

The study of Latino public opinion is a new endeavor. Major opinion surveys of large Latino populations have been undertaken only since the 1970s in response to growth in the Latino population and an increase in the number of Latino social scientists. Among the important findings is that Latinos share many of the same attitudes, beliefs, and values as non-Latino Americans. Empirical studies of Latino opinion have at least badly damaged, if not demolished, much of the conventional wisdom about Latinos' beliefs. Latinos are loyal, patriotic Americans. They believe in the work ethic and in being good citizens. Their loyalty is to the United States, not to their former homelands. Although Latinos feel a sentimental bond to people from their former homelands, they have not formed strong ethnic lobbies on behalf of their homelands, nor do they prefer that their children learn more about their ancestral homelands and their native language than about their chosen and current home. The one clear symbol of cultural pride among Latinos is their admiration for and desire to protect (if not themselves speak) the Spanish language. This is found in their support for bilingual education, something that is generally not shared by non-Hispanic whites or African American groups. However, Latinos also understand and greatly emphasize the importance of learning English at the earliest possible time.

With regard to public policy issues, Latinos overall have very much the same policy agendas as most Americans, with perhaps a little more emphasis placed on education, economic opportunity and security, and the war against crime and drugs, and with a little less emphasis on support for science and technology and environmental issues. However, differences on the domestic agenda are minor compared to the similarities. Political ideology may have less utility for Latinos than for non-Hispanic whites. The strong partisan ties within each Latino group may lessen the role of and need for political ideologies. Political party self-identification among Latinos (with the exception of Cubans) is very strongly Democratic, more so than that of non-Hispanic whites but less so than that of African Americans. Cuban Americans are more strongly Republican than any other major population grouping.

Perhaps the most important message in regard to Latino politics is that Latino public opinion is considerably diverse. A wide variety of opinions and attitudes exist within and across the Latino ethnic grouping. Differences in national origin are certainly a major cleavage within Latino opinion, but one must also be aware of the considerable variation in opinion caused by varying (and changing) socioeconomic status, immigration generation, and region of the country.

Obviously, much further work needs to be done in surveying, measuring, and analyzing Latino public opinion. One of the great unknowns is the opinion structure and content of some of the smaller Latino national origin groups. Very little work has been done to date on the opinions of, for example, Dominicans, Salvadorans, and Guatemalans. In addition, the continuing immigration of large numbers from Latin American countries, particularly Mexico, means that a new attitudinal environment is constantly being formed and re-formed in the Latino population of the United States.

Finally, one salutary effect of the burgeoning growth of Hispanics has been that there are now more major studies that either oversample Latinos in their national samples or undertake some surveys specifically focusing on Latinos. As Latinos grow increasingly important politically—as they most assuredly will—it is inevitable that more attention will be paid to their political, social, and economic orientations. As their economic potential increases, nonpolitical surveys, conducted by marketers and the commercial sector, will attempt to measure the preferences of Latinos as consumers. Surely, academic students and researchers will also find it important and interesting, indeed necessary, to study and advance the state of knowledge about an increasingly important segment of American society.

Notes

1. Examples of these surveys include the Mexican-American Political Attitudes and Behavior Survey (known as the National Chicano Survey, 1981–1982); the *Los Angeles Times* California Latino Poll (1984); and the Mexican American Electorate Studies (1981–1982), conducted by the Southwest Voter Registration Education Project and the Center for Mexican American Studies, University of Texas at Austin. Frequently cited early studies of Latino political orientations include: Antunes and Gaitz (1975); Buzan (1980); Cain and Kiewiet (1984); Comer (1978); de la Garza, Brischetto, and Vaughn (1983); de la Garza and Weaver (1984); F. C. Garcia (1973); Guzman (1976); Hirsch and Gutierrez (1977); Institute for Puerto Rican Policy (1984); Lamare (1982); Lovrich and Marenin (1976); MacManus and Cassel (1982); Miller, Polinard, and Wrinkle (1984); Portes (1984); Uhlaner, Cain, and Kiewiet (1989); Villareal (1979); and Welch (1977).

2. In some places this study is referred to as Mexican Origin People in the United States (1978). See J. Garcia (1982, 1987) for a fuller description and discussion of the results.

3. De la Garza's comments were made in the context of a conference (known as the Ignored Voices conference) held in October 1985 to address the lack of attention to Latino opinions. De la Garza added, "There is no systematic reliable source that tells us what Latinos think about issues or how they view the nation's political leaders" (1987, 3).

Part 2   Issue Attitudes

Surveys of political opinion typically include questions on a wide range of topics. Major national academic surveys may include a host of questions on public policy issues and scores of others on topics that might be thought of as political in some way. Yet, during election campaigns, one or more of four types of issues is always emphasized: economic issues, social or moral issues, foreign policy issues, and racial issues. Within these broad categories, of course, there are countless political issues. Economic issues can include tax rates, welfare payments, business regulation, and health care; social issues include abortion, gay rights, equal rights for women, school prayer, home schooling, and divorce laws; and foreign policy issues include spending on bombers and submarines, giving aid to foreign countries, imposing trade sanctions on other countries, and even going to war. Many issues fall into more than one category. Foreign trade, for example, involves both foreign policy and domestic economic policy. Equal pay for equal work laws, designed to eliminate wage discrimination against women, involve both social and economic policy. And policies that deny funding for international agencies that advocate abortion are at the intersection of foreign and social policy.

Scholars who study public opinion in a particular policy area ask many different questions. They may describe how opinions on racial discrimination have changed over the past several decades (Schuman, Steeh, Bobo, and Krysan 1997) or how an event like the Bosnian conflict has changed foreign policy views. Social scientists may study the changing sources of opinion on gay rights or the way certain groups, such as highly religious blacks, are torn on this issue as their religious views conflict with their strong belief in equality (Wilcox and Wolpert 2000). Researchers may investigate the impact of economic attitudes on vote choice or on the outcome of congressional elections.

Racial issues have been a major source of controversy in American politics since the founding of the nation. Early public opinion polls from the 1930s and 1940s found many white Americans expressing opinions that today most would classify as offensive (Schuman, Steeh, Bobo, and Krysan 1997). In recent decades, almost all Americans support the rights of minorities to equal treatment in schools, jobs, transportation, and housing. Questions of government actions to ensure equal treatment and to confront the economic gap between whites and minorities, however, evoke complex reactions from the American public. Edward Carmines and Paul Sniderman in their chapter explore the changing nature of American public opinion on racial issues and suggest three explanations for the complex set of racial attitudes held by Americans today.

Social issues also provoke complex, often emotional, reactions from the American public. Abortion has been a major issue in American politics since the 1973 Supreme Court ruling, *Roe v. Wade.* More recently, gay rights issues have come to the forefront of the national agenda. Despite these two issues sharing a number of similarities, public opinion on these issues has divergent trends, as Clyde Wilcox and Barbara Norrander demonstrate in their chapter. On abortion, public opinion has been mostly stable since the 1970s but undergoes shifts in the public mood with small movements in the liberal direction followed by small movements in the conservative direction. Opinion fluctuates as the public struggles over the competing values of when life begins versus individual freedom. On gay rights, the public became more liberal during the 1990s, perhaps because of the increasingly widespread view that sexual preferences are determined at birth and to increasing numbers of Americans knowing gays or lesbians in their social, family, or work environments.

Foreign policy attitudes in the post–cold war world are explored in John Mueller's chapter. For many years, Americans' attitudes on foreign policy were largely centered on containment of communism and the Soviet threat. The breakup of the Soviet Union left many Americans without this strong anchor to their opinion. One consequence is that it allows American presidents to mobilize the public behind moral imperatives, at least as long as the policy does not involve major American casualties.

5 The Structure of Racial Attitudes: Issue Pluralism and the Changing American Dilemma

Edward G. Carmines and Paul M. Sniderman

In the early years of the twenty-first century there is a new complexity in the politics of race in the United States. No longer does race revolve around the single overriding question of whether African Americans should be treated the same as other citizens. Issues of equal treatment were at the heart of the civil rights struggle a generation ago. At that time, regardless of the specific issue—segregated public schools, separate public accommodations, restricted voting rights—the underlying question was whether African Americans had the same rights as other citizens. The equal-treatment agenda centered on the role the government should play in fighting discrimination, defined as the intentional penalizing of blacks because they are black. With the ending of segregation—legally sanctioned, explicitly codified racial inequality—much (but not all) of this agenda has been achieved. The recent presidential election in Florida has reminded us that even the fundamental right to vote is not always guaranteed for African Americans.

Yet even as the United States struggles to resolve some persisting issues of equal treatment, new racial issues have emerged in American politics during the last several decades. These issues focus on two broad areas of public policy that have developed in the post–civil rights period. A "social welfare" agenda concerns the general role of the federal government in providing various forms of economic assistance to blacks, and a "race-conscious" agenda focuses on preferential policies—most notably affirmative action programs in employment and education. Race now involves not one but many policy agendas—an issue pluralism that makes racial politics in the United States today far more complicated than it was a generation ago.

The purpose of this chapter is to examine continuity and change in the racial attitudes of white Americans during the last half of the twentieth century. We first summarize the trends over time in whites' racial opinions during this period and then outline the major theoretical perspectives that have been proposed to explain these trends. We begin with a brief historical overview of the evolution of racial politics in the United States since 1950.

Historical Overview

During the 1950s and 1960s the principal goal of the civil rights movement was to establish legal and political equality for African Americans. This meant ending racial segregation in all areas of public life and ensuring that African Americans could participate fully in the political process. With the passage of the landmark Civil Rights Act of 1964 and the equally far reaching Voting Rights Act of 1965, this goal seemed to have been largely fulfilled—African Americans had finally acquired full American citizenship.

But even before black citizens and their white allies could properly celebrate this remarkable political victory, it became evident that an even more daunting challenge lay ahead. The legislative victories of the 1960s ended legal segregation and the widespread disfranchisement of black voters, but they did nothing to improve the deplorable socioeconomic conditions that most blacks confronted every day. The civil rights victories laid the foundations for economic progress but also underlined the fact that black economic empowerment would be a far more difficult and protracted undertaking. What the civil rights activist Bayard Rustin said about desegregating public accommodations could also be said about the larger civil rights movement:

In desegregating public accommodations, we affected institutions which are relatively peripheral to the American socioeconomic order and to the fundamental conditions of life of the American people. In a highly industrialized, 20th century civilization, we hit Jim Crow precisely where it was most anachronistic, dispensable, and vulnerable—in hotels, lunch counters, terminals, libraries, swimming pools, and the like. For in these forms, Jim Crow does impede the flow of commerce in the broadest sense: it is a nuisance in a society on the move (and on the make). (Quoted in Meier et al. 1971, 445)

Rustin understood that the next phase of the civil rights struggle would focus mainly on the economic sphere and would pose a fundamental challenge to the American socioeconomic order.

Two distinct though related racial agendas have emerged in the post–civil rights United States. First, there is a *social welfare* agenda organized around the general role that government should play to improve the social and economic position of blacks. Second, there is a *race-conscious* agenda, centered mainly on affirmative action programs, which is based on the idea that government should provide special benefits to African Americans because of the special burdens they have had to endure (see Sniderman et al. 1993; Sniderman and Piazza 1993; and Kinder and Sanders 1996, for this division of racial issues).

How have white Americans reacted to the new complexity of racial politics—multiple issues reflecting multiple policy agendas? It is to this question that we now turn.

Equal-Treatment Agenda

No area of American public opinion has undergone more dramatic change since the 1950s than white Americans' attitudes toward the equal treatment of African Americans— whether they believe that blacks should be treated equally regardless of race. During the 1940s and 1950s a clear majority of whites were unwilling to allow black citizens to exercise the basic rights that other Americans took for granted. A 1942 survey, for example, found that 54 percent of whites agreed that "there should be separate sections for Negroes in streetcars and buses"; only 46 percent disagreed. The same survey found that 68 percent of whites thought that black and white students should go to separate schools, while only 32 percent believed that they should attend the same schools.

In employment whites strongly supported overt discrimination. Asked in 1944 whether "Negroes should have as good a chance as white people to get any kind of job or do you think that white people should have the first chance at any kind of job?" 45 percent chose the former, 55 percent the latter. Indeed, on every racial issue on which public opinion was solicited during this period—from attitudes toward segregation and integration to support for a well-qualified black presidential candidate—a majority of whites openly expressed intolerant, discriminatory, and prejudicial attitudes toward African Americans. The message that was conveyed was clear and unmistakable—black citizens should not enjoy the same rights as whites and did not deserve to be treated as their equals.

These attitudes have undergone a fundamental transformation during the last half of the twentieth century. Gradually but steadily, white public opinion toward issues of equal treatment has moved from substantial opposition to overwhelming support. Figure 5-1 presents the evidence documenting this trend. The data show, for example, that support for black and white students attending the same schools has increased from 32 percent of whites in 1942 to 96 percent in 1995. Similarly, opposition to segregation in transportation nearly doubled between 1942 and 1970 (46 percent to 88 percent). To cite a third example: while in 1963, 39 percent of whites disagreed with the statement that "White people have a right to keep Negroes out of their neighborhoods if they want to," this was true of 86 percent in 1996. Overall, the results reported in Figure 5-1 reveal a picture of an increasingly racially tolerant white public, one that is strongly committed to the equal treatment of black citizens.

The attitudes measured in Figure 5-1 focus on the principle of equal treatment— whether whites favor the abstract idea that blacks should be treated the same as whites. A separate but related concern is the extent to which whites support efforts by government to enforce or implement this principle. In their personal dealings some whites may treat blacks as equals, but these same whites might be unwilling to support government policies that enforce equal treatment. Individual good will may not always translate into collective toler-

Figure 5-1 Trends in Whites' Attitudes Toward Principles of Equal
Treatment

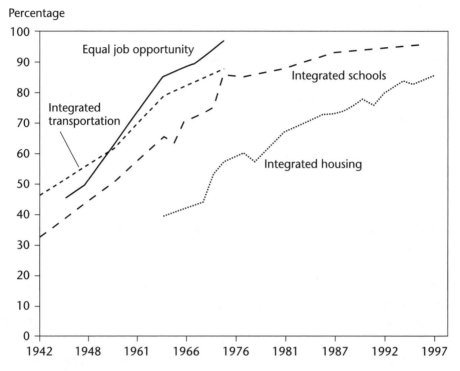

Percentage

Source: Adapted from Howard Schuman, Charlotte Steeh, Lawrence Bobo, and Maria Krysan, *Racial Attitudes in America: Trends and Interpretations,* rev. ed. (Cambridge: Harvard University Press, 1997), 104–107.

Note: Percentages represent those who supported a principle in a given year.

ance. Figure 5-2 shows support for government implementation of programs designed to promote equality in four areas.

Although this distinction between principle and policy is considered fundamental in the study of racial attitudes, public opinion surveys have not adequately illuminated this difference. Examining the survey archive, it is not easy to discover questions on the same racial topic with the only difference being the matter of government implementation. Schuman and his colleagues (1997, 122) suggest that only two racial attitudes have been measured with sufficient comparability to capture the principle–policy distinction. These are attitudes toward public accommodations and open housing.

By 1970, an overwhelming 88 percent of the white American public supported the principle that blacks "should have the right to use the same parks, restaurants, and hotels as white people." Equal treatment in public accommodations had seemingly won the day. But

Figure 5-2   Trends in Whites' Attitudes Toward Implementation of
Principles of Equal Treatment

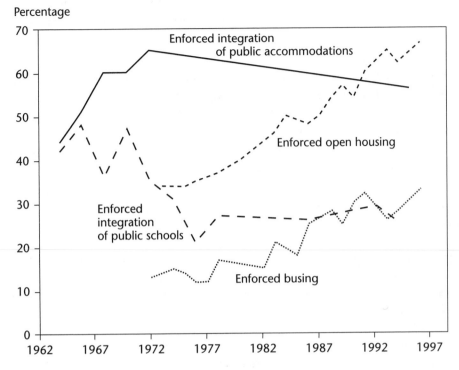

Source: Adapted from Howard Schuman, Charlotte Steeh, Lawrence Bobo, and Maria Krysan, *Racial Attitudes in America: Trends and Interpretations,* rev. ed. (Cambridge: Harvard University Press, 1997), 123–125.

Note: Percentages represent those who supported a policy of government enforcement in a given year.

were whites also willing to support government efforts to end segregation in public accommodations? And how have attitudes toward this issue changed over time? Beginning in 1964 the National Election Study posed the following question to respondents:

As you may know, Congress passed a bill that says that black people should have the right to go to any hotel or restaurant they can afford, just like anybody else. Some people feel that this is something the government in Washington should support. Others feel that the government should stay out of this matter. Have you been interested enough in this to favor one side over another? [If Yes] Should the government support the right of black people to go to any hotel or restaurant they can afford, or should it stay out of the matter?

The wording of this question closely parallels the wording of the question focusing on the principle of public accommodations—except that this item explicitly mentions government enforcement. In 1964, white Americans were almost evenly divided in their attitudes toward using the government to end racial discrimination in public accommodations: 44 percent supported government intervention, and 45 percent said the government should not become involved in this matter. By 1974, the distribution of opinion was heavily tilted toward the government enforcement position, with 65 percent of the white public favoring and only 21 percent opposing intervention.

The issue of open housing is another for which we can evaluate the difference between white support for an underlying principle and white support for government efforts to implement the principle. As we have noted, from the 1960s to the 1990s there was a dramatic increase in the proportion of whites who supported the principle that blacks should be able to buy a home in any neighborhood in which they could afford to live. But again the question can be raised—would white Americans support a law that guaranteed African Americans this right? Fortunately, beginning in the early 1970s the National Opinion Research Center at the University of Chicago posed the following hypothetical situation to respondents:

Suppose there is a community-wide vote on the general housing issue. There are two possible laws to vote on. One law says that a homeowner can decide for himself whom to sell his house to, even if he prefers not to sell to Negroes. The second law says that a homeowner cannot refuse to sell to someone because of their color. Which law would you vote for?

This item refers to the hypothetical integration of a neighborhood, and government enforcement takes the form of a local referendum. As Figure 5-2 indicates, there has been a steady increase in white support for such a law over the last two decades. In 1973, almost twice as many people said they would oppose such a referendum as said they would support it. By 1996, the ratio was almost exactly reversed: 67 percent of whites said they would vote for such a law.

These principle–policy comparisons in the areas of open housing and public accommodations support two basic conclusions. On the one hand, white support for both the principle of equal treatment and its implementation have shown an upward trajectory during the last several decades. It is not the case that most whites agree with the high-minded exhortations of a principle while opposing its implementation. Both principle and policy in these racial domains now command majority support—a position that represents a transformation in the racial thinking of white Americans.

At the same time, it is also true that support for implementation always lags behind support for the principle itself. This is not surprising. A liberal response to the implementation question implies that a person not only agrees with the underlying principle but also is willing to use the power of government to implement it. Those who agree presumably have a stronger, more intense opinion as well as a belief in the efficacy and appropriateness of government action.

The principle–policy gap is much larger for other issues in the equal-treatment agenda, but the comparison is muddled by the changing context of racial politics. A good example is school integration. As we saw earlier, there is now near-unanimous agreement among whites that black and white students should go to the same rather than separate schools. During the 1990s more than 90 percent of white Americans endorsed this view. But the policy question focusing on integrated schooling tells a very different story. Not only do whites not express overwhelming support for government implementation of school integration; they are sharply divided about this issue. A plurality says the government should "stay out of this area." Even more revealing, there has actually been a decline in white support for government-enforced school integration during the last thirty years. In the 1960s an average of 42 percent of whites favored this policy; this figure declines to 27 percent in the 1990s. It is tempting to conclude that this is a clear case of insincerity among many whites—a tendency to agree with the high-minded principle but to retreat from doing anything to put the principle into practice.

This seemingly straightforward interpretation, however, is confounded by the changing politics of race in general and school desegregation in particular during this period (Schuman et al. 1997, 127–128). During the 1950s and early 1960s the focus of attention was eliminating the system of racially separated schools that had developed in the South. But beginning in the later 1960s attention shifted to de facto school segregation that existed mainly in the North. And it became clear that there were no easy solutions to this situation—that, indeed, intercommunity busing was a necessary part of any solution given the extensive residential segregation existing throughout the country, North as well as South. In the face of these changing circumstances, white public support for government-enforced school desegregation plans, especially among northerners, plummeted. Does this principle–policy gap result from white insincerity or from the evolving nature of the policy itself? We know of no way to disentangle these competing explanations.

The difficulty of interpretation is even more acute when we consider the issue of busing. Whites have been notably unsympathetic to this means of achieving school desegregation since the policy was introduced in the early 1970s. Even very recently, less than one-third of whites express support for busing. Does this antipathy indicate a lack of genuine commitment to school integration or deep-seated misgivings about the policy itself? Again, both interpretations are plausible and we have no way of choosing between them.

In summary, all we can say with some confidence is that the principle–policy gap is much smaller when the means of implementation closely corresponds to the underlying principle. Conversely, when principle and policy diverge, the public often responds by endorsing the principle while rejecting the policy designed to implement it.

Social Welfare Agenda

During the past several decades race has focused increasingly on economic issues, notably on the role that government should play in improving the social and economic position of blacks. Figure 5-3 shows the results of two questions that tap the general attitudes of white Americans toward governmental assistance to blacks. The first question focuses on spending, specifically "whether we're spending too much money, too little money, or about the right amount . . . improving the conditions of blacks." Only a minority of whites says that the United States is spending too little money improving the condition of blacks. Indeed, as Figure 5-3 indicates, at no time have as many as one-third of whites felt that the country is spending too little money on blacks. The most frequent response by a substantial margin across all these years has been that Americans are "spending about the right amount," indicating a preference for the status quo over either increased or decreased spending.

Figure 5-3 also presents the results of a question that focuses not on spending but on the amount of effort that the government should expend in assisting blacks through programs and policies. This question is presented in a 7-point format in which the endpoints are anchored by the phrases "blacks should help themselves" and "government should help," respectively. Looking at those respondents who place themselves closer to the latter category (a response of 5 to 7), we find that only a small proportion of the white populace supports additional government programs and policies—a figure that has not changed appreciably since 1970.

Overall, these results suggest that although a majority of whites may favor current levels of government assistance to blacks, there is little support for increased assistance, an attitude that has remained largely stable during the last several decades. Furthermore, white support for government assistance quickly evaporates if it is seen as an alternative to blacks helping themselves.

Race-Conscious Agenda

We now turn to the most controversial dimension of contemporary racial politics: race-conscious policies, notably affirmative action involving preferential treatment in employment and education. We first examine a situation in which affirmative action is put in its most favorable light—namely, where previous discrimination provides the justification for preferential treatment. Beginning in 1985 the following question has been posed several times to respondents by CBS and the *New York Times:* "Do you believe where there has been job discrimination against blacks in the past, preference in hiring or promotion should be given to blacks today?" When an explicit justification for preferential treatment is mentioned without the inclusion of an opposing argument, as many as 35 percent of whites express support for the policy.

Figure 5-3 Trends in Whites' Attitudes Toward Government Assistance for Blacks

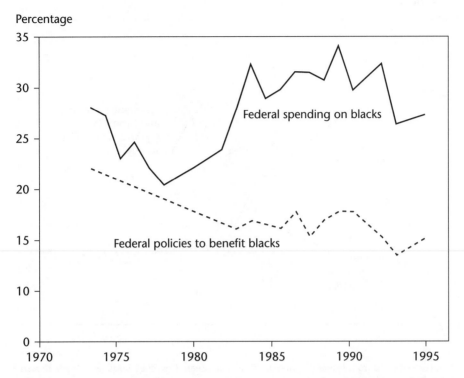

Percentage

Source: Adapted from Howard Schuman, Charlotte Steeh, Lawrence Bobo, and Maria Krysan, *Racial Attitudes in America: Trends and Interpretations,* rev. ed. (Cambridge: Harvard University Press, 1997), 172–176.

Note: Percentages represent those who favor more government spending or help in a given year.

Beginning in 1986 the National Election Study has asked the following question about racial preferences in employment:

Some people say that because of past discrimination, Blacks should be given preference in hiring and promotion. Others say that such a preference in hiring and promotion of Blacks is wrong because it gives Blacks advantages they haven't earned. What about you—are you for or against preferential hiring and promotion of Blacks? Do you (favor/oppose) preference in hiring and promotion strongly or not strongly?

The question is balanced in that it presents a reason for favoring preferences in employment as well as a reason for opposing them. When the question is framed in this manner, whites overwhelmingly oppose affirmative action. The high watermark for support is 17 percent; more than 80 percent of whites consistently oppose this form of affirmative action. More-

Figure 5-4 Trends in Whites' Attitudes Toward Affirmative Action

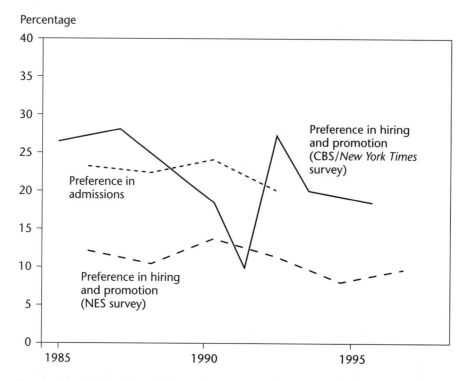

Percentage

Source: Adapted from Howard Schuman, Charlotte Steeh, Lawrence Bobo, and Maria Krysan, *Racial Attitudes in America: Trends and Interpretations,* rev. ed. (Cambridge: Harvard University Press, 1997), 172–176.

Note: Percentages represent those who supported a policy in a given year.

over, more than 60 percent of whites say that they strongly oppose the policy, indicating that white opposition is not only widespread but quite intense as well.

Whites also oppose racial quotas in higher education. Between 70 and 75 percent of whites oppose quotas, and about 50 percent say they strongly oppose them. Figure 5-4 indicates the lack of white support for affirmative action policies in college admissions and in employment. Overall, there is somewhat more support for racial preferences in higher education than in employment, a difference that may indicate, as Schuman and his colleagues argue, that "preferential treatment in education can be seen as an attempt to 'level the playing field,' whereas employment is seen as the final game itself" (1997, 180).

In sum, whites show little support for any kind of policy that involves preferential treatment for African Americans, a situation that has remained basically unchanged since affirmative action was introduced several decades ago. And with a majority of whites expressing strong opposition to race-conscious policies, this dimension of racial policy stands out as the most unpopular in the United States today.

Theoretical Perspectives

As we have seen, the racial attitudes of white Americans have become increasingly complex during the last fifty years. On issues most closely identified with the equal-treatment agenda, whites have become more tolerant and less prejudiced. But whites express little support for increasing government assistance to improve the social and economic circumstances of African Americans, while affirmative action policies involving racial preferences are extremely unpopular—indeed, such policies garner no more white support today than they did when first introduced several decades ago.

What explains this complex pattern of continuity and change over time in the racial attitudes of white Americans? Why have whites increasingly supported some racial issues, endorsed the status quo in other areas of race, and expressed strong opposition to still other racial policies? We review three explanations that have tried to bring theoretical order to this empirical complexity.

The New Racism Thesis

As its name implies, the new racism argument shares many characteristics with the older racism thesis. The older racism stressed the idea that whites discriminate against African Americans and oppose any policies intended to benefit them because they consider blacks to be biologically inferior to whites. This was racism in its most raw and most primitive form. It provided a justification for the ill treatment of African Americans because they were considered literally a race apart—a permanent and unalterable condition that put blacks at the bottom of American society.

The new racism differs from the old principally in its lessening preoccupation with biological determinism. The new racism theorists recognize that most whites no longer see African Americans as inherently inferior and as a consequence incapable of full membership in the human race. But this does not mean that racism itself has disappeared from the United States or that racist impulses do not dominate the political thinking of white Americans. Quite the opposite, in the words of Donald Kinder and Lynn Sanders: "As biological racism has declined, a new form of racial prejudice has appeared" (1996, 98).

What is the character of the new racism? At its core, it is a blend of racial animosity on the one hand and cherished American values, chief among them individualism, on the other (Kinder and Sears 1981). It is this combination—the capacity of racial hostility to become appended to American individualism—that makes the new racism such a potent force in white America.

The new racists do not claim that blacks are genetically inferior to whites. Instead, they believe that blacks lack the commitment to hard work, discipline, and self-sacrifice that are highly valued in white America. That is, African Americans are faulted because they are seen as not striving to live up to the central ideals of the American dream. "Today," Kinder and Sanders declare, "prejudice is expressed in the language of American individualism" (1996, 106).

Those who believe that a new racism has now taken root in the United States maintain that much of the opposition of whites to contemporary racial policies is based on this new form of racial resentment and animosity. Because it has become uncoupled from old-fashioned, biological racism, the new racism has gained a degree of acceptance and respectability. Today, whites who adhere to the new racism feel no hesitation in expressing negative attitudes toward African Americans.

The new racism is not only widespread in the United States today; according to new racism theorists, it is the most potent force shaping the attitudes of whites toward racial issues. As Kinder and Sanders put it, "Racial resentment is not the only thing that matters for racial policy, but by a fair margin racial resentment is the most important" (1996, 124).

Group Conflict Perspective

A second major theoretical perspective that has been proposed to explain the racial attitudes of white Americans grows out of an essentially sociological focus on the nature of group conflict. Herbert Blumer's (1958) work is foundational here because he first offered a sociological interpretation of prejudice as a "sense of group position." The key idea is that groups in society naturally compete with each other over scarce resources—not just those that are material in character, but also social and psychological values and benefits. The inevitable outcome of realistic group conflict is differential success, which leads to a hierarchical division of superior and inferior groups. A more controversial aspect of the theory is the assertion that dominant groups will employ all the means at their disposal to maintain their status, privileges, and resources to the detriment of subordinate groups. The degree of group competition and conflict depends on several factors, and is most intense when in-group identities are strong, out-group stereotyping is extreme, and the threat is seen as immediate and overwhelming.

Slavery and then segregation were once the preferred means by which whites could maintain their superiority over blacks. But as these institutions fell into disrepute, most whites did not suddenly become committed to racial equality. Instead, according to group-conflict theorists, they developed a belief system that allowed them to justify their superior status and dominant group position within the changing industrial economy so as to counter the increasing threat posed by the upward mobility and potential power of African

Americans (see Lawrence Bobo's concept of "laissez-faire racism" in Bobo, Kluegel, and Smith 1997 and in Bobo and Smith 1998).

Proponents of the group-conflict perspective see white opposition to racial policies intended to assist African Americans as being due to the threat these policies and their black beneficiaries represent to continuing white dominance. As Bobo puts it in explaining white opposition to affirmative action:

> The core argument here is that racial politics unavoidably involves a nettlesome fusion of racial identities and attitudes with racial group interests. It suggests that many whites will oppose affirmative action not so much because they see a race-based policy as contravening their loftiest values or because they have learned a new, politically relevant set of resentments of blacks; but rather because they perceive blacks as competitive threats for valued social resources, statuses, and privileges. (2000, 142–143)

It is important to emphasize that the seriousness of the threat is not necessarily derived from an objective assessment of the group's capacities or intentions but rather is based on the perceived threat posed by the group. Except perhaps for a brief moment during Reconstruction, African Americans, as a group, have never been large enough or powerful enough to represent a real threat in white America. But, according to the group-conflict perspective, this is beside the point: the key is that whites perceive blacks as a serious threat to their political and economic interests and so have devised an ideological system that justifies their privileged status and their treatment of blacks as an inferior group.

Politics-Centered Approach

The third position that we want to examine has been referred to as the politics-centered approach to the explanation of racial attitudes. This approach argues that the essential thing to understand in the argument about racial policy is that it "has become at its core an argument over politics" (Sniderman, Crosby, and Howell 2000, 236). From this perspective, the divergent trends in racial issues that we have observed are not due primarily to a new form of racism that has taken root in white America or to the inevitable clash of group interests but rather to the context of contemporary American politics. In particular, according to advocates of the politics-centered perspective, it is ideological conflict embedded in the American party system that shapes mass responses to racial issues.

The fundamental claim of the politics-centered approach is that race per se is no longer the issue in American politics; rather, issues of race are grouped together in the three policy agendas we outlined earlier—equal treatment, social welfare, and race conscious. This means there is not one overarching politics of race since the politics of the equal-treatment agenda is not the same as the politics of the social welfare agenda, and both differ from the politics of the race-conscious agenda.

This argument implies that no single factor—including racism—is the driving force determining white responses to all racial issues. Instead, racism is seen as one factor among the many that affect whites' attitudes toward racial policy; but racism does not influence the political thinking of all whites equally, nor is it equally relevant to all racial policies.

A second point concerns the crucial role that the logic of political choice plays within this theoretical framework. In particular, according to advocates of this perspective, white support for different racial policies is mainly a function of how these racial agendas line up with ideological conflict underlying the American party system.

Most issues of equal treatment, for example, are no longer on the front lines of the ideological battlefield in the United States: most conservatives as well as liberals and most Republicans as well as Democrats support the equal treatment of African Americans. And for the advocates of the politics-centered approach, it is precisely the fact that the equal-treatment agenda has become relatively free of ideological and partisan conflict that accounts for its increased support among whites.

By contrast, during the last several decades, issues centering on black social welfare have become increasingly incorporated into the main lines of ideological conflict in the United States. The basic contours of this conflict were established during the New Deal of Franklin D. Roosevelt, when the Democratic Party became associated with domestic liberalism while the Republicans emphasized limited government and market-oriented solutions to social problems. It took more than thirty years for racial issues to become part of the liberal–conservative framework, but today issues focusing on government assistance to blacks are an integral element of the extended New Deal issue agenda (Carmines and Stimson 1989).

Proponents of the politics perspective see issues of affirmative action in still a different ideological light. These issues are viewed neither as nonideological nor as a simple left–right matter. At the elite and activist levels of the party system, race-conscious policies are part of the broad ideological dimension separating Democrats and Republicans. But this partisan division is much less pronounced at the mass level of the party system, where many liberals as well as conservatives (and Democrats as well as Republicans) oppose affirmative action policies involving preferential treatment. Thus, affirmative action not only divides liberals and conservatives but, more important, it divides liberalism itself. As Paul M. Sniderman and Edward G. Carmines argue:

Rather than facing the opposition of the right but enjoying the backing of the left—which is the standard pattern for redistributive politics—affirmative action runs into trouble on both sides of the political aisle. . . . Instead of deepening the cleavage between the political left (liberals and the Democratic party) and the political right (conservatives and the Republican party), resentment over affirmative action has burst through the usual ideological channels. (1997, 44–45)

A New American Dilemma?

The purpose of this chapter has been to trace the trends over time in the racial attitudes of white Americans and to outline several theoretical perspectives that have been developed to account for racial politics in the United States today. Space does not allow us to offer a detailed assessment of these perspectives but it is clear that each has merits as well as limitations and that a comprehensive, fully satisfactory explanation will depend on a fruitful synthesis of the various approaches.

The task will not be easy because race has become more complicated and morally more ambivalent in recent American politics. In 1944 the Swedish social scientist Gunnar Myrdal posed the American dilemma concerning race: "Would the American Creed—the commitment to liberty, equality, and fair play—prevail over the prejudice and discrimination that were widespread in white America?" Myrdal was cautiously hopeful about ultimate success because, as he argued, "America is constantly reaching for . . . democracy at home and abroad. The main trend is the gradual realization of the American Creed" (1944, 1021).

The trends over time in public opinion that highlight the accelerating commitment of white Americans to the principle and practice of equal rights would seem to have finally resolved America's racial dilemma. Racial tolerance and enlightenment would seem to have won the day. But the situation is more complex than this sanguine conclusion would indicate. For, as we have seen, white Americans are largely unsympathetic to the new faces of racial politics. Not only do most whites not support increased government assistance to improve the social and economic position of blacks, they are adamantly opposed to affirmative action programs that involve the preferential treatment of African Americans.

The economic blight still so evident in much of black America constitutes a fundamental challenge in an increasingly prosperous United States. Whether this situation constitutes our new racial dilemma depends on whether the United States will launch new policy initiatives that will more fully realize racial justice, or, as now seems perhaps more likely, lacks the will to do so.

Edward G. Carmines thanks the Center for the Advanced Study in the Behavioral Sciences for its support during the writing of this chapter.

6 Of Moods and Morals:
The Dynamics of Opinion on Abortion and Gay Rights

Clyde Wilcox and Barbara Norrander

During the 2000 presidential election campaign and in the postelection analysis, much discussion centered on the role of moral issues in the campaign. A June 2000 *Los Angeles Times* survey revealed that more than three out of four respondents believed that the "moral climate in the country" was off on the wrong track. In a similar vein, national exit polls conducted on election day showed that nearly 60 percent of voters thought that the country was on the wrong moral track, and more than a third of voters thought that moral leadership was more important for a president than being competent to manage government. Such data imply that voters may respond to a general "moral mood" in their evaluations of parties and candidates. A moral mood also might influence voters' positions on social and moral policy issues, such as abortion, gay rights, divorce laws, and pornography.

The existence of a moral mood would fit with previous studies of American public opinion. James Stimson (1999) has written of a more general policy mood which moves both in swings and cycles. Liberalism surged in the early 1960s, conservatism peaked around 1980, and liberalism was once again on a general rise throughout the 1980s and into the early 1990s. Maybe the public's moral mood is but a component of a more general swing toward conservatism at the turn of the twenty-first century, or perhaps the public mood on moral issues moves independently of other policy preferences, sparked by events such as President Clinton's highly publicized affair with White House intern Monica Lewinsky.

Yet polls conducted by the *Los Angeles Times* reported very different stories about trends in two highly controversial and morally charged issues—abortion and gay rights. Survey data showed that attitudes on abortion in 2000 had become slightly more conservative than was the case in 1989 (when the newspaper asked many of the same abortion questions), whereas attitudes on gay rights had become dramatically more liberal since 1985 (when the newspaper asked many of the same gay rights questions).

Abortion and gay rights are emotional issues that involve personal beliefs on religious values, individual freedom, and human sexuality. Both issues spawned competing social movements. The associated interest groups engage in intense political mobilization efforts and high levels of campaign spending in hopes of shaping public opinion and electing candidates who share their views. Within the general public, attitudes toward abortion and gay rights are positively correlated—that is, if someone is more conservative on abortion it is likely that he or she is also conservative on gay rights. Yet in one case (abortion) opinion is moving slightly but significantly in the conservative direction, whereas the other (gay rights) opinion is moving rapidly and decisively toward a more liberal position. Such divergence challenges conventional understandings of public attitudes on moral issues. Why are opinions on these two issues moving in different directions?

This chapter will investigate the dynamics of public attitudes on abortion and gay rights from 1972 through 2000. In each case we will examine trends in attitudes over time and try to identify periods in which attitudes have become more liberal or more conservative. We also will look for generational differences in attitudes, which may help us predict future changes in attitudes, since the oldest generations will be replaced by younger ones. Finally, we will explore changing beliefs about pregnancy and homosexuality, which might ultimately influence the future of these issues in the public eye.

Accounting for Changes in Public Opinion

Public opinion changes over time in myriad ways. One type of change is characterized by quick movement in public attitudes. In February 1998 nearly two-thirds of Americans believed that Clinton should resign if he had lied about having sex with Monica Lewinsky. Over the next few months, the public increasingly came to accept that Clinton had in fact conducted an affair with Lewinsky and lied about it, but the public also came to define that affair as a private matter. By July of that year, 70 percent thought that Clinton should remain in office, whether or not he had lied about the affair (Andolina and Wilcox 2000).

Similarly rapid changes occur in public opinion about foreign policy. A Gallup poll in mid-January 1991 showed that only 46 percent of the public thought that the Iraqi invasion of Kuwait was worth going to war over, but a similar question asked at the end of the month, after the United States had begun the air war, showed that 71 percent supported the action. A year later, only 59 percent thought that the situation had merited going to war (Mueller 1994). This is an example of a more general phenomenon: the public tends to rally behind presidents in the event of military action, but that support often erodes either after the conflict ends or as casualties mount (Brody 1991).

Opinion moves relatively rapidly when enough Americans have changed their responses to survey questions. In some cases, events cause citizens to think of the issue in a new light, or political elites make arguments that persuade some members of the public to change their minds. The Clinton administration used its considerable persuasive resources to spin the Lewinsky story. With the Persian Gulf War, the first Bush administration carefully sought to build public support, and the administration had access to substantial polling data to help it shape its persuasive appeals. Yet not until the war actually began did the public rally to support the military effort.

A second type of change in public opinion involves a more gradual ebb and flow in attitudes. In response to the Soviet invasion of Afghanistan (1979) and the Iranian hostage crisis (1979–1980), public support for increased defense spending surged in the late 1970s and early 1980s, when almost one in four Americans changed his or her opinion to support a larger military budget. By 1982 real defense spending had dramatically increased, the media was full of stories of seemingly extravagant spending on hammers and toilet seats, and a nuclear freeze movement had mobilized. Support for increased military spending dropped from 60 percent in 1980 to only 31 percent in 1982 (Page and Shapiro 1992).

The ebb and flow of public support for various policies is often referred to as a public policy mood. Stimson (1999) argued for the existence of cycles of public policy moods and tracked these cycles from 1958 through 1996. Public policy moods and government actions are linked but somewhat out of sync, as the government overresponds to public opinion, causing public opinion to veer in the opposite direction. In the early 1960s, the Johnson administration pushed for many new liberal social welfare and racial policies, and public mood moved in a more conservative direction. In 1980, Ronald Reagan won office and pushed for more conservative policies, and the public mood became more liberal. More specifically, the burst of defense spending early in the Reagan administration was followed by a decline in public support for additional spending.

A third type of opinion change is evolutionary. Consider the position of blacks in American society. In the 1940s, surveys revealed that only a minority of white Americans favored equal job opportunities for African Americans and integrated transportation, housing, and schools. By the early 1980s, white support for this type of racial equality was overwhelming (Schuman et al. 1997). A similar pattern holds for women. In 1972 only 70 percent of the public indicated a willingness to vote for a woman for president if she were qualified and from their party, but by 1998 that number had increased to 90 percent. In both cases, opinion did not change suddenly, but rather gradually over time. Values also change in the longer run. After World War II, citizens of Western Europe were preoccupied with material needs and valued economic stability and prosperity above freedom and self-expression. Yet new generations took prosperity for granted and held "postmaterialist" values, meaning that they gave more weight to self-expression than material needs (Inglehart 1971; Abramson and Inglehart 1995).

Attitudes or values can change in the aggregate without everyone changing his or her opinions. Strong Republicans remained committed to impeaching and removing President Clinton in 1998, while Democrats, independents, and moderate Republicans became less supportive of impeachment. When elites of one party send a consistent signal on an issue, their arguments are likely to sway some of their own partisans but have little effect on supporters of the opposite party.

Moreover, citizens with little information or awareness of a policy issue seldom change their minds about that issue, although their responses to survey items may vary randomly. These individuals lack the cognitive framework to process news stories or statements made by political elites. People with more information on and awareness of an issue are more likely to respond to news reports. However, the most informed, having grounded their opinions in a large and complex network of facts, assumptions, and values, are not easily swayed (Zaller 1992). Thus, on many issues, attitude change is greatest among those with the capacity and background to process information from the media or arguments from political elites, but without internal reasons to discount the information or resist the arguments.

Periods, Generations, and Life Cycles

When we trace attitudes over a long period of time, we speak of three types of effects that might cause changes in opinion: period effects, generational effects, and life cycle effects. In period effects people from all segments of society alter their opinions, often in response to particular events. General policy mood is one type of period effect. Thus, support for welfare spending may decline because the public has become more conservative for a time, but this effect might disappear as the mood cycle reverses. Thus, some period effects, such as the public mood, may be relatively short-term swings in public opinion.

When we study attitudes over a long period, it is important to bear in mind that changes in aggregate attitudes may be at least partially a result of the process of generational replacement, when older generations die off and are replaced by younger generations who may have different experiences and values. For example, many Americans who came of age during the Great Depression became lifelong Democrats because of their support of Franklin D. Roosevelt's New Deal policies.

In this study, we will explore attitudes from 1972 through 2000. Generational replacement has been significant over this period, and the youngest generations have very different life experiences from those of the oldest ones. In 1972, fully 25 percent of respondents were from the Depression generation (who reached age eighteen before 1932), but by 2000 this oldest generation constituted only 1 percent of respondents. In contrast, in 2000, 15 percent of respondents had not yet been born in 1972, and more than 55 percent were less than eighteen years old in 1972. Thus, none of these younger cohorts are present in the 1972 data, whereas few from the older cohorts of the 1972 surveys are still alive in 2000.

Consider the different circumstances of this depression generation and the cohort that came of age during George Bush's presidency (1989–1992). The Depression generation came of age in a time without television, when travel was difficult, when many Americans still lived in rural areas, and when higher education was relatively rare. Throughout the twenty-eight years of the General Social Survey (GSS), nearly 60 percent of the Depression generation respondents indicated that they had less than a high school education, whereas only 9 percent claimed a college degree. In contrast, among those who came of age during the Bush administration, only 16 percent had less than a high school education, and fully 22 percent had a college degree. Forty-four percent of the Great Depression generation grew up in the country or on a farm, compared with only 19 percent of the Bush cohort.

For the purposes of this study, we have divided respondents into eight age cohorts: those who came of age during or before the Great Depression; those who came of age during World War II; those who came of age during the postwar period through 1960; those who came of age during the 1960s through 1972; those who came of age during 1970s after the Supreme Court's *Roe v. Wade* abortion decision; and those who came of age during the Reagan presidency, during the Bush presidency, and during the Clinton presidency. We will examine attitudes of these respondents over time, for we can gain some insight about future attitudes as we trace the decline of older generations and the rise of new ones.

The oldest generations came of age during a time of moral conservatism and material privation. The post–World War II era was one of great conformity; gender roles were clearly defined. The 1960s generation was one that rebelled, spawning the civil rights and antiwar movements, and one that pushed for reform of abortion laws. The post-*Roe* generation experienced a world with legal abortion and a growing feminist movement. Ronald Reagan's years were marked by a morally conservative rhetoric and a president who opposed abortion but who was not visibly anti-gay rights. George Bush's brief presidency is less easy to characterize, but Bill Clinton was a prochoice, pro-gay rights president with a strong feminist wife and partner. If there are generational effects to these issues, we can expect to find that the oldest cohorts are the most conservative; the 1960s, post-*Roe*, and Clinton cohorts the most liberal on abortion; and the youngest cohorts the most liberal on gay rights.

Yet it is also possible that attitudes change over an individual's life cycle, and if there are life cycle effects they may complicate generational considerations. Perhaps young people who worry about unexpected pregnancies think differently about abortion than do young married couples, who may in turn differ in their attitudes from parents of teenaged daughters and sons. The life cycle effect has great support in the popular lore of public opinion; many Americans assume that citizens become more conservative as they get older, for example. But the popular conception of life cycle changes is distorted. Surveys done in the 1990s find that age and ideology are only weakly correlated. Thus, we do not expect to find major life cycle differences on these issues.

The Static Nature of Abortion Opinion

Since the 1973 Supreme Court decision *Roe v. Wade* overturned state and national laws restricting abortions, abortion has been the single most explosive issue in American politics. Abortion has motivated ordinary citizens to take extraordinary political action, with one side picketing and blockading abortion clinics while the other tries to find ways to usher pregnant women through those blockades. At their most extreme, abortion attitudes have led to politically motivated murder. Most actions of the antiabortion and prochoice movements, however, are more conventional: organizing blocs of voters, engaging in peaceful marches, and contributing to campaigns. Interest groups on both sides of the abortion issue are among the largest and best funded in America, and both spend millions of dollars trying to influence public opinion and to elect their supporters to public office.

Yet seen from one perspective, what is most surprising about public attitudes on abortion is how static they are. Since 1972 the GSS has asked respondents six separate questions about whether abortion should be allowed under particular circumstances: when the woman's health is in danger, when the fetus would be severely defective, when the pregnancy was the result of rape or incest, when the family is too poor to support another child, when the mother is unmarried and does not want to marry, and when a married woman is pregnant but the couple wants no more children. Respondents can say yes or no to any or all of these, and from them we have created an additive scale ranging from 0 (permit abortions for none of these circumstances) to 6 (permit abortions for all of these circumstances).

Figure 6-1 shows the average score on this scale for all respondents in each year the survey has been conducted. In each year, the mean score rounds to 4 out of 6 items, with the mean usually hovering slightly below 4 (top line in Figure 6-1). Roughly speaking, the average American approves of abortion for the three physically traumatic circumstances of danger to the mother's health, of fetal defect, and of rape and incest, and then for about one other circumstance—usually poverty. Between 30 percent and 40 percent of respondents in various years have approved of abortions under all six circumstances, and between 5 percent and 9 percent of respondents have disapproved of abortion for all circumstances.

Figure 6-1 also shows different levels of support for two sets of abortion circumstances: physically traumatic reasons (woman's health, fetal defect, rape) and social reasons (poverty, unmarried, married but wants no more children). Public support is consistently higher for the physical reasons, with the mean response just below the maximum of three acceptable reasons (middle line in Figure 6-1). Support for abortion for social reasons is consistently lower, with a mean response between one and two acceptable reasons (bottom line in Figure 6-1).

Although abortion attitudes in Figure 6-1 appear to be quite stable, if we look at these trends more closely we can see small changes in support for legal abortion. Figure 6-2 pre-

Figure 6-1 Support for Legal Abortion, 1972–2000

Mean number of reasons

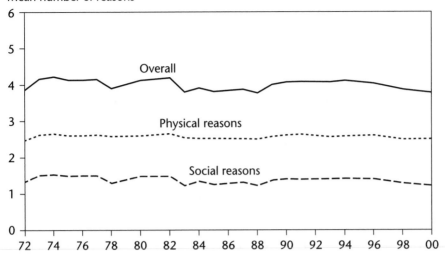

Source: General Social Survey, 1972–2000.

Note: Respondents could approve or disapprove of abortion under six conditions. Those who oppose abortion in all cases score 0, and those who approve of abortion in all cases score 6. The six reasons fall into two categories: physical (woman's health, fetal defect, rape) and social (poverty, unmarried, married but wants no more children).

sents the same information on overall support of abortion as Figure 6-1, but in this case the scale is magnified to allow us to look more closely at small changes in opinion. The GSS contains enough respondents to allow us to be confident that these small changes are real—they are not simply an accident of who was surveyed in any given year. The data show that support for abortion increased in 1973 after the *Roe* decision, stayed generally high until the early 1980s, dipped through 1989, and then increased and remained relatively high until the late 1990s, when it declined sharply. Thus, to understand the dynamics of abortion opinion, we must understand both its overall stability and the smaller cycles of opinion change.

Abortion attitudes have remained relatively stable over time because the issue lies at the intersection of two important and stable values—individual freedom and fetal life. The two movements that contest the abortion issue have chosen to emphasize one or the other of these issues and to deny the importance of the competing value. At prochoice rallies demonstrators chant, "Right-to-life, your name's a lie, you don't care if women die," while at antiabortion demonstrations marchers chant, "Prochoice your name's a lie, babies don't

Figure 6-2 Support for Legal Abortion, with Magnified Scale, 1972–2000

Mean number of reasons

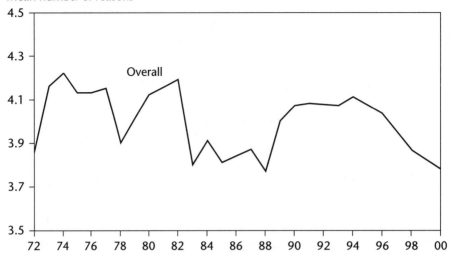

Source: General Social Survey, 1972–2000.

Note: Data are the average number of acceptable reasons (of six) for each year.

choose to die." This clash of absolutes in elite discourse might lead observers to expect to find a similar division in the general public.[1]

A majority of Americans embrace both values. A majority of Americans believe that the fetus is alive. In the *Los Angeles Times* 2000 poll, 49 percent of men and 63 percent of women indicated that life began at conception, and another 36 percent of men and 26 percent of women indicated that life began sometime between conception and birth. Moreover, the poll revealed that fully 60 percent of all respondents believed that abortion is murder. Yet the public also believes in the rights of individuals to make their own moral decisions. The *Los Angeles Times* poll asked respondents to agree or disagree with the statement: "No matter how I feel about abortion, I believe it is a decision that has to be made by a woman and her doctor." More than 70 percent of respondents agreed with this statement. More than half of those who strongly agreed that abortion was murder agreed that the decision must be made by a woman and her doctor, as did more than three-fourths of those who somewhat agreed that abortion was murder. Nearly four in ten women simultaneously believe that abortion is murder and that only a woman can make the decision whether to have an abortion.

This intersection of conflicting values—between the belief that abortion is murder and that only a woman can make the decision—is probably one of the sources of the stability of abortion attitudes over time. The basic arguments have not changed since the 1970s, and the key values are held by a majority of Americans. Torn between two absolutes, the average American draws subtle distinctions about when abortion should be permitted.

A majority of Americans in most surveys are situationalists whose most accurate reply to the question of whether abortion should be legal is "It depends" (Cook, Jelen, and Wilcox 1992). It depends on many things—the reasons the woman wants the abortion, whether she has consulted with her parents or partner, how far the pregnancy has progressed. When a woman seeks an abortion under physically traumatic circumstances—danger to her life or health, severe fetal defect, or pregnancy that has resulted from rape—large majorities of Americans support that choice. Even in the 2000 GSS survey, more than 75 percent of respondents approved of abortion for all three of these circumstances. The dividing line for the public debate is over whether abortion should be allowed for other reasons. Slightly more than half of all respondents in 2000 did not support abortion for any additional reason. Just over a third favored abortion for all three of the social and economic reasons for abortion (poverty, single motherhood, and married but wishing to have no more children). The rest selected one or two of these reasons as appropriate.

Public approval of abortion also depends on the gestational stage of the fetus. More than 65 percent of respondents to the *Los Angeles Times* survey supported a ban on abortions in the second trimester, and the 2000 National Election Study (NES) revealed that 77 percent opposed "partial birth" abortions, presumably in part because they occur in the third trimester. Finally, it depends on whom the woman has consulted about the abortion. Very large majorities favor requiring teenaged girls to inform their parents before obtaining an abortion, and somewhat smaller majorities would insist that girls get parental consent. A majority of both men and women would require that an adult woman obtain the consent of the biological father of the fetus before she could obtain an abortion (Riches and Wilcox 2001). These distinctions have remained largely unchanged over the course of the abortion debate.

The Hidden Dynamics of Abortion Attitudes

Figure 6-2 reveals clear period effects in abortion attitudes, with support ebbing and flowing around the margins of a generally static opinion. To better understand these changes, we have divided the years in the GSS data into five periods: pre-*Roe* (1972), post-*Roe* (1973–1982), the mid-1980s (1983–1988), post-*Webster* (1989–1994), and the late 1990s period (1995–2000). (The 1989 Supreme Court decision *Webster v. Reproductive Health Services* allowed states to impose more restrictions on abortion.) These periods correspond roughly to the changes in support for abortion shown in Figure 6-2. Table 6-1 shows the distribution of opinion on each of the six items from the GSS in each of the five

Table 6-1 Public Support for Abortion, by Time Period

	Pre-Roe (1972)	Post-Roe (1973–1982)	Mid-1980s (1983–1988)	Post-Webster (1989–1994)	Late 1990s (1995–2000)	Variation over Time
Abortion items						
Traumatic reasons						
Mother's health	87%	91%	89%	91%	89%	1.50
Fetal defect	79%	84%	79%	82%	80%	1.94
Rape	79%	84%	81%	84%	82%	1.90
Social reasons						
Poverty	49%	52%	45%	49%	44%	2.93
Single woman	43%	48%	41%	47%	43%	2.65
Married couple	40%	46%	41%	46%	43%	2.48
Abortion scales						
Overall abortion	3.85	4.13	3.84	4.07	3.88	0.12
Traumatic	2.47	2.61	2.52	2.59	2.53	0.05
Social	1.33	1.47	1.27	1.43	1.29	0.08

Source: General Social Survey, 1972–2000.

Note: The upper half of the table presents the percentage of respondents approving abortion for each reason. The traumatic reasons are when the mother's health is in danger, when the fetus would be severely defective, and when the pregnancy was the result of rape or incest. The social reasons are when the family is too poor to support another child, when the mother is unmarried and does not want to marry, and when a married woman is pregnant but the couple wants no more children. The bottom half of the table presents mean scores on abortion scales, for each period. The overall abortion scale ranges from 0 to 6; the traumatic and social scales range from 0 to 3. The last column measures change over time in each of these reasons and scales by presenting the standard deviation for each row.

periods, along with the mean values for the overall abortion scale and for the scales measuring support for abortion for traumatic and social circumstances.

Data in Table 6-1 reveal that changes in support for legal abortion in these five periods are greatest (that is, have the largest standard deviations) for abortions for social circumstances such as poverty, single motherhood, and for a married couple who wants no more children. Yet each of the six items changes at least slightly in the direction of the overall trend in each period. This pattern demonstrates that changes in overall support are not a result of changing attitudes toward one particular reason for having an abortion, but rather are more sweeping changes in overall attitudes.

Of course, the generational composition of the samples changes across these periods. We might expect that the generation that came of age during the 1960s, during the mobilization for abortion rights that led to changes in laws in many states, would be the most supportive of legal abortion, and that older generations would be the least supportive. Beyond those two groups, we might expect that the Reagan cohort might be distinctively less supportive of abortion and the Clinton cohort comparatively more supportive, if signals from presidents have any effect in molding generational attitudes.

Table 6-2 lists the average score on the six-item abortion scale for each generation for each period of the study. Some mild support is present for a generational model, for the 1960s cohort is the most supportive of legal abortion (has the highest mean score) in all but one period. But over the past decade the distinctiveness of the 1960s cohort has been unimpressive. Moreover, the Reagan cohort is essentially tied as the most liberal cohort in the late 1990s and is markedly more liberal than the Clinton cohort on abortion. The best case for a generational model of abortion attitudes lies in the consistently lower levels of support for abortion among the three oldest cohorts—all of which are declining in numbers. Thus the process of generational replacement is exchanging older, more conservative cohorts with younger, more liberal ones.

Some evidence exists for small life cycle effects. Note that in each period after 1972 the youngest cohort is less supportive of legal abortion than the cohort that came before it, but that in every case support eventually increases among the younger cohorts relative to older cohorts. This effect is strongest on two items: support for abortion when the fetus is severely defective, and especially support for abortions when a married couple wants no more children. Some respondents oppose abortion under these circumstances when they are young but come to support abortions for these reasons when they reach their thirties.

It seems likely that as younger Americans marry and take on career and family responsibilities, they become aware of the burden of caring for a child with birth defects. The desire of married couples to limit family size doubtlessly seems more compelling to married couples who understand the responsibilities and demands of extra children. Anecdotal evidence suggests that young single people may overestimate the reliability of contraception,

Table 6-2 Mean Approval of Abortion, Time Period and Age Cohort

Age Cohort	Pre-Roe (1972)	Post-Roe (1973–1982)	Mid-1980s (1983–1988)	Post-Webster (1989–1994)	Late 1990s (1995–2000)
Great Depression	3.33	3.78	3.41	3.50	3.63
World War II	3.76	3.97	3.51	3.81	3.54
Postwar	3.83	4.00	3.62	3.82	3.59
1960s	4.04	4.30	4.01	4.07	3.91
1970s		4.06	3.86	4.17	3.82
Reagan			3.83	4.04	3.90
Bush				3.84	3.90
Clinton					3.63

Source: General Social Survey, 2000.

Note: Cell entries are the average number of acceptable reasons for abortion out of six.

which may lead them to be less sympathetic to married couples seeking abortions to control family size. When one of us discussed these results with a freshman class, a student suggested that any married couple who unexpectedly became pregnant had no one to blame but themselves because of their sloppy use of contraception. In fact, the cumulative probability of contraceptive failure is surprisingly high: over twenty-two years, even those who use birth control pills regularly face a 20 percent chance of an unplanned pregnancy; the odds rise to more than 66 percent for the use of barrier methods. Older respondents are more likely to know someone who has experienced contraceptive failure, whereas young people may be overly confident in the effectiveness of contraception and thus be less sympathetic to this justification for abortion.

The data in Table 6-2 do nothing to help us understand the relatively small shifts in abortion sentiments. Indeed, the gradual replacement of the oldest cohorts by more liberal, younger Americans should produce a more prochoice opinion. But opinion is more conservative in 2000 than it was in the late 1970s; this trend suggests that something is going on under the surface to pull at least some Americans in a more conservative direction on abortion, and that change was partially offset by generational replacement.

Events and Issue Evolution

The ebbs and surges in support for legal abortion from 1972 to 2000 appear to be linked mainly to external events that helped to redefine the abortion debate in the public sphere.

After 1972, the Supreme Court's decision in *Roe v. Wade* produced an increase in support for abortion as many Americans confronted for the first time the abortion issue and came to agree with the Court (Franklin and Kosaki 1989). The increase in support in 1989 appears to be a reaction to the Court's *Webster* decision, which allowed greater leeway to states to regulate abortion.[2] Many observers, especially prochoice advocates, interpreted this decision as a sign that the Court might soon overturn *Roe;* those who feared that abortion might soon be made illegal were spurred to action. The decline in the late 1990s coincides with the debate over partial birth abortion, which focused the public's mind on a particularly unappealing procedure for third-trimester abortions.

Dips in abortion support in 1977 and in the mid-1980s are more difficult to explain. In 1977 the House and Senate passed the Hyde Amendment, which forbade using federal Medicaid funds to pay for abortions, and the Supreme Court upheld a state ban on Medicaid-funded abortions. These events received considerable media coverage, although it seems unlikely that public opinion was moved by them. In the mid-1980s, Congress debated a constitutional amendment declaring that human life begins at conception, the Reagan administration gave rhetorical support to the antiabortion movement, and many states began adopting requirements of parental notification.

Of course, the GSS items do not ask explicitly about any of these things. What is likely is that many Americans are ambivalent about at least one of the six items in the GSS list and that their response when asked these questions depends on what images of abortion are easily accessible to them (for a more general discussion of this effect, see Zaller 1992). If the most recent debate has been over teenaged daughters informing their parents or partial birth abortion, the public may respond more conservatively, but if recent debates have been over whether *Roe* could be overturned, the public may respond in a more prochoice manner.

Beneath the surface of this relatively static abortion opinion, some significant changes have occurred in what types of people hold the various opinions. Greg Adams (1997) argues that the abortion issue underwent an "issue evolution" in the 1990s. In the 1970s and into the early 1980s, Democrats were less supportive of abortion than Republicans, primarily because evangelical Protestants and Catholics were predominantly Democratic and Democrats generally had lower levels of education than Republicans. Yet, during this period, activists who favored or opposed abortion rights were very involved in recruiting and backing candidates in opposing political parties. Opponents of abortion chose the Republican Party because its elites were somewhat more sympathetic to abortion restrictions; in 1980 the antiabortion forces allied with Ronald Reagan to gain significant leverage in the national Republican Party and to write an antiabortion plank into the Republican platform. By the mid-1980s new GOP senators were significantly more opposed to abortion than earlier Sen-

Figure 6-3 Abortion Attitudes by Party and Education, 1972–2000

Mean number of reasons

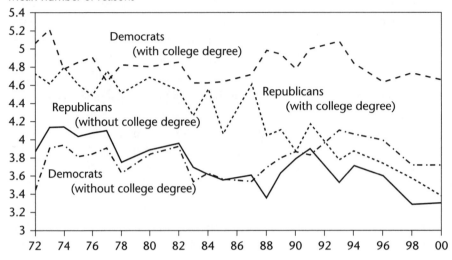

Source: General Social Survey, 1972–2000.

Note: Data are the average number out of six reasons to allow abortion, for Republicans with a college degree, Republicans with less than a college degree, Democrats with a college degree, and Democrats with less than a college degree.

ate classes had been. Meanwhile, prochoice forces were more active in Democratic politics, and by the mid-1980s newly elected Democratic House members were significantly more prochoice than those in earlier classes had been.

As party elites moved apart on abortion, voters gradually picked up their signals. Strong partisans for whom abortion was not salient changed their attitudes on abortion to fit cues coming from party leaders, and those for whom abortion was very salient changed their partisanship to match their attitudes. By the late 1980s Republicans were less prochoice than Democrats, and the gap has widened since. Figure 6-3 shows the average score on the six-point abortion scale for Republicans and Democrats, separately for those with college degrees and those without.

Reading the graph from left to right, the bottom two lines are Democrats and Republicans without college degrees. In the early years a large gap existed between the attitudes of those with less education and the attitudes of those in the same parties with college degrees. Those with less education in both parties were less supportive of abortion. Yet within each education group, the party patterns were different. Among those without college degrees, Republicans were slightly but significantly more prochoice, whereas among those with college degrees, Democrats were more liberal. Beginning in the mid-1980s college-educated Republicans began a rapid if jerky decline in support for legal abortion, so that by 2000 education had little impact on the attitudes of Republicans. In contrast, college-educated Democrats retained their general support for abortion, although their attitudes do follow the trends from Figure 6-3, with dips in support in the mid-1980s, a surge in the late 1980s and early 1990s, and a decline thereafter. In 2000, education mattered greatly to Democrats, with those with higher levels of education significantly more prochoice than those with less.

It is difficult to determine whether the overall pattern in Figure 6-3 means that highly educated Republicans changed their opinions on abortion or highly educated antiabortion citizens changed parties. Evangelical Protestants have become significantly more Republican during this period, and that party change was far more common among those who opposed abortion. By the late 1990s, abortion attitudes and partisanship of white mainline Protestant Christians and Catholics also began to line up with abortion attitudes, suggesting that some at least were changing their party to fit their abortion attitudes.

One final trend has occurred beneath the surface of abortion attitudes. The *Los Angeles Times* poll shows a sharp increase in the percentage of middle-aged women and men who now believe that life begins at conception. This is especially true among those in this age group with children. Although not enough evidence exists to be certain, it is possible that this pattern of changing beliefs about abortion may be triggering the most recent decline in support for abortion. More research is needed to determine the causes of this shift, but it is possible that the increased use of ultrasound technology to image fetuses early in pregnancy, combined with the vastly improved quality of those images, has begun to have an effect on beliefs about when life begins.

The power of beliefs about when life begins to move abortion attitudes is evident in Table 6-3, which shows the result of a regression model of abortion attitudes. The dependent variable is a scale composed of a number of items measuring abortion attitudes, and as independent variables we have included standard demographic variables—age, education, gender, race, marital status, and parenthood—along with religious variables, partisanship, and social ideology. The general findings support those of other research and suggest greater support for abortion among women, older Americans, single people, those with higher education, Democrats, and social liberals, when all other factors are held constant. Protestants and Catholics who frequently attend church, Pentecostal Christians, and those for whom religion has great saliency are less supportive of abortion. What we most want to illustrate, however, is the importance of beliefs about the start of life. The belief that life begins at conception has the strongest impact on attitudes (shown by the largest standardized coefficient), even controlling for a variety of religious attitudes and behaviors. Should the public continue to move toward this belief, it seems likely that support for legal abortion will decline still further.

Table 6-3 Regression Analysis Explaining Support for Abortion for Various Reasons

	Unstandardized Coefficient (b)	Standardized Coefficient (beta)	t-ratio
Demographic traits			
Sex (female)	.12**	.06	2.72
Black	−.01	−.00	−0.19
Hispanic	.07	.02	0.97
Age	.00**	.08	3.46
Married	−.24**	−.12	−5.18
Parent of child in home	.04	.02	0.87
Education	.08**	.14	6.54
Religious traits			
Frequently attending Protestant	−.31**	−.10	−4.50
Frequently attending Catholic	−.29**	−.07	−3.28
Pentecostal	−.22**	−.08	−3.55
Religious salience	−.25**	−.21	−9.10
Basic attitudes			
Party identification (Republican)	−.07**	−.14	−5.80
Social liberalism	.17**	.21	8.83
Specific attitude			
Life begins at conception	−.70**	−.35	−14.86
Constant	.39		1.92
R^2	.52		
Number of cases	1,128		

Source: *Los Angeles Times* survey, 2000.

Note: The dependent variable is coded with higher scores indicating greater acceptance of abortion under a wide variety of circumstances. Thus, positive coefficients show greater support for abortion and negative coefficients show less support.

**p ≤ .01

The Dynamic Nature of Public Attitudes on Gay Rights

In contrast to the static nature of public opinion on abortion, opinion on gay rights has changed dramatically in the past decade. Because gay rights were not generally on the public agenda in earlier years, it is difficult to trace attitudes over a longer period. But the GSS did ask respondents from 1973 to 2000 whether gays should be permitted to teach in col-

Figure 6-4 Support for Gays and Members of Other Groups Teaching in College, 1973–2000 (in percent)

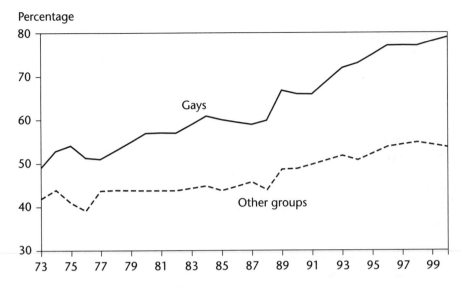

Source: General Social Survey, 1972–2000.

Note: Data are the percentage of respondents in each year who would allow gays to teach in college and the average percentage who would allow communists, atheists, racists, and militarists to teach in college.

leges and universities. Figure 6-4 shows the percentage that said yes. Because the public has become more tolerant of all kinds of groups and behaviors over this period, a comparison line is included which shows the average percentage in each year that would have allowed communists, atheists, racists, and militarists to teach in colleges and universities. This comparison allows us to see that tolerance for all groups has increased, but that it has increased more rapidly for gays and lesbians.

Table 6-4 provides data on policy attitudes from the National Election Studies (NES) from 1988 through 2000. Respondents were asked about laws that would ban discrimination against gays and lesbians in hiring and firing, about allowing gays and lesbians to serve openly in the military, and about allowing gay or lesbian couples to adopt children. For each of these questions, support has grown remarkably over time. For example, while in 1992 a third of all Americans strongly approved of allowing gays to serve in the military, by 2000 half approved of this policy.

Gallup polls also confirm changing attitudes toward gay rights. In 1977, 56 percent of respondents told Gallup that gays and lesbians deserved equal rights to a job, and in 2001 that figure was 85 percent. Between 1992 and 2001, Gallup showed a sharp increase in sup-

Table 6-4 Support for Gay Rights, 1988–2000 (in percent)

	1988	1992	1996	2000
Antidiscrimination laws				
Strongly approve	26%	33%	40%	40%
Approve	27	28	24	27
Neutral	3	n/a	n/a	n/a
Disapprove	16	15	13	14
Strongly disapprove	28	25	23	18
Gays in the military				
Strongly approve		32	44	51
Approve		26	24	25
Disapprove		9	7	5
Strongly disapprove		24	24	19
Gay couples adopt				
Approve		28		44

Source: National Election Studies.

Note: Percentages may not add to 100 because of rounding.

port for allowing gays into a number of professions: for clergy support increased from 43 percent to 54 percent, for elementary school teachers it increased from 41 percent to 56 percent.

We have argued in this chapter that many Americans are torn between two values on the abortion issue—the value of fetal life versus the value of a woman's right to control when she has children. Many Americans also hold clashing values in the debate over gay rights—traditional morality versus individual freedom and equality (Brewer 1997). Survey data reveal that Americans continue to believe that homosexual relations are morally wrong. The GSS has asked respondents since 1972 whether homosexual relations are always wrong, almost always wrong, sometimes wrong, or never wrong. Data in Figure 6-5 show the percentage that believe that homosexuality is always wrong, and for comparison we include the percentage that believe that extramarital sex is always wrong.

Although since 1992 the percentage that believe that extramarital sex is always wrong has increased, the percentage that says the same thing about homosexual activity has declined sharply. The magnitude of this change is remarkable. Yet it is also important to note that even in 2000, nearly 60 percent of respondents to the 2000 GSS believe that homosexual activity is always wrong. Confirming this trend are responses to *Los Angeles Times* polls in 1985 and 2000 that asked whether homosexual sexual relations are wrong. As in the GSS, a

Figure 6-5 Attitudes Toward Homosexual Sex and Extramarital Sex, 1972–2000 (in percent)

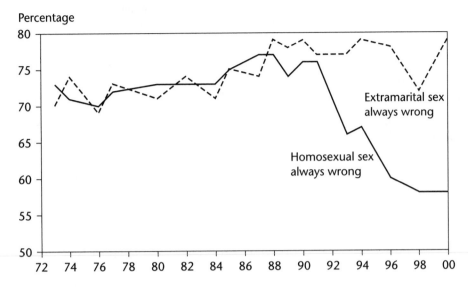

Percentage

Source: General Social Survey, 1972–2000.

sharp increase in acceptance occurred between these two surveys—those who believed that homosexual relations are always wrong declined from 72 percent to 55 percent—but those who agreed still constituted a majority. In the 1993 NES pilot survey,[3] half of the respondents indicated that homosexuality is against God's will, and more than half thought it is unnatural. Although these values are changing, they remain an important anchor in the gay rights debate.

Against these values of moral traditionalism are the values of individual liberty and of equality. In the 1970s and 1980s, gay rights activists focused on the former value, arguing that they were gay by choice and that sexual preference was a choice that all should be allowed to make. But by the 1990s, there was talk of a "gay gene," and the public gradually came to believe that homosexuality is an orientation that is present at birth. Gallup polls reveal that in 1977 only 13 percent thought that sexual orientation was fixed at birth, but by 2001 that figure had risen to more than 40 percent.

This change is important, for if Americans come to accept that gays and lesbians cannot change their sexual orientation, many citizens will feel bound to call on their equality values even if they do not approve of homosexuality (Wilcox and Wolpert 2000). If sexual orientation is fixed at birth, then it is difficult to justify denying gays and lesbians jobs, forbidding them to have sex with those they love, or even denying them the ability to enter into legal unions such as marriage. The increase in the number of people who believe that sexual orientation is fixed at birth doubtlessly explains the sharp increase in polls for allowing civil unions: Gallup reported in 2000 that a full 44 percent of respondents favored allowing civil unions for gays and lesbians (with 52 percent opposed), although only 36 percent would allow gays to marry.

Moreover, if sexual orientation is fixed at birth, then there is less reason to fear that gays or lesbians will try to seduce young, impressionable heterosexuals. Much of the opposition to gays serving in the military, adopting children, and teaching in elementary schools is based on a fear that gays and lesbians will seduce others. Indeed, opponents of allowing gays to serve in the military often used images of shared pup tents and showers. Research has shown that those who believe that homosexuals often try to seduce straight people are much less supportive of gay rights. Such a fear will become less intense if the public increasingly believes that sexual orientation is fixed at birth.

The public's switch to believing that sexual orientation is fixed at birth is an essential part of the explanation of the rapid attitude change during the 1990s on gay rights. Indeed, Christian Right groups in the late 1990s launched a "Truth in Love" campaign to try to persuade the public that sexual orientation could be changed—featuring men and women who claimed to have once been gay or lesbian but now live a heterosexual life. The ad campaign was withdrawn when some of the purported "ex-gays" admitted that they had never actually engaged in homosexual activity, whereas others left the heterosexual lifestyle to return to their same-sex partners.

Changing beliefs about the nature of homosexuality are only part of the explanation for changing policy preferences. A remarkable change also has occurred in public acceptance of homosexuality, along with a dampening of emotional reactions to gays and lesbians. At one time many Americans had a very strong, visceral reaction to the thought of homosexuality. In 1993, the NES pilot survey revealed that 36 percent of respondents were strongly disgusted by the thought of homosexuality and an additional 6 percent were mildly disgusted. The strength of that emotional reaction is evident in the NES feeling thermometers, where respondents are asked to rate groups from 0 degrees (very cold) to 100 degrees (very warm). In 1984 and 1988, more than 30 percent rated gays and lesbians at 0 degrees—a greater proportion than rated illegal aliens or Palestinians so low. Over the course of the 1990s the hostility declined: by 2000 only 12 percent assigned gays the lowest possible score.

Increasingly many Americans are becoming more comfortable with the idea of homosexuality. A 2000 Gallup poll revealed that for the first time a majority of Americans believed that homosexuality is an acceptable lifestyle.[4] The *Los Angeles Times* poll showed that the percentage who admitted to being uncomfortable around gays and lesbians declined from 41 percent in 1985 to 32 percent in 2000. But a more remarkable question asked respondents how upset they would be if they learned that their child was gay. In 1985, 65 percent indicated that they would be very upset, but by 2000 that figure had dropped to 38 percent.[5]

Events and Issue Evolution

Why has the public suddenly become more accepting of gays and lesbians? A likely source of the change is the increasing exposure to gays and lesbians on television and as key characters in movies. The 1993 film *Philadelphia* starred Tom Hanks as a gay man with AIDS who had been unfairly fired from his job and Denzel Washington as a homophobic lawyer who came to recognize Hanks's humanity. By 1997 Tom Selleck and Kevin Kline kissed on screen in *In and Out*. Sympathetic gay and lesbian characters on television were virtually unknown in the 1980s, but by 2000 the media project of Gay and Lesbian Alliance Against Defamation (GLAAD) was able to list a significant number of gay and lesbian characters in leading or regular supporting roles. Although many of these characters present one-dimensional portraits of gays and lesbians, their mere presence exposes more Americans to gays and lesbians.[6]

The AIDS crisis also may have humanized gay men for many Americans. As fears that AIDS would rapidly spread to the heterosexual community lessened, many Americans focused more on the ever increasing list of the dead—and over time more and more Americans knew someone who had died of the disease. The death of many highly respected celebrities and the large and emotional displays of the AIDS quilt also served to draw public attention to a disease that struck down so many in the prime of life.

Perhaps most important, surveys show that Americans are far more likely to be aware that they know a gay man or lesbian woman than in the past. The *Los Angeles Times* survey showed that in 1985 only 24 percent of respondents knew someone who was openly gay, and another 21 percent suspected that they knew someone who was gay. Fully 55 percent believed that they did not know a gay man or lesbian woman. By 2000, 74 percent knew someone who was openly gay, with only 7 percent suspecting that they knew a gay or lesbian. Only 19 percent believed that they did not know a gay man or lesbian woman.

These numbers are truly extraordinary—they suggest that half of all Americans since the mid-1980s have discovered that an acquaintance, friend, co-worker, or relative is gay. The effect of this change cannot be exaggerated. When someone is unaware that anyone they know is gay, the label "gays and lesbians" can conjure up negative images of strangers in other cities who live unimaginable lifestyles. But when someone comes out to them, suddenly the label "gays or lesbians" refers to Uncle Ted, or Mary and Sally who live down the street and who bake those great cookies, or Tom on the softball team.

In the 2000 *Los Angeles Times* poll data, for example, those who knew a gay man or lesbian woman held different attitudes from those who did not know anyone who is gay or who merely suspected that they knew someone. Fifty-two percent of those who knew a gay man or lesbian woman *strongly* supported antidiscrimination laws, and another 26 percent supported such laws. Among those who did not know a gay man or lesbian woman or who only suspected that they did, only 36 percent strongly supported antidiscrimination laws. Indeed, comparing these data with the results of a similar question in the 1985 *Los Angeles Times* survey suggests that much of the difference in attitudes between 1985 and 2000 can be accounted for by the increased awareness of gay friends, neighbors, and relatives. Of course, gays and lesbians are more likely to come out to those who they believe will be accepting of their identity. Nevertheless, the magnitude of these changes suggests that many gays over the past decade have come out to those who were not fully comfortable with homosexuality, and that these individuals came to accept their gay friends, co-workers, and family members.

The power of beliefs about the nature of sexual orientation and the knowledge that you know someone who is gay or lesbian is shown in Table 6-5. The dependent variables are one scale of support for antidiscrimination laws in hiring and housing and another scale of support for civil unions and marriage. The independent variables are generally the same as those in Table 6-3, but in place of attitudes of when life begins, we have included belief that sexual orientation is fixed at birth and whether the respondent knows a gay man or lesbian woman. Attitudes on antidiscrimination are more structured than those toward domestic partnership and marriage in that a greater proportion (shown by a larger R^2) of the variation across individuals in antidiscrimination attitudes can be explained by basic demographic traits, religion, and attitudes. Perhaps public opinion on antidiscrimination laws is better structured because these laws have been more publicly debated and involve fewer conflicting values.

Figures in Table 6-5 show that women and social liberals are more supportive of gay rights for both issues; Protestants who frequently attend church, Pentecostals, those for whom religion is salient, and Republicans are less supportive of both antidiscrimination laws and gay partnerships or marriages. Two contrasting results exist between support for gay rights and sources of abortion attitudes as shown in Table 6-3. Older respondents are more supportive of abortion, holding other attitudes and characteristics constant, but younger respondents are more supportive of gay rights. Catholics who frequently attend church are significantly more opposed to abortion than other Americans but are not more opposed to gay rights.

Turning to the specific attitudes of when sexual orientation is established and knowing a gay or lesbian person, both beliefs are significantly related to opinions on gay marriages and antidiscrimination laws. Belief that sexual orientation is fixed at birth is the strongest predictor of both attitudes, shown by the largest standardized coefficients. Knowing a gay man

Table 6-5 Regression Analyses Explaining Support for Gay Rights

	Approve of Marriage or Domestic Partner Laws for Gays			Favor Antidiscrimination Laws for Gays		
	Unstan-dardized Coefficient (b)	Stan-dardized Coefficient (beta)	t-ratio	Unstan-dardized Coefficient (b)	Stan-dardized Coefficient (beta)	t-ratio
Demographic traits						
Sex (female)	.36**	.17	7.18	.22**	.09	4.01
Black	−.00	−.00	−0.01	−.07	−.02	−0.70
Hispanic	−.11	−.03	−1.35	−.31**	−.08	−3.58
Age	−.00	−.04	−1.43	−.01**	−.14	−5.89
Married	−.09	−.04	−1.76	−.12*	−.05	−2.20
Education	.00	.01	0.27	.03	.04	1.67
Religious traits						
Frequently attending Protestant	−.32**	−.10	−4.03	−.18*	−.05	−2.07
Frequently attending Catholic	.05	.01	0.47	.01	.00	0.04
Pentecostal	−.20**	−.07	−2.81	−.20**	−.06	−2.71
Religious salience	−.07*	−.06	−2.19	−.30**	−.20	−8.57
Basic attitudes						
Party identification (Republican)	−.03**	−.07	−2.62	−.07**	−.13	−5.18
Social liberalism	.16**	.18	7.01	.16**	.16	6.50
Specific attitudes						
Sexual orientation fixed at birth	.56**	.26	10.45	.59**	.24	10.19
Know gay or lesbian	.18**	.07	3.04	.43**	.15	6.77
Constant	2.23**		9.63	2.37**		9.70
R^2	.25			.34		
Number of cases	1,371			1,410		

Source: *Los Angeles Times* survey, 2000.

Note: The dependent variables are coded with higher scores indicating greater acceptance of gay marriage and favoring of antidiscrimination laws. Thus, positive coefficients indicate greater acceptance of gay rights and negative coefficients indicate less acceptance.

*$p \leq .05$
**$p \leq .01$

Table 6-6 Men's and Women's Attitudes Toward Gay Rights, by Age Cohort and Time Period (in percent)

Age Cohort	1972–1980		1981–1991		1992–2000	
	Men	Women	Men	Women	Men	Women
Allow gays and lesbians to teach college						
Great Depression	27%	28%	35%	33%	44%	48%
World War II	45	46	44	44	58	53
Postwar	57	54	58	58	65	68
1960s	72	70	71	75	77	83
1970s	61	69	69	75	79	82
Reagan			67	73	80	84
Bush					81	85
Clinton					89	86
Homosexual activity always wrong						
Great Depression	88	88	90	91	82	87
World War II	79	82	86	85	80	83
Postwar	72	73	78	78	72	72
1960s	58	60	68	65	60	56
1970s	65	54	71	64	62	58
Reagan			75	68	60	51
Bush					54	41
Clinton					46	43

Source: General Social Survey, 1972–2000.

or lesbian woman also is a very important predictor, with an influence as important as partisanship or social liberalism. If more gays and lesbians come out over the next several years, and if the public continues to increase its belief that sexual orientation is fixed at birth, then it is likely that attitudes will continue to move in the liberal direction.[7]

It is worth noting that the issue evolution that we witnessed on abortion—with highly educated Republicans making a significant change toward the antiabortion direction—has not been duplicated on gay rights. The GSS data suggest that college-educated Republicans have not participated in the changing attitudes toward whether homosexual activity is always wrong, but neither have they become less accepting of homosexuality. College-educated Republicans have become increasingly accepting of allowing gays and lesbians to teach in colleges, although the rate of change is slower among them than among highly educated Democrats.

Table 6-7 Men's and Women's Attitudes Toward Gay Rights, by Age Cohort, 2000

	Men	Women
Mean feeling thermometer for gays		
Depression, WWII, postwar	34	43
1960s, 1970s, Reagan	44	50
Bush, Clinton	48	62
Support antidiscrimination laws		
Depression, WWII, postwar	56%	66%
1960s, 1970s, Reagan	62%	73%
Bush, Clinton	59%	79%
Support gays in military		
Depression, WWII, postwar	54%	76%
1960s, 1970s, Reagan	69%	80%
Bush, Clinton	77%	92%
Support gay adoption		
Depression, WWII, postwar	19%	36%
1960s, 1970s, Reagan	40%	48%
Bush, Clinton	59%	58%

Source: National Election Study, 2000.

Generational Replacement and the Future of Gay Rights Politics

Generational replacement is likely to continue to shape aggregate attitudes toward gay rights. Table 6-6 shows gay rights attitudes by cohorts across three periods: 1972–1980, 1981–1991, and 1992–2000. The data show that attitudes have changed for members of each cohort in the final period, so there is clearly evidence of a period effect. The data also show that there are clusters of cohorts whose attitudes track together. The World War II and Depression cohorts are the most conservative; the postwar cohort less conservative than those; and the 1960s, 1970s, and Reagan cohorts are less conservative than the postwar group. The Bush and especially the Clinton cohorts are the most supportive of gay rights and the least likely to condemn homosexual activity. Trends for men and women go in the same general direction, but within each generation women tend to be more accepting of gays than are men.

Table 6-7 presents data from the 2000 NES. This single survey does not contain enough respondents to divide into the eight age cohorts reliably, so we have combined groups that have similar attitudes. These data show a much larger gender gap than the combined GSS data, especially among younger respondents. There is little evidence for life cycle effects in these data, although some of our analysis (not shown) suggests that young men become more accepting of gays and lesbians as they move from their late teens into their early thirties. In general, these data show that younger respondents are more liberal than the oldest cohorts. This is especially true among women and on the issue of gay adoption. These patterns suggest that over time, generational replacement will make the public more supportive of gay rights.

Conclusion

Despite talk of a conservative moral mood in America, attitudes on gay rights are becoming much more liberal, whereas attitudes on abortion are moving slightly in the conservative direction. These two attitudes are correlated, meaning that in general those who are more opposed to abortion are also opposed to gay rights, and vice versa. Yet the dynamics of these two issues are clearly quite different.

We have argued that the debate over abortion has remained largely static and that the public values both fetal life and women's autonomy, leading many Americans to support abortion for some but not all reasons. As the political debate shifts and respondents call to mind different images as they answer abortion questions in surveys, small shifts in responses occur. Yet overall abortion attitudes are remarkably stable. Data from the *Los Angeles Times* polls hint that perhaps young married Americans have become slightly more likely to believe that life begins at conception; and if that trend continues it may lead to a continuance of the trend toward slightly more conservative abortion attitudes. In addition, the distribution of the "abortion pill," RU-486, may in some way redefine the abortion issue, although at this time that change appears unlikely (Riches and Wilcox 2001).

In contrast, gay rights have been redefined by two changes in attitudes. First, more Americans now believe that sexual orientation is fixed at birth, and this belief makes it harder to justify discrimination. Second, many more Americans today know someone who is openly gay, and this knowledge appears to be powerfully associated with more liberal attitudes.

The generational analysis in this chapter suggests that abortion attitudes might move slightly toward more liberalism as the oldest cohorts die off and are replaced by younger ones, but that the effect will be small. The youngest cohorts are more liberal than the oldest generations, but they are not more liberal than those who came of age in the 1960s or beyond. A more likely scenario might develop if the administration of President George W. Bush appoints judges who overturn *Roe v. Wade*. Such an event would likely lead to a swing in the public's policy mood toward greater support for abortion, although that effect could also be small and not permanent.

In contrast, as the oldest cohorts die off, attitudes toward gay rights are likely to become significantly more liberal. The impact of that change is best seen in the *Los Angeles Times* data. Only 35 percent of respondents overall favored allowing gays and lesbians to marry, but fully 60 percent of members of the Bush and Clinton cohorts supported marriage for gays and lesbians. This fact suggests that the politics of gay rights may move quite rapidly over the next decades, to the extent that policies that seemed impossible a decade ago may be likely a decade hence. When attitudes moved on racial and gender equality, they moved very quickly and much further than even civil rights and feminist activists might have predicted. This sort of rapid change might well occur with gay rights. It is unlikely to happen with abortion.

Notes

1. Laurence Tribe (1990) referred to the abortion debate as the "clash of absolutes."
2. Note that here we are arguing that one Supreme Court decision that liberalized abortion law led to more liberal public opinion, and one Court decision that decreased abortion rights also led to more liberal opinion. In the first instance, public opinion was largely unformed on abortion, and the large majority vote by the Court appears to have moved opinion. By 1989, opinions were formed and forces were mobilized. The *Webster* decision appears to have frightened moderately prochoice citizens. See also Goggin and Wlezien (1993).
3. The National Election Studies conducts pilot surveys to test the effects of new question wording.
4. Yet Americans tend to believe that other Americans are more prejudicial toward gays. Fully 75 percent of respondents believed that most Americans would not view gays and lesbians as living an acceptable lifestyle.
5. Of course, this change does not mean that all Americans have become accepting of homosexuality. Gay men and lesbian women remain the targets of hate crimes across the country.
6. For a list of gay and lesbian characters on television programs over the past several years, see http://www.glaad.org/org/projects/tv/index.html.
7. The empirical evidence on whether sexual orientation is fixed at birth is not yet conclusive, however. If a spate of scientific work were to suggest an opposite conclusion, the public might become less supportive of gay rights. Currently, this research is highly contested and politicized.

7 American Foreign Policy and Public Opinion in a New Era: Eleven Propositions

John Mueller

American foreign policy is being reshaped in the wake of the cold war (Mueller 1996). And, as in the past, public opinion will play an important role in this process—indeed, it has already shown itself to be a notable impelling factor in some of the key policy decisions of the 1990s (see also Holsti 1996, chap. 6).

I would like to advance a set of propositions about American public opinion, stressing ones that seem to have implications for the practice of foreign policy in the new era. Although I focus on opinion in the United States, many of the propositions may hold as well for other countries, particularly for other developed democracies.[1]

In general, it seems, Americans are inclined to pay little attention to foreign policy issues unless there appears to be a direct threat to the United States, though they have not become more isolationist in the wake of the cold war. They are also very sensitive to the degree to which a policy is likely to cost American lives. So long as American casualties are kept low, the president has quite a bit of leeway to deal with ventures that are not highly valued, such as humanitarian interventions. Because of public inattention, however, the long-term political consequences from such ventures—whether successful or not—are likely to be low. By the time of the next election, people will have forgotten all about them.

Proposition 1

The public generally pays very little attention to international affairs.

A useful way to assess the emphasis Americans place on foreign affairs is to consider the results generated by the frequently asked poll question, "What do you think is the most important problem facing this country today?" The question poses something of a contest: the hapless respondents are essentially asked to select the most notable irritant from the huge array of calamities arrayed daily in the news. Although they are allowed to give more than one response, the question does not encourage this.

The results of this question overstate concerns about political and international issues. A filter question asking the respondents whether they have given any attention to the country's problems would likely reduce the numbers of cited problems greatly—probably by half (Sterngold, Warland, and Herrmann 1994). Moreover, the responses would be quite a bit different if the question were broader, like the one asked by Samuel Stouffer in a classic study (1955, chap. 3): "What kinds of things do you worry about most?" The "big, overwhelming response," Stouffer found, "was in terms of personal and family problems." Indeed, 80 percent "answered *solely* in these terms." The poll then posed a follow-up question, "Are there other problems you worry or are concerned about, especially political or world problems?" Fully 52 percent responded they had nothing to add.[2]

The pattern of Americans' concerns can be seen by scanning Figure 7-1, which displays results derived from responses to the question about the country's most important problem as it was posed from 1935 until the beginning of 2001. The figure shows what percentage of respondents in each poll selected an international or foreign policy issue. It appears that the American public's natural tendency with regard to international issues is to pay them little heed: people principally focus on domestic matters when asked to designate the country's most important problem. Their attention can be diverted by major threats or by explicit, specific, and dramatic dangers to American lives, but once these concerns fade, people return their attention to domestic issues with considerable alacrity—rather like "the snapping back of a strained elastic," as Gabriel Almond once put it (1960, 76).

In the 1930s, domestic problems dominated even as the approach of a major war was signaled by such dangerous events as the Munich crisis of 1938. Only when war actually began in Europe in September 1939, and then when war against Japan approached in the Pacific—from late 1939 through November 1941—did foreign affairs come to dominate the public's professed concerns.

War presumably became the chief preoccupation after the Japanese attack at Pearl Harbor in December 1941. There are no exact data, but when the most important problem question was twice asked during the war, it was prefaced by the words, "Aside from winning the war . . ." (see Smith 1985; Niemi, Mueller, and Smith 1989, 39–46). Obviously and quite reasonably, the pollsters expected respondents overwhelmingly to mention the war if they posed the question in its original form.

Attention to international concerns dropped to almost nothing at the end of the war in 1945. It rose again only two years later, as the cold war was launched, and it reached highs during the Korean War and at the time of various cold war crises through the end of 1962.

Then, in mid-1963, what might be called the classic cold war came to an end with the Soviet-American détente surrounding the signing of the Partial Test Ban Treaty (Mueller 1989, 156–162). Again, as had happened at the end of the hot war in Europe and Asia in 1945, Americans' attention to foreign affairs dropped substantially.[3]

By 1966, Vietnam had come to dominate the public's attention, and the conflict there far outstripped all other foreign concerns. Attention to international issues declined by the 1970s as U.S. casualty rates in Vietnam were reduced and as troops began to be withdrawn.

Figure 7-1 Respondents Choosing a Foreign Policy Issue as the Most Important Problem, 1935–2001

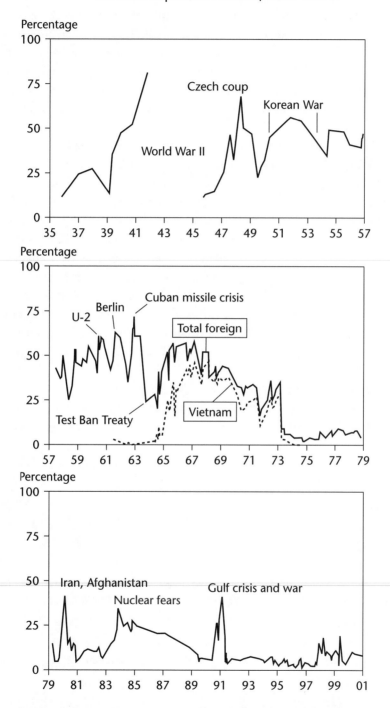

Source: Materials on deposit at the Roper Center for Public Opinion, Storrs, Conn., and Richard G. Niemi, John Mueller, and Tom W. Smith, *Trends in Public Opinion: A Compendium of Survey Data* (Westport, Conn.: Greenwood, 1989).

The Vietnam War essentially came to an end as far as the American public was concerned with the January 1973 agreement to halt direct American participation in the fighting and, in particular, with the consequent release of American prisoners of war. Even though the United States was still committed to the area, and even though the war continued for more than two years, attention to Vietnam remained low and did not revive even when America's long-time allies, the South Vietnamese, fell to Communist forces in the spring of 1975.

Since then, few events have been able to focus the public's attention on foreign affairs. Indeed, at no time from 1969 through 2000 did foreign policy issues outweigh domestic ones in the public's concerns.

Only three international issues notably intruded upon the American public's perceptions during that period. One was a rise in attention after the Soviet invasion of Afghanistan in December 1979, a concern apparently embellished by the Iran hostage crisis, which had begun in November 1979. Even this rise is more fleeting and less impressive than might be expected, however: there was a brief spike of heightened interest in January 1980, but then a speedy and very substantial decline during the rest of that year. Another instance was the remarkably heightened anxiety over thermonuclear war that materialized in the early and mid-1980s and then withered with the rise of the disarmingly agreeable Mikhail Gorbachev in the USSR (see also Oreskes 1990). Although the episode has been substantially forgotten, as late as 1986 and 1987 over a fifth of the American public designated the danger of war as the country's greatest problem.[4] The final attention-arresting international concern of the period was the Persian Gulf crisis and war of 1990–1991. Predictably, interest dropped precipitously as soon as the war was over.

This pattern of overall inattention was abruptly shattered in September 2001 by the devastating terrorist destruction at the World Trade Center and Pentagon. For the first time in over three decades, international concerns came to outnumber domestic ones (not shown in Figure 7-1).

In the past sixty years, then, the few events that have notably caused the public to divert its attention from domestic matters have been these:

- World War II
- Certain cold war crises before 1963
- The Korean War
- The Vietnam War
- Fleetingly, the Soviet invasion of Afghanistan in late 1979 (presumably embellished by the Iran hostage crisis of 1979–1981)
- The apparently heightened prospect in the mid-1980s of nuclear war
- The Persian Gulf crisis and war
- Terrorist bombings in New York and Washington, D.C., in 2001

The central conclusion from this survey of public opinion trends is that Americans show little interest in foreign and international matters unless they espy what appears to be a clear and present threat. It could be argued that the future of ordinary Americans today is likely to be significantly affected by international developments like globalization and the political direction that Russia and China take. But issues like that are unlikely to register on a survey, crowded out as they are by such parochial domestic concerns as education, crime, drugs, and the condition of the economy. A 1998 poll, for example, asked people to list not one, but two or three problems facing the country, and no international issue even made it into double percentage figures (Rielly 1999, 7–11). In fact, in some polls in the 1990s a few percent held the country's most important problem to be that it was spending too much time worrying about foreign concerns or was spending too much money on foreign aid—responses that were dutifully included in the "foreign policy" category for the purposes of Figure 7-1 (see also Rielly 1999, 11).

However, as Figure 7-2 suggests, people do voice concern about some international issues, as least when they are specifically asked about them. Nuclear weapons remain a potentially potent concern—even as the weapons themselves dwindle in number and relevance from cold war days. The same can be said for terrorism. Until the bombings of 2001, international terrorists had killed far fewer Americans than lightning or accidents caused by deer.[5] Yet, international terrorism registered as a top foreign policy concern in 1998. The bombings, obviously, will only heighten that concern.

Proposition 2

The public's agenda and attitude on foreign affairs are set much more by the objective content of the issue and by the position of major policymakers (including the political opposition) than by the media.

Given the public's limited attention span, the media are often given great credit for setting the political agenda (Iyengar and Kinder 1987; Iyengar 1993). However, it is difficult to argue that the media had much independent impact in whipping up interest in most of the eight international concerns that have notably diverted the public's attention away from domestic matters over the last several decades.[6] Rather, the chief determinant has been the often overwhelming weight and drama of the events themselves and opinion leadership exercised by the major policymakers, especially the president—who is, after all, in part elected explicitly to direct the country's foreign policy.

Thus, Franklin D. Roosevelt was important in leading the nation toward World War II, though he hardly had to do much to focus the public's concerns after Pearl Harbor (Cantril 1944, 1967) anymore than President George W. Bush had to after the terrorist destruction of 2001. President Harry S. Truman consciously led the country into the cold war, a mo-

Figure 7-2 Respondents Saying Foreign Policy Goals "Very Important"

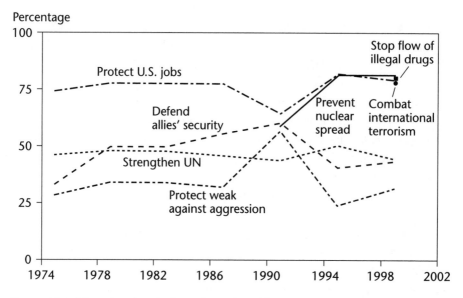

Source: Materials on deposit at the Roper Center for Public Opinion, Storrs, Conn., and Richard G. Niemi, John Mueller, and Tom W. Smith, *Trends in Public Opinion: A Compendium of Survey Data* (Westport, Conn.: Greenwood, 1989).

mentum that was continued by Dwight D. Eisenhower and John F. Kennedy (Lovell 1985, 122–123). As part of this process, Truman led the country into the Korean War, as did Lyndon Johnson into the Vietnam War and George Bush into opposing Iraq's invasion of Kuwait in 1990. In all these cases, the president found that he enjoyed a wide degree of backing among the political elite. Any notable independent impact by the media in these cases would be difficult to discern.

Much the same can be said for Jimmy Carter and his enveloping Iran hostage crisis. The president was acting within a wide consensus, though it seems possible in this case that he could have used his leadership position to dampen somewhat the concern which was, it could be argued, over something of less than massive importance (see Mueller 1984b, 1987). Following the lead of Carter—whose popularity ratings soared when the hostages were seized (Stanley and Niemi 1992, 280)—the media certainly hyped this issue, apparently in response to the actions of the president and to the demands of their customers.

The final attention-arresting international issue was the fear of war during the 1980s. Although the media unquestionably played a role by transmitting information about the issue to the public, they do not seem to have had an independent impact in this case either. After the end of the classic cold war in 1963, fears of nuclear war subsided substantially (Paarlberg 1973; Mueller 1977, 326–328). Renewed anxiety came almost out of the air: it was an old idea whose time had come again. Insofar as the issue was consciously promoted, credit must be given to the opposition parties in Europe (see Joffe 1987) and to their counterparts in the United States who were looking for an issue that they could use to undermine support for governments in office at the time—though such political exploitation of the issue seems to have come *after* nuclear concerns became popular, not before. The noisy cold war debate over missiles in Europe was also a central element in all this, it seems, as was Ronald Reagan's occasionally loose and casual verbiage about nuclear war (see Mueller 1989, 202–205).

Overall, the media seem not so much to act as agenda-setters as purveyors of information they hope will tantalize and, will, accordingly, boost sales and ratings. Like any other entrepreneurial organization, they are susceptible to the market, and they follow up on those proffered items that stimulate their customers' interest. In that very important sense, the media do not set the agenda; ultimately the public does.

For example, notable public concern over a famine in Ethiopia in the mid-1980s is often taken to have been media-generated because it was only after the suffering received prominent play in the media that the issue entered the public's agenda. But Christopher Bosso's study (1989) of the phenomenon suggests a different interpretation. At first the media were reluctant to cover the story because they saw African famine as a dog-bites-man story. However, going against this journalistic consensus, NBC television decided to do a three-day sequence on the famine in October 1984, something that inspired a huge public response. NBC then gave the story extensive follow-up coverage while its television and print competitors scrambled to get on the bandwagon, deluging their customers with information that, to the surprise of those in the media, was suddenly in demand. There is a sense in which it could be said that NBC put the issue on the public's agenda. But the network is constantly doing three-day stories, and this one just happened to catch on. It seems more accurate to say that NBC put the issue on the shelf—alongside a great many others—and that it was the public that put it on the agenda.[7]

Proposition 3

The "CNN effect" is vastly exaggerated.

It is often argued that television pictures set the public's agenda and policy mood: the so-called CNN effect. Usually pictures of horrors are said to cause the public to want to do something to relieve the situation, but sometimes the pictures are said to cause the public to be repelled and to want to avoid intervention. Or we get arguments on the one hand that violent pictures on television caused people to want to get out of Vietnam, and on the other that violent pictures on television have inspired people to go out and commit violence themselves.

At any rate, the CNN effect theory essentially assumes people are so unimaginative that they react only when they see something visualized. Yet Americans somehow managed to become outraged at and mobilized over the Pearl Harbor attack weeks—or even months—before they saw pictures of the event (see Mueller 1995a, 97–101). The Vietnam War was not noticeably more unpopular than the Korean War for the period in which the wars were comparable in American casualties, despite the fact that Vietnam is often seen to be a "television war" while Korea was fought during the medium's infancy (Mueller 1973, 167; Mandelbaum 1981; Hallin 1986).[8]

That the conventional wisdom about the CNN effect lingers on is impressive in light of the example of Bosnia during the first half of the 1990s. For years the public was deluged by vivid pictures of the problems there. Although these may have influenced the opinion of some editorial writers and columnists, they inspired remarkably little public demand to send American troops over to fix the problem (Sobel 1998; Larson 2000).

On those rare occasions when pictures have had—or seem to have had—an effect, as in Ethiopia in the mid-1980s, pundits espy a CNN effect. When pictures *fail* to have any notable impact, these theorists fail to notice—or they come up with other tortuous accountings. One explanation for the unwillingness of the American public to send troops to Bosnia is that the constant suffering shown on television did not "sensitize" the public but rather "inured" it to the violence (Orwin 1996, 49). Thus, whether the public in its collective wisdom concludes that troops should be sent or should not be sent, television always remains the convenient leader of public opinion (on this issue, see also Strobel 1997).

Proposition 4

The public applies a fairly reasonable cost-benefit analysis when evaluating foreign affairs, but it values the lives of Americans very highly and tends to undervalue the lives of foreigners.

In general, the American public seems to apply a fairly reasonable, commonsensical standard of benefit and cost when evaluating foreign affairs (see also Key 1966; Page and Shapiro 1992; Nincic 1992; Jentleson 1992; Holsti 1996, chap. 2). An assessment of probable and potential American casualties is particularly important in its evaluation (see also Wittkopf 1990, 229; Larson 1996; Klarevas 1999; Mueller 2000a).

After Pearl Harbor, the public had no difficulty accepting the necessity, and the costs, of confronting the threats presented by Germany and Japan. Then, during the cold war, it came to accept international communism as a similar source of threat and was willing to enter the wars in Korea and Vietnam as part of a perceived necessity to confront Communist challenges there—though as these wars progressed, the public engaged in a continuing reevaluation, and they had increasing misgivings about the wisdom of participating in the armed conflicts. This decline of support appears primarily to have been a function of accumulating American casualties, not of television coverage or antiwar protest: the decline of enthusiasm followed the same pattern in both wars, even though public protest and television coverage were uncommon in the Korean case (see Mueller 1973, chaps. 3–6).[9]

Policy in the Gulf War seems to have been subjected to a similar calculation. A fair number of Americans bought President Bush's notion that it was worth some American lives—perhaps a thousand or two, far fewer than were suffered in Korea or Vietnam—to use war to turn back Saddam Hussein's invasion of Kuwait. But it is clear from poll data that, led by Democrats who had opposed the war in the first place, support for the effort would have eroded quickly if very many casualties had been suffered (see Table 7-1). A similar pattern (at much lower casualty levels) is evident when the public was asked about peacekeeping in Bosnia (see Table 7-2).

Although concern about American lives often seems nuanced when the public assesses foreign affairs, there are times when public abhorrence of American casualties becomes so obsessive that policy may suffer.

For example, it could be maintained that the Vietnam War was essentially supported until the prisoners of war held by Hanoi were returned. Although it may not make a great deal of sense to continue a war costing thousands of lives to gain the return of a few hundred prisoners, it would be difficult to exaggerate the political potency of this issue. In a May 1971 poll, 68 percent agreed that U.S. troops should be withdrawn from Vietnam by the end of the year. However, when asked if they would still favor withdrawal "even if it threatened [not *cost*] the lives or safety of United States POWs held by North Vietnam," support for withdrawal dropped to 11 percent (Mueller 1973, 97–98).

The emotional attachment to prisoners of war was also central to the lengthy and acrimonious peace talks in Korea, and outrage at the fate of American POWs on Bataan probably intensified hatred for the Japanese during World War II almost as much as the attack on Pearl Harbor did. Concern about American prisoners and of those missing in action continued to haunt discussions about Vietnam for decades.

A dramatic case in point was the remarkable preoccupation by politicians and press with Americans held hostage by Iran during the crisis of 1979–1981, to the virtual exclusion of issues and events likely to be of far greater importance historically. Later in the 1980s, the fate of a few hostages in Lebanon seems to have held the Reagan administration hostage, an obsession that helped to generate the Iran-contra scandal. In another episode, until the Americans taken by Iraq after its invasion of Kuwait were released in December 1990, freeing them was a major concern among Americans—far more important in the public mind than liberating Kuwait (see Table 7-3).

Although Americans are extremely sensitive to American casualties, they seem to be remarkably *in*sensitive to casualties suffered by foreigners, including essentially uninvolved

Table 7-1 American Casualties and the Persian Gulf War

Question: Assuming Iraq leaves Kuwait, would you consider the war with Iraq a success if 500 American troops died, or not? (If yes) Would you consider it a success if 1,000 American troops died, or not? (If yes) Would you consider the war with Iraq a success if 5,000 American troops died, or not? (If yes) And would you consider the war with Iraq a success if 10,000 American troops died, or not? (If yes) And would you consider the war with Iraq a success if 20,000 American troops died, or not? (Accept "considers no American troops died as a success" as a volunteered response.)

Consider war with Iraq a success if Iraq leaves Kuwait and

No	American troops die	80%
500	American troops die	50
1,000	American troops die	37
5,000	American troops die	27
10,000	American troops die	20
20,000	American troops die	16
Don't know		13
Refused		7

Source: *Los Angeles Times,* Jan. 17–18, 1991.

Table 7-2 American Casualties and Bosnia

Question: Suppose you knew that if the United States sent U.S. troops to Bosnia as part of an international peacekeeping force, that no/25/100/400 American soldiers would be killed. With this in mind, would you favor or oppose sending U.S. troops to Bosnia?

Projected casualties	Favor sending troops	Oppose sending troops	Don't know
No soldiers killed	68%	29%	4%
25 soldiers killed	31	64	4
100 soldiers killed	30	65	6
400 soldiers killed	21	72	7

Source: Gallup/CNN/*USA Today* poll, Oct. 19–22, 1995.

Table 7-3 Reasons for Fighting Iraq

Question: Now that the U.S. (United States) forces have been sent to Saudi Arabia and other areas of the Middle East, do you think they should engage in combat if Iraq . . .

Date of poll	Engage in combat	Do not engage in combat	Don't know
A. invades Saudi Arabia?			
Aug. 9–10, 1990	67%	23%	10%
Oct. 18–19, 1990*	68	19	13
B. refuses to leave Kuwait and restore its former government?			
Aug. 9–10, 1990	42	40	18
Oct. 18–19, 1990*	45	37	18
Nov. 15–16, 1990*	46	40	14
C. continues to hold U.S. civilians hostage?			
Aug. 9–10, 1990**	61	30	9
Oct. 18–19, 1990*	57	32	11
Nov. 15–16, 1990*	55	34	11
D. kills American civilians in Kuwait and Iraq?			
Aug. 9–10, 1990	79	14	7
E. begins to control or cut off oil?			
Aug. 9–10, 1990	58	31	11
F. attacks U.S. forces?			
Aug. 9–10, 1990	94	4	2
Oct. 18–19, 1990*	93	3	4
Nov. 15–16, 1990*	91	6	3

Source: Gallup polls.

* Response items rotated from interview to interview to deal with the possibility that the order in which the items are asked affects the response.

** holds American civilians hostage

—that is, innocent—civilians. It may not be surprising to discover that there was little sympathy with the Japanese civilian population during World War II—many, after all, saw Japanese civilization as one huge war machine targeted against the United States.[10] But the Gulf War was radically different in this respect: for example, 60 percent of the American public held the Iraqi people to be innocent of any blame for their leader's policies (Mueller 1994, 316). However, this lack of animosity toward the Iraqi people did not translate into a great deal of sympathy among the American public for civilian casualties caused by air attacks. Extensive pictures and publicity about the civilian casualties resulting from an attack on a Baghdad bomb shelter on February 13, 1991, had no impact on support for bombing (Mueller 1994, 317). Moreover, images of the "highway of death" and reports that 100,000 Iraqis had died in the war[11] scarcely dampened enthusiasm at the various "victory" and "welcome home" parades and celebrations. Nor was much sympathy or even interest shown for the Iraqi civilian deaths that resulted from the severe sanctions imposed on Iraq by the United States during the 1990s (see Mueller and Mueller 1999, 2000; Mueller 2000a).

Proposition 5

The public has not become newly isolationist: it is about as accepting of involvement in foreign affairs as ever, but it does not have—and never has had—much stomach for losing American lives in ventures and arenas that are of little concern to it.

After the cold war, some people have become worried that the American public has turned—or may turn—isolationist since it has been able notably to contain its enthusiasm for sending American troops to police such trouble spots as Bosnia and Haiti. But it seems more likely that there has been little essential change in Americans' standards. Figure 7-3 displays the results for a set of questions designed to tap isolationism. As usual in public opinion surveys, the response percentages vary with the wording of the question. However, if we focus on consistently worded questions, we find that the ending of the cold war did not have much impact. There was some rise in isolationism after Vietnam in the mid-1970s, and something of a decline since then (an abrupt drop registered at the end of the Gulf War in 1991 was quickly corrected). For the most part, overall changes have been modest.

With respect to foreign interventions, the public seems to apply, as usual, a fairly reasonable cost-benefit calculus. A substantial loss of American lives may have been tolerable if the enemy was a threat like international communism or the country that bombed Pearl Harbor, but risking lives to police small, distant, unthreatening, and apparently perennially troubled countries has proved difficult for the public to accept.

For example, the international mission to Somalia in 1992–1993 helped to bring a degree of order to a deadly situation that was causing a famine reportedly killing at its peak thousands of people per day. Perhaps never before has so much been done for so many at

Figure 7-3 Isolationism Questions

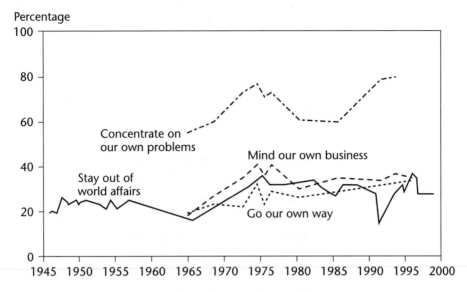

Percentage

Source: Materials on deposit at the Roper Center for Public Opinion, Storrs, Conn., and Richard G. Niemi, John Mueller, and Tom W. Smith, *Trends in Public Opinion: A Compendium of Survey Data* (Westport, Conn.: Greenwood, 1989).

such little cost. There seems to have been considerable support for the mission when Bush put it into effect in late 1992 (cautiously waiting, however, until after the presidential election). But it seems clear that the policy of nation building, shaped by the new Clinton administration in 1993 and much criticized by Republicans as unwise "mission creep," was dampening support for the venture even before eighteen Americans were killed in a firefight on the night of October 3–4, 1993 (Larson 1996; Strobel 1997, 166–183; Burk 1999, 66–67; Klarevas 1999). After that, support, already substantially reduced, it seems, to its hard-core supporters, dropped even further, and criticism became rampant.[12]

In essence, when Americans asked themselves how many American lives peace in Somalia was worth, the answer came out rather close to zero, as Table 7-4 forcefully suggests (see also Dole 1995, 41). The general reluctance to become involved in the actual fighting in Bosnia (despite years of the supposed CNN effect) suggests that Americans reached a similar conclusion for that trouble spot—as have, it seems, others in their own terms, including Britons, Germans, and Canadians.[13] It seems clear that policing efforts will be tolerated only as long as the costs in lives for the policing forces remain extremely low.

It is true that during the cold war Americans were willing, at least at the outset, to send troops to die in Korea and Vietnam, but that was because they subscribed to the contain-

Table 7-4 American Casualties and Somalia

Question: Nothing the U.S. could accomplish in Somalia is worth the death of even one more U.S. soldier.

Agree	60%
Disagree	35
Not sure	5

Source: Time/CNN/Yankelovich poll, Oct. 7, 1993.

ment notion which held communism to be a genuine threat to the United States. Polls from the time make it clear that the public had little interest in losing American lives simply to help out the South Koreans or South Vietnamese (see Table 7-5 and Mueller 1973, 44, 48–49, 58, 100–101). Similarly, as Figure 7-2 suggests, "protecting weaker nations against foreign aggression" (much less, fighting to do so) has usually achieved comparatively low ratings among foreign policy goals both during and after the cold war (though it did rise notably during the Gulf crisis of 1990). Thus an unwillingness to send Americans to die for purposes that are essentially humanitarian is hardly new.[14]

Proposition 6

Foreign policy has become less important in judging the performance of the president and of presidential contenders.

During the cold war, foreign policy was often a prominent theme in presidential campaigns. The Berlin Blockade accompanied the 1948 election; Korea was important in 1952;[15] the Suez crisis and Soviet intervention in Hungary were in the background in 1956; Kennedy and Nixon battled it out over who could stand up best to Khrushchev and Castro in 1960; and Vietnam was a notable concern in the elections of 1964, 1968, and 1972.

Thereafter, as is also suggested by the data in Figure 7-1, foreign policy declined in significance. It was of very little relevance in the 1976 election campaign between Carter and Ford (Mueller 1977, 328). It played more of a role in 1980, with the Iran hostage crisis, and in 1984 and 1988, with anxiety about nuclear war, arms control, and defense spending; overall, however, these elections were substantially dominated by domestic issues like inflation, unemployment, crime, government spending, and drug policy (Aldrich, Sullivan, and Borgida 1989).

In the wake of the cold war, any tendency by the American public to ignore foreign policy has surely been heightened. With his Gulf War success and with his opponent's complete lack of experience in foreign policy, George Bush tried very hard to make foreign affairs an

Table 7-5 Reasons for Continuing the Vietnam War

Question: Here is a list of arguments that have been given for our military effort in Vietnam. I'm going to ask you to read over this card carefully. Then I'm going to ask you to tell me which *two or three* of these you yourself feel are the *very* strongest arguments?

If we do not continue, the Communists will take over Vietnam and then move on to other parts of the world	49%
We must support our fighting men	48
If we quit now, it would weaken the will of other countries to defend their freedom	33
If we give up now, the whole expenditure of American lives and money will have been in vain	33
The United States should never accept defeat	24
If we do not continue, we will lose prestige and the confidence of our friends and allies abroad	23
We are committed to South Vietnam	19
If we pull out and the Communists take over, they will kill many of the Vietnamese who have opposed them	14
If we persevere, we are sure to gain our objectives	8

Source: Institute for International Social Research, February 1968.

important issue in the 1992 campaign. But he failed, as the public quickly refocused its attention on domestic matters (see Mueller 1994, 90, 103–107). Foreign policy was also substantially missing from the election campaigns of 1996 and 2000. Whether concern over international terrorism after the attacks of 2001 will change this in future elections remains to be seen.

Proposition 7

There is little or no long-term political gain from successful international ventures.

When American troops are sent abroad into dangerous situations, there is usually a "rally round the flag" effect: the commander in chief's approval ratings rise abruptly (Mueller 1973, 208–213). But it is important to note that this phenomenon tends to be fleeting. The public does not seem to be very interested in rewarding—or even remembering—foreign policy success.

If Bush found little lasting electoral advantage in a large dramatic victory like the Gulf War (or, earlier, for his successful intervention in Panama), lesser accomplishments seem to have been at least as unrewarding. Nobody gave Eisenhower much credit for a successful venture into Lebanon in 1958, to Johnson for success in the Dominican Republic in 1965, to Carter for husbanding an important Middle East treaty in 1979, to Reagan for a successful invasion of Grenada in 1983, or to Bill Clinton for resolving the Bosnia problem in 1995. Even Truman, who presided over the massive triumph in World War II, saw his approval plummet to impressive lows within months because of domestic concerns.[16]

At the time of the Kosovo bombings of 1999, press accounts argued that the presidential ambitions and political future of Clinton's vice president, Al Gore, hung in the balance and that the outcome would "make or unmake Clinton's much-discussed legacy" (Kettle 1999; Zelnick 1999; Page 1999; Balz and Neal 1999). From the standpoint of public opinion, the Kosovo venture seems to have been a success. But when he launched his campaign for the presidency a few months later, Gore scarcely thought it important or memorable enough to bring up, and Clinton's "much-discussed legacy" seems to have centered on rather different matters.[17]

Proposition 8

There is little or no long-term political loss from international failures when the perceived stakes are low unless the failure becomes massively expensive; this means that U.S. leaders can abruptly pull out of failed peacekeeping missions without having to worry much about political costs.

While Americans place a high, even sometimes exaggerated, value on the lives of other Americans, their reaction when Americans are killed varies considerably. In some cases the death of Americans leads to demands for revenge, in others for cutting losses and withdrawing. Which emotion prevails seems to depend on an evaluation of the stakes involved.

When Americans were killed at Pearl Harbor, the outraged call for revenge against the Japanese was overwhelming. But Japan was also seen as a palpable threat to the United States itself—indeed, many were anticipating an attack on the U.S. mainland. Much of this could also be seen in the public response to the terrorist attacks on New York and Washington in 2001. Similarly, although American decision makers apparently thought differently at the time, it seems clear from poll results like those in Table 7-3 that if Iraq had attacked American troops in the Saudi desert, where they were placed after Iraq's invasion of Kuwait, the Pearl Harbor syndrome would have been activated: Saddam Hussein would likely have been seen as an aggressor whose appetite knew no bounds and who must be confronted immediately (see also Mueller 1994, 123). Table 7-3 also suggests that if Saddam had killed some of his American hostages, his deed would have formed a major reason to go to war (far more than his cutting off oil supplies to the United States).

When the value of the stakes does not seem to be worth additional American lives, however, the public has shown a willingness to abandon an overextended or untenable position. Thus the public came to accept—even substantially to support—the decision to withdraw U.S. policing troops from Lebanon in 1983 after a terrorist bomb killed 241 U.S. marines in the chaotic civil war there. Public opinion data on the episode are sparse, but they tend to suggest that the Lebanon venture was never very popular with the public (Larson 1996, 48; Burk 1999, 65). In the two or three days after the marines were killed, the polls detected a sharp rise in the percentage calling for the sending in of more troops to avenge or deal with the tragedy; but this reaction dissipated within a few days. Meanwhile, the percentage advocating removal of the troops remained high and then grew considerably during the next weeks (see Table 7-6). Similarly, the deaths of eighteen U.S. soldiers in Somalia in 1993 helped lead to outraged demands for withdrawal, not for calls to avenge the humiliation. Unlike the problems with Japan in 1941 or Iraq in 1990, the situations in Lebanon and Somalia did not present much of a wider threat to American interests, and the public was quite willing to support measures to cut its losses and leave.

These episodes demonstrate that when peacekeeping leads to unacceptable deaths, peacekeepers can be readily removed with little concern about saving face. As Table 7-7 suggests, after the fact, Americans said that although they considered Reagan's expedition to Lebanon to have been a failure, many, with reasonable nuance, felt it still to have been "a good idea at the time." The lessons of Korea and Vietnam suggest that there can be electoral consequences if casualties are allowed to rise very substantially. But if a venture is seen to be of little importance, a president can, precisely because of that, cut and run without fear of inordinate electoral costs. As the experiences with Lebanon and Somalia suggest, by the time the next election rolls around, people will have substantially forgotten the whole thing. Thus, the situation does not have to become a quagmire.[18] Presidential adviser Dick Morris has argued that "if foreign policy is misplayed, it can hurt an incumbent's image faster than can domestic errors" (1999, 164). The tarnishing of the image may be swift, but it need not be debilitating in the long term.

Proposition 9

If they are not being killed, American troops can remain in peacekeeping ventures virtually indefinitely.

Although there is an overwhelming political demand that casualties in ventures deemed of little importance be extremely low, there seems to be little problem about keeping occu-

Table 7-6 U.S. Policy in Lebanon

Question: Would you say . . .

	the U.S. should send more troops to Lebanon	leave the number of troops about the same	or remove the troops that are there now	Don't know
Sept. 22–26, 1993	7%	48%	40%	5%
Oct. 23, 1993	241 Marines are killed in bomb attack			
Oct. 23, 1993	21	21	48	10
Oct. 24, 1993	Reagan gives press conference			
Oct. 25, 1993	31	26	39	5
Oct. 26, 1993	16	33	45	6
Oct. 27, 1993	Reagan gives speech on Lebanon, Grenada			
Oct. 28, 1993	17	41	37	5
Nov. 3–7, 1993	13	41	39	7
Dec. 8–13, 1993	9	38	48	5
Jan. 3, 1994	5	30	59	6
Jan. 4, 1994	8	29	57	6
Jan. 12–17, 1994	7	31	58	4
Feb. 1994	U.S. troops are redeployed to ships offshore			
Mar. 30, 1994	Reagan formally withdraws from peacekeeping			

Source: ABC, ABC/*Washington Post* polls.

pying forces in place as long as they are not being killed—for the most part, nobody will even remember that they are there. Thus, it is not important to have an "exit strategy," a "closed-end commitment," or "a time-certain for withdrawal," except perhaps to sell an interventionist policy in the first place.

After the Somalia fiasco, for example, the Americans stayed on for several months; since none were killed, Americans at home paid little attention and voiced little concern. Similarly, although there was little public or political support for sending U.S. troops to Haiti in 1994, there was almost no protest about keeping them there since no one was killed—in fact, when the last of them were withdrawn in March 1996 the story was given eleven inches in a lower corner of page 14 of the *New York Times* (Mitchell 1996). Although Clinton sug-

Table 7-7 Success and Failure in Lebanon

Question: Do you think the removal of the U.S. Marines from Lebanon means that Ronald Reagan's policies were a success or failure?

Success	19%
Neither (volunteered)	15
Failure	54
Not sure	15

Question: Which of the following statements come closest to your opinion about sending U.S. Marines to Lebanon?

It was a big mistake to send them at all	33%
It was a good idea at the time but it didn't work	45
We should have sent more of them to begin with	15
Not sure	7

Sources: NBC News, March 8–11, 1984, and CBS/*New York Times,* Feb. 21–25, 1984.

gested that policing troops sent to Bosnia in 1995 might be withdrawn after one year, there was hardly any protest when their stay was extended. And Americans tolerated—indeed, hardly noticed—the stationing of hundreds of thousands of U.S. troops in Europe, Japan, and South Korea for decades on end. If they are not being killed, it scarcely matters whether the troops are in Macedonia or in Kansas.

On the other hand, if American troops start being killed in low-valued ventures, there will be public and political demands to get them out, whatever the initial plans for withdrawal had been. Thus, despite calls for knowing in advance what the endgame will be (see Powell 1992/93; Sciolino 1993), the only exit strategy required is a tactical arrangement to yank the troops abruptly and painlessly from the scene should things go awry.

Therefore, presidents would be wise to sell low-valued ventures not with cosmic internationalist hype, but rather as international social work that can be shrugged off if necessary. For all his high-flown rhetoric about the importance of Bosnia, Clinton was never able to increase the number of Americans who saw wisdom or value in sending U.S. policing troops there, even though it was expected that there would be few casualties (Sobel 1998; Larson 2000; see also Mueller 2000b, 2000c). Similarly, his echoing in 1994 of Bush's earlier amazing hyperbole about the antidemocratic coup in Haiti—that it posed "an unusual and extraordinary threat to the national security, foreign policy, and economy of the United States"—seems to have had no resonance with the American public, which may very well see such hyperbole as nonsense and an insult to their intelligence.

Fortunately, the public often seems more sensible than its leaders. When he sent the marines to help police Lebanon, Ronald Reagan declared that "in an age of nuclear challenge and economic interdependence, such conflicts are a threat to all the people of the world, not just to the Middle East itself" (1983, 1096). Despite having gotten such an overblown sales pitch from the president, however, the public had no difficulty accepting Reagan's later decision to have the marines "redeployed to the sea" after 241 of them had been killed by a terrorist bomb.

Proposition 10

A danger in peacekeeping missions is that Americans might be taken hostage, something that can suddenly and disproportionately magnify the perceived stakes.

Because of the overriding importance Americans place on American lives, as discussed in proposition 4, policy remains vulnerable to hostage taking. I have argued that peacekeeping ventures need not become quagmires because a president can still abruptly withdraw troops from an overextended position with little long-lasting political cost. However, this principle can be dramatically reversed if even a small number of Americans are taken hostage.

The process is illustrated best by some evidence from the Somalia episode. After the debacle of October 1993, a Somalia group captured one American soldier. The public's determination to remain until the prisoner was recovered (and then to withdraw) is clear from Table 7-8.

Policymakers seem well aware of this problem. Much of the reticence about bombing in Bosnia stemmed from fear that West European peacekeepers might be caught in the crossfire or taken hostage. Accordingly, extensive bombing was begun in 1995 only after troops had been quietly removed from vulnerable areas. The same thing happened with bombing campaigns against Iraq in 1998 and against Serbia in 1999.

Proposition 11

The degree to which notable international events linger in the public mind after they are over varies rather curiously and does not appear to depend on their inherent historical importance.

As is clear from the preceding analysis, few international events and issues have managed to arrest the public's attention substantially. The degree to which notable and noted events have had a long-range impact varies in a sometimes rather puzzling manner. Some linger on more or less continuously in the public consciousness, some vanish quickly and never revive, some linger for a while and then suddenly vanish, and some vanish for a while but then become revived in memory.

Table 7-8 U.S. Policy in Somalia

Question: Which of these three policies do you most favor for U.S. policy in Somalia?

Withdraw all U.S. troops immediately	11%
Withdraw all U.S. troops but only after all U.S. servicemen are returned	67
Or stay in Somalia until political stability is restored	19
Not sure	3

Source: NBC News, Oct. 6, 1993.

Events That Linger

The best example of an international event that continued uninterruptedly to live in memory long after it was over is undoubtedly World War II. The war was a massive affair, affecting all strata of society, and it continued, and continues, to affect popular perceptions. On the domestic side, something somewhat comparable could probably be said for the Great Depression—an unpleasant event that had a long, lingering impact.

Events That Vanish

The Gulf War seems prototypical of international events that vanish. On the eve of the war, half of the American people claimed that they thought about the crisis at least once an hour (Mueller 1994, 214). But when it was over, it quickly, and apparently permanently, vanished from sight and recall—as its author, George Bush, ruefully found out in his unsuccessful reelection campaign a year later. In this, public opinion may appropriately be reflecting historical reality: it is difficult to escape the conclusion that from the standpoint of world history the war was really quite a minor event (Mueller 1994, chap. 9). However, the cold war cannot so easily be dismissed as a historical sideshow. Yet it seems already to be picking up a patina of quaintness as it recedes from memory.[19]

Events That Linger, Then Vanish

The Korean War may well have been the most important event since World War II. It was the most costly war in the period (Small and Singer 1982), and it essentially crystallized the cold war (see Gaddis 1974; Jervis 1980; May 1984; Mueller 1989, chap. 6). Moreover, it seems to have importantly affected public perceptions throughout the 1950s (see Mueller 1979, 314–315). The War of 1812 also lingered for quite a while and influenced several elections. Yet both wars eventually sagged from public consciousness, and both, interestingly enough, have inspired books with titles labeling them "forgotten" conflicts (Blair 1987; Hickey 1989).

Events That Vanish, Then Revive

The Vietnam War was the great nonissue of the 1976 election campaign—just a year after the war concluded—and it continued to be neglected by the public for several years (see Lovell 1992, 389–391). Americans, it seemed, did not want to think about a costly and unpleasant failure like Vietnam—in part, perhaps, because they did not want to have to consider doing something about the consequent Khmer Rouge genocide in Cambodia, a catastrophe that garnered a total of less than twenty-nine minutes of coverage on all three networks at the time (Adams and Joblove 1982). Yet, by the 1980s, Vietnam had become a fabled and memorable event, even a haunting one, in the American consciousness, and it seems likely to remain one for a long time. Something similar happened with the Civil War—probably the most important event in American history. For twenty years there was a considerable desire to forget the conflict, but then the building of myths—and of memorials and monuments—began (see Linderman 1987).

Overall, then, neither the scope of the event nor its objective historical importance seems precisely to determine the pattern it takes in public recall.

Notes

1. Unless otherwise indicated, all data come from materials on deposit at the Roper Center for Public Opinion, Storrs, Conn., and from Niemi, Mueller, and Smith (1989). This paper is dedicated to the memory of John Lovell and was written in part while the author was a guest fellow at the Norwegian Nobel Institute in Oslo. The institute's support is gratefully acknowledged.

2. Results like these frequently elicit disapproving tongue-clicking. It is not clear, however, why one should expect people to spend a lot of time worrying about national or international problems, particularly when democratic capitalism not only leaves them free to choose other ways to get their kicks but in its seemingly infinite quest for variety is constantly developing seductive distractions. Some people are intensely interested in government and world affairs, but it verges on the arrogant to suggest that others are somehow inadequate or derelict unless they share the same curious passion (see Mueller 1999, chap. 6).

3. For an analysis of American expectations of war during the classic cold war period, see Mueller (1979).

4. For data, see Mueller (1994, 211–212). It could be argued that, objectively speaking, thermonuclear war is the most important problem facing the country, considering the potential devastation. Clearly, however, the poll respondents are not unreasonably building an estimate of probability into their responses. For example, it appears that no one has ever suggested that the explosion of the sun might be the country's most important problem.

5. In almost all years, fewer than 10 Americans die at the hands of international terrorists (U.S. Department of State 1998, 85). By contrast, an average of 90 Americans are killed each year by lightning (National Safety Council 1997, 120), and about 100 die in accidents caused by deer (Revkin 1998). The destructiveness of the 2001 bombings in which thousands perished is thus unprecedentedly extreme.

6. Nor, it might be added, has the speed with which the public receives news significantly increased in recent decades. Once the telegraph was established in the nineteenth century, information

that had previously taken days, weeks, months, or even years to travel could be relayed almost instantly, reaching ordinary citizens within a very few hours as newspapers came out with special editions. With the arrival of radio and, much later, television, the information delay was further reduced—at least for those who happen to have their radio or television sets turned on at the time. But this is a comparatively minor improvement.

7. In some important respects, the Gulf War experience also calls into question, or at least delimits, the notion that the media has a great independent impact in agenda-setting in international affairs. Throughout, journalists and editors reported what was going on, and they correctly doped out what their public wanted (especially supportive, uncritical news during the war itself). So instructed, they supplied that need, but they did not invent it nor did they invent the issues that, for a while, so engrossed the public. Then, following their customers, the media dutifully shifted their attention to domestic concerns at the end of the war, despite the strenuous efforts of the previously influential president to keep the war euphoria and glow alive. The message and the customer dominated, even intimidated, the medium. For a fuller discussion, see Mueller (1994, 129–136).

8. During World War II an experiment was made to determine whether "realistic" war pictures would hurt morale. It found that those who were exposed to such pictures were not any more or less likely to support the war than an unexposed control group. Those exposed, however, did become more favorable to showing people realistic war pictures (National Opinion Research Center 1944). Other studies found that efforts of the military to use propaganda films to indoctrinate new draftees were ineffective (Kinder and Sears 1985, 706).

9. This conclusion is principally derived from trend data on the percentage holding the wars to have been a mistake. Opinion data concerning policy options does not permit a precise trend assessment about whether the public came to support withdrawal or escalation during the course of the wars because the polling agencies constantly changed the wording of the relevant questions in important ways (for an extensive display and analysis of such data, see Mueller 1973, chap. 4). For an analysis that seems to be insensitive to this issue, see Schwarz (1994); for a correction, see Larson (1996).

10. Asked what should be done with the Japanese after the war, 10 to 15 percent volunteered the solution of extermination. And after the war was over, 23 percent said they regretted that many more atomic bombs had not "quickly" been used on Japan before it "had a chance to surrender" (Mueller 1973, 172–173).

11. This figure is almost certainly much too high, probably by a factor of more than 10; see Mueller (1995b).

12. The popularly accepted notion that the debacle was importantly caused by the UN (Dole 1995, 37) is not only wrong but grotesque; see Gordon and Friedman (1993). Despite the criticism of the UN that this episode inspired, especially from Republicans, there has been no notable decline in public support for the UN (Murray, Klarevas, and Hartley 1997; see also Figure 7-2).

13. After Spanish troops had suffered some 17 deaths in the Bosnian war, their government indicated that this was enough, and they withdrew from further confrontation, something that greatly encouraged the Croat gangs the Spanish had been dealing with (Hedges 1997). Similarly, Belgium abruptly withdrew from Rwanda—and, to save face, urged others to do so as well—when 10 of its policing troops were massacred and mutilated early in the genocide (Gourevitch 1998, 114, 149–150). For the remarkable conclusion, based on a single poll question, that Americans might be willing, on average, to sacrifice 6,861 U.S. military deaths in order to stabilize a democratic government in Congo, see Feaver and Gelpi (1999). For a similar take, see Kull and Destler (1999, 106–108), critiqued by Larson (1999, 625).

14. Actually, this is not such an unusual position for humanitarian ventures. If Red Cross or other workers are killed while carrying out humanitarian missions, their organizations frequently threaten

to withdraw, no matter how much good they may be doing. Essentially what they are saying, then, is that the saving of lives is not worth the deaths of even a few of their service personnel.

15. The Republican presidential campaign apparently was able to raise the salience of the Korean War as an issue, however; see Harris (1954, 25).

16. The truly big electoral loser of World War II was Britain's Winston Churchill, voted out of office even as he was attending a peace conference at the end of the war. Nor did Woodrow Wilson or his party derive long-term benefit from victory in World War I. There may be some partial exceptions to this pattern, however. Eisenhower benefited from the Korean War, but that was not because he had instituted it. Rather, his achievement was in apparently bringing it to an end within six months of his inauguration in 1953, something that may well have been the most significant achievement turned in by any postwar president: it was still remembered as a great accomplishment seven years later when Eisenhower was leaving office, and it was pointedly brought up again by Republicans in the 1968 election, a full fifteen years after the event (Mueller 1973, 234). A good case for an exception seems to be the War of 1812, which apparently benefited the Republicans who had instituted it (see Mueller 1994, 108–111), and something similar may have happened after the Civil War. The successful Falklands War of 1982 may have helped British prime minister Margaret Thatcher in the elections of 1983, but the effect is confounded by the fact that the economy was improving impressively at the same time; see Norpoth (1987a, 1987b).

17. Conceivably, a successful venture will help if it comes close enough to the next election—Bush might have benefited, perhaps, if he had been able to stage the Gulf War so that it wrapped up within a few days or weeks of the election. There may have been such an effect in the March 2000 presidential election in Russia, where the popular invasion of Chechnya seems to have boosted Vladimir Putin's election prospects even higher than they might otherwise have been.

18. Most remarkably in this regard, the utter collapse of the American position in Vietnam in 1975 was actually used by the man who presided over it, Gerald Ford, as a point in his favor in his reelection campaign of 1976. When he came into office, he observed, "We were still deeply involved in the problems of Vietnam" but now "we are at peace. Not a single young American is fighting or dying on any foreign soil" (Kraus 1979, 538–539; see also Mueller 1984a).

19. In 1945, the Western victors of the war faced two major international problems: what to do about the defeated countries, Germany and Japan, and what to do about the emerging conflict with the USSR. Since it involved a lot of interesting conflict, the latter problem has inspired a much greater literature. But it seems quite possible that in time the cold war will be remembered as something of a historical curiosity. By contrast, the successful solution of the Japan–Germany problem—making those countries over into moderate and prosperous allies and peaceful competitors whose view of the world is much like that of the Western victors—may well come to be seen as a much more momentous development historically.

Part 3   Organization of Attitudes

During the 2000 presidential elections, George W. Bush and Al Gore used ideology, values, and party to appeal to voters. Bush won the GOP primaries in part by arguing to strong Republicans that only he could beat Gore in November. The image he sought to portray to the general electorate was one of a "compassionate conservative"—a label that modified an ideological label (conservative) with the value of compassion. Gore's appeal to the Democratic base was complicated by his efforts to distance himself from Bill Clinton because he did not want to be tarnished by an association with Clinton's moral values. After the election was decided by the Supreme Court, many Democrats argued that Gore should have embraced the Clinton policy legacy and allowed Clinton to campaign for him in key states.

The campaign themes and images developed by Bush and Gore were based on public opinion research by pollsters and focus-group moderators. The details of policy positions are often too complex for most citizens to sort out, so candidates communicate by stressing basic orientations such as partisanship, ideology, and values, and each of these is used by at least some citizens to organize their political attitudes and to help them process information about candidates and issues.

The earliest academic research on public opinion found the public to have strong partisan preferences but more sketchy ideological identities. Party identification is defined as a long-term psychological attachment to a political party (Campbell et al. 1960, chap. 6). Ideology is normally viewed as a sophisticated and abstract orientation toward government and its role in society: in the United States the predominant ideologies are liberalism and conservatism. Theoretically, both ideology and party identification shape our viewpoints on specific issues and candidates. Although much of the early political science research questioned the meaning of ideology for the American public, more recent works question the meaning of party identification in a candidate-centered election era.

The classic studies of ideology, based on surveys from the 1950s, concluded that the American public was incapable of abstract ideological thought (Campbell et al. 1960; Converse 1964). Most Americans conceived of politics in terms of which groups benefit or lose from certain policies or in terms of "the nature of the times"—whether they thought that things were getting better or worse. Very few voters seemed to use ideology to shape their opinions and influence their candidate choices.

Public opinion researchers beginning in the 1980s started to question the classic interpretation of ideology. One group of scholars began to suggest that ideological labels had more to do with symbolism than with specific issue positions (Conover and Feldman 1981; Levitin and Miller 1979). Americans' reactions to the label "conservative" may be more a function of their feelings about the police, military, and businesses; definitions of liberalism are influenced by reactions to the challenges that women, students, and minority groups made to the 1950s traditional lifestyle (Conover and Feldman 1981). Indeed, George Bush's presidential campaign in 1988 sought to define liberalism (and therefore Michael Dukakis) by associating the ideological label with unpopular causes and groups.

Other scholars argued that the search for ideology in the American public should not be limited to identifying liberals and conservatives (Maddox and Lilie 1984). Other possible ideologies include populism (a preference for expanded social welfare programs coupled with stricter government controls to maintain social order) and libertarianism (the rejection of government intervention in economic and social issues). Both populists and libertarians would appear to be inconsistent on the traditional liberal–conservative scale. The American public may be equally divided into liberals, conservatives, populists, and libertarians (Janda, Berry, and Goldman 1995, 26, 165). Green party presidential candidate Ralph Nadar argued in 2000 that Bush and Gore were similar ideologically and that his candidacy and party offered a new way of thinking about American politics.

For many Americans, however, values may be far more salient than ideology (see Sniderman 1993 for a summary). Basic values include beliefs on economic individualism (whether hard work leads to success), equality of opportunity (judgments on whether it exists or is necessary), and the free enterprise system (government's role in regulating the economy) (Feldman 1988). Other core values could include political tolerance, patriotism, and desire for social order. Preferences and competition between a number of core values could produce within each citizen a variety of sometimes apparently inconsistent opinions, depending on which value dominates in each case (Tetlock 1986). William Jacoby's chapter fits into this last alternative to the classically defined ideology. In his chapter, Jacoby asks whether a structure exists among competing core values and what consequences this might have for an individual's political attitudes.

The classic voting behavior studies from the 1950s viewed party identification as the key element to understanding the American electorate. Party identification influenced whether someone voted and which candidate they voted for. Partisans were more likely to vote than were independents, and partisans voted overwhelmingly for their party's candidates, especially for lower level offices. Partisanship was vastly more stable than any other attitude. The

New Deal generation had strong partisan preferences and passed these identifications on to their children.

Yet, beginning in the 1960s, the dominant role of party identification in elections began to decline. More people adopted an independent identification, more voters split their tickets between Republicans and Democrats, partisans defected more often from their party's candidate, and more citizens began to develop negative attitudes toward both parties (see Gant and Luttbeg 1991 for a summary and explanation of these changes). Political scientists described this as a process of dealignment, where old partisan alignments were broken down and not replaced by new preferences.

By the 1990s the picture of partisanship began to change once again. With the passage of time, political scientists began to realize that some of the elements of the dealignment of the 1960s and 1970s were actually a very slow realignment of partisan preferences. The South had been solidly Democratic since the Civil War, but as the Democratic Party took more explicit positions on civil rights and expanded social welfare programs in the 1960s, southern Democrats began to move away from the party. But rather than taking a dramatic jump from Democratic to Republican preferences, many southerners adopted the independent label or defected from their Democratic partisanship to vote for Republican candidates, especially for president. Gradually, more southerners were willing to declare themselves Republicans. Preferences changed outside the South as well. These slow partisan changes are what political scientists term a secular realignment (Key 1959). By the end of the twentieth century, partisanship and ideology were aligned more closely; conservatives became Republicans while liberals were Democrats. This realignment also produced the gender gap, as men moved into the Republican Party while women were more likely to remain in the Democratic Party (Kaufman and Petrocik 1999; Norrander 1999). In their chapter, Alan Abramowitz and Kyle Saunders write about the consequences of this ideological realignment for congressional elections.

8 Core Values and Political Attitudes

William G. Jacoby

Since the 1960s, research on public opinion and mass behavior has demonstrated repeatedly that citizens' attitudes on policy issues are determined primarily by their more general orientations and feelings. The exact nature of these general orientations varies. Some researchers have stressed the "perceptual screen" that is generated by personal attachments to political parties (Campbell et al. 1960), while others have emphasized the broad "evaluative yardstick" provided by ideological abstractions (Converse 1964). Various broadly applicable reasoning routines have also been suggested. These include the "likability" of the social groups involved in issue controversies (Brady and Sniderman 1985; Link and Oldendick 1996) and judgments about recent societal economic performance (Fiorina 1981; Popkin 1991). Still another such general orientation is a person's set of core values, which should provide each individual with immediate guidance for developing his or her own reactions toward policy controversies.

Although mass behavior researchers generally pay some lip service to the concept of values, they have not devoted anywhere near the level of empirical scrutiny to values as to the other general orientations. From one perspective, the rather cavalier treatment of values by political scientists is a bit surprising. After all, values are widely believed to be a fundamental building block of human behavior (Rokeach 1973). Philosophers, collective action theorists, and policy analysts seem to agree that political conflict inherently involves clashes of competing value systems (Berlin 1969; Chong 2000; Stone 1997). Similarly, values determine the institutional structure of political systems (Lipset 1967; Bell 2000) as well as the general belief systems of the citizens that live within them (Lane 1973; Feldman 1988). Thus, the connection between values and politics seems to be pervasive and obvious.

But there is also a different, and largely contradictory, perspective on the relevance of personal values to public opinion. For example, some psychologists point out that regardless of theoretical expectations, actual research has often shown that the relationships between values, attitudes, and behavior are often contradictory, weak, or even nonexistent (Kristiansen and Hotte 1996; McCarty and Shrum 2000). Similarly, a long line of research in mass political behavior stresses the distinct separation between personal concerns and political phenomena (Sniderman and Brody 1977; Kinder and Kiewiet 1981; Sears and Funk 1990); if this is the case, then individual value orientations could well be irrelevant for political purposes, in just the same ways that self-interest and personal economic experiences do not coincide with distinctive issue attitudes. Finally, some analysts stress that many individual combinations of value orientations, from an "objective" standpoint, seem to be contradictory in nature (Alvarez and Brehm 1998). If this kind of ambivalence is, in fact, widespread, then it is difficult to see how value choices could provide any systematic guidance on political matters.

There is currently no clear scholarly consensus on the role of values in public opinion. To put it differently, there is much more to be learned on this topic, and the objective of the present chapter is to take a few steps in that direction. Specifically, I will employ some unique data from a 1994 nationwide sample survey to examine value orientations within the American public. We will see that citizens do have coherent preferences for particular values; there is not very much ambivalence to be found. Further, choices between two particularly prominent values—liberty and equality—have a strong impact on public attitudes toward a salient political issue—government spending. Taken together, the results from the analysis in this chapter suggest that values should receive more attention from scholars interested in uncovering the underlying sources of public opinion and mass political attitudes.

Background

Let us begin by defining terms. *Values* can be defined as each individual's abstract, general conceptions about the desirable and undesirable end states of human life.[1] As such, values provide criteria for evaluating external stimuli and interacting with other elements of the social environment. They effectively define what is "good" and "bad" in the world. Good things are those that facilitate, promote, or are consistent with positive values. Bad things either promote negative values or inhibit the attainment of positive values.

Values are closely related to, but still different from, a number of other important social, psychological, and political phenomena. For example, some of the early sociological treatments of values seem to regard them as equivalent to *norms* (Parsons 1951; Spates 1983). But the latter comprise acceptable forms of behavior within specified social settings. In contrast, values refer more to the goals toward which any such behaviors are oriented.

Some of the recent political science literature uses *values* and *beliefs* more or less synonymously (Feldman 1988; McCann 1997; Goren 2001). But there are fairly significant differences between these concepts, at least within the confines of social psychological theory (and, by implication, in its political science relatives, as well): beliefs are fairly specific in content; they attach an attribute to a particular stimulus object (Fishbein and Ajzen 1975). Values are nonspecific; the term used by Shalom H. Schwartz (1996) is "transsituational." In other words, values ". . . transcend specific situations" (Schwartz and Bilsky 1987, 551).

Values and *ideology* are often portrayed in ways that suggest intersecting relationships between them (Peffley and Hurwitz 1985; Chong 2000). To oversimplify a bit, this view suggests that a person's values comprise his or her ideology and vice versa. But this perspective does not really do justice to either concept. Ideologies represent a view of the ideal society along with the means of achieving it (Hinich and Munger 1994). As such, ideologies are inherently social in nature. Values are much more general than this; they refer to any kinds of environmental or personal states that humans may regard as objectives for personal conduct.

It is worthwhile to consider the relationship between *values* and another critical social psychological construct—*attitudes*. Functionalist theories contend that attitudes are external manifestations of inner value states (Katz 1960; Murray, Haddock, and Zanna 1996). More cognitively oriented treatments define an *attitude* as a predisposition to respond positively or negatively toward some object (Fishbein and Ajzen 1975; Eagly and Chaiken 1993). As such, an individual's attitude is based upon the cognitions that he or she holds about the object. Each cognition is weighted by an affective evaluation. And values are an important source of the positive or negative feelings in such evaluations. So, regardless of one's specific theoretical perspective, it is reasonable to assert that values exert an important and fundamental influence on individual attitudes.

Finally, what about *values* and *culture*? Indeed, "culture" could, itself, be defined largely by the values that are salient in society at any given time (Inglehart 1990; Abramson and Inglehart 1995). Within the bounds defined by current cultural standards, there is also likely to be conflict between values. The problem is that the desirable end states implied by values are, themselves, a limited commodity. They are in short supply, and there are not enough to go around. Therefore, the attainment of one value (such as liberty) will almost certainly restrict or inhibit the degree to which some other desirable end state (such as equality) can be achieved. This basic tenet of societal interaction explains why values are of fundamental importance to politics: as stated in the well-known phrase from David Easton, political conflict inherently involves disagreements about the "authoritative allocation of *values*" (Easton 1965a, emphasis added).

The purpose of this somewhat extended explication of the term *values* is to justify the basic approach I am taking in this chapter: that is, treating values as a phenomenon that is conceptually distinct and substantively separate from other influences on mass political attitudes. Let us next consider three lines of prior research that have important implications for our understanding of the ways values impinge on American public opinion. These are:

(1) social psychological investigations into the structure of human values; (2) studies that emphasize values drawn from the ideological foundations of American political culture; and (3) analyses of value ambivalence within citizens' contemporary political orientations.

Value Structures

Most contemporary understandings of human values can be traced to the pioneering work of social psychologist Milton Rokeach, carried out in the 1960s and 1970s. Earlier social scientific treatments of values proceeded at a fairly high level of abstraction (Blake and Davis 1964; Parsons 1966). The resultant theories were not grounded in observable phenomena and therefore provided little in the way of testable hypotheses about human behavior (Glaser and Strauss 1967; Spates 1983).

Rokeach's Values Survey (1973) helped to change the focus of scholarly research in this field. It demonstrated that individual feelings about values could be measured empirically. In fact, Rokeach found that people seem to possess value *hierarchies*, which summarize their personal assessments about which values are more important and which ones are less important. Furthermore, these value preferences seem to be quite reliable (that is, they are stable over time) and comparable from one person to the next (it is meaningful to examine the placement of particular values across individuals). Perhaps most important, Rokeach demonstrated that personal value systems are related in reasonable ways to other interesting aspects of human behavior, such as social class distinctions, racial prejudice, and religious preferences, as well as many other attitudes and behavior.

Subsequent research on values has proceeded in a wide variety of directions (Rokeach 1979; Spates 1983; Seligman, Olson, and Zanna 1996). But one general idea drawn from this research tradition deserves particular emphasis: this is the basic notion that value *structures* are the key to understanding human behavior (Schwartz and Bilsky 1987; Schwartz 1992). In other words, people rarely consider single values in isolation from other values. Instead, values are almost inevitably arranged into personal hierarchies, with each individual holding some values more dearly than others. The impact of values on behavior stems from this juxtaposition: "Indeed, values may play little role in behavior except when there is value conflict—when a behavior has consequences promotive of one value but opposed to others that are also cherished by the person" (Schwartz 1996, 2).

So the research implies that it makes little sense to examine the impact of a single, particular value on public opinion. Instead, it is necessary to observe how *sets* of values impinge on political orientations. But, as we will see, the fact that values operate in sets makes it more difficult to elicit empirical information on values in the first place. So, the importance of value structures rather than individual values may have, in itself, contributed to the relative dearth of information about the effects of values on public opinion.

Values and Political Culture

Up to this point, the discussion has considered values from a generic perspective. But exactly what values are we talking about? Which ones affect public opinion? These are serious questions, precisely because the potential range of values is vast, indeed. For example, Rokeach included thirty-six different values in his original Values Survey (1973). Subsequent researchers have followed suit, often by simply adapting Rokeach's values to other purposes (Ball-Rokeach, Rokeach, and Grube 1984; Seligman and Katz 1996) or by examining individual preferences among other sizable sets of distinct desirable end states for human existence (Kamakura and Mazzon 1991; Schwartz 1992).

For present purposes, it is probably sufficient to examine a more limited subset of values—those with immediate relevance to political concerns. These relevent values can be extracted from the content of American political culture. For example, Herbert McClosky and John Zaller (1984) and Stanley Feldman (1988) emphasize that the underlying philosophy of the American political system—classical liberalism—has great utility for understanding both contemporary political rhetoric and the ways citizens react toward society and politics. Two values are particularly important: (1) personal freedom (or individual liberty), derived from the expectation of individual self-fulfillment inherent in the capitalistic economic tradition, and (2) equality of opportunity, a vital component of the democratic norms that have dominated American culture at least since the nineteenth century.

Along with the ideas inherited fairly directly from John Locke, Thomas Jefferson, and Adam Smith, other values should also be taken into account. For example, economic security for all is a commonly espoused value, although there remain many citizens who cannot compete in the "marketplace" of socioeconomic interactions (Hochschild 1995). Another is social order. Traditional conservative philosophy has always emphasized the need to enforce fairly strict norms of social behavior (Rossiter 1962); otherwise, any form of orderly, interactive human existence would be impossible.

Hence, it seems appropriate to include basic economic security and social order as fundamental values, along with freedom and equality. Virtually all contemporary domestic political issues can be traced to the problem of how to achieve these four values. So it is important to consider how ordinary citizens feel about them and to evaluate their effects on subsequent political attitudes.

Value Ambivalence

Surprisingly, there is a fundamental question that has never been directly addressed in the vast amount of research on human values: Do people possess fully ordered value hierarchies in the first place? It seems possible, at least on intuitive grounds, that some individuals may believe that two or more values are equally important.

The problem is that most past research has used methods that prevent such "tied" value choices from occurring (Alwin and Krosnick 1985; McCarty and Shrum 2000). Most measurement instruments (including Rokeach's Values Survey) simply ask people to rank-order a prespecified set of values according to their importance. Experimental subjects and survey respondents are usually willing to comply cheerfully with interviewers' instructions, regardless of whether their overt responses are truly indicative of some meaningful underlying psychological trait (Schuman and Presser 1981). In other words, some people may specify that one value is more important than another simply because there is no way to indicate that two values are equally important.

The failure to measure *value ambivalence* is a serious shortcoming, precisely because the inability to choose between competing values may have systematic consequences. For example, Philip Tetlock's theory of value pluralism is based upon the idea that individuals' internal conflicts between important personal values have direct effects on the nature of human reasoning, including manifestations of political ideology (Tetlock 1984, 1986; Tetlock, Peterson, and Lerner 1996).

In a somewhat different vein, Feldman and Zaller (1992) suggest that modern American liberals experience ambivalence stemming from the inherent conflict between the values of freedom and equality. This internal conflict has immediate political consequences because it places liberals at a disadvantage relative to conservatives (who experience no such value conflict). Conservatives favor freedom over equality. Therefore, they possess relatively clear cut value hierarchies, with very little internal conflict.

More generally, R. Michael Alvarez and John Brehm argue that value ambivalence may contribute to the apparently ephemeral quality of many citizens' issue attitudes. Specifically, conflicts in feelings about underlying values make it much more difficult for an individual to select a personal stand on salient, but difficult, policy issues like abortion and racial equality (Alvarez and Brehm 1995, 1997). As a result, the person may give inconsistent responses to questions about such an issue. Although inconsistent responses are frequently interpreted as evidence of unsophisticated, politically naive behavior (Zaller 1992), apparent inconsistencies may actually reflect the inherent difficulty of reconciling personal values with political choices. From this perspective, the ability to recognize the potential for conflicts between values indicates a fairly high degree of political comprehension and sophistication.

In any event, it does seem important to incorporate the possibility of value ambivalence into any analysis of value effects in public opinion. At the very least, it should be possible to identify people who *cannot* rank-order their feelings about specific values into a complete hierarchy. But again, designing a study that accounts for value ambivalence requires relatively complex data collection strategies—basically, methods that are not commonly incorporated into public opinion surveys. Thus, the actual prevalence and impact of value ambivalence remains largely unknown at present.

Data for Measuring Value Preferences

Unfortunately, it is quite difficult to find the kind of data that are required to examine the presence and impact of values in American public opinion. The standard sources available to the scholarly community generally do not address the points raised in this chapter so far. For example, the biennial National Election Studies often contain a few items that purport to measure particular values (for example, individual commitments to equal opportunity and to moral traditionalism). But they rarely incorporate enough distinct values to tap the presence of value *structures* in any meaningful way. At the same time, it is difficult to trace the origins of some of these values (such as moral traditionalism) back to the components of American culture and its underlying ideology. Finally, the formats of the survey questions often vary from one value to the next, thereby inhibiting valid individual-level comparisons across different values.

For all of these reasons, the study presented in this chapter relies on data from a different source: the 1994 Multi-Investigator Study (MIS), carried out by the University of California-Berkeley's Survey Research Center. The MIS is based upon a nationwide random sample of 1,464 American adults. It combines the factor manipulations of experimental designs with the broad coverage and external validity of public opinion surveys (Sniderman, Brady, and Tetlock 1994). So, along with a variety of more or less standard survey questions (for example, party identification and ideology sequences, a battery of feeling thermometer ratings, and standard demographic characteristics), many innovative items are included in the interview schedule. Among the latter, the MIS asked respondents to make paired-comparison choices among the four values discussed earlier: equality, liberty, economic security, and social order.

The introduction to and content of the questions is a bit lengthy. But this is a unique set of items, so it is useful to go over them in some detail. Respondents were contacted by telephone and presented with the following introductory statement and battery of questions:

Now let's talk about things that are important for our society such as liberty, equality, economic security, and social order. Before we get to the questions, let me first explain what we mean by these ideas.

By LIBERTY we mean a guarantee of the widest freedom possible for everyone to act and think as they consider most appropriate.

By EQUALITY we mean narrowing the gap in wealth and power between the rich and the poor.

By ECONOMIC SECURITY we mean the guarantee of a steady job and a decent income.

By SOCIAL ORDER we mean being able to live in an orderly and peaceful society where the laws are respected and enforced.

All four of these ideas are important, but sometimes we have to choose between what is more important and what is less important. In your opinion, as things stand right now, which is more important for our country—liberty or equality?

How about economic security or social order? As things now stand, which do you feel is more important for our country?

How about liberty or economic security?

How about equality or social order?

How about liberty or social order?

How about equality or economic security?

Several features of this question battery deserve particular emphasis. First, all possible pairs of values are represented. In other words, each value is compared with every other value. The direct comparison makes the judgmental task particularly easy for the survey respondents. If people really do distinguish among these different values, then there should be no difficulties in sorting them out when they are considered two at a time. Certainly, the cognitive tasks involved in formulating the responses should be far easier than the rank-ordering of several dozen values that occurs in other instruments, such as the Rokeach Values Survey.

A second, and closely related, advantage of this question format is that it makes the very existence of value hierarchies within the mass public an empirical question. That is, to the extent that these hierarchies actually do exist, they can be reconstructed from the responses to the pairwise value choices (Coombs 1964; Weller and Romney 1988). In contrast, more traditional value measurements implicitly presuppose the existence of value hierarchies. Without such an a priori assumption, there would be no validity in subjects' rank-ordered choices among the values.

Third, note that the four terms—liberty, equality, economic security, and social order—are explicitly defined for the respondents. These values are, by nature, very broadly conceived, so each value could mean different things to different people. Providing a single definition for each one, and asking respondents to use that in their choices, minimizes the effects of varying definitions on the responses. Therefore, the observed variability in the pairwise choices is likely to result from actual differences in beliefs about the relative importance of the values rather than to individual differences in how people understand the language.

Clearly, the MIS respondents had little difficulty answering the questions in the values battery. Only about 5 percent refused to make the choices (not an atypical refusal rate in survey research). And on each pair of values, a few people (between six and sixteen—never more than 1 percent of the sample) insisted that both values were equally important. Thus the vast majority of respondents were willing to state that one value was more important than the other in each of the pairs. This is precisely the kind of information that is useful for examining values in public opinion.

Value Structures in the Mass Public

The information provided by the paired comparisons is used to determine each MIS respondent's beliefs about the relative importance of the separate values. To do so each value is assigned a score showing the number of times the person selects that value over any other value. As a simple example, consider three values: *A, B,* and *C*. Assume that these are presented to respondents in pairwise fashion. A hypothetical respondent indicates that *A* is more important than *B*, *A* is more important than *C*, and *B* is more important than *C*. In this case, *A* would receive a score of 2, since it was chosen over two other values (*B* and *C*); *B* receives a score of 1 (it was chosen only over *C*); and *C* receives a 0, since it was not chosen over any other values. Since the MIS data include four values, the scores for each value can range from 0 to 3.

Do Value Hierarchies Really Exist?

Let us begin by considering a fundamental question: Do people possess value hierarchies in which they fully distinguish the relative importance of different values? This is not a trivial concern. When confronted with lofty and emotion-laden terms like *equality, liberty,* and so on, many citizens could easily state that all are equally important (even though the survey question used to measure value choices does not offer this as an alternative). If people were to refuse to choose among values, it would be impossible to rank-order individual values in the ways that are implied by the concept of a value hierarchy.

The scores assigned to the separate values enable us to test for the existence of value hierarchies. If people really do distinguish the importance of the values, then the pairwise choices should be *transitive*. That is, for any set of three values (*A, B,* and *C*), choices on two of the pairs imply the choice that will be made on the third pair. So, if *A* is chosen over *B*, and *B* is chosen over *C*, then transitivity implies that *A* is chosen over *C*. An individual with a transitive ordering of values might report that equality was more important than freedom, that freedom was more important than social order, and that equality was more important than social order.

If an individual's choices among the values are fully transitive, then each of the values will receive a distinct score. Therefore, it is possible to assemble that person's pairwise choices into a complete rank-ordering of the values. A complete rank-ordering is strong evidence for the existence of a true value hierarchy.[2]

Now consider a person who believes that our three hypothetical values are equally important. Remember that the format of the MIS survey question requires respondents to select one value over the other—ties are not permitted (even though about 1 percent of the sample insisted on this response in each pairwise comparison). Instead, the inability to rank the separate values would likely be manifested as *intransitivity*. An individual with an intransitive set of preferences might tell us that equality was more important than freedom, that freedom was more important than social order, and that social order was more important than equality. In this case, it would be impossible to identify any single value as the most important in that individual's hierarchy. Because each value is selected over a single other value, all three receive scores of 1. This result should not occur if people really do maintain complete value hierarchies.[3]

Turning to the MIS data, 1,352 respondents answered all six of the pairwise value choice questions. For now, the important result is that 1,063 people, or 78.6 percent of the total respondents, gave fully transitive choices. From this result we can conclude that the vast majority of Americans do distinguish among salient values.

Of course, there remains a nontrivial subset—about one-fifth—of the respondents with intransitivities among their choices. It is important to emphasize that this result does not necessarily signal inconsistent or irrational behavior; instead, it may simply mean that these people regard some of the values as equally important for American society. But are certain subsets of values particularly difficult to distinguish? Table 8-1 shows the percentages of tied scores for each pair of values. Overall, there is very little variation across the pairs: the percentages of ties range from 7.62 percent to 11.61 percent. The only systematic pattern in the table (and it is a fairly weak tendency) seems to be that social order is involved in fewer ties than any of the other three values. Closer inspection of the specific choices reveals that social order is generally considered to be less important than the others. Among the remaining pairs, just about one-tenth of the respondents fail to give clear rankings on each comparison.

Another relevant question is whether there are particular kinds of people who manifest an inability to rank-order the values. Here, previous research suggests two distinct possibilities. First, Feldman and Zaller (1992) argue that liberals should have more difficulty than moderates or conservatives in reconciling their feelings toward the full spectrum of values inherent in American political culture. Second, many studies have shown that political sophistication affects the clarity and consistency of individual political orientations; this might also be the case with respect to value choices. Tables 8-2 and 8-3 present the data for testing these two hypotheses.

The information in Table 8-2 shows that liberals are only slightly more likely than conservatives to exhibit tied value rankings. And both of these self-identified ideological groups are more likely to do so than are moderates. However, none of these differences are statistically significant. Thus, it is reasonable to conclude that personal ideology is unrelated to the presence or absence of individual value hierarchies.

Table 8-3 shows the proportion of respondents with tied value rankings, broken down by education level. Here, there is a clear pattern: As years of schooling increase, the proportion of tied rankings decrease. The difference is statistically significant, and quite sizable

Table 8-1 Tied Importance Scores for Each Pair of Values (in percent)

	Liberty	Equality	Economic security
Equality	10.13		
Economic security	10.58	11.61	
Social order	8.06	7.62	8.06

Source: Multi-Investigator Study, 1994.

Note: Table entries show the percentage of MIS respondents with tied importance scores for each pair of values.

Table 8-2 Tied Versus Fully Ranked Value Importance Scores, by Ideological Self-Placement

	Liberal	Moderate	Conservative
Fully ranked importance scores	78.95%	83.86%	80.68%
Ties present in importance scores	21.05	16.14	19.32
Total	100.00	100.00	100.00
(N)	(228)	(316)	(316)

Source: Multi-Investigator Study, 1994.

Table 8-3 Tied Versus Fully Ranked Value Importance Scores, by Education Level

	Less than High School	High School Graduate	At Least Some College
Fully ranked importance scores	67.26%	71.53%	83.80%
Ties present in importance scores	32.74	28.47	16.20
Total	100.00	100.00	100.00
(N)	(113)	(418)	(821)

Source: Multi-Investigator Study, 1994.

by absolute standards: The proportion of college graduates with tied value rankings is only about half that of people who did not graduate from high school (16.20 percent versus 32.74 percent, respectively). Education definitely affects individual abilities to differentiate the values.

The results presented in this section are important for several reasons. First, the fully ranked value importance ratings manifested by the vast majority of the MIS respondents verify that value hierarchies do exist on a widespread basis within the mass public. Despite all of the attention that value structures have been accorded in the previous research literature in several academic disciplines, this rather fundamental point has, apparently, never been tested empirically. Instead, previous studies of value hierarchies have relied upon small, nonrandom samples and simply assumed that everyone is capable of ordering their personal beliefs about different values.

Second, these findings suggest that value ambivalence is not a serious problem for most citizens. Once again, the MIS respondents have little trouble distinguishing the values that they consider to be more, or less, important; this would certainly not be the case if people experienced conflicted feelings about these values. So the empirical results raise some questions about the relevance of theories that posit value conflict as a fundamental influence on subsequent attitudes and behavior.

Third, there do not seem to be particular value choices that are problematic for citizens. Various commentators and analysts have stressed the ongoing tension in American political culture between liberty and equality. But there is no such problem in the MIS data: respondents have no more difficulty distinguishing between these two values than between any of the other pairs. And this is as true for liberals as for anyone else. The ideological imbalance in value ambivalence that has been hypothesized by some researchers fails to materialize in these data. Self-professed liberals and conservatives are roughly equal in their willingness to designate certain values as more important than others.

Finally, these results indicate an alternative explanation for tied value importance ratings, apart from ambivalence: the inability to assess the importance of certain values probably stems from low levels of sophistication. Stated simply, education enables people to see the connections between different ideas. This distinction has been demonstrated repeatedly with respect to more abstract political orientations, such as issue attitudes and the use of ideological concepts. What is particularly striking about the present results is that similar relationships seem to exist in more immediate and personal phenomena like value preferences.

The Importance of Specific Values

The results described in the previous section establish that there is variability in public beliefs about value importance. But which values are considered more important than others? Table 8-4 provides information about the value scores. Recall that an individual's score

Table 8-4 Distribution of Importance Scores for Each Value

Importance Score	Value			
	Liberty	Equality	Economic Security	Social Order
0	22.71%	20.71%	15.38%	27.44%
1	25.52	32.10	25.89	28.33
2	23.89	34.17	33.36	26.18
3	27.88	13.02	25.37	18.05

Source: Multi-Investigator Study, 1994.

Note: Cell entries give the percentage of respondents with each importance rating for each value. The number of observations is 1,352.

for each value is the number of times that value is chosen over the other values. So, for example, the value in the bottom left cell of the table shows that 27.88 percent of the 1,352 MIS respondents specified that liberty was more important than either equality, economic security, or social order; the entry in the cell just above that reveals that 23.89 percent selected liberty over two of the remaining values, and so on.

The most striking feature of Table 8-4 is the wide variability in the scores for all four of the values. There are a few weak patterns among the cell entries. For example, equality received more middle (1 and 2) scores than scores of 0 or 3. And social order seems to be considered less important than the other values, since it received a higher proportion of low scores (0 or 1). But it is fair to say that each of the four values shows up in every possible position within the value hierarchies of a substantial number of people.

The dot plot shown in Figure 8-1 summarizes succinctly the distribution of importance ratings for each value. Specifically, the horizontal position of the point plotted within each row corresponds to the mean importance score for that value; the solid bar around each point represents a 95 percent confidence interval. From the figure, it can be seen that economic security is considered (on average) to be the most important value of the four, by a statistically significant margin. Liberty receives the second-highest mean importance rating and it, in turn, significantly exceeds the mean scores for the remaining two values. Equality has a higher mean than social order, but the confidence intervals overlap, so this difference may simply be due to sampling error.

There are several interesting—and somewhat unexpected—points to be drawn from the information in Table 8-4 and Figure 8-1. The American ethos is based directly upon the philosophical principles drawn from capitalism and classical liberalism. Accordingly, one

Figure 8-1 Mean Importance Ratings for Each Value

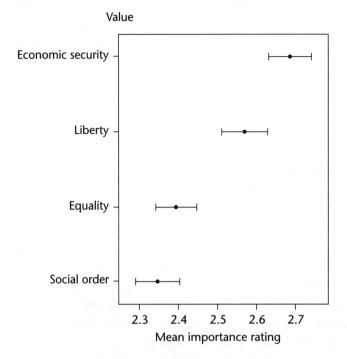

Source: Multi-Investigator Study, 1994.

Note: The plotted points correspond to the mean importance rating assigned to each of the values, on a scale ranging from a minimum of 0 to a maximum of 3. The horizontal error bars show 95 percent confidence intervals for each of the means. Nonoverlapping confidence intervals imply that the means are reliably different from each other; that is, their difference is probably *not* merely due to sampling error.

would expect liberty and equality to rise above the other values in popular esteem. But, as we have just seen, they do not. Instead, economic security is placed higher in the average value hierarchy than any other value. This is particularly surprising, given that the 1994 MIS was carried out during a time of relative prosperity—precisely when people should be least worried about their own financial well-being.

The American public does seem to exhibit a fairly clear ordering of the four values. They range from economic security as most important, through liberty and equality, down to social order as least important. But this ranking of values must be qualified by the previously noted fact that there is wide variability in the rankings from one person to the next. Therefore, it would not be appropriate to assert that there is a broad consensus about the relative salience of these four values in American society. Apparently, value pluralism exists at the aggregate level, even though individuals are generally capable of fully sorting out their own feelings about the personal importance of each value.

There is some noticeable variability in the value importance ratings across different groups within American society. Table 8-5 shows the mean scores for the values, broken down by several demographic and political characteristics. Touching briefly on some of the salient features in the table: white MIS respondents consider liberty to be most important (although economic security is a close second), while African Americans are far more attentive to both equality and economic security. Gender differences—consistent with some common stereotypes—also emerge, with males rating both liberty and economic security significantly higher than females. Women, like African Americans, place a greater emphasis on equality. Education and family income show similar relationships to value hierarchies: as either of these increases, liberty and social order are rated more important while equality and economic security become less important.

Political orientations correspond to value preferences as well. Republicans and conservatives lean toward liberty, and Democrats and liberals stress equality. Interestingly, Republicans and Democrats differ on economic security (the latter rate it higher than the former), but they are nearly identical in their ratings of social order. Conservatives place social order higher than liberals do, and they rank social order comparably to economic security.

These group-based differences in value priorities are all fairly predictable. In fact, they largely confirm common stereotypes about social and political differences within American society. But these empirical patterns are important for more than intrinsic reasons. The fact that the expected relationships actually do appear in the data attests to the validity of the value rankings.

Value Choices and Issue Attitudes

A great deal of the theoretical importance of personal values lies in their impact on subsequent aspects of human behavior. Presumably, values underlie an individual's reactions to the world by helping to define what is "good" and what is "bad" in the external environment. In this capacity, values provide a potential structuring mechanism for citizens' political orientations. Because values can be understood by everyone, they could be employed as a general evaluative standard for reactions to issues. Furthermore, political rhetoric about issues is almost always phrased in terms of values. Thus, individual citizens do not need to make the connection between issues and values on their own; instead, it is often done for them by public figures and opinion leaders. In this section, we will examine the effect of value preferences—along with symbolic orientations, different issue frames, and several

Table 8-5 Mean Value Importance Ratings, by Demographic and Political Characteristics

	Value			
	Liberty	Equality	Economic Security	Social Order
Race				
White (1,118)	2.67	2.34	2.65	2.34
African American (129)	1.94	2.83	2.94	2.30
Gender				
Male (647)	2.73	2.30	2.55	2.42
Female (705)	2.42	2.48	2.81	2.28
Education				
Less than high school (113)	2.44	2.53	2.93	2.10
High school graduate (418)	2.54	2.40	2.84	2.23
At least some college (821)	2.60	2.38	2.58	2.44
Family income				
Less than $30,000 (478)	2.47	2.45	2.77	2.31
$30,000–$49,999 (363)	2.60	2.41	2.69	2.30
More than $50,000 (466)	2.67	2.31	2.60	2.42
Party identification				
Democratic (622)	2.38	2.57	2.80	2.50
Independent (125)	2.58	2.50	2.68	2.24
Republican (576)	2.78	2.17	2.57	2.48
Ideological self-placement				
Liberal (228)	2.50	2.64	2.57	2.30
Moderate (316)	2.69	2.33	2.61	2.37
Conservative (352)	2.81	2.15	2.58	2.47

Source: Multi-Investigator Study, 1994.

Note: Cell entries give mean value importance scores. Figures in parentheses after row labels are numbers of observations.

background characteristics—on citizens' attitudes concerning a prominent political issue: government spending.

Public Attitudes Toward Government Spending

Stated simply, government spending is an important political issue. It is a constant feature of the major party platforms; candidates for public office routinely address spending concerns in their campaign rhetoric; and partisan or ideological debates over the proper allocation of governmental revenues often occupy a central position on the public agenda. More generally, questions about the government's ability and/or willingness to fund programs cut to the heart of the basic distinction between liberal and conservative ideologies (Jacoby 2000). Government spending also seems to lie at the core of predominant trends in macro-level public opinion—the characteristic that has come to be known as the public mood (Jacoby 1994; Stimson 1999). Thus, the political prominence and substantive importance of government spending make it important to understand public opinion on this issue.

The dependent variable in this analysis consists of a two-item scale. At an early point in the MIS interview schedule, respondents were asked the following question:

Some people think that it is necessary to decrease government spending, even though it would mean cutting back on services. Other people think that it is necessary to increase government spending in order to provide more services. If you had to choose, do you think government spending on services should be decreased or increased?

Follow-up questions asked how much spending should be decreased/increased, and the resultant responses are combined to form a five-point scale, with successive integer scores ranging from 1 for "spending should be increased a great deal" through 5 for "spending should be decreased a great deal."

At a later point in the interview schedule, respondents were asked another spending question (with follow-ups), similar but not exactly identical to the first. In this case, the targets of government spending were specified more explicitly in the first sentence of the question. Three different versions were presented to randomly determined subsets of respondents: the first mentions "social services for the needy," the second mentions "social services for minority groups," and the third mentions "spending on crime, the environment, and public education."[4] Regardless of question version, the coding scheme for responses is identical to that used on the first spending question.

Each person's responses to the two spending items are combined to form a single index. The reliability of this summary variable (Cronbach's alpha) is an acceptable, but not overwhelming, 0.59. Undoubtedly this rather low value reflects the variation in question wording across the two items. As we will see, this wording difference can be incorporated into the regression model. So we will regard this two-item index as a measure of individual attitudes toward government spending.

Independent Variables

The independent variables are divided into four substantively distinct subsets. The first subset is composed of value choices, which are measured by the signed difference in the importance rating scores assigned to the values *liberty* and *equality*. The resultant variable ranges from -3 (for a person who rates equality more important than, and liberty less important than, all other values) to $+3$ (for a person who rates liberty more important than, and equality less important than, all other values). A value of 0 indicates identical scores for the two values and, therefore, the absence of an unambiguous ranking across them.

This measurement strategy does not take into account individual preferences with respect to the other values, economic security and social order. But the approach is justifiable for several reasons. On the one hand, liberty and equality are considered the central components of political ideologies in general (Rokeach 1973) and American political culture in particular (McClosky and Zaller 1984). On the other hand, feelings about economic security and social order have no impact on spending attitudes, once liberty and equality are taken into account. So, there are both theoretical and empirical justifications for omitting the two values from this portion of the study.

The second subset of independent variables consists of two symbolic predispositions: party identification and ideological self-placement. A long line of previous research shows that these variables have strong, pervasive effects on the formation of issue attitudes (Sears 1993). Therefore, they provide a useful standard of comparison for the magnitude of influence that personal value preferences may have on attitudes toward government spending. Here, party identification and ideology are both measured using the standard seven-point scales, coded so that larger values indicate more Republican identifications and conservative self-placements, respectively.

The third subset of variables consists of two dummy variables that take into account the question-wording manipulation in the dependent variable. The first is coded 1 for those respondents who were presented with the "services for the needy" version of the second spending item, and 0 for everyone else. The second dummy variable identifies respondents who received the "services for minority groups" form of the question. Respondents who were asked about spending on "crime, the environment, and public education" were left as the reference category (that is, they were coded 0 on both dummy variables). Note that these dummy variables effectively provide a test of the effects of issue framing (different presentations of a policy controversy correspond to systematic variations in public reaction toward that issue) in public opinion toward government spending.

The fourth group is made up of several socioeconomic variables that represent background influences: family income (in thousands of dollars), race (a dummy variable for African Americans), gender (a dummy variable for females), and education (two dummy variables for fewer than twelve years of schooling and at least some college, respectively). These variables are included primarily as controls, to improve the overall model specification. Therefore, they are probably of somewhat less interest than the other variables, at least for present purposes. Instead, the more important question is whether values join the other, more explicitly political, factors in shaping citizens' responses to questions of public policy.

Influences on Attitudes Toward Spending

Table 8-6 shows the ordinary least squares (OLS) coefficient estimates from a regression analysis in which the four sets of independent variables are used to predict individual attitudes toward government spending. The equation's fit is quite good for public opinion data, with an R^2 of .393. Most of the coefficients are statistically different from 0, and the separate variables' effects all make sense in substantive terms.

The most important result here is the positive coefficient for the variable measuring value choices. Given the coding of the variables, this shows that people who believe liberty is more important than equality are also more likely to favor reductions in government spending. Conversely, those who value an egalitarian society apparently recognize the relevance of government spending and services for achieving this objective.

Among the other independent variables in Table 8-6, party identification and ideology exhibit their typical strong effects on issue attitudes. Precisely as expected, Democrats and liberals favor increased spending and services, while Republicans and conservatives prefer decreases.

The empirical results also reveal some fairly substantial issue framing effects. The significant coefficients on the question wording variables indicate that people who were asked about spending for the needy or for minority groups were less supportive than those who were asked about other policy areas. This finding confirms other research, which demonstrates that public reactions to government spending are strongly affected by the specified targets of that spending (Eismeier 1982; Sanders 1988; Jacoby 2000).

Among the background variables, two have significant effects while two others do not. African Americans are more likely to favor increases in government spending and services, while people with higher family incomes are more opposed. In contrast, the coefficients for gender and education fail to achieve statistical significance. All in all, the regression results suggest that citizens' spending preferences are more a function of political loyalties and personal value orientations than of position within the social structure. This general conclusion is quite consistent with the vast literature on the symbolic sources of political conflict within American public opinion.

Value preferences clearly do affect public opinion toward government spending. And the

Table 8-6 Influences on Attitudes Toward Government Spending

	OLS Regression Coefficient	Standard Error
Values		
Differential importance of liberty and equality	0.114*	0.019
Symbolic predispositions		
Party identification	0.157*	0.018
Ideological self-placement	0.120*	0.017
Issue frame		
Spending on services for the needy	0.518*	0.075
Spending on services for minority groups	0.601*	0.073
Sociodemographic factors		
Family income	0.003*	0.001
African American	−0.455*	0.062
Female	−0.055	0.062
Less than 12 years of education	0.183	0.152
More than 12 years of education	0.054	0.076
Intercept	1.626	
R^2	0.393	

Source: Multi-Investigator Study, 1994.

Note: * = Coefficient is statistically different from zero at the 0.05 level.

magnitude of this effect is sizable: the coefficient for liberty–equality importance ratings is only slightly smaller than those for party identification and liberal–conservative ideology—the two variables with the strongest, most consistent impact on mass attitudes. Apparently citizens can translate their personal feelings about core values into stands on matters of public policy. This finding is even more significant because people make the connection entirely on their own; the values in question—liberty and equality—were not mentioned in the question about government spending. These results constitute strong evidence that values should be regarded as a prominent influence on American public opinion.

Another Look at Value Ambivalence

Before concluding the analysis, let us return briefly to a topic that was discussed earlier—value ambivalence. The reason for doing so is that ambivalent feelings may affect not only choices among the values themselves but also the relationship between value choices and issue attitudes. For example, the theory of value pluralism asserts that conflicts among core values should lead to more complex forms of reasoning (Tetlock 1986); in turn, complex reasoning should inhibit a person's ability to express his or her policy stands in a single response to an issue question on a public opinion survey. Similarly, Feldman and Zaller (1992) argue that liberals experience value conflict between their feelings about individual liberty and equality; the conflict makes it more difficult for them to translate their general ideological stance into a specific position on issues that involve these concerns—like government spending. Alvarez and Brehm (1998) provide a more general statement of this kind of effect. According to their analyses, ambivalent feelings about values have an adverse effect on the degree to which people express crystallized, consistent feelings about issues, because a number of conflicting considerations come more readily to mind when people formulate their own responses to public policy controversies.

All of the preceding hypotheses can be tested in the regression model predicting attitudes toward government spending. However, the relevant tests involve the *residuals* from the equation rather than the coefficients associated with the separate independent variables. Residuals are the difference between the value for each respondent predicted from the regression equation and the actual observed response of that individual. To the extent that value ambivalence exerts the expected effects on the development of government spending attitudes, we should find that the equation's fit to the data is significantly worse among self-identified liberals and among those people who believe that potentially conflicting values are equally important. This lack of fit would be manifested empirically by larger residual variances for these subsets of the MIS respondents.

Table 8-7 presents the relevant information, divided into three separate comparisons. First, the residual variance for liberals is, in fact, significantly larger than that calculated for moderates and conservatives. This result is consistent with Feldman and Zaller's hypothesis about value ambivalence. Second, the table also compares the residual variances for those who rated liberty and equality equally important and those who gave them different ranks in their personal value hierarchies. Here, the difference not only fails to achieve statistical significance (in a one-sided test); it actually goes in the wrong direction. Contrary to the value ambivalence hypothesis, the residual variance for the people who assign identical importance scores to liberty and equality is *smaller* than the variance for those who rated them differently! Finally, Table 8-7 also compares the residual variances for people who gave fully ranked importance ratings across the complete set of four values and for people who had intransitive importance ratings (there were ties among the four importance scores). The difference between the residual variances is very small, and the ratio of the two is definitely not significantly greater than 1.

Taken together, the information presented in Table 8-7 provides only very meager sup-

Table 8-7 Assessing Value Ambivalence by Comparing Residual Variances Across Subgroups of MIS Survey Respondents

Subgroup	Variance of OLS Residuals	F Statistic (ratio of variances)	Observed Probability of F Statistic
Comparison 1			
Liberals	0.909		
		1.235	0.025
Moderates and conservatives	0.736		
Comparison 2			
Tied importance scores for liberty and equality	0.688		
		0.871	0.769
Different importance scores for liberty and equality	0.790		
Comparison 3			
Intransitive value importance scores	0.780		
		1.005	0.474
Fully ranked value importance scores	0.776		

Source: Regression analysis performed on data from the 1994 Multi-Investigator Study.

Note: The first column of the table gives the within-subgroup variances of the OLS residuals from the regression reported in Table 8-6. The second column gives the ratio of the two variances in each comparison. This ratio is the test statistic for a homogeneity of variances test. The third column gives the observed probability value from this test. Entries smaller than 0.05 indicate that the ratio of variances is significantly larger than 1 (at the 0.05 level of significance).

port for the value ambivalence hypothesis, or for the more general idea that internal value conflict fosters complexity in subsequent political orientations. There is an ideological asymmetry in the crystallization of attitudes toward government spending, just as Feldman and Zaller would predict. But the overall size of this effect is fairly small (the correlation between the ideology variable and size of the squared residual from the regression equation is only −.097).[5] And it is difficult to link this liberal–conservative imbalance specifically to value conflict because the expected patterns in the residual variances do not appear when we focus our attention on those people who are unable to completely differentiate their feelings about the importance of the respective values. The earlier results presented in this chapter showed that value ambivalence is not very widespread within the mass public. The analyses in this section demonstrate that, to the extent ambivalence *does* exist, it has little impact on citizens' abilities to formulate their own stands on public policy issues like the question of government spending.

Conclusions

This study makes several contributions regarding the importance of values for understanding American public opinion. First, it demonstrates that people do possess meaningful value hierarchies. There appears to be a great deal of coherence and consistency in public views about what is good and bad in everyday life and society. This finding is definitely not a foregone conclusion. The set of four values presented to the MIS survey respondents were selected precisely because of their prominence in American political culture. Therefore, many people could well find it impossible to make consistent choices between them. The easy rationalization for such behavior would be to say that all of the values are equally important.

And yet, the vast majority of the respondents made consistently transitive judgments about the values' relative importance for American society. This consistency would not exist if value conflict or ambivalence were widespread throughout the mass public. Instead, most citizens do seem to recognize that some values are more important than others, and they make the requisite choices between them.

Second, the results from this study show that there is extremely wide variability from one person to the next in judgments about value importance. From one perspective, this is not particularly surprising. The heterogeneity of the American public implies that people will experience vastly different socialization experiences and patterns of social interaction. It would be incredible if this did *not* have some noticeable effect on individuals' feelings about desirable and undesirable states of existence—that is, about values.

But, from another perspective, the variation in value preferences seems to be somewhat at odds with the studies that emphasize the lasting primacy of freedom and equality in American political culture. Perhaps elites and intellectuals value freedom and equality above other values, but such conclusions do not reflect the feelings of ordinary citizens. Their judgments contain a mixture of lofty principles (for example, liberty is often ranked quite highly) and more immediate concerns (for example, economic security is often the most important value). It seems reasonable to assert that values are neither strictly personal nor strictly social concerns. Instead, they stand at the juncture between the individual and the society within which he or she exists.

Third, this study shows that individuals' general value choices have direct relevance for understanding their issue attitudes. As we have seen, personal feelings about liberty and equality are strongly related to reactions toward government spending. This basic finding is particularly striking because it holds up across several specific presentations of the spending issue, none of which explicitly mentions either of these two values. In this sense, values function in a manner similar to a variety of other symbolic predispositions or evaluative criteria such as party identification and liberal–conservative ideology. However, an important and fundamental distinction remains, because the last two orientations possess much more overt political content than do the four values under investigation in this study. So values represent a fundamental step in the translation from the nonpolitical aspects of human existence to the explicitly political domain of policy issues.

In conclusion, the analysis presented in this chapter provides firm support for a number of ideas that have been widely held, but seldom tested in previous research efforts—for example, the existence of value hierarchies and the effects of value preferences on issue attitudes. However, some of the analytic results present challenges to previous work—particularly, the extreme variability in value preferences and the apparent absence of value conflict within individuals. So I believe that this study represents only an initial effort to tackle a potentially vast subject area. It would be useful to extend this kind of analysis to other prominent values in American society (such as racial equality, justice, free expression, and so on). At the same time, it is important to understand the perceptual structures that undergird value choices (for example, do people view the contrast between, say, liberty and equality in similar ways even though they may express different feelings about which one is more important?). It would also be useful to determine whether values influence attitudes on other kinds of political issues; for example, those that are relatively distant from everyday life and experience for most citizens (foreign affairs) or those that involve fundamental questions about living conditions (protection from violence and criminal activity), lifestyles (legal protections for gays and lesbians), or moral concerns (abortion rights). Thus, there is much that remains to be done in unraveling the viability of personal value choices as an organizing principle for individual political orientations and American public opinion more generally.

Notes

1. Milton Rokeach (1973) distinguishes between terminal values and instrumental values. The former correspond to the definition of values employed in this chapter. The latter refer to modes of conduct and behavior that are appropriate for achieving desirable terminal values.

2. The more common approach in the research literature on personal values simply has the subjects rank a (frequently sizable) set of values from most to least important. But the resultant rank-ordered list of values is transitive by construction; in other words, there is simply no way that intransitive choices could occur. Hence, the rank-ordering strategy cannot be used to test for the presence of value hierarchies.

3. Let us consider how beliefs might be translated into intransitive value choices. Assume that a person's "true" importance judgment about value A is represented as $I(A)$. Further, assume that this

person believes values A, B, and C to be equally important. Thus, $I(A) = I(B) = I(C)$ for this individual. Now, any person's overt response to the survey question about the relative importance of the two values is shown as $R(A, B)$. And if $I(A) > I(B)$ then $R(A, B) = A$; that is, if the person judges A to be more important than B, then he or she will select A when given the choice between them. But, as explained in the text, the question format does not allow for tied values. Hence, even if $I(A) = I(B)$, the person must still choose either A or B (or refuse to answer the question at all). But since he or she really feels the values are equally important, the empirical response is just "error," which is conceptualized as a random answer—in effect, the result of a mental coin flip. Over the long run, if the person were repeatedly asked about A versus B, then he or she should select each one about an equal number of times. But still, on any single choice, one of these values is chosen over the other. Intransitivity can occur when this error response exists across three value pairs: Say, on A versus B, the error moves the person toward A; on B versus C, the person responds B (again, because of the random fluctuation, and not because of an innate preference); then finally, on A versus C, a third "flip" of the mental coin causes the person to answer C. Combining these three choices produces the intransitivity.

4. The first variant of the second spending question was worded as follows: "Some people feel that it is necessary to decrease government spending, even if it would mean cutting back on services like food stamps, Medicaid, and other forms of assistance for the needy. Other people feel that it is necessary to increase government spending in order to provide more of these services. If you had to choose, do you think government spending on services like food stamps, Medicaid, and assistance for the needy should be decreased or increased?" The second variant was "Some people feel that it is necessary to decrease government spending, even if it would mean cutting back on services like food stamps, Medicaid, and other forms of assistance for minority groups. Other people feel that it is necessary to increase government spending in order to provide more of these services. If you had to choose, do you think government spending on services like food stamps, Medicaid, and assistance for minority groups should be decreased or increased?" The third variant was "Some people feel that it is necessary to decrease government spending, even if it would mean cutting back on programs like fighting crime, protecting the environment, and public education. Other people feel that it is necessary to increase government spending in order to provide more of these services. If you had to choose, do you think government spending on services like fighting crime, protecting the environment, and public education should be decreased or increased?" There was also another question-wording experiment built into this series of items. A randomly selected half of the sample was given the questions worded as shown here. For the other half of the sample, the locations of the words *decreased* and *increased* were switched around in the question. This manipulation produced no significant differences in the response distributions.

5. Ideological self-placement is correlated with the squared residual because the correlation with the raw residual is 0, by definition (as a byproduct of the OLS regression).

9 Ideological Realignment and U.S. Congressional Elections

Alan I. Abramowitz and Kyle L. Saunders

For fifty years following the Great Depression and the New Deal, the Democratic Party enjoyed a major electoral advantage over the Republican Party because far more Americans identified with the Democratic Party than with the Republican Party. According to data from the National Election Studies, between 1952 and 1980 an average of 54 percent of American adults identified with the Democratic Party (including independents who leaned Democratic), while only 34 percent, on average, identified with the Republican Party (Wayne 1996, 73).

Although the GOP was able to win a majority of presidential elections from the end of World War II through the 1980s because of the greater popular appeal of its candidates and issue positions, the Democrats' edge in party identification helped them to maintain control of the House of Representatives and the Senate throughout most of this period: between 1946 and 1994, Republicans controlled the Senate for only twelve years and the House for only four years. After 1980, however, the Democratic Party's advantage in voter identification began to shrink. Despite the Democrats' victory in the 1992 presidential election, the difference between the percentage of Democratic and Republican identifiers in the electorate declined from nineteen points in 1980 to ten points in 1992.

In the 1994 midterm election, Republicans shocked almost all of the pundits and prognosticators by taking control of both the House and the Senate. Two years later, voters proved that the results of the 1994 elections had not been a fluke by reelecting Republican majorities to the House and Senate for the first time since before the New Deal. Despite Bill Clinton's decisive victory in the presidential election, Republicans lost only nine seats in the House of Representatives and gained two seats in the Senate. The results of the 1994 and 1996 elections raised important questions for students of American politics: Was the era of Democratic domination of Congress over and, if so, why did it end?

Ideological Polarization and Party Realignment

We believe that the Republican takeover of Congress in 1994 and the subsequent GOP victories in the 1996, 1998, and 2000 congressional elections reflected a long-term shift in the relative strength and bases of support of the two major parties. This shift in the party loyalties of the electorate was, in turn, based on the increased ideological polarization of the Democratic and Republican Parties during the Reagan and Clinton eras. Clearer differences between the parties' ideological positions made it easier for citizens to choose a party identification based on their policy preferences. The result, according to our theory, was a secular realignment of party loyalties along ideological lines that reduced the Democratic advantage in voter identification and strengthened the connection between party identification and ideology (Abramowitz and Saunders 1998).

The election of Ronald Reagan, at the time the most prominent leader of the American conservative movement, resulted in a marked increase in ideological polarization among party leaders and activists in the United States (Stone, Rapoport, and Abramowitz 1990). Reagan's program of tax cuts, increased military expenditures, and reductions in domestic social programs divided the nation along ideological lines and produced the highest levels of party unity in Congress in decades. Liberal Republicans and conservative Democrats found themselves under increasing pressure to follow the party line on key votes. Some went along with their party's leadership at the risk of losing support in their own constituencies. Others switched parties or retired. The result was an increasingly liberal Democratic Party and an increasingly conservative Republican Party (Rohde 1991).

The results of the 1992 elections accelerated the movement toward ideological polarization. Although he campaigned as a "new Democrat" rather than a traditional liberal, Bill Clinton moved quickly to reward liberal interest groups that had supported his candidacy by announcing policies such as permitting gays and lesbians to serve in the military and ending the ban on abortion counseling in federally funded health care clinics. The president further antagonized conservatives with his proposals to raise taxes on middle- and upper-income Americans and dramatically expand the role of the federal government in providing health insurance (Quirk and Hinchliffe 1996).

The actions of the Republican Party in the House of Representatives may have contributed even more to ideological polarization in the 1990s than the president's policies. At the beginning of the 103d Congress (1993–1995), House Republicans chose Rep. Newt Gingrich of Georgia as their minority whip. The election of Gingrich as the minority whip and heir apparent to Minority Leader Robert Michel, R-Ill., reflected a long-term shift in the distribution of power within the House GOP. The older, relatively moderate wing of the party, based in the Midwest and the Northeast, and represented by pragmatic leaders such as Michel, was gradually losing influence to a younger, more conservative wing, based in the South, and represented by leaders such as Gingrich who preferred confrontation to accommodation in dealing with the Democrats (Wilcox 1995).

The 1994 election campaign was a direct result of the Republican leadership changes in the 103d Congress. The "Contract with America," a compendium of conservative issue positions chosen for maximum public appeal, was the brainchild of Newt Gingrich and Richard Armey, R-Texas, another hard-line conservative and Gingrich's top lieutenant. They decided what issues to include in the contract and they persuaded the overwhelming majority of Republican House candidates to publicly endorse its contents. The result was one of the most unified and ideological campaigns in the history of U.S. midterm elections: Republican candidates across the country ran as members of a party team committed to enacting a broad legislative program (Wilcox 1995).

The Republican takeover of the Senate and House in the 1994 election and the subsequent ascension of Newt Gingrich to the House speakership marked the beginning of an era of intense partisan and ideological conflict in American politics. Republican congressional leaders were determined to advance their conservative agenda; the president and his Democratic allies in Congress were just as determined to resist that agenda. With few moderates left on either side of the aisle, bipartisan compromise became much more difficult than it had been during earlier periods of divided party control. For the next six years, President Clinton and the GOP Congress would engage in a continuous battle for control over national policy—a battle that led, first, to the shutdown of the federal government during late 1995 and, eventually, to the impeachment and trial of the president during 1998–1999.

James L. Sundquist has argued that one of the conditions for a party realignment is the emergence of party leaders who take sharply contrasting positions on the realigning issue (Sundquist 1983, chap. 3). In order to choose a party based on issue positions, voters must recognize the differences between the parties' positions. We believe that the increased ideological polarization of Democratic and Republican party leaders and activists since 1980, and especially since 1992, has made it easier for voters to recognize the differences between the parties' positions and to choose a party based on its proximity to their own ideological position.

Congressional Elections in the 1990s

If our theory of ideological realignment is correct, the results should have been evident in voting patterns in U.S. congressional elections during the 1990s. In this chapter, therefore, we will examine the impact of ideological realignment on voting in U.S. congressional elections. Specifically, we will explore how this realignment affected the size and ideological composition of coalitions supporting Democratic and Republican incumbents in U.S. Senate and House elections during the 1990s.

The advantage of incumbency in U.S. House and Senate elections has received extensive treatment in the literature on voting behavior. Political scientists have devoted considerable time and effort to measuring the size of this advantage and to explaining its sources (Jacobson 2001, 21–40). Based on this literature, it is clear that the advantage of incumbency has two principal components, one personal and one political.

The personal advantage of incumbency is based on the electorate's perceptions and evaluations of the congressional candidates themselves—the incumbents and their challengers. It is this aspect of the incumbency advantage that has received the most attention in the scholarly literature (Jacobson 2001, chap. 3). Numerous studies have documented the fact that Senate and, especially, House incumbents are generally much better known than their challengers. In part, this disparity reflects the ability of most incumbents to vastly outspend their challengers during the campaign. In addition, incumbents in both chambers have numerous resources that they can use to cultivate their constituencies between elections and build a favorable reputation among the public (Mayhew 1974). As a result, most incumbents are able to add a personal vote to their party's base vote by attracting support from independents and even opposing partisans (Erikson 1971; Ferejohn 1977; Mann 1977; Mann and Wolfinger 1980; Abramowitz 1980).

In addition to the personal vote, however, most House and many Senate incumbents enjoy an additional advantage based on the political composition of the electorate in their constituency. Regardless of the activities of the incumbent or the challenger, the voters in most House districts and many states are already inclined to favor the party of the incumbent due to their partisan loyalties and ideological orientations. Most Democratic incumbents represent relatively liberal constituencies dominated by Democratic identifiers while most Republican incumbents represent relatively conservative constituencies dominated by Republican identifiers. This phenomenon is similar to Fenno's concept of the "reelection constituency," the voters whose support an incumbent expects to receive even in a difficult reelection battle against a strong challenger (Fenno 1978). It is this political component of the incumbency advantage that should be affected by the realignment of the electorate since 1980.

We are interested in how ideological realignment has affected voters' decision making in House and Senate elections and how changes in voters' decision making have in turn affected the size and composition of the base or normal vote for Democratic and Republican incumbents in the House and Senate. The normal vote, here, refers to the vote that a Democratic or Republican incumbent can expect to receive based only on the partisan and ideological composition of his or her constituency, with the personal vote removed. Specifically, we will test three hypotheses about the consequences of ideological realignment for House and Senate elections.

1. As a result of the increased ideological polarization of the parties and growing public awareness of ideological differences between the parties, we expect to find an in-

crease in the influence of ideology on voters' decision making in House and Senate elections.

2. We expect to observe an increase in the size of the base vote for Republican incumbents and a decrease in the size of the base vote for Democratic incumbents since 1990 in both House and Senate elections.

3. We expect to observe a shift in the partisan and ideological composition of the base vote for Republican incumbents in both the House and Senate. The base vote for Republican incumbents should become increasingly Republican in party identification and conservative in ideology. As a result of both of these trends, we expect Republican incumbents in the 1990s to be much less dependent on support from moderate and independent voters than Republican incumbents in the 1980s and earlier.

Data and Methodology

The data used in this study come from the cumulative file of the National Election Studies. We will analyze data from the 1972–1996 National Election Studies. By combining data from all of the elections in each decade (1972–1980, 1982–1990, and 1992–1996), we should have enough cases to identify major shifts in the behavior of the electorate over time. We begin in 1972 because it is the first election that includes our measure of ideology—the 7-point liberal–conservative scale.

The concept of a base or normal vote in this study is somewhat different from that developed by Philip Converse (1966) and subsequently used by many other election scholars (Kabaker 1969; Miller 1979; Petrocik 1989). For Converse, the normal vote for a party was based on the distribution of party identification in the electorate, the turnout proclivities of the various partisan subgroups, and the typical rates of loyalty and defection among these subgroups. However, we will modify Converse's concept in two respects. First, we take voter turnout as a given and look only at the behavior of actual voters. Second, and more important, we add an additional variable to party identification in calculating the normal vote: ideological identification. We believe that since 1980, as a consequence of ideological realignment, ideology has become a fundamental determinant of voters' decision making in American elections. Therefore, in calculating the normal vote we must take into account the distribution of ideological identification in the electorate along with the distribution of party identification.

To calculate the normal vote, we begin by dividing the electorate into nine subgroups, combining party identification and ideological identification. The nine subgroups are liberal Democrats, moderate Democrats, conservative Democrats, liberal independents, moderate independents, conservative independents, liberal Republicans, moderate Republicans, and conservative Republicans. To measure the normal voting tendency of each subgroup in the 1970s, 1980s, and 1990s, we remove the influence of incumbency on voters' decision making by weighting the subgroup samples for each decade to equalize the proportions of respondents in districts or states with Democratic and Republican incumbents. This step gives us an "incumbency free" measure of partisan voting for each subgroup in each decade. By multiplying the partisan voting tendency of each subgroup by its relative size and summing across the nine subgroups, we can calculate the normal or base vote for Republican or Democratic incumbents in each of our three decades.

Ideology in this chapter is measured simply by a respondent's position on the 7-point liberal–conservative identification scale. However, to avoid ending up with large quantities of missing data and to keep from overestimating the influence of ideological identification in relation to other explanatory variables, we assigned all respondents who did not place themselves on the 7-point scale to the middle position (4). We would have preferred to use a more sophisticated scale incorporating a variety of policy-based items to measure the ideological orientations of voters. Unfortunately, no such questions were available throughout the time period under study. Moreover, ideological self-identification has a consistently high correlation with a wide variety of policy-based items, and we feel confident that it provides a reasonably accurate gauge of voters' ideological orientations.

Results

Our previous research on ideological realignment in the U.S. electorate concluded that the increasing ideological polarization of the major parties during the Reagan and Clinton eras (Rohde 1991, King 1997) made it easier for voters to recognize the differences between the policy stands of the parties. This should allow voters to choose House and Senate candidates based on their own ideological preferences to a greater extent than in the past.

Table 9-1 shows the trends in the percentages of liberals, moderates, and conservatives voting for Republicans in House and Senate elections between 1972 and 1996. Over this time period, in House elections, we see that the percentage of liberals voting for Republican candidates fell from 25 percent to 20 percent, while the percentage of conservatives voting for Republican candidates rose from 58 percent to 70 percent. The correlation between ideology and House vote increased by over half, from .31 to .47, demonstrating a growing alignment of ideology and House voting over time.

The results for Senate elections form a similar picture. Over the same time period, we see a decrease, from 26 percent to 17 percent, in the percentage of liberals voting for Republican candidates along with an even larger increase, from 62 percent to 74 percent, in the percentage of conservatives voting Republican. As in House elections, the correlation between ideology and the vote increased by over half, from .33 to .54.

These results support our hypothesis that the increased ideological polarization of the

Table 9-1 Republican Votes for House of Representatives and
Senate by Ideology, 1972–1996 (in percent)

Ideology	House of Representatives		
	1972–1980	*1982–1990*	*1992–1996*
Liberal	25	22	20
Moderate	34	33	34
Conservative	58	60	70
Correlation	.31	.36	.47
(Number of cases)	(4,029)	(3,536)	(2,528)

Ideology	Senate		
	1972–1980	*1982–1990*	*1992–1996*
Liberal	26	24	17
Moderate	36	37	35
Conservative	62	65	74
Correlation	.33	.38	.54
(Number of cases)	(2,696)	(2,446)	(1,777)

Source: American National Election Studies, 1972–1996.

Note: The correlation coefficient (Kendall's tau-c) measures the strength of the relationship between ideology and the vote.

parties during the Reagan and post-Reagan eras has affected voting in House and Senate elections. To provide a more thorough test of our hypothesis, we conducted logistic regression analyses of House and Senate voting decisions over three different time periods, 1972–1980, 1982–1990, and 1992–1996, using party identification and incumbency as predictors, along with ideology. The results of the logistic regression analyses are shown in Table 9-2.

With regard to voting in House elections, we see that the effects of partisanship and incumbency show little change over time. However, the coefficient for ideology more than doubles in size between the 1970s and the 1990s. The results are even more striking for Senate elections. Again the effects of partisanship and incumbency show little change over time while we see a dramatic increase in the influence of ideology, with the coefficient almost tripling in size between the 1970s and the 1990s.

Table 9-2 Estimates for Three-Variable Model of Vote Choice in Senate and House Elections, 1972–1996

	House of Representatives		
	1972–1980	*1982–1990*	*1992–1996*
Independent Variable	*B (S.E.)*	*B (S.E.)*	*B (S.E.)*
Party identification	.614 (.024)	.618 (.024)	.627 (.028)
Ideology	.175 (.039)	.298 (.042)	.370 (.046)
Incumbency	.536 (.025)	.658 (.026)	.546 (.029)
Constant	−4.736 (.197)	−5.630 (.216)	−5.632 (.232)
Predicted correctly	77.8%	80.4%	80.4%
(Number of cases)	(3,741)	(3,899)	(3,125)

	Senate		
	1972–1980	*1982–1990*	*1992–1996*
Independent Variable	*B (S.E.)*	*B (S.E.)*	*B (S.E.)*
Party identification	.600 (.040)	.633 (.025)	.583 (.030)
Ideology	.158 (.065)	.265 (.042)	.459 (.053)
Incumbency	.253 (.045)	.388 (.026)	.233 (.033)
Constant	−3.682 (.324)	−4.935 (.221)	−5.010 (.267)
Predicted correctly	76.5%	77.3%	79.2%
(Number of cases)	(1,138)	(3,225)	(2,165)

Source: American National Election Studies, 1972–1996.

Note: *B* is the estimated logistic regression coefficient for each independent variable. *S.E.* is the estimated standard error for each coefficient. All of the coefficients are highly statistically significant ($p < .01$).

The results presented in Table 9-2 strongly support our hypothesis concerning the increased influence of ideology on voting in House and Senate elections. In the remainder of this chapter we will analyze the consequences of ideological realignment for electoral coalitions in House and Senate elections. Specifically, we are interested in how ideological realignment and the growing influence of ideology on voting in House and Senate elections have affected the size and composition of the normal vote for Republican and Democratic

Table 9-3 Partisan and Ideological Contributions to Normal Vote for House Republican Incumbents, 1972–1996

Group	1972–1980 Contribution	1982–1990 Contribution	1992–1996 Contribution	Change
Liberal Democrats	.152 × .101 = .015	.145 × .089 = .013	.155 × .118 = .018	+.003
Moderate Democrats	.203 × .162 = .033	.201 × .167 = .034	.201 × .118 = .024	−.009
Conservative Democrats	.239 × .053 = .013	.276 × .059 = .016	.236 × .049 = .012	−.001
Liberal Independents	.351 × .066 = .023	.346 × .046 = .016	.280 × .056 = .016	−.007
Moderate Independents	.458 × .159 = .073	.459 × .124 = .057	.497 × .126 = .063	−.010
Conservative Independents	.567 × .103 = .058	.569 × .088 = .050	.670 × .109 = .073	+.015
Liberal Republicans	.781 × .027 = .021	.694 × .028 = .019	.698 × .017 = .012	−.009
Moderate Republicans	.798 × .134 = .107	.737 × .129 = .095	.764 × .104 = .079	−.028
Conservative Republicans	.789 × .195 = .154	.829 × .270 = .224	.881 × .302 = .266	+.112
Total	.497	.524	.563	+.066

Source: American National Election Studies, 1972–1996.

Note: Contribution of each group to normal Republican vote = loyalty of group to Republican Party × size of group in the electorate. Entries shown are proportions.

incumbents in House and Senate elections. The normal vote in this analysis is the vote that the incumbent's party would expect to receive in the absence of any personal advantage of incumbency.

Tables 9-3 through 9-6 present our analyses of the partisan and ideological composition of the normal vote for incumbents of both parties in Senate and House elections over time. The contribution of each subgroup to the normal vote during a given time period is a function of two factors—the size of the group and the loyalty of its members to one party or the other. In Table 9-3, for example, we see that liberal Democrats comprised just over 10 percent (.101) of the voters in House districts represented by Republican incumbents between 1972 and 1980 and that the average Republican vote among this group was just over 15 per-

Table 9-4 Partisan and Ideological Contributions to Normal Vote for Senate Republican Incumbents, 1972–1996

Group	1972–1980 Contribution	1982–1990 Contribution	1992–1996 Contribution	Change
Liberal Democrats	.138 × .091 = .013	.126 × .109 = .014	.086 × .111 = .010	−.003
Moderate Democrats	.192 × .203 = .039	.170 × .229 = .039	.180 × .158 = .028	−.011
Conservative Democrats	.248 × .094 = .023	.269 × .079 = .021	.303 × .059 = .018	−.005
Liberal Independents	.331 × .079 = .026	.321 × .058 = .019	.246 × .064 = .016	−.010
Moderate Independents	.488 × .167 = .081	.457 × .126 = .058	.469 × .127 = .060	−.021
Conservative Independents	.620 × .118 = .073	.634 × .083 = .053	.691 × .111 = .077	+.004
Liberal Republicans	.773 × .015 = .012	.759 × .012 = .009	.621 × .016 = .010	−.002
Moderate Republicans	.773 × .085 = .066	.712 × .120 = .085	.726 × .100 = .073	+.007
Conservative Republicans	.818 × .148 = .121	.824 × .184 = .152	.877 × .253 = .222	+.101
Total	.454	.450	.514	+.060

Source: American National Election Studies, 1972–1996.

Note: Contribution of each group to normal Republican vote = loyalty of group to Republican Party × size of group in the electorate. Entries shown are proportions.

cent (.152). By multiplying these two proportions together, we find that the contribution of liberal Democrats to the normal Republican vote was .015.

The results presented in Table 9-3 show, as we hypothesized, that the normal vote for House Republican incumbents increased dramatically between the 1970s and the 1990s. Between 1972 and 1980, the normal Republican vote in House districts represented by Republican incumbents was just under 50 percent—after removing the personal vote, these districts actually leaned slightly toward the opposition party. By 1992–1996, however, the normal Republican vote had risen to over 56 percent.

The entire increase in the size of the normal Republican vote was a consequence of the increased size and loyalty of one subgroup of voters—conservative Republicans. During

Table 9-5 Partisan and Ideological Contributions to Normal Vote for House Democratic Incumbents, 1972–1996

Group	1972–1980 Contribution	1982–1990 Contribution	1992–1996 Contribution	Change
Liberal Democrats	.848 × .124 = .105	.855 × .136 = .116	.845 × .152 = .128	+.023
Moderate Democrats	.797 × .240 = .191	.799 × .260 = .208	.799 × .203 = .162	−.029
Conservative Democrats	.761 × .073 = .056	.724 × .086 = .062	.764 × .078 = .060	+.004
Liberal Independents	.649 × .057 = .037	.654 × .057 = .037	.720 × .061 = .044	+.007
Moderate Independents	.542 × .149 = .081	.541 × .136 = .074	.503 × .151 = .076	−.005
Conservative Independents	.433 × .101 = .044	.431 × .094 = .041	.330 × .098 = .032	−.012
Liberal Republicans	.219 × .012 = .003	.306 × .015 = .005	.302 × .008 = .002	−.001
Moderate Republicans	.202 × .092 = .019	.263 × .089 = .023	.236 × .073 = .017	−.002
Conservative Republicans	.211 × .151 = .032	.171 × .126 = .022	.119 × .176 = .021	−.011
Total	.568	.588	.542	−.026

Source: American National Election Studies, 1972–1996.

Note: Contribution of each group to normal Democratic vote = loyalty of group to Democratic Party × size of group in the electorate. Entries shown are proportions.

the 1970s, conservative Republicans made up less than 20 percent of the electorate in districts represented by GOP incumbents and gave an average of 79 percent of their votes to Republican candidates; by the 1990s, they made up more than 30 percent of the electorate in these districts and gave an average of 88 percent of their votes to Republican candidates. In the rest of the electorate, the normal Republican vote actually declined over time. As a result, the proportion of the normal Republican vote provided by conservative Republicans rose from 31 percent during the 1970s to 47 percent during the 1990s.

The results in Table 9-4 show very similar trends in Senate elections involving Republican incumbents. Once again, the size of the normal Republican vote rose substantially—from just over 45 percent during the 1970s to just over 51 percent during the 1990s—and

Table 9-6 Partisan and Ideological Contributions to Normal Vote for Senate Democratic Incumbents, 1972–1996

Group	1972–1980 Contribution	1982–1990 Contribution	1992–1996 Contribution	Change
Liberal Democrats	.862 × .128 = .110	.874 × .119 = .104	.914 × .136 = .124	+.014
Moderate Democrats	.808 × .229 = .185	.830 × .210 = .174	.820 × .199 = .163	−.022
Conservative Democrats	.752 × .066 = .050	.731 × .068 = .050	.697 × .058 = .040	−.010
Liberal Independents	.669 × .050 = .033	.679 × .048 = .033	.754 × .045 = .034	+.001
Moderate Independents	.512 × .180 = .092	.543 × .146 = .079	.531 × .128 = .068	−.024
Conservative Independents	.380 × .102 = .039	.366 × .102 = .037	.309 × .109 = .034	−.005
Liberal Republicans	.227 × .017 = .004	.241 × .019 = .005	.379 × .009 = .003	−.001
Moderate Republicans	.227 × .085 = .019	.288 × .107 = .031	.274 × .081 = .022	+.003
Conservative Republicans	.182 × .144 = .026	.176 × .181 = .032	.123 × .235 = .029	+.003
Total	.558	.545	.517	−.041

Source: American National Election Studies, 1972–1996.

Note: Contribution of each group to normal Democratic vote = loyalty of group to Democratic Party × size of group in the electorate. Entries shown are proportions.

once again, the increase was due entirely to the increased size and loyalty of the conservative Republican subgroup. Conservative Republicans provided 43 percent of the normal Republican vote in the 1990s, compared with only 27 percent in the 1970s.

While Republican incumbents benefited from an increase in the size of the normal Republican vote during the 1990s, Democratic incumbents experienced a decline in the size of the normal Democratic vote in their constituencies. The data in Tables 9-5 and 9-6 show that the normal Democratic vote in House districts represented by Democratic incumbents fell from almost 57 percent during the 1970s, and almost 59 percent during the 1980s, to just over 54 percent during the 1990s. Similarly, the normal Democratic vote in states represented by Democratic senators fell from almost 56 percent during the 1970s to just below 52 percent by the 1990s.

In contrast to the situation for Republican incumbents, the decline in the size of the normal Democratic vote was not attributable to a dramatic change in the contribution of any single subgroup of voters. Instead, the shrinkage of the normal Democratic vote was due largely to an increase in the size of the conservative Republican subgroup and a corresponding decrease in the size of the moderate independent and/or moderate Democratic subgroups. Despite the overall decline in the size of the normal Democratic vote during the 1990s, there was little change in the relative contributions of various partisan and ideological subgroups to the Democratic coalition. Liberal Democrats made up only a slightly larger component of the normal Democratic vote during the 1990s than during the 1970s.

Compared with the Republican electoral coalition, the Democratic electoral coalition remained quite ideologically diverse during the 1990s. Whereas conservatives provided over 62 percent of the normal Republican vote in House districts represented by GOP incumbents, liberals provided only 32 percent of the normal Democratic vote in House districts represented by Democratic incumbents. Similarly, conservatives provided almost 62 percent of the normal Republican vote in states represented by GOP senators while liberals provided only 31 percent of the normal Democratic vote in states represented by Democratic senators.

Discussion and Conclusions

The ideological realignment of the electorate and the growing salience of ideological differences between the parties have had important consequences for congressional elections in the 1990s. While the personal advantage of incumbency remains substantial, especially in House elections, Democratic and Republican identifiers are more clearly divided along ideological lines and ideology has a stronger direct influence on candidate preferences in House and Senate elections than in the past. As a result, there have been important changes in the size and composition of the normal vote in House and Senate elections involving Republican and Democratic incumbents.

The most obvious change affecting these elections is that Republican incumbents are more secure than in the past while Democratic incumbents are less secure. Despite the increased number of Republican seats in the House and Senate, seats that were formerly held by Democrats, the normal Republican vote is somewhat larger than it was during the 1970s and 1980s. At the same time, the normal Democratic vote has declined in the districts and states still represented by Democratic incumbents. These results suggest that despite the narrow Republican majorities in the House and Senate, it will not be easy for Democrats to regain control of either chamber.

In addition to the increased size of the normal Republican vote, there has also been a substantial change in the composition of that vote. Conservatives in general, and conservative Republicans in particular, comprise a much larger portion of the GOP base than in the past. As a result, Republican incumbents, especially in the House, are now much less dependent on votes from moderates, independents, and Democrats. The growing conservatism of the normal Republican vote may help to explain the strong support by House Republicans for impeachment and other conservative causes in recent years—causes that were highly popular with the GOP base if not with the rest of the country.

Note

A previous version of this chapter was presented at the annual meeting of the American Political Science Association, Washington, D.C., August 31–September 3, 2000.

Part 4   Electoral Connections

George W. Bush chose to govern in 2001 as though he had won a mandate in the 2000 election—as though voters had sent a clear signal of support for the policies that he had supported. Bush's behavior is not unusual, for all presidents try to argue that their victory constitutes an endorsement of their policies by the electorate. If political attitudes have consequences, they are most easily seen in elections. Voters choose one candidate over another, and the winner then seeks to enact new policies.

Professional pollsters are especially interested in the behavioral consequences of public opinion in the electoral arena. They need to know what kinds of people are likely to vote in a given election and which attitudes are most likely to influence voters' choices. These pollsters also seek to determine which existing attitudes might be activated to help the candidate who hired them, which attitudes might be changed, and in some cases whether a new attitude might be developed. In the 2000 presidential elections, Al Gore's pollsters advised him to adopt a more populist theme to appeal to working-class voters and to tone down his aggressive stance after the first debate, which offended some women voters (Johnson 2000; Macintyre 2000).

Political scientists are not interested in manipulating public opinion, but they do want to study the impact of public opinion on political behavior. How do opinions and resources influence rates of political participation? Among those who do participate, how do attitudes influence the decisions that citizens make—for which candidate to vote, which group to join or to give money, for which cause to volunteer? In recent years the definition of participation has broadened considerably, and scholars now explore the role of resources and opinions in shaping contributions to candidates (Brown, Powell, and Wilcox 1995), voluntarism in communities (Verba, Schlozman, and Brady 1995), and unconventional political actions such as blocking entrances to abortion clinics (Maxwell 1994). But the vast majority of research remains centered on an individual's decision on whether or not to vote in caucuses, primary elections, and especially in general elections.

Turnout in American elections is quite low by international standards, and it has been declining since 1960. Some scholars also suggest that involvement in civic and organized social groups has fallen (Putnam 2000). The chapter by Henry Brady, Kay Lehman Schlozman,

Sidney Verba, and Laurel Elms asks if, inside this picture of declining participation, the causes of involvement remain the same. In particular, they investigate the continuing role of socioeconomic status in political and civic engagement.

When political scientists study political choice, they most often focus on decisions about which candidate to vote for. For many years, a social-psychological model (Campbell et al. 1960) dominated voting behavior studies. This model examines the interplay of demographic traits, partisanship, and opinions on candidates and issues in the selection of the Democratic or Republican candidate. A second school of thought, the rational choice model, focuses on efficient methods for selecting between candidates when voting is a low-cost, low-benefit activity (Aldrich 1993). One method of rational decision making is retrospective voting, where voters compare the record of the incumbent president to that which the opposition party may have accomplished (Downs 1960; Fiorina 1981). A major portion of the incumbent president's record is his or her handling of the economy. Thus, Paul Brewer in his chapter examines economic voting in recent elections.

10 Who Bowls?
The (Un)Changing Stratification of Participation

Henry E. Brady, Kay Lehman Schlozman, Sidney Verba, and Laurel Elms

Americans are participants. Although they are less likely than citizens in other democracies to go to the polls, Americans are in other ways generally more active than their counterparts elsewhere. They get in touch with public officials; they belong to political organizations; they take part in local community politics. And beyond political activity, they are active in organizations and associations of all kinds, from sports and garden clubs to fraternal, veterans', and homeowners' organizations. The religious sphere is perhaps most distinctive: more than citizens elsewhere, Americans not only attend services but also take part in many other activities associated with religious institutions. A high level of civic participation—observed most notably by Alexis de Tocqueville in the nineteenth century and remarked by visitors ever since—is a source of distinction and pride in the United States.

Recent years have witnessed considerable discussion in the popular media as well as in academic publications about the crisis in civic involvement. Robert Putnam's resonant image of Americans bowling alone, in his book of that title, has inspired heated and extended debate, as well as considerable hand wringing, about whether there has been a decline in civic engagement in the United States over the past generation.[1] In the discussion of the decline in civic involvement, what matters about the condition of civil life is the overall level of citizens' voluntary involvement. The fact that civic participation is very unevenly distributed across society is barely mentioned. Indeed, a 1998 report of the National Commission on Civic Renewal, *A Nation of Spectators,* focuses almost exclusively on the problem of decline and does not devote even a single paragraph to the marked inequalities in civic participation across various sectors of society. In short, by concentrating on asking how many people are bowling and whether they do so solo or in leagues, we are neglecting to ask "Who bowls?"

Civic participation in the United States is and has long been unequal. Not only are many people inactive, but participation is very unevenly distributed among those who do take part. In fact, we can measure that unevenness by adapting a technique developed by economists to measure the extent of income inequality. If we array Americans in terms of their scores on an 8-point scale measuring political activity in 1990, we find that the top fifth of the population on the participation hierarchy is responsible for 44 percent of all participatory acts. In contrast, the bottom fifth of the population is responsible for only 1.5 percent of all participatory acts.[2] An admittedly somewhat crude comparison with income inequality in 1990 shows that the top fifth of families in terms of income received 44 percent of all income, a figure identical to that for the top fifth's share of participation. The bottom fifth received only 4.6 percent of all income—a somewhat larger portion than their share of political activity.

Furthermore, citizens who take part in politics are unrepresentative of the American public in a number of ways. Most important, they are socioeconomically advantaged: better educated, more affluent, and more likely to hold high-status jobs. They are also disproportionately likely to be Anglo-white rather than African American or, especially, Latino; middle-aged, rather than elderly or, especially, young; and men rather than women. In this chapter we bring to the matter of changes over time in the equality of participation the same concern with longitudinal change that has been at the root of the controversy over erosion in the total amount of civic activity. We demonstrate that the well-known inequalities on the basis of class that characterize political activity in the United States have prevailed since the middle 1970s and confirm that, although political participation declined from 1973 to 1994, the extent to which political activity was structured by socioeconomic status remained more or less unchanged.

Why Do We Care Who Takes Part?

The dialogue about civic disengagement often proceeds as if the reasons for concern about the health of civil society are self-evident, and proof that civic involvement is on the skids is interpreted as cause for anxiety. However, we might care about participation in voluntary activity for three broad categories of reasons: the creation of community and the cultivation of democratic virtues, the development of the faculties of the individual, and the equal protection of interests in public life.[3]

The first justification for concern about a decline in civic involvement, that involvement fosters community and democracy, rests on the notion that when people work together as volunteers, they become more trusting,[4] more cooperative, and more willing to make sacrifices on behalf of collective goals.[5] Communities characterized by high levels of voluntary activity are in many ways better places to live: the schools are better, crime rates are lower, tax evasion is less common.[6] The second line of argument on behalf of civic involvement shifts the focus from the community to individuals and directs us to consider the educational effects of civic activity and the ways that civic engagement fosters individual capacities such as independence, competence, respect for others, the willingness to take responsibility, and the ability to assess the interests of the self and the community.[7] For these two goals of civic involvement—the creation of community and the development of the individual—the overall level of engagement is key. What matters is how much voluntary activity there is, not whether the activity is political in character.

Our concerns change somewhat when it comes to the equal protection of interests—that is, the ability of all citizens, on an equal basis, to have their opinions and needs considered by public officials. Through the medium of political participation, citizens communicate information about their preferences and needs for government action and generate pressure on public officials to heed what they hear. Of course, we know that public officials act for many reasons—only one of which is their assessment of what the public wants and needs. And policymakers have ways other than the medium of citizen participation to learn what citizens want and need from the government. Nonetheless, what public officials hear clearly influences what they do. Therefore, as long as citizens differ in their opinions and interests, we should care about whether political participation communicates those interests accurately. We have learned from survey research that obtaining an accurate picture of public opinion requires consulting only a relatively small fraction of the public—as long as that group is randomly selected. Thus, it is the representativeness of participation, not the level of participation, that matters for the equal protection of interests.

It is well known, however, that the relatively small group of those who are active in politics constitutes anything but a random sample.[8] Of course, departures from randomness along dimensions that are truly unrelated to politics—Coffee or tea in the morning? Dogs or cats at home?—can be ignored without jeopardizing the equal protection of interests.[9] However, the politically active differ from those who are politically quiescent along a variety of dimensions germane to politics: in their demographic characteristics, in their needs and preferences for government action, in their policy priorities.[10] Since those who take part are not representative of the citizenry as a whole—and there is ample evidence that in crucial ways they are not—then the political needs and preferences of the quiescent may not be voiced in the political process. Thus, when we focus on the equal protection of interests, the relevant forms of voluntary activity are necessarily political. Furthermore, what matters is not so much the level of civic involvement as its distribution, not so much *how much* participation there is but *who* is active.

The Changing Relationship of Class to Participation: Our Expectations

With respect to whether the social class stratification of political activity has changed over the past two decades, we might entertain opposing expectations. On one hand, political participation has traditionally been extremely low among those on the lowest rung of the socioeconomic ladder; therefore, the recent decline in overall rates of political activity cannot come solely from erosion at the bottom. Furthermore, in recent decades the nation has become more affluent and better educated. The result of these processes—when combined with the political mobilization of evangelical Protestants, a group that is not especially affluent or well educated—might be to facilitate the political activation of those at the bottom of the SES (socioeconomic status) hierarchy and produce greater class convergence in participation. On the other hand, it has been demonstrated that increasing education does not produce commensurate increases in activity.[11] Moreover, since 1980, several factors— among them the attenuation of the labor movement and the increasing concentration of wealth at the top—have conspired to exacerbate class stratification, though not class conflict. These trends would suggest a more pronounced pattern of class stratification in political activity.

Data Sources

This inquiry relies principally upon an exciting new dataset, the Roper Social and Political Trends Data, 1973–1994, from Roper Starch Worldwide. From the end of 1973 to the middle of 1994, the Roper Organization (now Roper Starch Worldwide), a commercial polling firm, conducted ten polls each year with about 2,000 Americans in each survey, for a total of more than 400,000 respondents over the two-decade period. Each poll used an identical battery of twelve items (reproduced in Appendix 10-1) covering many different types of political participation. These data contain important information about the political participation of Americans; no other set of data includes so many forms of participation over such a long time interval with such frequent (almost monthly) surveys.[12] Unfortunately, the data have certain weaknesses for our purposes: the coverage of important variables measuring the factors associated with participation is spotty, and the categories used to measure certain important demographics—including age and income—are inconsistent and insufficiently fine-grained. We supplement the Roper surveys with data about nonpolitical forms of activity from the General Social Survey. The General Social Survey (GSS), conducted by the National Opinion Research Center on a regular basis since 1972, is the largest national survey of the social behaviors and attributes of the American public.

Studying Participatory Inequality

To investigate participatory inequality we must specify a dimension of participatory inequality that is politically relevant and we must focus on political attributes that have relatively stable meanings over time and that have been measured in the same way over a series of surveys. The first of these tasks is easier than the second. While the headlines can change in a flash, issues engaging certain fault lines of conflict—among them, social class—are never long absent from the political agenda in the United States. The particular manifestations of these enduring conflicts change over time: controversies over establishing a graduated federal income tax, legislating unemployment insurance, and guaranteeing labor the right to organize have given way to debates about the end of welfare and the abolition of es-tate taxes. Nevertheless, even as specific issues come and go, not only has class been a per-sistent feature of American politics, but cross-sectional studies of political participation have documented over and over again that political activity is stratified along class lines.

Longitudinal analysis also requires measures that are available over time. Each of the existing datasets containing measures of participation has a shortcoming from our point of view. The Citizen Participation Study contains a rich array of measures of voluntary ac-tivity as well as politically relevant needs, attitudes, and demographics, but the survey was conducted only once—in 1990. Of the longitudinal datasets, the General Social Survey con-tains repeated measures only of nonpolitical involvement and the American National Elec-tion Study (ANES) contains repeated measures of electoral activity only. In contrast, the Roper Social and Political Trends Data contain a detailed battery of participation items mea-sured over two decades, but the Roper measures of respondents' politically relevant attri-butes are thin and inconsistent.[13]

Measuring SES over Time

Measuring socioeconomic status is notoriously complicated, and the complexities are multiplied when longitudinal concerns are introduced. To make the task manageable, we might simply use a fixed set of categories—for example, to compare over time those who never finished high school with college graduates or professionals and managers with lower blue-collar workers. Since SES is ordinarily considered to be multidimensional—composed of education, income, and occupation—we could even make combinations of categories, say those with graduate degrees and family incomes over $75,000 or high school dropouts with incomes below $15,000.

The problem with this approach is that categories that look the same over time are not really the same. The meaning of such nominal categories and the proportion of respondents in each category may change over time. Obviously, as inflation erodes the value of the dol-lar, the purchasing power of any particular income decreases. At the same time there has been steady escalation in the standard of living considered to be minimally adequate—or comfortably middle class (Rainwater 1974, chap. 3). With respect to education, in 1960 41.1 percent of American adults had completed high school; by 1990 that figure had risen to 77.6 percent (U.S. Bureau of the Census 1996, 159). With the rising level of education in the population has come a transformation in the social meaning of any particular level of educational achievement. Over the twentieth century, the person with a high school diploma and no further education moved from a relatively high position on the educational hierarchy to a much lower one. In fact, Norman Nie, Jane Junn, and Kenneth Stehlik-Barry (1996) demonstrate that what matters for activity in politics is not the absolute level of edu-cational attainment but the level of education relative to one's peers and, therefore, that a college degree was associated with much greater political activity a generation ago, when graduating from college was less common than it is today.

Our strategy was to rank the respondents in each survey by their SES and divide them into hierarchical SES groups of equal size—in our case, quintiles (groupings of fifths). This approach required us to make a number of discretionary decisions. Of the three components of SES—education, family income, and occupation—only the first two are available for (almost) all respondents in the Roper surveys. No occupation is listed for the 40 percent of respondents who are not in the labor force, a group that has changed substantially in its composition in recent decades as many women have entered the work force and older people have retired earlier. Because including occupation in the measure of SES would entail omitting a large and changing group of people, our measure of SES uses only education and income.

For two reasons we have combined measures of education and income into a composite SES index. First, in the Roper surveys, income levels and, to a lesser extent, educational attainment, have been measured only in ranges, creating, in some cases, as few as four categories.[14] It is obviously impossible to create quintiles from a measure with only four categories. By combining two measures we can increase substantially the number of distinct rankings that are possible.[15] In addition, there are good reasons to expect that any errors of classification will not be correlated across the two measures, so that the summary index will be less error prone and will produce a better ranking than the measures taken separately.[16]

SES Quintiles: Associated Characteristics

As displayed in Table 10-1, the Roper data show that the respondents in each of the five quintiles differ dramatically in their demographic characteristics and partisan commitments.[17] The top quintile is composed disproportionately of males, almost entirely of whites, and largely of those between thirty and fifty-nine years of age. Those in the top quintile are disproportionately likely to be married and to be employed. Although a bare majority is Protestant, people in the top quintile are, in fact, somewhat less likely than the entire population to be Protestant. Although roughly the same percentages profess Democratic and Republican leanings, those in the upper quintile are markedly more Republican than the others. Those in the bottom quintile are most distinctive when it comes to age and employment: compared with those at the top, they are four times as likely to be sixty or over and less than half as likely to have a job. The bottom quintile is also disproportionately female and African American. In addition, those in the bottom quintile are somewhat less likely to be married or unionized yet more likely to be Protestant and to be Democratic than the population at large.[18]

As shown in Table 10-2, some demographic characteristics of the quintiles have changed

Table 10–1 Characteristics of SES Quintiles

| | SES Quintile | | | | | |
Characteristic	Bottom 20 percent 1	2	Middle 20 percent 3	4	Top 20 percent 5	Total Sample
Male	43.4%	44.4%	46.1%	48.3%	55.0%	47.5%
White	75.2	86.6	92.1	93.9	95.5	88.7
Black	24.8	13.4	7.9	6.1	4.5	11.3
Under age 30	20.0	31.4	30.6	30.0	25.1	27.4
Ages 30–59	36.1	44.2	53.9	57.8	64.6	51.3
Age 60 and older	43.8	24.4	15.5	12.2	10.3	21.2
Married	47.6	60.2	70.4	71.6	75.0	65.0
With job	32.7	54.3	64.4	71.3	78.6	60.2
Protestant	66.0	59.2	54.8	52.6	50.1	56.5
Catholic	23.0	27.6	30.8	31.3	29.4	28.4
No religious affiliation	5.3	6.2	6.2	7.0	9.0	6.8
Union members	7.0	12.5	16.0	15.9	12.7	12.8
Democratic	54.6	47.8	44.4	40.8	36.7	44.8
Republican	16.4	21.2	25.1	29.7	35.6	25.6
Independent (vol.)	7.8	11.0	12.5	13.6	15.1	12.0
No particular party (vol.)	16.3	16.6	15.3	13.8	10.8	14.6
Number of respondents (N)	(75,713)	(75,835)	(75,836)	(75,735)	(75,754)	(378,973)

Source: Roper Social and Political Trends Data, 1973–1994.

Note: Religious affiliation was not included on Roper surveys conducted in 1993 and 1994.

considerably over the past two decades. In the bottom quintile, the proportion of respondents age sixty and older has fallen while the proportion under age thirty has increased, trends that are reversed for the top quintile. The marriage rate for the bottom three quintiles has dropped over time; it has fallen far less sharply for the top quintile. Levels of unionization for the bottom quintiles have also plunged over the twenty years of the Roper studies, but the proportion of union members among the top quintile has remained nearly constant.

Table 10-2 Selected Characteristics of SES Quintiles over Time

Characteristic	Year	Bottom 20 percent 1	2	Middle 20 percent 3	4	Top 20 percent 5	Total Sample
Black	1974	20.1%	12.8%	5.1%	4.8%	2.9%	9.1%
	1984	28.4	12.3	6.9	4.9	4.0	11.3
	1993	27.5	17.4	11.9	7.1	5.0	13.6
Under age 30	1974	13.7	32.6	32.6	33.6	33.2	29.2
	1984	21.6	32.0	33.3	34.0	27.0	29.6
	1993	24.2	28.9	24.9	21.3	14.9	22.8
Age 60 and older	1974	47.4	20.6	12.0	11.7	7.8	19.9
	1984	41.1	25.3	17.0	12.1	11.0	21.3
	1993	38.4	25.5	18.1	13.1	11.2	21.3
Married	1974	60.6	71.0	80.7	75.9	81.3	74.5
	1984	46.4	57.5	67.6	68.2	70.7	62.1
	1993	37.4	48.5	62.0	69.2	74.1	58.2
Union members	1974	11.8	18.5	22.0	18.7	12.7	16.8
	1984	6.6	11.1	14.6	14.5	12.6	11.9
	1993	3.0	7.7	10.5	12.8	12.5	9.3
Number of respondents (N)	1974	(3,835)	(3,842)	(3,840)	(3,842)	(3,836)	(19,192)
	1984	(3,964)	(3,970)	(3,969)	(3,970)	(3,967)	(19,840)
	1993	(3,214)	(3,218)	(3,218)	(3,218)	(3,216)	(16,084)

Source: Roper Social and Political Trends Data, 1973–1994.

SES and Continuing Participatory Inequality

In its frequent surveys, the Roper Organization asked about a wide range of participatory acts.[19] The proportion of respondents who reported having engaged in each of these acts in the previous year varies widely—from a low of just under 1 percent who indicated that they had held or run for office to just about a third who reported having signed a petition. On average, across the two-decade period, respondents indicated having engaged in 1.13 political acts. Figure 10-1 uses the Roper Trends data to show, for each of the five socioeconomic groups, the change in the average number of activities over the period from 1973 to 1994.[20] Figure 10-1 makes clear several aspects of political participation in the United States. First, for every quintile, there is an overall decline in participation between 1973 and 1994. Respondents in the bottom three quintiles increase their participation during the mid- to late 1980s but eventually fall to a level below where they had been twenty years earlier.

Figure 10-1 Political Activities, by SES Quintile

Mean number of activities

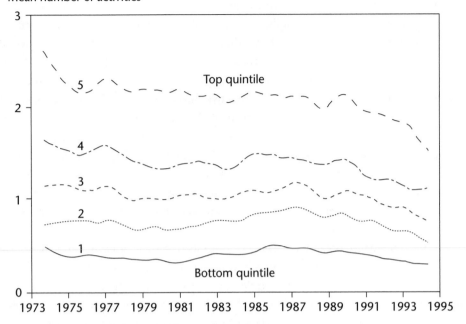

Source: Roper Social and Political Trends Data, 1973–1994.

Second, political activity is structured by SES. The five quintiles array themselves neatly in order with discernible differences between adjacent quintiles. The lines move more or less in tandem and never cross. Those at the highest level of SES are roughly five times more active than those at the bottom—undertaking on average about 2.1 acts, compared with 0.4 acts for the lowest quintile. In short, over the past twenty years public officials have consistently heard much more from those who are high on the SES hierarchy.

Third, those at the very top of the SES ladder participate even more than we would expect based upon a simple linear extrapolation from the lower quintiles. The most affluent and well-educated group is significantly different from the rest. Moving up the SES ladder, the gain in political activity is approximately the same from one quintile to the next among the four lower quintiles (about 0.35 acts); however, the gain is larger when we move from the fourth quintile to the fifth (about 0.7 acts). Thus, the top quintile is especially politically active.[21]

Figure 10-1 uses a scale summarizing twelve different political activities. When we consider these acts separately, some distinctive patterns do appear. Quite notable is the continuous and substantial decline in participation for electoral activities during this period. The most striking finding, however, is that all the activities move in tandem—showing decline over time and continuity in their stratification by social class.

Earlier we presented a set of conflicting expectations about the way that class stratification has changed over time. On one hand, those in the lower quintiles are better educated and more affluent than they once were. These higher absolute levels of two of the most crucial resources for political participation, education and income,[22] might lead us to expect those in the lower quintiles to become more active and close the participation gap based on class. Furthermore, two other developments might have the effect of diminishing stratification in political participation. First, white evangelical Protestants—a group that is neither particularly well educated nor particularly well-off financially—have been mobilized politically, which might raise activity levels among those in the lower rungs of the SES ladder. In addition, the fact that many of the well-educated women who once might have devoted themselves to volunteer activities are now in the work force might erode activity levels among those higher up on the SES hierarchy.[23]

On the other hand, because the evidence suggests that educational attainment relative to one's peers rather than absolute years of education determines participation, we might expect the rising level of aggregate education not to have the hypothesized effect. Furthermore, increasing income polarization and the widely recognized weakening of the institutions most effective in mobilizing the working class—unions and political parties—would suggest an increase in representational inequality over time.

To measure representational inequality, we create what we call a representation ratio by taking the ratio of average participation by the top SES quintile to average participation by the bottom SES quintile. This ratio can range from 0 to infinity; a ratio of 1 indicates representational equality between the two quintiles (or any two groups). Ratios greater than 1 indicate that the top quintile is more active than the bottom quintile. Based on what we have seen, it is hardly surprising that the representation ratios presented in Figure 10-2, which range between 4 and 7, show an ongoing pattern of participatory dominance by the highest SES quintile. What is surprising, however, is the absence of any clear secular trend. Participatory inequality rises somewhat in the late 1970s, falls during the early 1980s, and ends the two-decade period almost exactly where it started.[24]

The Nonpolitical Domain: Organizations and Churches

We can deepen our understanding of the socioeconomic stratification of civic involvement by looking beyond political participation. As we indicated at the outset, Americans have a long tradition of secular and religious voluntary activity outside politics, and a large part of the concern about declining civic engagement has focused on these nonpolitical do-

Figure 10-2 Political Activities Ratio, Top Fifth to Bottom Fifth

Ratio: top fifth/bottom fifth

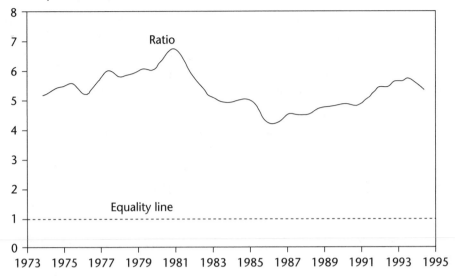

Source: Roper Social and Political Trends Data, 1973–1994.

mains. Although issues of the distribution of activity, as opposed to the amount of activity, pose themselves less starkly for religious and nonpolitical organizational activity, it matters who takes part in these arenas for several reasons. For one thing, religious institutions and nonpolitical organizations often provide direct benefits to their members only. These benefits, which range from education to health benefits to various kinds of charitable assistance—parallel those provided by governments. In addition, institutions that are ordinarily nonpolitical often get involved in politics. In recent years religious institutions and nonpolitical organizations of all sorts have spoken out on behalf of their members on public policy issues as diverse as world peace, school prayer, and the minimum wage. Finally, because activity within churches and nonpolitical organizations develops civic skills that can be transferred to politics and generates requests for political involvement, these institutions operate in various ways to foster political participation. In short, for several reasons the concerns about equal protection of interests that we raised originally with respect to political participation are germane to the nonpolitical forms of civic engagement.

In order to assess how the stratification in secular and religious nonpolitical involvement has changed over time, we turn to the General Social Survey, which has asked about organizational membership and church attendance over a twenty-year period.[25] As before, we divide the respondents in each survey into quintiles on the basis of socioeconomic level. We begin with the nonpolitical organizations that form the heart of civil society. The data in Figure 10-3—which displays the average number of nonpolitical memberships for each of the SES quintiles from 1974 to 1994—echo those we saw in Figure 10-1 and confirm the well-known structuring of organizational activity by socioeconomic advantage. There is a clear difference between the top and bottom quintiles, with the other socioeconomic levels lining up in between. Without exception, those in the lowest quintile are the least, and those in the highest SES quintile the most, organizationally active. Figure 10-4, which shows the ratio of the number of memberships of those in the top quintile to those at the bottom, highlights that the association between socioeconomic advantage and membership in nonpolitical organizations is more or less constant across the time period we cover. Although there are perturbations here and there, throughout the time period those at the top of the hierarchy belong to about three times as many organizations as those at the bottom.

Finally, we can consider another form of nonpolitical involvement that fosters political participation, religious engagement. The average attendance at religious services, measured in weeks per year, for each of the five quintiles, is roughly the same. The lines representing the average number of weeks of attendance for each quintile cross and re-cross each other over the years. Religious attendance is not stratified by social class, a pattern that persists throughout the time period of our data. In striking contrast to its distinctiveness in both political participation and organizational membership, the top socioeconomic quintile is not consistently the most churchgoing; in fact, in some years, the lowest quintile is. Figure 10-5 shows the ratio between the top and bottom SES quintiles for religious activity. Figure 10-5 also uses the same vertical scale as Figures 10-2 and 10-4 to allow for comparisons of the representation ratios. The message is simple: the ratios for religious activity hover around the 1.0 line of equality, with no particular pattern to the small deviations.[26] Unlike political participation or organizational memberships, religious activity constitutes a rare source of continuing participatory equality in the United States.

Conclusion: Continuing Stratification in Political Participation

As students of political participation with a special interest in political stratification, we have been intrigued by the evidence for—and the debate about—diminishing civic engagement in the United States. But we have been struck by the extent to which concern with "How much?" has eclipsed attention to "Who?" when it comes to civic involvement. In the discussion about whether people are bowling alone or in leagues, we must not forget to find out who bowls and to understand the implications of participatory stratification on the basis of class for the equal protection of interests in a democracy. In this chapter we have used

Figure 10-3 Organizational Memberships, by SES Quintile

Mean number of memberships

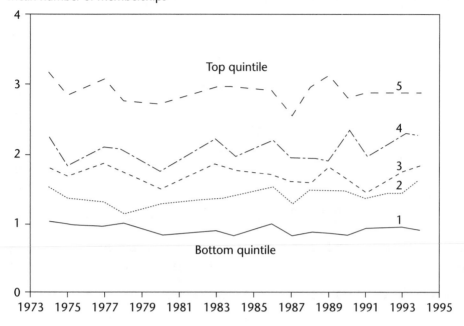

Source: General Social Surveys, 1972–1994 [Cumulative File]

Figure 10-4 Organizational Memberships Ratio, Top Fifth to Bottom Fifth

Ratio: top fifth/bottom fifth

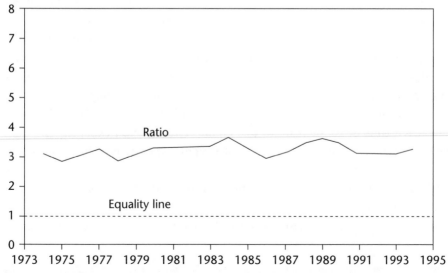

Source: General Social Surveys, 1972–1994 [Cumulative File]

Figure 10-5 Religious Attendance Ratio, Top Fifth to Bottom Fifth

Ratio: top fifth/bottom fifth

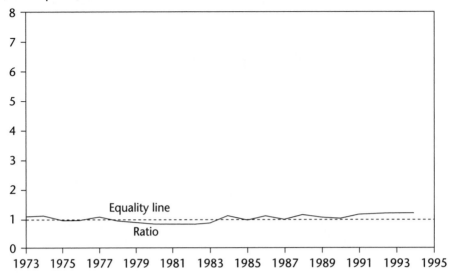

Source: General Social Surveys, 1972–1994 [Cumulative File]

a significant new data set, the Roper Social and Political Trends Data, supplemented by data from the General Social Surveys, to consider longitudinal trends in the stratification of civic activity.

The Roper data demonstrate two unambiguous trends in political participation over the past two decades. The first is a decline in political participation, particularly in forms of activity related to the political parties; this finding confirms what others have shown. The other is a continuing pattern of political participation strongly structured on the basis of SES. When we stratify the public into socioeconomic quintiles, the repeated surveys and consequent large samples from the Roper studies demonstrate not only that year after year the quintiles are arrayed in order in terms of participation, but also that the highest SES quintile is even more active than expected on the basis of a linear extrapolation from the lower four quintiles. The fact that the highest SES group is especially politically active and, therefore, that so much of all political participation originates in this high-status group, suggests that to approximate an answer to the question, "Who participates in politics?" we would be better off asking, "Who plays polo?" than asking, "Who bowls?" The stratification in political participation contrasts sharply with the extraordinary equality in religious attendance, and the stratification in organizational membership is roughly midway between the inequality in political participation and the equality in religious attendance.

We also investigated the nature of changes over time in SES stratification, with less unambiguous results. At the outset, we had entertained conflicting expectations with respect to whether the upper-SES dominance in political activity would have been strengthened or eroded over the period. Such factors as rising levels of education and income suggested that the pattern of class inequality would be ameliorated. Other factors, such as the decline in unions and political parties and greater economic polarization, suggested the opposite. In fact, the data show a pattern of fluctuation in the extent to which the top SES quintile outparticipates the bottom quintile; the data also show that the stratification in activity in the mid-1990s is not much different than it was in the mid-1970s.

We cannot conclude without suggesting an important qualification to our findings. We have been considering a scale that includes a variety of kinds of political activity. However, the Roper surveys do not include information about an especially significant form of political activity, campaign giving. The stability in the level of socioeconomic stratification that we found for overall political participation may not pertain to political contributions, for which the SES gap may be growing. Cross-sectional data from the Citizen Participation Study demonstrate that contributors are, on average, more affluent than other kinds of political activists, who are in turn more affluent than those who are politically quiescent. Not surprisingly, the affluent are not only more likely to give, but they write larger checks when they do: among those who make contributions, those at the top of the economic ladder give, on average, fourteen times more than those at the bottom.[27] Thus, when we move from considering contributors to considering contributions, we see that, as a form of political input, contributions are much more socioeconomically skewed in their origins than are other kinds of participation, such as contacts with public officials.

It is well known that, even when measured in constant dollars, campaign giving has risen rapidly over the last generation.[28] In particular, soft money donations—which are raised at the national level and channeled to state parties and which are not subject to limits—have increased especially dramatically. Although we have no longitudinal data to assess the consequences of this configuration of circumstances, there is reason to presume that, when it comes to campaign finance, socioeconomic stratification of participatory input has been exacerbated in recent decades.

These considerations multiply the ironies of what we saw for religious activity. In contrast to political and nonpolitical secular activity, religious activity is distributed more or less evenly across socioeconomic groups with little variation over time. Thus, it is ironic that, even though many religious institutions are hierarchically governed and democracy is supposed to provide a level playing field on which all citizens are equal, it is religious activity that has consistently been distributed relatively equally across socioeconomic groups.

Notes

1. On the erosion of civic engagement, see Putnam (2000) and, for a much less persuasive contrary view, see Ladd (1999). While it is widely acknowledged that electoral turnout has decreased, Rosenstone and Hansen (1993) demonstrate convincingly that certain other forms of political participation have also declined.

2. These figures are calculated from the Citizen Participation Study, described in detail in the appendices to Verba, Schlozman, and Brady (1995), and from U.S. Bureau of the Census (1996), 467.

3. Robert Putnam (1996, 27) makes the point that many discussions of the decline in civic engagement proceed from the unstated assumption that civic engagement is beneficial to society and that its decline is to be regretted.

There are a number of helpful discussions about why we care about civic engagement, among them Mansbridge (1980, chap. 17); Parry, Moyser, and Day (1992, chap. 1); Putnam (1993); Skocpol (1996); Newton (1997); Edwards and Foley (1997); Warren (1998); and Putnam (2000, esp. sec. 4). We should make clear that there is variation across authors with respect to the way they categorize the beneficial consequences of civic involvement. In proposing three kinds of benefits from voluntary activity, we make no claims of either novelty or definitiveness. For elaboration of the various reasons for concern about declining civic engagement, see Schlozman, Verba, and Brady (1999).

4. This perspective clearly draws from Coleman's (1988) concept of social capital. For a rare empirical test of this hypothesis, see Brehm and Rahn (1997).

5. Many commentators point out that the inevitable result of collective action is not necessarily to foster community and democracy. Some groups, such as militias, hardly promote democratic values. Moreover, organizations of likeminded individuals beget conflict as well as cooperation. See, for example, the arguments and references contained in Foley and Edwards (1997), Berman (1997), and Putnam (2000, chap. 22).

6. For elaboration of this theme, see Putnam (2000, sec. 4).

7. See, for example, Bachrach (1967); Pateman (1970); and Parry (1972).

8. For discussion and extensive references, see Milbrath and Goel (1977); Bennett and Bennett (1986); and Conway (2000).

9. Our flippant examples should not obscure our understanding that *any* attribute or preference can become relevant for politics. For example, a preference for dogs or cats as pets is irrelevant to politics until the local governing council proposes stricter leash laws for dogs.

10. See Verba, Schlozman, and Brady (1995, part 2).

11. See, Nie, Junn, and Stehlik-Barry (1996).

12. We are grateful to Henry Brady, Andrea Campbell, and Robert Putnam, who—with support from the Pew Charitable Trusts—acquired these data from the Roper Center at the University of Connecticut and shared them with us. Readers may be familiar with these data from the work of Rosenstone and Hansen (1993), who used the frequencies from the printed Roper record to make a very convincing argument about the decline in many forms of participation.

13. The Roper measures of age, education, and income posed some problems for making comparisons over time. The age and education variables had response categories that varied over time, but always in the direction of including more specific categories as time passed. For example, when the number of education categories increased from four (no school, grade school, high school, college) to seven (no school, 0–8, 9–11, 12, 13–15, 16, 17+ years of education), some of the earlier categories were simply divided into narrower ranges. Thus, it is possible to collapse categories from later studies to ensure comparability with earlier ones. The income variable posed a greater problem because inflation caused income ranges to change dramatically over time, and the ranges changed in a rather haphazard way. It is, therefore, not possible simply to collapse categories to make a later mea-

sure comparable to an earlier one. As will be discussed, however, our method for constructing SES quintiles has been designed to overcome this problem by combining education and income measures and using them to construct rankings of respondents within studies. These rankings can then be used to compare respondents across studies.

14. For comparability, we also combined measures of income and education for the GSS, although far more categories were available for each measure.

15. It is usually possible to get at least as many categories as one less than the sum of the number of categories from each measure. This follows if the first measure is scored 1 to m and the second 1 to n. Then the possible sums of the combined measure are all integers between 2 and $(m + n)$. This amounts to $(m + n - 1)$ categories. If the two measures are perfectly correlated, then there can be no more categories than the smaller of m and n, but in the usual case with imperfect correlation, the number of categories is at least $(m + n - 1)$ and usually more.

16. The initial decision to combine the measures immediately raised three additional issues: First, over what time period should we construct SES ranks? Second, how should each separate measure be scored to make maximum use of the information it contains? Third, how should the two scorings be combined? Because we want rankings for each separate national sample, the answer to the first question is that the index should be constructed separately for each study, and quintiles should be constructed for each study from this index. There is no question about this, but there is some question about how to obtain the information needed for scoring each measure separately and combining the two measures. For elaboration of the methods used to create the quintiles, see Appendix 10-2.

17. Wherever possible, we used other datasets to validate results based on the Roper data. American National Election Studies data confirm the Roper findings in Table 10-1. Furthermore, unemployment data reported in the Roper surveys track quite closely analogous data from the census. Using unemployment levels to evaluate the accuracy of the Roper data has at least two virtues: very good monthly data are published by the Bureau of Labor Statistics, and the unemployment rate varies substantially over time so that we can see that the nearly monthly Roper surveys do track these changes. One drawback is that the Roper Organization used interview quotas for employed people.

18. Obviously, these simple data obscure complex social relationships that would involve a separate research enterprise to disentangle. For example, it is well known that African Americans are disproportionately Protestant. Hence, the fact that Protestants are overrepresented in the bottom quintile may be related to the overrepresentation of African Americans in that category.

19. See Appendix 10-1 for question wording.

20. The lines in Figures 10-1 and 10-2 are locally weighted scatterplot smooths (LOWESS) fit to the 207 Roper studies of 2,000 respondents per study (a total of over 400,000 respondents). LOWESS is a compromise between using linear (or polynomial) fits to time series data, which tend to obscure important ups and downs by "oversmoothing" and simply connecting the average value for each survey, which results in a noisy (and sometimes uninterpretable) picture of overall trends dominated by sampling error. LOWESS makes this compromise by calculating a curve based upon more than just one study but fewer than all of them. See Hardle (1990, 43). The smoothing parameter for Figures 10-1 and 10-2 is .10, and the number of iterations is 2.

21. Replicating the analysis for deciles rather than quintiles produces the same patterns. The deciles move in tandem and do not cross. In addition, those at the very top of the SES scale are even more active than we would expect by extrapolating from the relationship for the lower parts of the scale.

22. On the role of resources in political activity, see Verba, Schlozman, and Brady (1995, esp. chaps. 9–12).

23. The reality with respect to the political activity of women who are in the work force is much more complicated. According to Putnam (2000, 194–203), the march of women into the work force in recent years has diminished the social forms of civic involvement more than the political ones. In

fact, cross-sectional data demonstrate that women who are in the labor force are more politically active than are women at home. For an analysis that demonstrates why this is so, see Schlozman, Burns, and Verba (1999).

24. Analogous data from the American National Election Studies for the representation ratios for electoral activity tell a story that is similar in its broadest outlines: there is no clear secular trend of either increasing or decreasing class inequality in electoral participation. For reasons that elude us, however, in its particulars the pattern for the ANES is quite different from that shown in Figure 10-2. In the ANES data, participatory inequality falls during the late 1970s and rises again during the 1980s—the opposite of what emerged from the Roper data. In contrast, levels of inequality in organizational memberships from the General Social Survey (discussed in the next section) roughly follow the pattern of inequality in the Roper participation data.

25. The measure of religious involvement is frequency of attendance at religious services. See Appendix 10-1 for question wording. The February 1998 edition of the *American Sociological Review*, vol. 63, features a symposium on the measurement and the debate over possible overreporting of Americans' church attendance. For organizational involvement, we use a measure of the number of types of organizations to which an individual belongs, which is the best repeated measure available in the General Social Surveys. For a discussion of the complexities involved in measuring organizational membership and activity, see Verba, Schlozman, and Brady (1995, App. 3.1).

26. Analysis of a somewhat differently worded item, weekly church attendance, from the Roper data also indicates near equality among SES quintiles. The average equality ratio over time is 1.2 for the Roper measure, only slightly higher than the 1.0 for the GSS.

27. See Schlozman, Verba, and Brady (1999, 433), as well as Verba, Schlozman, and Brady (1995, chap. 7).

28. See Corrado (2000, esp. chaps. 3 and 6).

Appendix 10-1 Question Wording and Measures

This appendix lists the names and the question wordings of the variables from the Roper Social and Political Trends Data and the General Social Surveys. The name of each variable as it appears in the dataset is in capital letters. The wording of each question as it appears on the survey questionnaires is given in quotes. When the wording of a question changed over the years, we have indicated the alternate versions and the time period each version was used.

Roper Social and Political Trends Data, 1973–1994, from Roper Starch Worldwide
Political Activities Series (Included in all 207 Roper Surveys)

"Now here is a list of things some people do about government or politics. (HAND RESPONDENT CARD) * Have you happened to have done any of those things in the past year? (IF 'YES') Which ones?"

CONTACT: "Written your congressman or senator"

ATTRALLY: "Attended a political rally or speech"

PUBMTG: "Attended a public meeting on town or school affairs"

OFFICE: "Held or run for political office"

ORGCMTE: "Served on a committee for some local organization"

ORGOFCR: "Become an officer of some club or organization" [Studies 73-09 through 75-08]
"Served as an officer of some club or organization" [Studies 75-09 through 94-06]

LETTER: "Written a letter to the paper"

PETITION: "Signed a petition"

PARTYWRK: "Worked for a political party"

SPEECH: "Made a speech"

ARTICLE: "Written an article for a magazine or newspaper"

ORGMBR: "Been a member of some group like the League of Women Voters, or some other group which is interested in better government" [Studies 73-09 through 84-10]
"Been a member of some group like the League of Women Voters, or some other group interested in better government" [Studies 85-01 through 94-06]

---

* Interviews for the Roper surveys were all conducted in person. Long lists of items, such as the participation series, age ranges, and income, were printed on a card to be shown to respondents rather than read by interviewers.

Responses to all twelve of these items were summed to create the political activities index we use. "Don't know" responses were added to the "No" category.

Respondent's Level of Education

"What was the last grade of regular school that you completed—not counting specialized schools like secretarial, art, or trade schools?"

EDUC: (studies 73-09 through 78-02)		EDUCNEW: (studies 78-03 through 94-06)	
1	No school	1	No school
2	Grade school (1-8)	2	0-8
3	High school (9-12)	3	9-11
4	College (13-16+)	4	12
		5	13-15
		6	16
		7	17+

Respondent's Household Income

HHINC: "Now here is a list of income categories. (HAND RESPONDENT CARD) Would you call off the letter of the category that best describes the combined annual income of all members of this household, including wages or salary, pensions, interest or dividends, and all other sources?"

The dollar amounts of the response options changed frequently over time—there are six different sets of response options.

When a respondent refused to answer HHINC, we used INTVUINC, the interviewer's estimate of household income level. However, INTVUINC is only available for studies 74-03 through 86-10.

Respondent's Sex

SEX: Recorded by interviewer (respondent was not asked).

Respondent's Race

RACE: Recorded by interviewer (respondent was not asked).

Respondent's Age Range (Observed or Given)

AGE, AGEOBS: For studies 77-02 through 94-06, respondents were asked:
"Here is a list of age groups. (HAND RESPONDENT CARD) Would you call off the

letter of the age group you happen to be in? (IF REFUSED, INTERVIEWER ESTIMATE GROUP)"

For studies 73-09 through 77-01, respondents were not asked to provide their ages. Their age groups were estimated by the interviewer.

Respondent's Marital Status

MARITAL: "Are you married, single, widowed, separated or divorced?" (Studies 73-09 through 89-06, 89-10, and 90-01)

"Are you married, widowed, separated, divorced, or have you never been married?" (Studies 89-07, 89-08, 89-09, and Studies 90-02 through 94-06)

Respondent's Employment Status

JOBFTPT: "Are you at present employed, either full time or part time?"

Respondent's Religious Affiliation

RELIG: "What is your religious affiliation, if any—Protestant, Catholic, Jewish or what?"

Respondent's Union Membership

UNION: "Do you, or does anyone in your family living here at home belong to a labor union?"

Respondent's Party Identification

PID: "Regardless of how you may have voted in the past, what do you usually consider yourself—a Democrat, a Republican, some other party, or what?"
Recorded responses:
Democrat
Republican
Other specific party
Independent (volunteered)
No particular party (volunteered)
Don't know
Refused

Weights

For about half of the 207 separate surveys that comprise the Roper Trends Data, the Roper Organization calculated weights to adjust the demographic composition of the samples to match Census Bureau figures for the population of the U.S. As these weights were not included in all surveys and were not calculated consistently over time, we did not use them to adjust the Roper data.

General Social Surveys, 1972–1994 [Cumulative File]
Organizational Membership Series (Included in 1974, 1975, 1977, 1978, 1980, 1983, 1984, 1986, 1987, 1988, 1989, 1990, 1991, 1993, 1994)

"Now we would like to know something about the groups or organizations to which individuals belong. Here is a list of various organizations. Could you tell me whether or not you are a member of each type?"

MEMFRAT:	"A. Fraternal groups."
MEMSERV:	"B. Service clubs."
MEMVET:	"C. Veterans' groups."
MEMPOLIT:	"D. Political clubs."
MEMUNION:	"E. Labor unions."
MEMSPORT:	"F. Sports groups."
MEMYOUTH:	"G. Youth groups."
MEMSCHL:	"H. School service groups."
MEMHOBBY:	"I. Hobby or garden clubs."
MEMGREEK:	"J. School fraternities or sororities."
MEMNAT:	"K. Nationality groups."
MEMFARM:	"L. Farm organizations."
MEMLIT:	"M. Literary, art, discussion or study groups."
MEMPROF:	"N. Professional or academic societies."
MEMCHURH:	"O. Church-affiliated groups."
MEMOTHER:	"P. Any other groups."

Responses to all fifteen of the nonpolitical organizations were summed to create the index of organizational membership we use. MEMPOLIT was excluded from the index. "Don't know" responses were added to the "no" category.

Religious Service Attendance (Included in 1972, 1973, 1974, 1975, 1976, 1977, 1978, 1980, 1982, 1983, 1984, 1985, 1986, 1987, 1988, 1989, 1990, 1991, 1993, 1994)

ATTEND: "How often do you attend religious services?"

Original Response Option	Conversion to Weeks per Year
0 Never	0

1 Less than once a year	.5
2 Once a year	1
3 Several times a year	6
4 Once a month	12
5 Two to three times a month	30
6 Nearly every week	41
7 Every week	52
8 More than once a week	52
9 Don't know, NA	Missing data

We recoded the original values of ATTEND to approximate the number of weeks per year respondents attended religious services. The values we assigned are listed above.

Respondent's Level of Education

EDUC: "What is the highest grade in elementary school or high school that you finished and got credit for?"

Respondent's Total Family Income

INCOME (1973–1976), INCOME77 (1977–1980), INCOME82 (1982–1985), INCOME86 (1986–1990), and INCOME91 (1991–1994): "In which of these group did your total family income, from all sources, fall last year before taxes, that is? Just tell me the letter."

Identical wording was used for all the family income items. However, the dollar amounts of the response options changed over time.

Weights

We used the variable OVERSAMP to weight the GSS surveys. OVERSAMP adjusts the data to compensate for the intentional oversampling of African American respondents in 1982 and 1987.

Appendix 10-2 Creating SES Quintiles

For both the Roper and the GSS data, we created socioeconomic status (SES) quintiles using the measures of education and income described in Appendix 10-1. We did not include occupation because it was not available for everyone. The education and income questions provided two different rankings of people based on their education or income. Our goal was to combine these rankings into one SES dimension. But how do we compare years of education with dollars of income? Our solution was to use a statistical technique called *principal components* that constructs a ranking of individuals along one common component that does the best job (according to the well-known statistical criterion of maximizing the explained variance) of reproducing the rankings in the original measures of education and income. We applied this method to the data from each group of studies that used education and income measures with identical categories.* We chose to analyze groups of studies, rather than individual surveys, because we worried that analyzing each study separately would lead, because of sample variability, to quite different principal components. Invariably, we found that the two measures contribute about equally to the common component, and this component explains about 70 to 73 percent of the variance in each measure for the Roper Trends Data and the General Social Surveys. Furthermore, the method led to very stable component loadings across studies.

The scores on the principal component from the two measures provided enough separate categories so that approximations to quintiles of between 16 and 24 percent per quintile were possible for the Roper data. The GSS includes more categories for both education and income, making the initial quintiles more precise. Groups of exactly 20 percent for either dataset could not be created directly because the discrete categories had many tied cases. To break these ties, we added a very small random number (on the order of .000001) to the principal component to break the ties. With this modification, true quintiles became possible because the people in the tied category were randomly divided into the two nearest quintiles, although each quintile includes some people who might really belong in the quintile above or below them. Because we do not have enough information to make the proper assignment, it is clearly better to assign ambiguous cases randomly to "finish up" a quintile than to have quintiles of uneven sizes.

---

*This discussion focuses on the problem of finding a common SES ranking. There is also another problem of "scoring" each category in an optimal fashion because, for example, one year of college might mean much more on an SES scale than one year of grammar school. We "solved" this problem in a mechanical fashion by simply assigning integers starting with 1 from the lowest to the highest category. It seems unlikely that this is the best scoring for the categories, especially for the income measure, which might be scored according to the number of dollars at the midpoint of the income category, but it is hard to think of a better approach.

11 Public Opinion, Economic Issues, and the Vote: Are Presidential Elections "All About the Benjamins"?

Paul R. Brewer

In a 1998 hit song, rapper Sean Combs argued that "it's all about the Benjamins"—that money (in this case, $100 bills) is what really matters. Although the artist formerly known as Puff Daddy presumably did not have presidential elections in mind when he wrote these lyrics, many political observers have used his logic to explain how voters make up their minds. What voters really care about, according to what we might dub the Puff Daddy theory of presidential elections, are dollars-and-cents issues: national economic conditions, budget deficits, taxes, and so forth. In 1996, for example, voters rewarded the incumbent, President Bill Clinton, with another four years in office because the national economy was doing well, just as they had punished incumbent George Bush in 1992 for a recession and a broken promise not to raise taxes. Or so the argument goes.

On the other hand, 2000 did not seem to be a good year for either Puff Daddy himself (he was indicted for bribery and unlawful possession of a handgun) or the Puff Daddy theory of presidential elections. Despite a booming economy and budget surpluses, the candidate of the party in the White House—Clinton's vice president, Al Gore—won the popular vote by only the slimmest of margins and lost the electoral vote. If voters attach more weight to economic issues than anything else, then why did Gore not win by a wide margin? Was the 2000 election not all about the Benjamins after all?

"The Economy, Stupid!"

The following account examines how public opinion on economic issues shapes the presidential vote. It focuses on the three most recent presidential elections: 1992, 1996, and 2000. First, though, it takes a closer look at what we know—or at least what previous research tells us—about public opinion, economic issues, and presidential voting. A good place to begin is with the most obvious economic issue: the performance of the national economy.

American history is sprinkled with presidents who lost reelection campaigns after the economy soured during their tenure. Martin Van Buren was swept out of office in the wake of the Panic of 1837. The Great Depression doomed Herbert Hoover's chances in 1932. In

1980 the winning candidate, Ronald Reagan, quipped: "A recession is when your neighbor loses his job and a depression is when you lose your job. Recovery is when Jimmy Carter loses his" (Boller 1996, 359). By contrast, presidents who served during economic good times typically have fared well in their bids for reelection. The moral seems clear: voters reward prosperity and punish economic hardship. As Clinton's chief strategist, James Carville, put it, "It's the economy, Stupid!"

That's a neat slogan. But which economy is it that matters? People could base their votes on national economic conditions or on personal economic circumstances. The former type of voting is sometimes called *sociotropic voting,* the latter, *pocketbook voting* (Kinder and Kiewet 1979). This distinction is not necessarily one between selfish pocketbook voters and altruistic sociotropic voters. People who vote on the basis of national economic circumstances may be acting on their own individualistic motives: they may care about how the national economy performs because that will ultimately influence their own financial fate as well.

To complicate matters, voters also may think *prospectively* or *retrospectively* about both the national economy and their personal finances. When people vote retrospectively, they base their votes on their perceptions of what has happened already—whether the economy has gotten better or worse, whether their personal fortunes have increased or decreased. When people vote prospectively, on the other hand, they base their votes on their expectations about what will happen to the national economy or to their own financial situation in the future. Put more simply, retrospective voting is about looking back, while prospective voting refers to looking forward.

Figure 11-1 summarizes the four types of economic voting. The conventional wisdom is that that sociotropic voting is more common than pocketbook voting (see, for example, Kinder and Kiewet 1979) and that retrospective voting is more common than prospective voting (see, for example, Fiorina 1981; Norpoth 1996). Not everyone agrees, however (Kramer 1983; MacKuen, Erikson, and Stimson 1992), so a look at the recent evidence is in order. Did voters in the past three presidential elections look back at the national economy?

The implications of economic voting—particularly retrospective, sociotropic voting—are intriguing, though controversial. Some observers, such as the late political scientist V. O. Key, have argued that "voters are not fools"—that the electorate acts as a "rational god of vengeance and reward" (1964, 568). Other commentators, however, have worried that if citizens vote on the basis of national economic circumstances, their faulty attributions of responsibility for those circumstances may mislead them. For example, Stephen Ansolabehere, Roy Behr, and Shanto Iyengar (1993, 203; see also Fiorina 1981) have noted that although "[President] Carter was widely blamed for the rampant inflation in the United States that was produced by the sudden surge in energy costs" during his term, there was "not much [he] could do to prevent the OPEC cartel from raising oil prices."

Figure 11-1 Types of Economic Voting

	Pocketbook voting	Sociotropic voting
Retrospective voting	Did I get a raise? Did I lose my job?	Did the economy grow? Did unemployment increase?
Prospective voting	Will I get a raise? Will I lose my job?	Will the economy grow? Will unemployment increase?

In any event, one point seems clear: voters take the economy into account when they choose between candidates for the White House. Some pundits and election forecasters have even suggested that *all* one truly needs to know in order to predict the outcome of a presidential campaign is the state of the economy. If the economy is in good shape, the party in the White House will stay; conversely, if the economy is in bad shape, out it goes.

Two Things in Life Are Certain (Maybe): Deficits and Taxes

Throughout U.S. history, a variety of other dollars-and-cents issues have played major roles in presidential campaigns. At the dawn of the twentieth century, for example, the debate over the gold standard dominated politics. "In two presidential campaigns," party boss George Washington Plunkitt (Riordan 1995, 88) once complained, "The leaders talked themselves red in the face about silver bein' the best money and gold bein' no good." He was referring to "free silver" advocate William Jennings Bryan, who won two Democratic nominations (and lost two presidential elections) by vowing that gold standard supporters "would not crucify mankind upon a cross of gold!" As for Plunkitt, he favored "all kinds of money—the more the better."

In recent years, tax proposals and budget deficits have loomed large in presidential politics. For decades the Gallup Organization has asked survey respondents, "Do you consider the amount of federal income taxes you have to pay as too high, about right, or too low?"[1] From the early 1960s onward, most respondents (always a majority, and often over 60 percent) have said they pay too much in taxes, while hardly any (never more than 2 percent) have said that they pay too little. This point has not been lost on presidential candidates, who have tried to woo voters with promises of tax cuts, "no new taxes," or (in one ill-fated case, that of Walter Mondale) tax increases. As federal budget deficits rose in the 1970s and 1980s—and with them, the national debt—they, too, became a major issue in presidential campaigns.

What role have these three critical economic issues—the performance of the national economy, taxes, and budget deficits—played in recent presidential elections? Is money the root of all presidential election outcomes? Admittedly, other factors also matter: for example, noneconomic issues (such as abortion and gay rights), candidate images (Bill Clinton as "Slick Willie"; Al Gore as "stiff"), and longstanding partisan loyalties. But there is ample evidence to suggest that the Puff Daddy theory was not far off in every election from 1976 to 1988.

1976–1988: From W.I.N. Buttons to "Read My Lips"

In 1976, the economy presented Republican president Gerald Ford with a major hurdle on his path to reelection. One problem facing the nation was inflation. As Barbara Holland (1989, 268) related, with tongue only slightly in cheek:

Ford tackled the situation head-on. He had millions and millions of big round buttons printed up that said "W.I.N.," which stood for "Whip Inflation Now," and he promised that if we wore them every time we went out in public, pretty soon prices would stop going up and then slowly but surely start going down. Unfortunately not enough people remembered to wear them—you know how it is when you're dressing in a hurry in the morning—so it didn't work, but it might have.

High unemployment compounded Ford's dilemma. In 1976, the unemployment rate was about 8 percent, and Ford's opponent, Jimmy Carter, "won seven of eight votes from persons who held unemployment to be the major issue" (Pomper 1977, 75). Carter won the election, buoyed by voters' negative perceptions of business conditions and of the government's performance on economic policy and inflation (Fiorina 1981, 48).

In 1980, Carter's reelection bid was hampered by a weak economy. During a debate the challenger, Ronald Reagan, summed up his campaign theme by asking viewers:

Are you better off than you were four years ago? Is it easier for you to go and buy things in the stores than it was four years ago? Is there more or less unemployment in the country than there was four years ago? . . . if you don't agree, if you don't think this course that we've been on for the last four years is what you would like to see us follow for the next four, then I could suggest another choice that you have.

Most voters answered Reagan's question in the negative, and Reagan won the election. "Despite their partisanship," Pomper wrote (1981, 88–89), "those Democrats suffering economically defected to Reagan. . . . Jimmy Carter was not defeated in the marketplace of ideas; he was trounced in the marketplace of food and gasoline and mortgages."

Four years later, Reagan posed the same question: "Are you better off now than you were four years ago?" This time, though, he was an incumbent presiding over a growing economy. His opponent, Walter Mondale, tried to shift the focus of the campaign to two other economic issues—budget deficits and, most famously, taxes. "Mr. Reagan will raise taxes," the Democratic challenger said in his nomination acceptance speech, "and so will I. He won't tell you. I just did." Mondale's announcement inspired more ridicule than popular support. A *Saturday Night Live* sketch, for example, portrayed an incredulous reporter stating that no candidate who had promised to raise taxes had ever won an election, then asking Mondale why he pledged to raise taxes; "I don't know," is all he could say in reply. In the end, Reagan crushed Mondale, winning 59 percent of the popular vote and every electoral vote except those of the District of Columbia and Mondale's home state of Minnesota.

Again, economic issues played a key role. Fewer than one in four Americans had approved of the way Ford was handling the economy in 1976 or Carter was in 1980. In 1984 a majority approved of Reagan's economic performance. Those who did by and large voted for Reagan, just as those who had disapproved of Ford's and Carter's performances by and large voted against them (Abramson et al. 1985). Moreover, among voters who considered taxes the most important issue in deciding whom they voted for, an overwhelming majority preferred Reagan to Mondale (Keeter 1985). Mondale did win a majority among voters who chose the deficit as the most crucial issue, but their numbers were far too small to help him.

As Reagan's second term wound down, inflation, unemployment, and interest rates were still low. His political heir, Vice President George Bush, capitalized on the economic situation in his campaign:

The Republicans . . . started with a strong anti-Carter television spot to remind people of how angry they had been eight years ago. Black-and-white stills of former President Carter were interspersed with pictures of gas lines and unemployment lines; the old song "I Remember You" played in the background. Voters were warned not to take the Reagan successes for granted. (Farah and Klein 1989, 118)

Bush also vowed in his acceptance speech at the Republican convention: "Read my lips: no new taxes," a "one-liner he would repeat almost daily during the fall" (Hershey 1989, 79). His Democratic opponent, Michael Dukakis, could not persuade voters that he would make a better economic manager than Bush. Most Americans thought they were better off in 1988 than they had been in 1980 (Farah and Klein 1989, 118). Bush's tax pledge also resonated with the public: two-thirds of the voters endorsed it, and many were influenced by it (Pomper 1989, 150). Bush won the election, garnering 54 percent of the popular vote.

So far, so good, then, for the proposition that presidential elections are all about the Benjamins. But have economic issues played the same role in more recent presidential elections? The elections of 1992, 1996, and 2000 provide a useful mix of scenarios: an incumbent president running under poor economic conditions, an incumbent president running during economic growth, and an incumbent vice president running during a continued economic boom.

1992–2000: Three New Tests of the Puff Daddy Theory

The analysis that follows uses data from a variety of sources but focuses in particular on the results of the National Election Studies (NES). These surveys asked voters to rate all four "economies," retrospective and prospective, personal and national. Thus we can see how many people judged each economy favorably or unfavorably, how people who made a specific judgment (for example, "the national economy has gotten worse") tended to vote, and whether one type of economic voting mattered more than others. The studies also measured public opinion about budget deficits and taxes, allowing us to gauge these issues' effects on the outcomes, too.

1992: A Bad Economy, a Broken Pledge, and Ross Perot's Storm

The economic outlook was bleak when President Bush launched his 1992 reelection effort. Whereas disposable per capita income had grown 8.5 percent and 6.6 percent, respectively, during Reagan's two terms in office, it grew a net of 1 percent during Bush's tenure (Alvarez and Nagler 1995). The deficit, meanwhile, grew much more rapidly. Bush had even agreed to "new taxes" as part of a 1990 budget deal designed to reduce the deficit.

The Economy in the 1992 Election. Placed on the defensive, Bush struggled to defend his economic record. On January 18, 1992, he spoke to New Hampshire voters about the recession:

That guy over there at Pease—a woman actually—she said something about a country-Western song, you know, about the train, a light at the end of the tunnel. I only hope it's not a train coming the other way. Well, I said to her, "well, I'm a country music fan. I love it, always have . . . But nevertheless, I said to them you know there's another one the Nitty Ditty Gritty Great Bird [Nitty Gritty Dirt Band]— that they did. And it says if you want to see a rainbow you've got to stand a little rain. We've had a little rain. (Boller 1996, 398)

The Clinton campaign's message about the economy was simpler: "The economy, Stupid!" On the stump, Clinton repeatedly criticized Bush's handling of the economy and touted his own economic plans, as did independent candidate Ross Perot.

How did voters react to the economy in 1992? In a word, negatively. For starters, the American public perceived the national economic climate as dire. Gallup polls consistently found that the percentage of respondents who rated "economic conditions in this country today" as "poor" far outnumbered the percentage rating conditions as "excellent" or "good." Americans were also pessimistic about the future of the economy. When Gallup asked, "Right now, do you think that economic conditions in the country as a whole are getting better or getting worse?" the public's verdict invariably favored "getting worse." Fig-

Figure 11-2 Perceptions of Current and Future Economic Conditions,
January 1992–October 2000

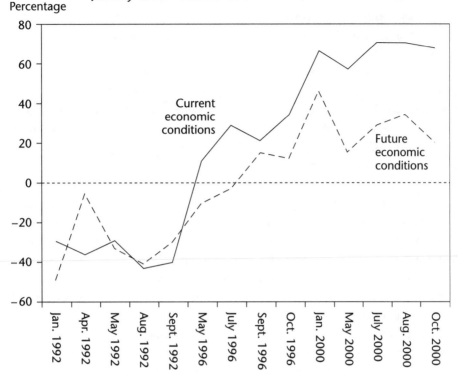

Source: Gallup Organization.

Note: "Current economic conditions" represents the percentage of respondents who said the economy was in excellent or good condition minus the percentage of respondents who said the economy was in poor condition. "Future economic conditions" represents the percentage of respondents who said the economy was getting better minus the percentage of respondents who said the economy was getting worse.

ure 11-2 charts the trends in the Gallup poll findings, represented as the percentage of favorable economic evaluations minus the percentage of economic unfavorable evaluations.

The respondents in the 1992 NES rendered a similar verdict. More than 70 percent said that the economy had gotten worse over both the past year and the past four years; more than a third answered "much worse" to each question. Only 5 percent said the economy had improved over the past year or the past four years. NES respondents were somewhat more optimistic about the future; even so, half of them expected the national economy to stay the same (that is, bad) and 19 percent expected it to get worse.

When it came to their own pocketbooks, Americans were also unhappy. At first glance, judgments of personal economics do not seem as harsh. When asked whether they were "better off or worse off financially than they were a year ago," NES respondents were more likely to say "worse off" (35 percent) than "better off" (30 percent)—but not by much. They were fairly optimistic about their own financial future: 34 percent expected to be better off in 1993, whereas only 10 percent expected to be worse off. Below this surface, though, were signs of personal economic anxiety: for example, about half of those surveyed said that their income had fallen behind the cost of living over the past year. Perhaps most crucially, Americans saw the federal government as hurting rather than helping them economically. Many NES respondents (29 percent) attributed worsening personal finances to "the economic policies of the federal government," but only 3 percent attributed improving personal finances to government.

Given their perceptions of economic circumstances, it is hardly surprising that voters saw the economy as the biggest problem facing the nation in 1992. Figure 11-3 tracks responses to a Gallup question—"What do you think is the most important problem facing the country today?"—over the course of the Bush presidency. The percentage of respondents who answered that "the economy," "unemployment," or "jobs" was the most important problem rose from only 6 percent in September 1989 to 64 percent in late August and early September 1992. The 1992 NES included a similar question: "What do you personally feel are the most important problems the government in Washington should try to take care of?" Two-thirds of the interviewees cited economic issues as the most important issue for the federal government, with 23 percent specifically mentioning unemployment or the recession (Abramson et al. 1995, 174). These percentages represented dramatic increases from 1988 (when the figures were 45 percent and 5 percent, respectively). Clearly, Americans were becoming more and more concerned about the performance of the economy as the 1992 election approached.

Respondents were also highly dissatisfied with Bush's performance on this most important issue. When the NES respondents were asked, "Do you approve or disapprove of the way George Bush is handling the economy?" 79 percent disapproved. Indeed, 62 percent disapproved strongly, whereas only 7 percent approved strongly. The American public saw Clinton as a more promising economic manager. Upon being asked, "Which presidential candidate do you think would do a better job at handling the nation's economy—George Bush, Bill Clinton, or wouldn't there be any difference?" those naming Clinton outnumbered those naming Bush by almost a two-to-one margin.

Voters who expressed dissatisfaction with the national economy tended to favor Clinton—and because those outnumbered the ones who were happy with the national economy, this issue gave Clinton an electoral advantage. Of the NES respondents who said that the nation's economy had gotten better over the past year, 71 percent voted for Bush and 16 percent voted for Clinton; unfortunately for Bush, such people were rare. In contrast,

Figure 11-3   Most Important Problem Facing the Nation,
September 1989–September 1992

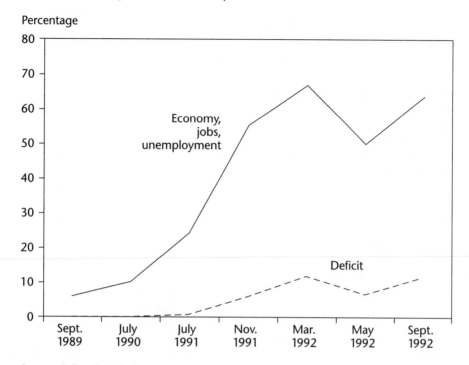

Percentage

Source: Gallup Organization.

among the interviewees who thought that the economy was getting worse (72 percent of the sample), Clinton trounced Bush, 55 percent to 26 percent. Similarly, whereas the few respondents who thought they were better off now than they had been four years earlier preferred Bush, the much greater number of respondents who thought otherwise preferred Clinton. When respondents were asked to look forward, rather than backward, the pattern persisted: those who saw rosy days ahead for the national economy chose Bush by a slim margin (43 percent to 40 percent), but those who saw dark clouds picked Clinton overwhelmingly (49 percent to 29 percent).

What about voters' perceptions of personal, rather than national, economic circumstances? Among NES respondents who thought they were better off in 1992 than in 1991, Bush won narrowly, 43 percent to 35 percent; among those who thought they were worse off, Clinton won 58 percent to 21 percent. Expectations about personal finances were not strongly related to voter preferences: respondents preferred Clinton to Bush regardless of whether they expected to be better off or worse off in 1993.

A closer look at the NES data reveals that one type of economic voting was more com-

Table 11-1 Influences on Votes for Bush in 1992 (Bush and Clinton Voters Only)

Independent Variable	Coefficient	Standard Error
Favorable retrospective evaluation of national economy	1.45**	.39
Favorable prospective evaluation of national economy	0.38	.30
Favorable retrospective evaluation of personal finances	0.56*	.25
Favorable prospective evaluation of personal finances	−0.46	.35
Republican partisanship (7-point scale)	5.49**	.34
Conservative ideology (7-point scale)	4.26**	.56
Gender (1 if female, 0 if male)	0.35	.20
Race (1 if African American, 0 otherwise)	−2.32**	.50
Education (7-point scale)	−0.06*	.02
Income (in \$/100,000)	−0.48	.40
Age (in years/100)	−0.40	.61
Constant	−5.21	.59
Number of cases	(1,234)	

Source: American National Election Study, 1992.

Note: Coefficients represent the impact of the independent variables on the dependent variable, vote choice. Variables are coded so that a positive coefficient indicates a positive relationship between the independent variable and voting for Bush. Respondents who did not vote for Bush or Clinton are excluded from the analysis. Except where noted otherwise, all variables are coded to range from 0 to 1.

The coefficients were estimated by using logistic regression. The model correctly predicts how 87.68 percent of the respondents voted; the χ^2 for the model is 961.25 (significant at the .01 level). See the Appendix for more information about statistical techniques.

* The impact of this independent variable is statistically significant at the .05 level (that is, the chance that an effect this large would occur by random chance is less than 5 percent).
** The impact of this independent variable is statistically significant at the .01 level.

mon than other types in 1992. Table 11-1 reports the results of a logistic regression analysis of influences on voters' preferences in 1992. As the table shows, retrospective judgments of the national economy had a stronger effect (statistically significant at the .01 level) on the vote than did prospective sociotropic judgments (not significant), retrospective pocketbook judgments (significant at the .05 level), or prospective pocketbook judgments (not significant). Put another way, voters tended to focus on the big picture, not their personal fortunes, and they tended to look backward rather than forward. The conventional wisdom about economic voting was right in this case.

By looking only at the impact of the economy, might we be overlooking other forces that influenced both public opinion about the economy and voters' candidate preferences? For example, Republicans' party loyalties could have shaped their economic perceptions in

Bush's favor, while Democrats looking for a reason to support Clinton might have been predisposed to think the worst about the economy. However, this relationship was no mere illusion. Opinions about the economy influenced the vote even when a host of other forces that might influence voter preferences were taken into account—not only party loyalty but also ideology, gender, race, education, age, and income.

Indeed, voters themselves identified the economy as the single most important factor in the election. In a *Los Angeles Times* exit poll that asked voters what issues were most important to them in deciding how to vote, 69 percent of Clinton voters and 72 percent of Perot voters said "jobs" or "the economy." No other issue came close to matching those figures (see also Alvarez and Nagler 1995).

Deficits and Taxes in the 1992 Election. Ross Perot, the wild card in the 1992 election, won 19 percent of the vote as an independent candidate. Public opinion about the economy is not a persuasive explanation of the Perot phenomenon: support for Perot did not vary dramatically between those who thought the economy was doing well and those who thought it was doing poorly. One of the Texas billionaire's favorite campaign themes, however, was another economic issue: the budget deficit, which served as the focus for the following ad script:

The national debt. It is a massive storm that is clouding America's future. It is a debt so enormous that it will take one-third of the federal income tax collected this year just to pay the interest. . . . When will it end? When we choose a candidate who understands that deficit spending is an irresponsible act of government, not an uncontrollable force of nature. . . . The candidate is Ross Perot.

Perot told the public he could solve the problem "without working up a sweat. It's just that simple" (Boller 1996, 396).

In July 1990, Perot's pet issue was almost completely absent from the public's radar screen: in a Gallup poll that month, fewer than 1 percent named the deficit as the most important issue facing the nation. Over the next two years, though, the deficit began to weigh more heavily on the public's mind: by August of 1992, 12 percent chose it as the nation's biggest problem (see Figure 11-3). It is difficult to say whether Perot was responsible for the public's increasing attention to deficit spending or merely took advantage of it; a mixture of the two seems likely. What is clear is that concern over the deficit boosted public support for Perot. Forty percent of Perot voters in a *Los Angeles Times* exit poll said that the federal budget deficit was an important issue in deciding their vote, four times the proportion of Clinton and Bush voters (Brownstein 1992). In particular, the issue won Perot support among NES respondents who otherwise would have preferred Bush (Alvarez and Nagler 1995).

Finally, let us not forget Bush's 1988 pledge, "Read my lips, no new taxes." Indeed, many Clinton supporters remembered it well. In the documentary *The War Room*, James Carville referred to the statement (hyperbolically, perhaps) as the most famous broken campaign promise in history. One in four Clinton voters surveyed in the *Los Angeles Times* exit poll said that Bush's flip-flop on raising taxes had a major influence on their vote.

The Verdict. The election of 1992 *was* all about the Benjamins. It would be an exaggeration to say that voters made their decisions entirely on the basis of economic issues, for other factors mattered, too. Yet the evidence strongly indicates that dollars and cents trumped all other issues in determining Bill Clinton's 43 percent to 37 percent victory over incumbent George Bush.

1996: A Good Economy Beats Bob Dole's 15 Percent Tax Cut

As Clinton prepared for his reelection bid in 1996, economic reports were as bright as they had been gloomy in 1992. During Clinton's first term, the economy averaged a 2.5 percent growth rate; by the second quarter of 1996 it was growing at a 4.8 percent clip (Herrnson and Wilcox 1997). Unemployment was at a seven-year low, inflation at a thirty-year low (Pomper 1997). Even budget deficits were declining.

The Economy in the 1996 Election. Americans' perceptions of the national economy reflected the good news. As the 1996 campaign progressed, public opinion on the economy became increasingly positive (see Figure 11-2). By October, 47 percent of Gallup poll interviewees rated the economy as excellent or good, whereas only 13 percent rated it as poor. Thirty-nine percent of NES respondents said that the nation's economy had improved over the past year, and only 17 percent said it had worsened. Americans also became increasingly optimistic about the future of the national economy. In May 1996, more Gallup interviewees expected a downturn than expected continued growth, but by the eve of the election these expectations had flip-flopped. Sixty-two percent of NES respondents expected the economy to stay the same (that is, good) and 25 percent expected it to get better. Only 13 percent expected it to get worse.

Americans were just as pleased with their personal finances. Asked whether they were better or worse off than they had been a year before, Gallup interviewees who said the former outnumbered those who said the latter by a twenty-point margin. Optimism about the future was even greater. When Gallup and NES asked people whether they expected to be better or worse off in 1997, they were overwhelmingly more likely to say better off.

Americans were happy not only with the economy but also with Clinton's handling of it. Two in three NES interviewees approved of his performance on the economy. One in three approved strongly. Americans still cared deeply about the issue, too; respondents in a Voter News Service exit poll, for example, ranked the economy as the top campaign issue (Sabato 1997).

Clinton was quick to take credit for the economic gains. He trumpeted them in the first presidential debate: "Four years ago I ran for president at a time of high unemployment and rising frustration. Now there's a record: 10½ million more jobs, rising incomes. . . . We are better off than we were four years ago. Let's keep it going."

Dole, asked to reply, wisecracked, "Well, he's better off than he was four years ago." His dilemma was that most Americans felt that they were, too.

In the end, the economy was the number one reason voters gave for supporting Clinton. Half of the Clinton voters polled by the *Los Angeles Times* named the economy or jobs as one of the two most important issues to them in deciding how they would vote (Brownstein 1996); 61 percent of the Clinton voters in the Voter News Service poll said the same thing (Sabato 1997). The 1996 NES survey provides further evidence that the performance of the national economy benefited Clinton. The relatively few voters who said that the economy had worsened since 1995 or would worsen in 1997 favored Dole over Clinton by a two-to-one margin. On the other hand, the more numerous voters who saw past improvement and expected future improvement favored Clinton by an even wider margin. The logistic regression analysis reported in Table 11-2 shows that one of these differences remains statistically significant even after accounting for the effects of party loyalty, ideology, and demographics. As in 1992, voters thought about the national economy more retrospectively than prospectively: backward-looking judgments had a stronger effect on voter preferences than did forward-looking ones.

Voters also paid more attention to the national economy than to personal finances—another echo of 1992. Whereas Clinton won 71 percent support from voters who said the national economy had improved, he won a smaller majority (62 percent) among voters who said their own financial situation had improved. Dole won a 27 percentage point victory among voters who said the national economy had gotten worse, but he barely beat Clinton among voters who said their own financial situation had gotten worse. Furthermore, the effects of pocketbook judgments disappear entirely when sociotropic judgments and other relevant factors are taken into consideration (see Table 11-2). The conventional wisdom was right again in 1996: retrospective sociotropic voting not only mattered, it mattered more than any other type of economic voting.

Deficits and Taxes in the 1996 Election. Aware that he needed an issue to counterbalance the performance of the national economy, Dole chose to campaign on a pledge to cut taxes by 15 percent, even selecting tax-cut champion Jack Kemp to be his running mate. This campaign theme was somewhat awkward for Dole, who was not known as a tax cutter. His opponents highlighted the inconsistency and stressed the dangers of such a plan: during the vice presidential debate, Al Gore repeatedly called the 15 percent tax cut a "risky scheme" that would "blow a hole in the deficit" and "knock our economy off track."

Table 11-2 Influences on Votes for Clinton in 1996 (Clinton and Dole Voters Only)

Independent Variable	Coefficient	Standard Error
Favorable retrospective evaluation of national economy	1.80**	.38
Favorable prospective evaluation of national economy	.79	.42
Favorable retrospective evaluation of personal finances	−.10	.33
Favorable prospective evaluation of personal finances	.52	.45
Support for a tax cut	−.76*	.34
Republican partisanship (7-point scale)	−5.22**	.41
Conservative ideology (7-point scale)	−4.25**	.72
Gender (1 if female, 0 if male)	.52*	.24
Race (1 if African American, 0 otherwise)	4.06**	1.08
Education (7-point scale)	−.24	.21
Income (in $/100,000)	−.16	.41
Age (in years/100)	−.56	.74
Constant	4.12	.64
Number of cases	(987)	

Source: American National Election Study, 1996.

Note: Coefficients represent the impact of the independent variables on the dependent variable, vote choice. Variables are coded so that a positive coefficient indicates a positive relationship between the independent variable and voting for Clinton. Respondents who did not vote for Clinton or Dole are excluded from the analysis. Except where noted otherwise, all variables are coded to range from 0 to 1.

The coefficients were estimated by using logistic regression. The model correctly predicts how 89.56 percent of the respondents voted; the χ^2 for the model is 832.81 (significant at the .01 level). See the Appendix for more information about statistical techniques.

* Statistically significant at the .05 level.
** Statistically significant at the .01 level.

Dole's appeal produced mixed results. Many voters did not care about tax cuts either way. When asked what they thought about the idea of a 15 percent tax cut, half the NES respondents said they had no opinion or had not thought much about the issue. Of those who did have an opinion, 41 percent said federal income taxes should not be cut at all. Furthermore, in a poll conducted by the *New York Times* and CBS, 64 percent of respondents expressed skepticism about whether Dole could actually implement his proposal if elected (Berke 1996). The public's lack of awareness about the proposal was yet another obstacle for Dole. Ten percent of NES interviewees thought he *opposed* tax cuts, and a *Washington Post* poll found that almost one in three voters was unaware that *either* candidate had proposed a 15 percent tax cut (Keeter 1997).

Nevertheless, Dole's plan did appeal to some voters. Even taking other factors into account, including the national economy, NES respondents who favored a tax cut preferred Dole to Clinton. As Table 11-2 reports, the impact of support for a tax cut was significant at the .05 level (see also Alvarez and Nagler 1998). Indeed, voters in the Voter News Service exit poll who listed taxes as the top issue preferred Dole to Clinton, 73 percent to 19 percent (Sabato 1997). However, these voters were outnumbered two to one by those who cared more about the economy than taxes.

What of Ross Perot and his call for deficit reduction? In 1996, Perot was a voice in the wilderness. Voters who were worried about the deficit still liked him; they constituted 25 percent of his supporters, according to the *Los Angeles Times* exit poll (Brownstein 1996). Those supporters, however, were few and far between this time, and Perot won only 9 percent of the vote. As for Dole and Clinton voters, relatively few of them named the deficit the most important issue in deciding how they would vote.

The Verdict. In 1996, the Puff Daddy theory of presidential election outcomes triumphed again. Voters cared about both the economy and taxes, but Clinton's economic record beat Dole's tax cut. Clinton won, 49 percent to 41 percent. It was *still* all about the Benjamins.

2000: What Happened?

On August 14, 2000, Bill Clinton spoke at the Democratic National Convention about the state of the economy:

Today, we are in the midst of the longest economic expansion in our history. More than 22 million new jobs, the lowest unemployment in 30 years. . . . For the first time in decades, wages are rising at all income levels. . . . Today, we have gone from the largest deficits in history to the largest surpluses in history—and if we stay on course, we can make America debt-free for the first time since 1835.

He then presented his vice president as the person to maintain this economic growth, "Al Gore and Joe Lieberman will keep our prosperity going. . . . In stark contrast, Republicans want to spend every dime of our projected surplus and then some on big tax cuts." Clinton's message was clear: a vote for Gore was a vote for a strong economy.

The Economy in the 2000 Election. Americans shared Clinton's view that the economy was in great shape. According to Gallup polls, public perceptions of the national economy in 2000 were considerably more favorable than the already positive perceptions of 1996 (see Figure 11-2). In the month of Clinton's speech, for example, 74 percent said that national economic conditions were excellent or good, whereas only 4 percent said they were bad. Gallup respondents also foresaw good times ahead for the national economy. Those who expected the national economy to get better consistently outnumbered those who expected it to get worse, as Figure 11-2 shows. The same patterns held among NES interviewees. Forty percent of them said that the national economy was stronger than it had been a year ago, whereas only 17 percent said it had worsened; similarly, 81 percent of them expected national economic conditions to stay the same or even improve.

Americans saw themselves as better off, too. Compared with their 1996 counterparts (let alone their 1992 counterparts), the Gallup interviewees of 2000 were more likely to call their personal financial situation excellent or good, and they were overwhelmingly optimistic about their future financial situation. As of October 2000, those who expected their own situation to improve outnumbered their pessimistic peers by a 57 percentage point margin. Of the NES respondents, 33 percent said they were better off financially than a year earlier and 12 percent said they were worse off. Those expecting to be better off a year in the future outnumbered those expecting to be worse off, 40 percent to 6 percent.

All in all, economic circumstances portended a Gore victory. Recall the simple rule offered by pundits: if the economy is in good shape, the party in the White House will stay there. Because Gore ran to succeed Clinton under the most favorable economic circumstances in recent memory, one might have expected him to win by a landslide. Yet he and GOP nominee George W. Bush virtually tied in the popular vote, and Bush won a narrow (albeit contested) victory in the electoral college. In the aftermath of the election, many observers wondered whether voters really cared about the economy that year.

Voters did, in fact, cast their ballots partly on the basis of the economy, or at least on the basis of their retrospective sociotropic evaluations of it. Among NES respondents who thought that the national economy had improved, Gore won a two-to-one victory. Among the less numerous voters who thought it had worsened, he lost by the same margin. A logistic regression analysis of the 2000 NES data (Table 11-3) shows that backward-looking evaluations of the national economy influenced voters' preferences, even controlling for other factors. Other types of economic voting were inconsequential in 2000, but people who thought the national economy had improved were significantly more likely to vote for Gore than those who thought it had worsened. Why, then, did Al Gore not win the presidency?

Put simply, economic voting did not matter enough to give him the victory. Although voters cared about the economy, they did not care enough about the economy to make it *the* decisive issue. When Gallup respondents were asked to name the *most* important problem facing this country, the "economy in general" was tied for fifth, with 8 percent; even adding the 3 percent who said "unemployment/jobs," it still only tied for third. When voters in a *Los Angeles Times* exit poll were allowed to list two issues that were important to them in deciding how they voted for president, only 26 percent chose the economy. Even among Gore voters, only 36 percent named the economy.

That begs the question of why voters placed less weight on the economy than they had in

Table 11-3 Influences on Votes for Gore in 2000 (Gore and Bush Voters Only)

Independent Variable	Coefficient	Standard Error
Favorable retrospective evaluation of national economy	1.00**	.32
Favorable prospective evaluation of national economy	.26	.35
Favorable retrospective evaluation of personal finances	−.63	.36
Favorable prospective evaluation of personal finances	.40	.40
Support for a tax cut	−.92*	.23
Republican partisanship (7-point scale)	−6.40**	.42
Conservative ideology (3-point scale)	−1.00**	.34
Gender (1 if female, 0 if male)	.19	.22
Race (1 if African American, 0 otherwise)	1.57*	.63
Education (7-point scale)	.52	.45
Income (in $/100,000)	−.12	.28
Age (in years/100)	−.55	.70
Constant	3.49	.71
Number of cases	(1,017)	

Source: American National Election Study, 2000.

Note: Coefficients represent the impact of the independent variables on the dependent variable, vote choice. Variables are coded so that a positive coefficient indicates a positive relationship between the independent variable and voting for Gore. Respondents who did not vote for Gore or Bush are excluded from the analysis. Except where noted otherwise, all variables are coded to range from 0 to 1.

The coefficients were estimated by using logistic regression. The model correctly predicts how 87.91 percent of the respondents voted; the χ^2 for the model is 802.41 (significant at the .01 level). See the Appendix for more information about statistical techniques.

* Statistically significant at the .05 level.
** Statistically significant at the .01 level.

the previous two elections. One answer is that the prosperity of the 1990s eroded the public's concerns about the economy, allowing other issues to rise to the top of the agenda. Economic considerations are less likely to be decisive during a long period of prosperity, when the economy is less on people's minds as an issue, than they are in a bad economic period or during a period of recovery, when the bad times are still on people's minds. Indeed, some citizens had even forgotten why they were so upset with Bush's father back in 1992. By the end of Clinton's tenure, according to Gallup pollster David Moore (2000), Americans had "revised their dour views of almost a decade ago, giving a retrospective rating of the 1992 economy that [was] much more positive: 52 percent remembered it as excellent or good, and only 12 percent as poor" (compare with Figure 11-2). They also judged Bush's economic performance less harshly than they had at the time: in a June 1999 Gallup poll,

58 percent said they approved of the elder Bush's handling of the economy, whereas only 36 percent disapproved.

Moreover, polls found that Americans did not give Gore much credit for the rosy state of the economy. When Gallup asked respondents who deserved the most credit for the good economy—"the Clinton-Gore administration, Congress, Alan Greenspan and the Federal Reserve, or the American entrepreneur and worker"—only 22 percent chose Clinton-Gore. Only 8 percent of interviewees said that Gore himself deserved a "great deal" of credit for the improvement of the state of the economy; although 37 percent gave him "a fair amount" of the credit, 33 percent gave him "not much" credit and 17 percent gave him none. Just as people were dubious about Gore's attempt to claim responsibility for inventing the Internet, so too were they skeptical about assigning him responsibility for inventing the prosperity of the 1990s.

Some have argued that the Gore campaign could have done more to capitalize on the economic gains of the 1990s. Gore did point to the administration's economic record on occasion. For example, in his acceptance speech at the Democratic convention he proclaimed:

For almost eight years now, I've been the partner of a leader who moved us out of the valley of recession and into the longest period of prosperity in American history. I say to you tonight: millions of Americans will live better lives for a long time to come because of the job that's been done by President Bill Clinton.

At the same time, however, he also attempted to distance himself from Clinton: "This election is not an award for past performance. I'm not asking you to vote for me on the basis of the economy we have. . . . I stand here tonight as my own man." Was Gore casting away his most powerful advantage? We can only speculate about how the election would have turned out if Gore had campaigned more aggressively on the administration's economic record. In the election that really happened, though, the state of the economy did not give him enough of a boost to carry him to victory.

Taxes in the 2000 Election. Gore and Bush clashed repeatedly on the issue of tax cuts. Each offered a tax-cutting plan. Each criticized his opponent's plan. In the first presidential debate, Gore asserted:

Under Governor Bush's tax cut proposal, he would spend more money on tax cuts for the wealthiest 1 percent than all of the new spending that he proposes for education, health care, prescription drugs and national defense all combined. Now, I think those are the wrong priorities.

Gore repeated this charge seven more times in the first debate alone. Bush replied that Gore was using "fuzzy math": "[Gore] says he's going to give you tax cuts. Fifty million of you won't receive it. He said in his speech he wants to make sure the right people get tax relief.

That's not the role of a president to decide right and wrong. Everybody who pays taxes ought to get tax relief." The same themes reappeared in subsequent debates and in the candidates' television commercials.

Did the tax issue give Bush an advantage? At first glance, the answer appeared to be yes. In a Pew Research Center survey, few of those who preferred Gore cited the tax issue as a reason for liking him, but many Bush supporters specifically mentioned taxes as a reason for liking their candidate. Twenty-five percent of the Bush voters surveyed by the *Los Angeles Times* listed taxes as one of the two most important issues in deciding how they voted for president; only 9 percent of Gore voters mentioned taxes. Moreover, as Table 11-3 reports, NES respondents who approved of using the federal budget surplus to cut taxes preferred Bush to Gore (effect significant at the .05 level).

Other poll results, however, cast doubt on whether the public bought Bush's tax cut plans. When the Pew Research Center asked whether Bush or Gore would do a better job with taxes, respondents split almost evenly. Gallup poll interviewees actually preferred Gore's plan to Bush's by an eight- or nine-point margin. Moreover, when Gallup asked whether respondents preferred "broad, across-the-board tax cuts, (or) targeted tax cuts to alleviate specific problems (or) no tax cuts at all," 44 percent favored targeted tax cuts and 10 percent favored no tax cuts. Only a minority, 44 percent, endorsed the broad, across-the-board tax cuts that Bush promised. Voters cared about taxes, but neither candidate had a clear edge on the issue.

The Verdict. The third time was not the charm for the Puff Daddy theory of presidential election outcomes. With the new surplus, the deficit issue was nowhere to be seen.[2] The tax issue led to a draw. Even the traditional powerhouse, retrospective evaluations of the national economy, failed to prove decisive: if the election had been all about the economy, Gore would have won. Instead, this time it was *not* all about the Benjamins.

Conclusion: Two out of Three Ain't Bad

The evidence suggests that the Puff Daddy theory provides a compelling explanation of the outcomes of the 1992 and 1996 elections, but not of the 2000 election. What should we make of this? Are presidential elections really all about the Benjamins?

One answer is simply no. From this perspective, the 2000 results put to rest the idea that economic considerations always exercise the decisive impact on the outcome of presidential elections. Although there are numerous explanations for why the pattern was broken in 2000, the most intriguing one lies in the changing dynamics of economic evaluations. Eight years, it seems, was sufficient time for voters to forget past economic woes. Perhaps this was because voters took the recent prosperity for granted because their most recent point of reference, the 1991–1992 recession, was too distant in memory to matter; then again, perhaps they discounted prosperity because Al Gore failed to stake a persuasive claim that he deserved credit for it.

From another perspective, the answer is that presidential elections *are* all about the Benjamins, the premise being that the 1992 and 1996 results fit the normal pattern and that the 2000 result was a rare exception to the rule. In looking for regularities in politics, we cannot realistically expect to be right every time. Having begun with a 1990s Puff Daddy lyric, it seems fitting to end with 1970s lyric by Meat Loaf: "Two out of three ain't bad." Even though special circumstances that prevailed in 2000 worked against the emergence of economic issues as decisive, they still influenced voters' choices. Furthermore, the 1992 and 1996 elections pose further confirmation of what political analysts have long known: that such issues are generally a crucial determinant of how presidential elections come out. That this is a tendency—albeit, it would seem, a strong one—rather than a universal truth is made clear by the 2000 election.

Notes

1. Except where noted, the survey data reported in this chapter were obtained from the Web pages of the Gallup Organization, the National Election Studies, the Pew Research Center for the People and the Press, and the *Los Angeles Times.*

2. Only 1 percent of Gallup poll respondents named the deficit as the most important issue in 2000.

Part 5   Governmental Connections

In February 1999 the president of the United States was tried in the U.S. Senate, after he had been impeached in the House. Although the issues surrounding the impeachment were complex (Rozell and Wilcox 1999), at its core was Bill Clinton's denial of an affair with Monica Lewinsky. Clinton told television viewers directly that "I did not have sexual relations with that woman"; later he admitted to having encounters with Lewinsky that he claimed did not meet the definition of "sex." Republicans were deeply angered by Clinton's behavior, but the public response caught many pollsters by surprise. Many Americans reported high levels of satisfaction with Clinton's professional performance but dissatisfaction with his personal conduct.

The health of a democracy might be judged by how much confidence its citizens have in the government. A high level of trust would seem to indicate that the public is pleased with the performance of the government or at least has confidence that the government will act fairly in solving society's problems. High levels of trust allow governments the flexibility to tackle society's most difficult problems, which often have short-term costs and do not produce benefits until sometime in the future. In addition, reserve public trust allows government officials to fail—for example, when the economy falters or an international intervention results in military casualties.

Since the early 1960s the American public has become very cynical toward the government. Only about one-third of Americans in 1998 felt that they could always or most of the time trust the federal government to do "what is right," according to the National Election Study's survey. Two-thirds of Americans felt that the government was run for the benefits of a few big interests, and a similar number believed that government officials waste a lot of the taxpayers' money. One in four Americans felt that there were quite a few crooked people running the government.

In light of events since 1960 (Vietnam, Watergate, the troubled economy of the 1970s–1980s, and a series of personal and financial scandals involving members of Congress), such cynicism is understandable. The government does not stand alone in this crisis of confidence. The public has less faith today than in the recent past in a wide variety of institutions, including big business, schools, doctors, and organized religion (Lipset and Schneider 1987).

Some public skepticism may arise from a greater awareness by the public of politicians' efforts to shape public opinion to their advantage. Kathleen McGraw in her chapter examines the outcome of deliberate attempts by elected officials to mold public opinion. Modern presidents use a strategy of "going public" (Kernell 1997), in which they use speeches and appearances to shape the political agenda and influence public opinion. All officials, at times, use a strategy of "crafted talk," wherein they use public opinion polls to find ways to fit the politician's preferred policy outcome to public preferences. When politicians err and cast unpopular votes or get caught in scandals, they need to engage in explanations. McGraw relates results of several of her experiments that judge the effectiveness of various types of explanations: concessions, excuses, justifications, and denials.

Over the past two decades, many programs formerly under the purview of the federal government have been ceded, at least in part, to state and local governments. In addition, local governments in the United States traditionally play a strong role in education, transportation, crime control, and land development policies. Wendy Rahn and Thomas Rudolph in their chapter examine public support for local governments. They find that the American public has somewhat more trust in local governments than in the federal government but that those who trust one level of government also tend to have trust in the other. Variations in levels of trust in local government can be explained by both traits of the individual and characteristics of the community.

John Hibbing in his chapter takes a closer look at Americans' distrust of the federal government. He carefully delineates which aspects of government the American public supports (institutions) and which aspects Americans distrust (government officials). Hibbing also looks at the change and continuity in public trust since the 1960s. Moving beyond survey data, Hibbing presents results from a focus group study that provides greater insight into why individual Americans may be displeased with their government's performance.

Finally, political trust may be an even more important factor for governments moving toward democracy. With the fall of communism in the 1990s, a host of countries in Eastern Europe and the former Soviet Union have begun the transition to more democratic forms of government. At the same time, these countries have been moving from state-planned economies to market economies. The stress of both economic and political transitions has been great. Given these adverse conditions, how do citizens of these countries evaluate their governments? William Mishler and Richard Rose in their chapter find that citizen evaluations of the performance of these governments, and to a lesser extent their evaluations of the former Communist regime, shape public confidence in these new democratizing governments.

12 Manipulating Public Opinion

Kathleen M. McGraw

In an essay concerned with the relationship between public opinion and policymaking, Benjamin Page (1994) recounted Lance Bennett's (1989) "gloomy conjecture" that about one-third of the time, American policymaking is the result of a "bottom-up" process, wherein public officials are responsive to public opinion; about one-third of the time public officials ignore public opinion; and in the remaining third of the time, public opinion is managed or manipulated to ensure that the public supports policies that are pursued by public officials for reasons other than "the will of the people." Bennett's pessimistic division of the possible links between public opinion and policy may or may not be an accurate parsing of political reality, but it does provide a useful framework for making sense of these complex, interactive relationships. Research providing support for the first causal linkage—a systematic relationship between public opinion and policymaking, such that public opinion exerts a substantial influence on policy—is plentiful and increasingly sophisticated, yielding a portrait of representation that is generally consistent with normative theories of democratic responsiveness (Erikson, Wright, and McIver 1989, 1993; Page and Shapiro 1983, 1992; Stimson, MacKuen, and Erikson 1995). However, the presence of democratic responsiveness—public officials responding to the will of the people when formulating policy—does not rule out the other two possibilities. Much less is known about the conditions under which political elites ignore public opinion (Bennett's 1989 argument is that they instead attend to institutional voices). The goal of this chapter is to provide a selective overview of theory and research on the third possibility, namely elite manipulation of public opinion.

The consideration of elite manipulation of public opinion in effect treats *public opinion* as the dependent variable in the analytic framework (Margolis and Mauser 1989), rather than as the independent variable posited in the democratic responsiveness relationship. Of course, a complex construct like public opinion necessarily results from multiple factors, including early socialization forces (Sears 1983), personal experiences, and political and social events such as war, economic fluctuations, domestic crises, and so on (Page and Shapiro 1992). This chapter focuses on a specific set of factors that have an influence on public opinion, namely, rhetorical strategies, or verbal communications, used by public officials to move public opinion in a direction that serves the official's own purposes.[1]

A brief clarification of the core concepts is critical. Following V. O. Key, I adopt an expansive view of *public opinion* as "those opinions held by private persons which governments find it prudent to heed" (1961, 14). These "opinions" can be about public policy alternatives, but also include attitudes and beliefs about public officials, political institutions, and normative principles. *Manipulation* is a term that often has pejorative connotations, with the implication that the act of manipulation entails unfair or deceptive strategies. But the meaning of the term is actually broader than that. *Webster's* defines the verb *to manipulate* as "to manage or utilize skillfully; to control or play upon by artful, unfair, or insidious means especially to one's own advantage; to change by artful or unfair means so as to serve one's purpose" (*Webster's Online Dictionary*). In short, manipulation can be either "artful" or "unfair." If it is artful, observers may feel admiration; if it is unfair, the reaction may be outrage. I adopt this broader linguistic usage by reviewing theory and research more generally directed toward understanding how public officials strive to influence public opinion through rhetorical strategies. In the concluding section, I devote special attention to rhetorical manipulation that involves deliberate deception and misleading the public.

In calling upon the relevant literature, I have chosen to focus on three research domains that illustrate in a convincing manner, with a variety of methodological approaches and theoretical frameworks, the central claim that political rhetoric can and does have systematic consequences for public opinion. The three domains are presidential strategies of "going public" (Kernell 1997); Lawrence Jacobs and Robert Shapiro's (2000) analysis of "crafted talk" as a strategy to change public opinion; and experimental research on the effectiveness of political explanations to manage the damage associated with political predicaments (McGraw 2001). In the final section, I consider the occurrence and normative implications of the deliberate use of deception in political rhetoric.

Presidential Rhetoric and *Going Public*

Walter Lippmann (1922) was one of the first scholars to argue that politicians attempt to "manufacture consent" through strategic appeals to the public. Samuel Kernell provides a prominent and detailed analysis of strategic presidential practices in his model of *going public,* which he defines as "a class of activities that presidents engage in as they promote themselves and their policies before the American public" (1997, ix). These strategies include televised press conferences, special prime-time television addresses, radio addresses, and travel to make local appearances. Contemporary American presidents have made increasing use of these communication strategies, starting with the Eisenhower administration. Certainly, advances in communication and travel technology account for some of these trends, but Kernell argues that the strategy of "going public" is also fundamentally rooted in the declining influence of the major parties in American politics. In the absence of strong party loyalties and collective political interests, the president is uniquely poised to act as an individual to mobilize public opinion in support of his positions, with the ultimate goal of increasing his chances of success in Washington.

In short, influencing public opinion is the linchpin in securing support in Congress for presidential policy initiatives. Kernell argues that five conditions are required for these dynamics to be effective. First, a necessary prerequisite is that the president is generally popular, enjoying some measure of public support.[2] Second, the president must accurately communicate his preferences to the public. Third, citizens evaluate the policy initiative according to their general evaluation of the president (which is why general popularity is necessary). Fourth, citizens communicate support for the president's initiative to their elected representatives, who, fifth, strategically align their preferences with the president in the service of electoral security.

As should be obvious, the process of going public is complex and ultimate success is contingent on a number of specific steps. Empirical evidence for some of the steps in the model exists, but there are still many open questions. Three sets of findings regarding the president's ability to lead public opinion appear to be robust. First, presidents are able to influence their general popularity ratings through dramatic political events such as travel and making speeches, but those boosts tend to be short-lived (MacKuen 1983; Ragsdale 1984, 1987) and contingent upon the type of speech and trip (Brace and Hinckley 1992). Second, popular presidents can sway public opinion on specific policies, but unpopular presidents have little influence (Edwards 1983; Kernell 1997; Mondak 1993; Page and Shapiro 1984, 1992; Sigelman 1980). Third, presidents can shape the public's views about the most important political problems, with the president's ability to shape the public agenda apparently not being dependent upon popularity (Behr and Iyengar 1985; Cohen 1995).

An important practical and normative question that follows from these analyses is, What matters more for sustaining the president's standing with the public—rhetoric or actual political performance (that is, satisfying political and economic conditions), public relations or political substance? Kernell's conclusion is that "both do" (1997, 241), a conclusion that is supported by experimental evidence. That is, systematic and independent manipulation of rhetorical strategies and policy consequences—"what they say and what they do"— in an experimental context revealed that both sets of factors have a statistically significant and substantively meaningful impact on evaluations of public officials (McGraw, Best, and Timpone 1995). The implication here is clear: modern presidents must work hard to solve political problems *and* be skilled practitioners of public relations in order to sustain public support for their policy goals. A final note: Kernell's analysis is explicitly concerned with presidential strategies, and presidents have certainly been the earliest and foremost practitioners of "going public." However, other public officials such as members of Congress have come to recognize the power and necessity of enlisting public support for their policy initiatives (see, for example, T. Cook 1989), a trend that suggests that the practice of "going public" will increase in a variety of political arenas.

Simulated Responsiveness and *Crafted Talk*

The negative interpretation of the democratic responsiveness thesis is that elected politicians "pander" to public opinion by tailoring their policy positions to poll results and other indicators of public opinion. As *New York Times* columnist Maureen Dowd, in reference to the Clinton administration's heavy reliance on polls, famously lamented, "Polling has turned leaders into followers" (1997). Jacobs and Shapiro point to an intriguing paradox: although the use of public opinion polling has increased since the 1970s (contributing to the "pandering" charge), at the same time there has been a "widening gulf between politicians' policy decisions and the preferences of the American people" (2000, xii). Jacobs and Shapiro's solution to this paradox is to identify a set of electoral motivations and tactics by which public officials—both presidents and legislators—increasingly make use of public opinion polls to create the *appearance of responsiveness* to public opinion that at the same time allows public officials to pursue their own policy ends. One of the key motivations for trying to change public opinion, rather than be responsive to it, is that this strategy allows politicians to satisfy both their electoral and policy objectives. Public officials can both sustain public support and enact policy initiatives that they prefer and/or that are preferred by activists, special interest groups, and campaign donors.

Politicians pursue this two-pronged goal by a strategy of *crafted talk* that is aimed to change public opinion in order to minimize the risk of appearing unresponsive to the wishes of the voters. As a consequence, politicians make use of public opinion polls "to determine how to craft their public presentations and win public support for the policies they and their supporters prefer" (Jacobs and Shapiro 2000, xiii). Jacobs and Shapiro identify three specific techniques in this strategy. First, politicians make use of polls and focus groups to determine the arguments and symbols about specific policies that the public finds most appealing. Second, they influence press coverage by "staying on message," by making their simple, crafted message the dominant—and, ideally, the only—story the media are able to cover. Third, politicians make use of a "priming" strategy that is aimed not at changing the public's fundamental values and preferences but rather at maximizing the weight and priority the public assigns to considerations that already exist in the policy realm. For example, in the health care debate between the Clinton administration and the Republican-led House of Representatives in the mid-1990s (the case that is the centerpiece of Jacobs and Shapiro's analysis), Republican opponents to health care reform claimed that the Clinton plan would increase "big government," while the Clinton administration's message emphasized "security for all." The point, of course, is that the public already has views about big government and security, and the battle between the two sides was over which criteria would be used to evaluate the policy proposals.

Jacobs and Shapiro make use of what they call an insider research strategy that emphasizes an in-depth analysis of elites' strategic calculations and decisions, relying on interviews with key players, official memoranda and records, and content analysis of statements and official communications. This insider strategy is contrasted with an "outsider" approach that focuses on aggregate relationships and is unable to delve into the "black box" of policy decision making. Ultimately, the integration of the two approaches will provide the most compelling support for this, and for any other, model of the relationship between public opinion, policy, and elite communication strategies. Nonetheless, the Jacobs and Shapiro case studies marshal an impressive body of evidence that refutes the simple pandering claim and that supports the more complex and nuanced model of simulated responsiveness. Indeed, the resulting model does not fit easily into the tripartite framework introduced at the outset of this chapter. Rather than a simple unidirectional causal flow between public opinion and policymaking, the Jacobs and Shapiro model suggests that the causal arrow moves in both directions: public opinion provides the basis for elite strategies, which are then used to move public opinion to be congruent with public officials' own policy preferences.

The Effectiveness of Explanatory Rhetoric in Shaping Public Opinion

What is the content of the verbal communications that public officials use to influence public opinion, under what conditions are these communications made, and which are more or less effective? In turning to these questions now, I limit the discussion to a particular type of verbal communication—accounts, or explanations (used interchangeably)—for two reasons. The first is that explanation is a fundamental manifestation of accountability in a representative democracy, and so a particularly significant form of political rhetoric. According to Hanna Pitkin, representation implies "acting in the interest of the represented, in a manner responsive to them. . . . the representative must act in such a way that there is no conflict, or if it occurs an explanation is called for" (1967, 209–210). Richard Fenno also emphasized the centrality of explanation to theories of representation when he proclaimed: "Theories of representation will always be incomplete without theories that explain explaining" (1978, 162). The second reason for the focus on political explanations is that no systematic work exists in other rhetorical domains that consider all of the important elements—content, antecedents, and effectiveness. I hope that this overview will prompt more systematic investigation of the content, antecedents, and consequences of other types of political communications.

John Kingdon (1973) was the first congressional scholar to draw attention to the importance of "explaining the vote." Soon after, Fenno's classic analysis of congressional "home style" (1978) outlined three basic strategies used to cultivate constituent support and public opinion, namely resource allocation, self-presentation, and explanation of Washington activity. A sizable experimental literature concerned with the consequences and effectiveness of political explanations exists (I turn to this later), but there is less systematic research on the motivations and constraints that shape the expression of political explanations (see Austen-Smith 1992; Bianco 1994; Willey 1998, for exceptions).

A central theme in the literature is reflected by the adage, "If you have to explain, you're in trouble" (Fenno 1978). In other words, explanation occurs when the public official's actions have negative implications, be it personal misconduct or an unpopular policy vote or decision (Pitkin's discussion also assumes that explanation follows "conflict" or unpopular actions).[3] And, in fact, the anecdotal evidence is very clear that when politicians violate their constituents' expectations, through policy decisions or personal misconduct, they respond with explanations or *blame-management strategies* (McGraw 1991, 2001) to contain the political fallout and shore up public opinion. A good example of a recent political explanation in response to public outrage was former president Clinton's op-ed column in the *New York Times* (February 18, 2001), titled "My Reasons for the Pardons," and beginning with the statement: "Because of the intense scrutiny and criticisms of the pardons of Marc Rich . . . I want to explain what I did and why."

Although explanations of unpopular decisions and misconduct are widespread, explanations can be provided in other circumstances, such as in the context of positive actions. William Bianco has argued that "explanations appear to have political value" (1994, 53), for example, by strengthening perceptions of accessibility and as a mechanism for position taking. This argument is key, as it suggests a link between political explanations and the electorally useful activities identified by David Mayhew (1974). Although Mayhew did not discuss explanations directly, it is not much of a theoretical stretch to argue that explanations of positive outcomes can serve as *advertising* (for example, a public official may issue a press release explaining a popular vote in the hopes of garnering media attention and strengthening public support); as *credit claiming* (for example, explaining a vote that will yield particularized or generalized benefits for constituents); and as a component of *position taking,* defined by Mayhew as "the public enunciation of a judgmental statement on anything likely to be of interest to political actors" (1974, 61). In fact, it is difficult to imagine a public statement of a position—"I will support the president," "I am opposed to this bill"—without an accompanying explanation of the reason behind the position.

Little systematic work has delved into the antecedents of the decision to explain, particularly work considering whether explanations are more likely to be prompted by electoral troubles or offered as an act of self-promotion. A recent analysis of explanations for a high-profile, controversial vote—the House of Representatives' votes on the articles of impeachment against President Bill Clinton in December of 1998—yielded results that have intriguing implications for this question (McGraw, Anderson, and Willey 2000). My co-authors and I examined explanations posted to House members' personal web pages, an increasingly common medium used by legislators to communicate with their constituents. Forty percent of the House members posted an explanation of their impeachment votes. Results of that analysis were complex, but generally consistent with the argument that explanations were used to elaborate and capitalize on an action that was positively received by constituents. That is, House members were more likely to post an explanation of their impeachment votes when their votes were consistent with their districts' preferences (level of support for Clinton), not when they voted in a way that violated district preferences.[4] In other words, House members voluntarily offered an explanation when they were communicating good news to supportive districts; they avoided communicating unpopular news to districts that would be more critical of their decision. The conclusion to be drawn from this study is not that political explanation is limited to self-promotion; it is clear that politicians are frequently forced—by the media, their colleagues, and a disgruntled public—to explain their behavioral violations. Rather, results of the impeachment explanation study suggest that scholars broaden the theoretical framework within which explanation and representation are understood, recognizing that a host of motivations, not simply blame management, can contribute to the decision to explain.

Understanding the consequences of political explanations for shaping public opinion requires a theoretical framework that is both capable of linking specific opinion consequences to particular types of explanations and capable of specifying the underlying psychological mechanisms. A number of typologies have been proposed (among them Goffman 1971; Schlenker 1980; Schonbach 1990; Scott and Lyman 1968; Sykes and Matza 1957; Tedeschi and Reiss 1980; Tetloc 1985), but there is widespread agreement that four types of accounts are fundamental. I have argued that the four types can be conceptualized within a 2×2 framework, as summarized in Figure 12-1 (McGraw 2001).[5] If a public official finds himself or herself in a political predicament, the disapproving audience is implicitly making two accusations: (1) a negative or objectionable event has occurred, and (2) you—the official being criticized—are responsible for the event. The first dimension is concerned with perceptions of the negativity of the event, whereas the second dimension concerns attributed responsibility for the event.

Within this framework, *concessions* involve an acknowledgment that the negative event occurred and an implicit or explicit acceptance of responsibility. For example, Attorney

Figure 12-1   A Framework for Political Explanations

	Accept event is negative	Deny event is negative
Accept responsibility	Concessions	Justifications
Deny responsibility	Excuses	Denials

General Janet Reno, after the Branch Davidians' deaths in Waco, Texas, in 1993, stated: "I made the decision. I'm accountable. The buck stops with me." Concessions often, but not always, include expressions of regret, apologies, and even offers of restitution. *Excuses,* like concessions, acknowledge that an offense has occurred, but reject full responsibility for the event. Common political excuses include a denial of intent or foreseeability, diffusion of responsibility to other actors, and claims of mitigating circumstances. (Consider, as an example, Oregon Senator Bob Packwood's response to allegations of sexual misconduct in 1992: "Whether alcohol was a factor in these incidents, I do not know. In any event, alcohol at best can only be a partial explanation.")

Whereas concessions and excuses at least implicitly acknowledge that a problem exists, *justifications* are characterized by attempts to deny or minimize the negative implications of the event. Justifications can emphasize positive objective consequences; or the opinions of prominent others who support the action (in the *New York Times* op–ed column referred to earlier, Clinton noted that "the case for the pardons was reviewed and advocated . . . by three distinguished Republican attorneys"); or moral principles through which the event may be reinterpreted. An example of a moral justification was Democratic Senator Harry Reid's explanation of his unpopular vote against Clarence Thomas's nomination to the Supreme Court in 1991 to his Nevada constituents: "The polls in the state clearly favored him. From a political standpoint, I badly wanted to vote for Clarence Thomas. However, my conscience wouldn't let me do it. I thought she [Anita Hill] was telling the truth." Finally, *denials* are not technically an explanation at all, but a refutation on the part of the official that the event even occurred. President Clinton's televised refutation, finger wagging—"I did not have sex with that woman"—at the beginning of the Lewinsky scandal is perhaps the most prominent denial in recent political history.

Ultimately we are interested in the public opinion consequences of political explanations, assuming that they are not simply empty rhetoric. The method of choice for systematically investigating the consequences of political explanations has been experimentation, for three reasons. First, it is enormously difficult, if not impossible, to disentangle the independent influences of the explanation itself, the to-be-explained event, and the history and characteristics of the explainer with a naturalistic research strategy. Most political predicaments in the real world involve one or at most a handful of public officials, rendering systematic quantitative analysis of the independent impact of the event and accompanying rhetoric impossible. Experimentation is ideal for decomposing complex phenomena into independent conceptual parameters and isolating their independent impact on some outcome variable. Moreover, a serious problem with the analysis of real political predicaments is the lack of variance on the key independent variable, that is, the explanation. The underlying question involved in understanding the impact of a political explanation (or any political rhetoric, for that matter) involves the implicit "compared to what?" question. What if Clinton had continued to stonewall via "no comment" responses, or conceded immediately, or blamed Ms. Lewinsky, or invoked childhood traumas, instead of making the "I did not have sex" denial? Experimentation facilitates theoretically meaningful comparisons to shed light on the "compared to what?" question. Finally, experimentation is ideally suited for probing the underlying reasons by which outcomes occur (Kinder and Palfrey 1992; McGraw 1996).

In elaborating on causal mechanisms, it has been useful to consider political explanations as a kind of persuasive communication—verbal appeals aimed at changing or influencing public opinion about some political event. Accordingly, citizens' reactions to accounts can be understood in terms of the steps that are necessary for successful persuasion (McGuire 1985; Zaller 1992): (1) citizens must be *exposed* to the explanation; (2) they must *pay attention* to it; (3) they must *comprehend* it; and (4) they must *accept* the explanation as legitimate and credible. This fourth step is critical, because a citizen must be satisfied with an explanation before it can have its desired—from the perspective of the politician— ameliorative impact. Given the centrality of acceptance in effective persuasion, it is not surprising that our research has consistently indicated that satisfaction with a proffered account is the key factor in predicting subsequent evaluations of the public official.

Table 12-1 summarizes the varying degrees of satisfaction elicited by different explanations from two studies in this research program. In the top panel, research participants read about a controversial political decision (a reprimand of a member of Congress for behavior modeled after Barney Frank's homosexual relationship with a male prostitute in 1990), and asked to imagine that their representative had provided one of two explanations for his vote (McGraw, Timpone, and Bruck 1993). The explanations were drawn from Fenno's (1978) interviews with real members of Congress. The alternatives were designed to examine whether principled justifications rooted in different roles were more or less effective with the public. In a delegate role (explanation 2 in Table 12-1), the representative votes according to public wishes in the district. In the trustee role (explanation 1), a member of

Table 12-1 Satisfaction with Explanation Type from Member of Congress: Evidence from Two Experiments

---

Appeals to Conscience[a]

Trustee/individualistic justification. "But to base this decision on politics and public opinion would violate my own conscience, as to what I feel is the proper course of action. I know this vote may damage my political career. But that pales into insignificance when weighted against my duty to vote as my conscience dictates. Therefore, I voted my conscience, against the acknowledged wishes of many of my constituents."   **Mean = .66**

Delegate/communitarian justification. "But I know the people of my district. I am one of you and the issue is our conscience as a community. I imagined how the people of this district would vote if they were in my shoes. We are a compassionate, forgiving people. I have voted as I believe this community would vote, in a compassionate and forgiving manner."   **Mean = .64**

Excuses and Justifications[b]

Mitigating circumstances excuse. "These kinds of decisions are always difficult. I didn't feel I had a choice on this one because a change was necessary. The failure of this nation's previous education policies requires drastic solutions such as those included in the education bill."   **Mean = .40**

Diffusion of responsibility excuse. "These kinds of decisions are always difficult, and very complicated. Unfortunately, my staff failed to provide me with complete information about the likely consequences of the bill and therefore I wasn't made fully aware of all of its possible ramifications."   **Mean = .22**

Party loyalty. "These kinds of decisions are always difficult. I agree with the leaders of my party that the passage of this bill is in the nation's best interest, and I voted accordingly."   **Mean = .35**

Benefits justification. "These kinds of decisions are always difficult. I voted for the education bill because I think that it also brings with it real benefits for this district. For example, as part of the same package of legislation, funds have been set aside for research on improving science education and reducing dropout rates."   **Mean = .43**

Normative justification. "These kinds of decisions are always difficult. I voted for the education bill because I believe that under the new allocation criteria the distribution of education funds is fairer, going to those who need the funding most. I followed my conscience and did what I thought was the best thing to do."   **Mean = .42**

Hypothetical comparison justification. "These kinds of decisions are always difficult. This education bill could have been a lot worse. For example, other versions of the bill were considered that would have resulted in much more serious cuts in funding for this district."   **Mean = .33**

Note: The values after each explanation are the mean level of satisfaction elicited by each explanation, coded on a 0 to 1 scale, where higher values reflect more satisfaction.

[a] The to-be-explained controversy in this experiment was a vote for a congressional reprimand; see McGraw, Timpone, and Bruck (1993) for details. The average levels of satisfaction elicited by the two explanations do not differ ($F < 1$).

[b] The to-be-explained controversy in this experiment was a vote for a reduction in federal funding for education; see McGraw, Best, and Timpone (1995) for details. The differences among the mean levels of satisfaction elicited by the explanations are significant ($F[3,305] = 9.26, p < .001, \eta^2 = .135$).

Congress votes according to what he or she sees as best for the nation. In fact, as Table 12-1 indicates, both justifications were highly, and equally, acceptable.

However, many of the explanations that we have used in our research are not nearly as effective as those principled justifications. The second part of Table 12-1 summarizes the effectiveness of a wider range of explanations. In this study (McGraw, Best, and Timpone 1995), research participants read about a complex and controversial bill involving the distribution of grant-in-aid funding for education which would result in cuts in such funding for their district, and they were asked to imagine that their elected representative provided one of six explanations (systematically manipulated) for his vote. Justifications claiming real benefits (explanation 4) or rooted in normative claims (explanation 5) were significantly more satisfactory than other types of explanations, in particular an excuse attempting to diffuse responsibility to the member's staff (explanation 2). In fact, excuses laying full or partial responsibility on other parties are consistently among the least effective explanations we find.

More generally, our experimental work examining the effectiveness of various types of political justifications and excuses suggests a number of broad conclusions about what makes for a satisfactory explanation.[6] One principle points to the general characteristic of commonness: explanations that are more common in political rhetoric tend to be more satisfactory (Bennett 1980; McGraw 1991). This finding is in line with the more general argument that the public responds more favorably to political rhetoric that is simple and familiar, when political arguments and themes fit categories the public already accepts (Edelman 1988; Margolis and Mauser 1989). A second principle points to individual characteristics of the citizen: trusting and less sophisticated individuals tend to be more satisfied with political explanations, all else being equal (McGraw and Hubbard 1996). Third, existing attitudes about the public official (Gonzales et al. 1995) or the to-be-explained decision (McGraw, Best, and Timpone 1995) serve as an anchor for acceptance of subsequent rhetoric: simply, citizens are more satisfied with explanations provided by public officials whom they like or for decisions or behaviors that they feel positively toward. Fourth, at least in the political realm, justifications appealing to normative principles—particularly personal ethical standards like fairness or moral conscience, as well as collective social benefits—consistently are the most positively evaluated explanations (Chanley et al. 1994; McGraw 1991; McGraw, Best, and Timpone 1995; McGraw, Timpone, and Bruck 1993). In contrast, excuses involving a diffusion of responsibility are consistently unacceptable.[7] These determinants of satisfaction with political explanations are critical, as satisfaction is a key determinant of subsequent evaluations of the public official: satisfactory accounts boost public support whereas accounts that are rejected can do further damage to the official's reputation.

In addition to the link between acceptance/rejection of political explanations and subsequent evaluations of the public official, three other consequences are noteworthy. In line with the conceptual framework summarized in Figure 12-1, excuses and justifications influence different types of judgments about the predicament. Because excuses attempt to deny full responsibility for a decision and its consequences, effective (satisfactory) excuses shift assignment of blame away from the public official (McGraw 2001). An important caveat here: many excuses are inherently unsatisfactory and only those that are acceptable can ameliorate blame. In contrast, because justifications are an attempt to redefine perceptions of the act and its consequences, successful justifications are most effective in persuading citizens to change their opinion about a controversial act or policy (McGraw, Best, and Timpone 1995). Third, political explanations have consequences for inferences about specific dimensions of political character (Kinder 1986; Miller, Wattenberg, and Malanchuk 1986). For example, a *trustee* justification, such as "In the end, I used my own judgment as to what is in your best interests," increases perceptions of leadership (the traits "commands respect," "[not] easily influenced," "[not] weak"), whereas a *delegate* justification, such as "I owe it to my constituents to vote according to their wishes, and that is what I did," increases perceptions of empathy (comprised of the traits "compassionate," "[not] out of touch," and "really cares"; McGraw 2001).

In summary, political explanations have systematic and theoretically meaningful public opinion consequences. They can influence attributions of responsibility, inferences about political character, and opinions about controversial policies. Most important, political explanations have an impact on citizens' evaluations of the public official who is the source of the communication; in other words, the political messages citizens receive greatly affect their opinions of public officials. Of course, a number of important questions remain to be addressed, questions that will require methodologies other than experimentation. For example, how do politicians translate their electoral goals—namely, to be supported and eventually reelected—into specific communication strategies? How do they accommodate potentially conflicting goals (such as to be truthful and to be reelected)?

It is also evident that many political explanations fail spectacularly. For example, less than one-quarter of the American public reported being satisfied with the explanations provided by their members of Congress to account for their overdraft checks in the House bank scandal of 1991 (Hugic 1992). Why do seemingly rational actors provide such poor explanations? An important principle may be the timing of the accountability pressures, or *when* public officials anticipate the need to explain. Erving Goffman (1959) identified two strategies involved in impression management (or "facework"). The first, *preventive practices,* are the steps taken prior to making a decision, in anticipation of a valued audience's response. The role of such preventive practices is well established in the congressional literature, where it has frequently been noted that legislators' decisions are influenced by their need to eventually justify the decision to their constituents (Arnold 1990; Austen-Smith 1992;

Fenno 1978; Kingdon 1973; Mayhew 1974; Weaver 1986, 1988). In contrast, *corrective practices* are steps taken after a decision that an audience finds to be inappropriate or objectionable. It is here that the official must use "damage control tactics" or blame-management strategies (McGraw 1991, 2001) to restore public support. It may well be that preventive practices are more effective than corrective practices, because the official who takes accountability seriously and considers that before making a decision is more likely to make a vigilant analysis of options and thus employ more reasonable rhetorical strategies (Tetlock 1992).

Deceiving the Public

The three research programs just reviewed—presidential strategies of going public, the use of crafted talk, and the use of political explanations to manage the fallout from political predicaments—provide solid support for the proposition that elite rhetoric can effectively shape public opinion. The potency of elite rhetoric poses few normative problems if we can safely assume that the arguments that are espoused by public officials are accurate and sincere articulations of the true reasons for the behavior or position being advocated. If public officials provide correct and useful information that will help citizens reach more fully informed opinions, then officials are providing a service by educating the public (Page and Shapiro 1992). But if we have reason to believe that politicians sometimes deceive the public by providing false or misleading information and arguments, then the normative implications are enormously disconcerting. Most scholars would probably take as a given that politicians on occasion deceive the public, although they may disagree about the frequency (Bok 1989; Jacobs and Shapiro 2000; Jamieson 1992; Page 1996; Page and Shapiro 1989, 1992). It is difficult, as an epistemological matter, to identify instances of truth and deception in political rhetoric, and social scientists who attempt to do so wander into "minefields of subjectivity and controversy" (Page and Shapiro 1989, 308). Shapiro and his colleagues have notably braved these minefields and have specified a number of instances in contemporary American politics where the public appears to have been misled or manipulated by public officials (Jacobs and Shapiro 2000; Page and Shapiro 1989, 1992).[8]

The disquieting normative implications of elite deception are magnified by the proposition that the public finds it enormously difficult to detect deceptive political rhetoric. There are both psychological and political mechanisms that play a role in this dilemma (McGraw 1998). The psychological literature on deception suggests that people are simply not very good at detecting deception under most circumstances (Friedman and Tucker 1990). Nonverbal indicators provide moderately reliable cues to deception, but the mediated nature of most political rhetoric renders these cues less useful, particularly if the visual medium is stripped away, as is the case in newspapers or radio news. Finally, detecting deception presupposes a willingness on the part of the audience to consider the possibility that a statement is not truthful. In part, this willingness to be suspicious about the veracity of political communication is rooted in citizens' evaluation of the politician and the content of the communication (McGraw, Lodge, and Jones 2000). Despite the well-documented declines in levels of trust in government (Hibbing and Theiss-Morse 1995), opinions about specific public officials still tend to be positive in the aggregate (Sears 1983). Simply stated, if a citizen holds a positive opinion about the politician, he or she will be predisposed to accept the sincerity of the politician's arguments.

If citizens are disinclined to be suspicious of political rhetoric if left to their own psychological devices, suspicion and scrutiny may be prompted by political forces, in particular by other elites and public officials charging deception. But in fact, there are several reasons to believe that this kind of countercharge does not happen very frequently. First, it is widely recognized by scholars, public officials, and the public that political rhetoric is "heavily ritualized" (Graber 1976, 12), and that exaggerated and even false claims are part of the political spectacle (Edelman 1977; Bennett 1980). Respect for the ritual is a key reason that politicians rarely challenge each other, because they participate in the same ritual themselves. Second, to declare someone to be a liar is often a no-win situation for the accuser. W. Peter Robinson argues, "To call someone a liar is potentially dramatic, and even if true, can rebound on the challenger. Conventionally, it appears that it is the challenger and not the alleged liar who has broken the stronger rule" (1993, 364). Kathleen Hall Jamieson's (2001) recent analysis of "civility in the House of Representatives" provides support for this claim that allegations of "liar" are risky. Explicit use of the word *liar* is quite rare on the floor of the House, making its most frequent appearance in 1988 with only 2.4 utterances per every 1,000 pages of the *Congressional Record*. The 106th Congress in 2000 was at the low end of the scale with about 0.6 utterances of the word *liar* for every 1,000 pages of the *Record*. Moreover, on the rare occasion the word *liar* is used in the House, it is most frequently directed toward foreign nationals (41 percent of the uses), not American public officials.[9]

Although it is an important step to recognize that deceptive and misleading political communication is used to manipulate public opinion, prescribing feasible solutions for the problem is a far thornier issue (see Jacobs and Shapiro 2000, for specific recommendations). The goal for social scientists and citizens alike should be to recognize that elite rhetoric can be rooted in both laudatory and unscrupulous motives, and to be willing to try to tell the difference. For social scientists, achieving this goal requires a more systematic understanding of the parameters that elicit and sustain elite deception as well as the conditions and opportunities citizens have to limit such manipulation. For citizens, the requirement is constant vigilance against instances of "elite domination" (Zaller 1992) of public opinion and a steady insistence "that politicians follow the popular will and allow citizens to engage in unfettered public debate" (Jacobs and Shapiro 2000, 339).

Conclusion

The evidence reviewed here, obtained from a variety of research methodologies and informed by an assortment of theoretical frameworks, provides solid support for the proposition that elite rhetoric can be used to shape and move public opinion. This is probably not a surprising conclusion to many readers. But the undeniable emphasis in the past twenty years of research has focused on democratic responsiveness, where the causal arrow flows from public opinion to public policy. The role of elite strategies and communications has been downplayed, if considered at all. The research programs reviewed in this chapter flip the democratic responsiveness relationship on its head in various ways. We are still a long way from understanding the frequency with which these various models are utilized (the Bennett conjecture noted at the outset), and the conditions that lead them to be utilized successfully. As Page has argued, multiple research methods will be appropriate and necessary to disentangle the complex interrelationships among policy, public opinion, and rhetoric, to understand the conditions under which these effects are larger or smaller (1994, 28). Nevertheless, if we want to understand how democracy works in the United States, and elsewhere, it is important to understand how often, and under what circumstances, public officials follow, lead, or manipulate public opinion.

Notes

1. I ignore research on the mass media as the conduit by which public opinion is shaped and research on the effects of campaigns as mechanisms of persuasion aimed at shifting public opinion about political candidates.

2. As Kernell notes, the model "is silent on what an unpopular president should do to restore the public's confidence" (1997, 129).

3. The emphasis in political science has its roots in Goffman's seminal work on self-presentation and the use of accounts as "remedial tactics" to minimize the negative repercussions of undesirable behavior (1959, 1971).

4. In addition to the district preferences, more junior members were more likely to explain (consistent with Fenno's and Kingdon's arguments linking seniority to attentiveness), as were House members in leadership positions.

5. Note that this analytic framework has been limited to explanations of predicaments, or negative outcomes. In addition, the four account types are regarded as superordinate categories, each of which includes a number of subcategories (note that Schonbach's 1990 typology contains more than 100 types of accounts).

6. We have focused on excuses and justifications as explanations for explaining policy decisions because they are the most commonly occurring accounts (in politics and other domains; Austin 1961; Bennett 1980) and because concessions and denials for policy decisions are quite uncommon.

7. These conclusions are limited to comparisons of the effectiveness of a variety of excuses and justifications for policy decisions. As Cody and McLaughlin (1990) make clear in a comprehensive review, the evidence as to which of the four types of accounts are more or less effective outside the political realm is decidedly mixed, with different patterns of results obtained in different contexts (for

example, interpersonal, legal, and organizational). Moreover, all four types of explanations have effective and ineffective variants.

8. Page and Shapiro distinguish between *misleading* the public, which they define as "providing false, incorrect, biased or selective information" and *manipulating* the public, which occurs when public officials mislead "consciously and deliberately, by means of lies, falsehoods, deception, and concealment" (1989, 308). This is a narrower conception of manipulation than the one used in this chapter.

9. Consideration of close synonyms for the word *liar* in its various forms (such as *hoax, farce,* and *prevaricate*) increases the occurrence rate to about 150 utterances for every 1,000 pages of the *Congressional Record* (Jamieson 2001).

13 Trust in Local Governments

Wendy M. Rahn and Thomas J. Rudolph

Understanding the sources of public confidence in political institutions has taken on renewed importance in recent years as both new and established democracies cope with the challenges of economic, technological, political, and social change. Institutions that enjoy citizen support are better able to respond to such change effectively and equitably because political leaders have room to maneuver in the implementation of policies (Gamson 1968). In addition, citizens' trust in and support for representative institutions are importantly related to citizens' compliance with governmental demands, such as taxpaying (Scholz and Lubell 1998) and military service (Levi 1997). Furthermore, people's views about government also have implications for attitudes beyond the realm of politics. For example, John Brehm and Wendy Rahn (1997) find that Americans who have more confidence in national political institutions also have higher levels of social trust, the belief that even those who are strangers can be trusted. Social trust, in turn, appears to be linked to important indicators of the quality of life, such as health and personal happiness (Putnam 2000).

Because citizens' trust in democratic institutions is thought to affect how well such institutions function, it is a source of concern that governments in many democratic countries seem to be experiencing declines in citizen confidence (see Putnam, Pharr, and Dalton 2000; Klingemann 1999; Dalton 1999). In some places, such as the United States, these declines have been quite dramatic. Figure 13-1 reports the percentage of respondents in the biennial National Election Studies who said that they trust the "government in Washington" always or most of the time to "do what is right." In the mid-1960s, a sizable majority of Americans had confidence in the national government, but by 1980 this sentiment was held by less than a quarter of those surveyed. Trust rebounded somewhat in the mid-1980s, but this recovery proved to be short-lived as trust declined again in the late 1980s and reached a new low in 1994. As the twentieth century came to a close, Americans again were feeling somewhat more confident in their government. But the events surrounding the protracted political and legal battle over the outcome of the 2000 presidential election appear to have slowed this modest rise in confidence.

Unlike many European nations, the United States is a federal system in which sub-

Figure 13-1 Trust in the "Government in Washington," 1964–2000

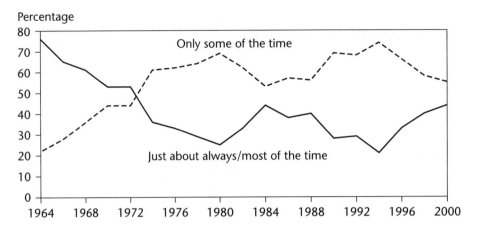

Percentage

Source: National Election Studies.

Note: The graph shows the percentage of respondents who gave a particular response to the following question: "How much of the time do you think you can trust the government in Washington to do what is right—just about always, most of the time, or only some of the time?"

national levels of government have autonomy, and, in the case of the American states, sovereignty. Citizens are taxed by both state and local authorities and are obligated to follow the laws made by the representative institutions at these levels, such as state legislatures, city councils, and public school boards. Some of the most intense conflicts in American politics are waged at the subnational level as political opponents vie to control the content of school curricula or regulate the institution of marriage, for example. And subnational governments have been called upon to play an increasing role in the federal system as several federal programs, such as aid programs for the poor, have been devolved to states since the 1990s. The Supreme Court, too, in a series of recent decisions, has substantially altered the federal–state relationship in favor of state authority vis-à-vis the national government.

The "devolution revolution" has greatly expanded the powers and responsibilities of subnational governments. Many services once provided by the federal government have been transferred to state and local governments. With greater powers and responsibilities, however, come greater expectations. As subnational governments are increasingly entrusted with the task of providing governmental services, the public may begin to hold them to a higher standard. These heightened expectations, if not fulfilled, may erode public confidence in subnational governments. For as David Kimball and Samuel Patterson (1997) have demonstrated at the national level, public support for political institutions is heavily influenced by the gap between expectations and performance. If subnational governments are truly the laboratories of democracy, it is imperative that we develop a deeper understanding of public attitudes toward them.

The ability of subnational governments to cope with their new responsibilities will depend, in large part, upon the political contexts in which they operate. States, for example, have great variation in their social (Hero 1998), cultural (Elazar 1966), economic (Brace 1993), electoral (Jewell and Morehouse 2001), ideological (Erikson, Wright, and McIver 1993), and institutional contexts (Fiorina 1994). Local governments are even more diverse, and, as one scholar has noted, their importance is on the rise:

If policymaking authority is devolved to the states, local governments will become more important, too. Most states rely heavily on their local governments to maintain law and order, educate children, and care for the needy. States also work with local governments to build and maintain roads, attract businesses, and protect the environment. The extensive partnership means that any increase in state activity is bound to affect local governments in significant ways. (Hanson 1999, 52)

Contextual conditions shape a government's ability to satisfy public expectations, which in turn may shape public confidence in those governments. To develop a better understanding of public attitudes toward subnational governments, we must take some of these sources of contextual variation into account.

Despite the importance of subnational institutions in the federal system, public opinion scholars know surprisingly little about how citizens view them. In part this failing reflects the fact that in comparison with the information available on Americans' views of the national government, data on the public's evaluations of subnational levels of government is not as rich, nor has information been collected at regular intervals. In addition, most research on American public opinion is based on *nationally* representative samples. When national surveys include questions about subnational governments, researchers can discover why some people, such as homeowners in general, might be less supportive of, say, local governments, although few people have done such analysis (for an exception, see Jennings 1998). However, with a nationally representative sample, it is not possible to study the characteristics of different communities and why people in different places might have more or less favorable views of their local or state governments. In nationally representative samples, so few respondents are interviewed from any given state or locality that comparisons across states or communities cannot be made with any statistical reliability.

Samples that are drawn from specific localities, of course, can be compared. For example, Paul Allen Beck, Hal Rainey, and Carol Traut (1987) compared citizen views of local government using data drawn from three Florida cities. Ruth Hoogland DeHoog, David Lowery, and William Lyons (1990), in an analysis similar in spirit to the one we undertake in this chapter, explained the origins of satisfaction with local government using data gathered from surveys done in ten localities in Kentucky. Their analysis included not only individual-level factors, such as a respondent's race and age, but also characteristics at the city level, such as average income and type of local government structure. While the De-Hoog, Lowery, and Lyons (1990) study employs, in our view, the right type of research design for studying the origins of trust in local government (see also Oliver 2001), its conclusions are limited by the fact that the researchers studied only ten communities.

Fortunately, a new source of data on Americans' views of their local communities has become available. This study, sponsored by the Saguaro Seminar of Harvard University in collaboration with the Ford Foundation and several local community foundations, does not have the same limitations as other sources of information on Americans' views of subnational governments. In addition to a nationally representative sample, the project, known as the Social Capital Community Benchmark Survey (SCCBS), included interviews with people drawn from forty different subnational representative samples. These samples had different geographic boundaries, including states and regions within states. However, most of the samples were drawn from a specific local community (city or county) or a metro area that includes a large core city. Respondents were queried about a number of different aspects of their communities, including how much trust they had in their local governments. In our analysis, we make use of data both from the nationally representative sample and from thirty-two of the forty community samples.[1] The community samples are drawn from a variety of American places, including Los Angeles, Seattle, Detroit, Boston, and Chicago.

Trust in Local and National Governments: Ideology and Interests

As we have noted, few national surveys have included questions about local governments. From the limited evidence that exists, it is apparent that support for state and local governments has not undergone the kind of downward slide that characterizes the trend shown in Figure 13-1 for the national government (Jennings 1998). As a consequence of these different patterns of change, Americans now have more faith in their subnational political institutions than in the national government. A survey conducted in the summer of 2000 by National Public Radio (NPR) and the John F. Kennedy School of Government, for example, found that only 29 percent of the public trusted the national government to do what is right "almost always" or "most of the time." State and local governments enjoyed slightly more support than the national government, although only 39 percent of the public expressed confidence that these governments would do what is right almost always or most of the time.

In the SCCBS data, we find a similar pattern for local and national government trust: relatively more trust in local governments but low to moderate levels of trust in both arenas. In the national sample portion of the survey, 29 percent of respondents said they

Table 13-1 Trust in Local and National Government

	National		
Local	*Hardly Ever/ Some of the Time*	*Always/Most of the Time*	*Row as % of Total*
Hardly ever/some	73.5	20.0	58.0
Always/most	26.5	80.0	42.0
Column as % of total	71.0	29.0	100.0

Source: Social Capital Community Benchmark Survey.

Note: The question was "How much of the time do you think you can trust the national (local) government to do what is right—just about always, most of the time, only some of the time, or hardly ever?"

trusted the national government just about always or most of the time, while 42 percent of respondents said they trusted their local governments. As Table 13-1 shows, however, confidence in one level of government seems to extend to another. For example, 80 percent of those respondents who said they trust the national government always or most of the time said the same thing about their local governments. The Pearson's correlation coefficient of .49 indicates that this relationship is a strong one.

People's judgments of local and national government may be intertwined for a number of reasons. One simple explanation is the respondent's desire to appear consistent to the interviewer. People were asked the local government question immediately following the question on trust in the national government, and so they may have felt pressure to give a similar response. More substantively, people's responses to the two questions may reflect a general orientation toward "government," and this broader attitude influences their responses to both questions. A third possibility is that people may use their experiences at one level of government to make inferences about another level of government with which they are less familiar. Whatever the mechanism, in our statistical model (as presented later in the chapter) we control for respondents' beliefs about the national government in order to isolate the variation in opinion of local government that is not due to variation in opinion of national government.

While as a whole the public is more supportive of local institutions than of the national government, the relative position of local and national governments could be influenced by a number of factors. Consider, for example, ideology. Philosophically, conservatives are more suspicious of government power in general than liberals, but historically they have viewed state and local governments as less of a threat to individual freedom and have tended to champion state and local prerogatives over national power. Liberals, on the other hand,

Figure 13-2 Ideology and Trust in Government

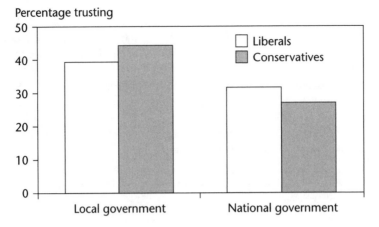

Source: Social Capital Community Benchmark Survey.

Note: The graph shows the percentage of liberals (conservatives) who said they trusted local (national) government "just about always" or "most of the time."

have often viewed subnational governments as accomplices to prejudice and inequality, and they are less reluctant to use the authority of local governments to further such causes as civil rights and the redistribution of wealth.

As Figure 13-2 shows, these ideological principles have their counterpart in public attitudes, although the differences are slight. Among people who identified themselves as conservatives (48 percent in the national sample), 27 percent said they trusted the national government just about always or most of the time, which compares with 44 percent who said the same about their local governments. Among liberals (26 percent of the national sample), on the other hand, support for the national government was somewhat higher, at nearly 32 percent, and support for local government was somewhat lower, at about 39 percent, than the corresponding figures among conservatives. The simple correlation between ideology and trust in local government, −.05, is very weak, indicating that the views of ideological elites about the relative trustworthiness of different levels of government are not well reflected in mass opinion.

If political principles do not get us very far in explaining levels of support for different levels of government, perhaps considerations of self-interest do. One of the main tasks of modern government is to redistribute resources among different groups of people. Naturally, because some people stand to gain and others stand to lose as a result of governmental decisions, people's views of government may well depend on whether their material well-being is advanced by government policy. Different levels of government in the U.S. federal system extract resources in different ways. Local governments depend primarily on property taxes to finance their activities, such as running the public schools, whereas the U.S. government generates its revenues principally through corporate and individual income taxes. Considerations of self-interest might lead homeowners to be more resentful of the authority of local government than nonhomeowners. But home ownership may be positively related to trust in the national government, as homeowners are the beneficiaries of a substantial tax break in the U.S. tax code that allows homeowners to deduct their local property taxes and the interest on their mortgages from their federal taxable income. The same kind of calculation may lead wealthier individuals to view the national government with more distrust (see Brehm and Rahn 1997), but the rich, except insofar as they are also homeowners, might not be expected to oppose the activities of local government to the same degree. If we consider the positive side of the government transfer ledger, parents with school age children benefit quite substantially from the activities of local governments, whereas senior citizens, through spending on social security and Medicare programs, benefit more from federal government programs.

Table 13-2 displays the correlations of each of these four indicators of self-interest with trust in national and local government. By this simple reckoning, self-interest tells us little about why some people might trust one level of government more than another. Homeowners are actually more likely to trust local government than nonhomeowners, and wealthier individuals are not necessarily less supportive of the national government than the less well off are. Having children eligible to attend public schools does not make people any more inclined to view local governments positively, nor do older Americans appear to view the national government any more positively than younger Americans, even though spending on social security and Medicare represent a substantial fraction of total federal spending.

These findings, or rather nonfindings, are consistent with a large body of research that demonstrates that self-interest is a surprisingly weak influence on public opinion (see Sears and Funk 1990). Group identities and interests, on the other hand, are often much more potent predictors of policy attitudes (Kinder 1998). Whites, for example, are more opposed to busing for school integration and affirmative action in education and hiring than blacks are, regardless of whether they actually stand to be affected by such policies (see Sears and Funk 1990 for a review of several studies). For example, R. Michael Alvarez and Tara Butterfield (1998) found that whites were much more likely than blacks to vote for Proposition 209, a successful California ballot initiative to dismantle affirmation action in many state agencies, including universities. Another issue that may pit groups against each other is immigration, especially illegal immigration. Native-born Americans may resent, for example, that their local taxes are used to educate the children of people who are in the United States

Table 13-2 Self-Interest and Trust in Government

	National Government	Local Government
Home ownership	−.01	.07*
Income	.01	.05*
Number of children	.00	−.02
Age	.03	.13*

Source: Social Capital Community Benchmark Survey.

Note: Cell entries are Pearson's r.

*p < .01
N = 2,993

illegally. Indeed, such resentment seemed to be the impetus for another successful California initiative, Proposition 187, which denied many government services to illegal aliens. With respect to support for different levels of government, African Americans, a majority of whom continue to reside in the South, may view local governments with suspicion because those governments actively supported racial segregation and discrimination in the past (Beck, Rainey, and Traut 1990). During the 1960s, when the national government was seen as advancing the civil rights agenda, blacks actually had higher confidence in the national government than whites did. In more recent periods, however, surveys indicate that there is little to distinguish the views of whites and blacks on the trustworthiness of the federal government (Lawrence 1997).

Table 13-3 confirms that whites and blacks continue to hold very different views on the trustworthiness of local governments. Over 70 percent of blacks, but only 52 percent of whites, said they trust local government only some of the time or hardly ever. Consistent with other surveys, data in Table 13-3 show that distrust of the federal government was equally widespread. Contrary to expectations that noncitizens would have greater trust in local government, both citizens and noncitizens share similar evaluations. Noncitizens, however, are less inclined than citizens to distrust the federal government.

M. Kent Jennings (1998) argues that local governments enjoy more support from citizens than the national government because they are viewed as being more accessible, more amenable to citizen influence, and less complex than the more remote federal government, qualities he terms the linkage function. The NPR study mentioned earlier confirms this wisdom. For example, in this survey half of the respondents thought that if they contacted their U.S. representative, he or she would pay either a lot or some attention to their opinions. State legislators were viewed as more responsive than Congress (58 percent), and local gov-

Table 13-3 Group Membership and Distrust of Government

Group	National Government	Local Government
Blacks	73.4%	70.9%
Whites	71.8	51.9
Citizens	71.7	57.9
Noncitizens	61.0	56.9

Source: Social Capital Community Benchmark Survey.

Note: Entries are the percentage of respondents in each group who reported that they trust local or national government only some of the time or never.

ernment representatives were seen to be the most amenable of all. Fully 67 percent of respondents in the survey said that city council members would pay either a lot or some attention to their opinion.

The Saguaro Seminar study did not compare different levels of government on the linkage dimension. Respondents were asked, however, to agree or disagree with the statement: "The people running my community don't care what happens to me," a question that taps what political scientists call external efficacy. A sizable majority, 62 percent, *rejected* the sentiments expressed by the statement, indicating that people generally viewed their local leaders as having benevolent motivations; that is, at the local level people had a fairly high degree of external efficacy. As might be expected, people who believed their local representatives lacked empathy for them were much less likely than people who held the opposite view to trust local governments (see Table 13-4). Among the former, only slightly more than a quarter (27.5) trusted local government just about always or most of the time, while among the latter, over half (50.8 percent) did. The correlation between local trust and local political efficacy is .14, indicating a moderately positive relationship.

Further Explorations of the Origins of Trust in Local Government

In this section, we turn from a consideration of the relative positions of the federal and local governments in the public's mind to a more focused, and multivariate, investigation of the origins of people's views about their local governments. A number of explanations have been offered for why trust in government varies across location and time. Most of the explanatory frameworks have been based on the analysis of survey questions that ask people in different countries to evaluate their national governments or specific national political in-

Table 13-4 Local Political Efficacy and Trust in Local Government

Local Trust in Government	Local Political Efficacy		
	Low	High	Row as % of Total
Some/never	72.5%	49.2%	57.9
Always/most	27.5	50.8	42.1
Column as % of total	35.7	62.1	100.0

Source: Social Capital Community Benchmark Survey.

Note: Low-efficacy respondents are those who agreed with the statement "The people running my community don't care about me." High-efficacy respondents disagreed with the statement.

stitutions, such as legislatures or courts. We draw on this literature to help us identify causes for variation in attitudes toward local political authorities. Our aim in this section is to develop a comprehensive model of the origins of support for local government that takes advantage of the fact that the Social Capital Community Benchmark Survey allows us to investigate factors at both the individual and the community level of analysis.

Performance. An important class of theories focuses on the performance of governments. In these sorts of accounts, political actors and institutions are judged by their ability to advance valued collective goals such as economic prosperity, law and order, and international security. Of these, the role of economy has received the most attention from analysts. Although the health of the national economy would appear to be a plausible basis for levels of public trust, when trends in objective measures of economic welfare, such as inflation or unemployment rates, are matched with trends in public opinion, the correspondence is surprisingly weak (see, for example, Lawrence 1997; Miller and Listhaug 1999; MacAllister 1999; Pharr 2000). The linkages appear to be stronger, however, when subjective rather than objective measures of economic performance are used (Craig 1993). In one recent study, for example, Virginia Chanley, Thomas Rudolph, and Wendy Rahn (2000) traced variation in levels of trust in the U.S. national government during the 1980–1997 period to a variety of factors, one of which was a measure of subjective economic optimism. They found that the U.S. public's trust in the national government was higher when optimism about the economy was widespread. Chanley and her colleagues also found, however, that concern about crime was even more important than the economy in explaining fluctuations during this time period (see also Mansbridge 1997), suggesting that people focus on more than simply economic criteria when appraising government's ability to "do what is right." For example, at the local level, DeHoog, Lowery, and Lyons (1990) found that citizen satisfaction with local government is affected by government performance as measured by perceptions of the quality of service delivery in such areas as public transportation, trash collection, and police protection.

The Social Capital Community Benchmark Survey did not ask people to judge local economic conditions or the quality of government services. However, it did include two questions that we would expect to be related to these evaluations. In one question, respondents were asked to rate how satisfied they were with their own financial situation. Brehm and Rahn (1997) found in their study of confidence in national institutions that respondents who had seen improvements in their personal economic fortunes were more trusting. In another, more directly relevant question, respondents were asked to rate the quality of their communities. We view responses to this question as a summary rating that encapsulates many of the performance dimensions upon which local governments could be expected to be judged, such as crime, the quality of schools and other public services (such as street maintenance and public libraries), and the local economy.

Integrity. Another set of explanations focuses on the integrity of governmental actors and institutions. Government corruption and the scandals that result have been shown to affect how much trust people have in their national governments in such diverse places as the United States (Chanley, Rudolph, and Rahn 2000), Italy, Germany, France (della Porta 2000), and Japan (Pharr 2000). Rates of political corruption do vary across U.S. localities (Meier and Holbrook 1992), but we lack the data at present to incorporate this dimension of integrity into our analysis, either at the individual or the community level of analysis. Another aspect of integrity, briefly mentioned in the previous section, is how well political institutions and the actors within them respond to citizens' demands and seem to care about the interests of citizens. We use the question about local political efficacy already discussed to capture these kinds of evaluations.

Media. Another popular explanation for variation in levels of confidence, particularly their declines over time, focuses on the role of the media. Media coverage of politicians and government has grown increasingly negative (Patterson 1994). So, too, have the campaigns of candidates for public office (Finkel and Geer 1998). Larry Bartels and Wendy Rahn (2000) found that higher levels of exposure to either network TV news or to negative political advertising reduced American respondents' levels of trust in the national government. The media thesis is controversial, however, and other researchers contend that it cannot account adequately for why political support varies over time; further, only in scattered countries do heavy viewers of television have lower levels of institutional confidence (Norris 2000). The SCCBS contains two measures of media exposure, newspaper reading (in days per week) and general TV watching (in hours per day).

Interests. Even though self-interest did not appear to influence levels of trust in local government when we considered bivariate relationships, we nonetheless retain these variables because others have found, for example, that homeowners or wealthier individuals are less satisfied with local government (DeHoog, Lowery, and Lyons 1990) and more likely to favor property tax reductions (Sears and Citrin 1982). We also include variables designed to tap group interest and identities: race and citizenship.

Control Variables. In addition to the individual-level variables already discussed, we include several control variables at the individual level: the respondent's opinion of the national government, sex, education level, marital status, and political ideology.

Community-level Variables. The chief virtue of the SCCBS is that respondents were interviewed in a number of different localities. Thus, we are able to incorporate into our model information not only about each individual respondent but also about the communities in which the respondents live. There are, of course, numerous dimensions upon which towns and cities in the United States differ. We consider two classes of variables, community socioeconomic development and community heterogeneity.

Two relevant aspects of a community's socioeconomic context are the education and income levels of its denizens. Of course, these two are related: wealthier communities have more educated people and vice versa. Indeed, the simple correlation between average community income and average education is a sizable .73. Our argument, however, is that each of the aspects at the community level can influence the performance of local governments and their ability to extract resources from citizens efficiently and fairly, although perhaps in different ways. Consider, first, education levels. Education is a form of what economists call human capital. Places with more human capital may be more prosperous, among other things, than locations that lack these human resources; higher human capital may in turn contribute to higher levels of trust in local government. In addition, at the individual level, education contributes to the acquisition of democratic norms.

Formal education is important to the development of enlightened democratic citizens because it fosters the recognition that their fate is controlled in fundamental ways by the actions and policies of democratic government. At the same time, education encourages in citizens both the recognition that their fate is intimately connected with their fellow citizens and the recognition that the goals of fairness and equality are important to the long-run stability of the democratic system. (Nie, Junn, and Stehlik-Barry 1996, 18)

Thus democratic norms are more widespread in communities characterized by high education levels. Because the ideals of fairness and equality are more widely shared in such places, local governments may be able to function more equitably, thereby affecting people's perceptions of their trustworthiness. The communities in our analysis differ widely on average education, and we expect this community-level variation to affect levels of political trust across communities.

The effects of community prosperity, as measured by average income levels, are potentially countervailing. We have already mentioned the standard self-interest explanation for why wealthier individuals might be more suspicious of government. The community-level analog of this proposition is that in wealthier communities, people may be less favorable toward government because fewer citizens in these places actually benefit from local government spending. For example, in communities characterized by higher income levels, more people may send their children to private school or be less dependent on public services such as transportation. Therefore, according to this hypothesis, more prosperous communities will have lower average levels of trust.

Our model also includes two measures of community heterogeneity: racial and ethnic diversity and political polarization. As we will explain, both of these characteristics pose challenges for communities and for the ability of governments to perform well and equitably. In other words, places characterized by high levels of heterogeneity may have poorer-functioning governments, and thus, may indeed be less worthy of citizen's trust.

We are writing this chapter in the midst of the Census Bureau's release of state-by-state information on the demographic make-up of American places. These data make it abundantly clear that the United States is a very diverse place socially, even more diverse than many analysts had predicted, mostly as a result of greater than expected growth in the number of Hispanics. Of course, some places are more diverse than others. For example, in our set of communities, whites are no longer the majority race in Los Angeles (Hispanics are). On the other hand, the area around Bend, Oregon, is predominantly white; but just to the north, the population of Yakima, Washington, is over 30 percent Hispanic.

So the experience of social diversity is not evenly spread across American states, towns, and cities. There are many reasons to believe that social diversity makes it more difficult to achieve cohesion within a community and may make it more difficult for local governments to function fairly. High levels of social diversity can contribute to the process of social categorization in which perceptions of between-group differences are magnified and within-group differences minimized (Gaertner et al. 1999).

Perceptions of between-group dissimilarity are no doubt exacerbated by the fact that many diverse American cities are also characterized by a high degree of residential segregation. By choice or by circumstance (such as discrimination), people may wind up living in racially homogeneous neighborhoods, with most whites, for example, residing in predominately white neighborhoods and most blacks living in predominantly black neighborhoods (Farley 1996; Cutler, Glaeser, and Vigdor 1999).

Social categorization encourages ethnocentrism, or in-group favoritism and out-group hostility. Donald Kinder, Cindy Kam, and Claudia Deane (2000), for example, find that ethnocentrism is strongly related to negative attitudes toward immigrants. With respect to politics, Alberto Alesina, Reza Baqir, and William Easterly argue that in communities characterized by sharp ethnic divisions, the provision of such local public goods as public libraries and roads is lower than is optimal: "Representatives of interest groups with an ethnic base are likely to value only the benefits of public goods that accrue to their group, and discount the benefits for other groups" (1997, 2). Alesina, Baqir, and Easterly find, for example, that in ethnically diverse places, local governments spend less money per pupil on public education, one of the most productive forms of government spending because it increases human capital. Yet total government spending is actually higher in diverse places. But because local tax revenues do not correspondingly increase, ethnically diverse places have higher government deficits, a measure of poor government performance that has been shown in cross-national research to adversely affect citizens' views of government trustworthiness (Miller and Listhaug 1999). We measure ethnic diversity in a community using a commonly used index of ethnic fractionalization, which is defined as the probability that any two randomly chosen individuals from a community will *not* belong to the same racial or ethnic group.[2] The higher this probability, the greater the ethnic diversity.

Ethnic diversity may contribute to another aspect of community heterogeneity, political polarization (Alesina, Baqir, and Easterly 1997). Polarization can occur in the absence of social diversity, however, and that is why we consider it separately. For example, by our measure, Boulder, Colorado, is among the most polarized communities in our set, but it is not especially diverse socially. Political polarization can contribute to perceptions of government untrustworthiness in two ways, by contributing to beliefs that government policy is unrepresentative and by decreasing government effectiveness.

With respect to the first of these, consider the two hypothetical opinion distributions in Figure 13-3. The mean and the median of each of these distributions are the same, but in distribution A a higher proportion of the population holds opinions that are found in the middle of the spectrum, that is, opinions are more tightly clustered around the average opinion. In contrast, the second distribution is flatter, or more dispersed: a smaller fraction of people lies in the middle of the distribution and more people, in comparison to Distribution A, are characterized by extreme opinions. In statistical parlance, we say that Distribution B has a higher standard deviation than Distribution A. The higher the standard deviation of an opinion distribution, the more polarized it is (DiMaggio, Evans, and Bryson 1996). Another way of conveying the importance of the shape of the opinion distribution is to note that any randomly chosen individual from a community characterized by polarized opinion is more likely to be further from the average opinion than a randomly chosen individual from a more politically homogeneous community (Alesina, Baqir, and Easterly 1997).

How, then, does political polarization affect government confidence? Here, following

Figure 13-3 Two Hypothetical Opinion Distributions with the Same Mean and Median

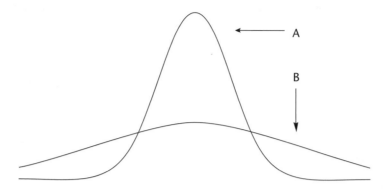

Alesina and colleagues (Alesina, Baqir, and Easterly 1997; Alesina and Wacziarg 2000), we make use of the logic of the median voter theorem. According to median voter models of party competition, if political parties or political candidates care about winning elections and voters are concerned with getting their preferred policies enacted, the policy positions advocated by competing candidates will converge on the opinion held by the median voter, the person who is exactly in the middle of the opinion distribution. The predictions of the median voter theorem hold regardless of the shape of the opinion distribution. However, even though the median voter model would predict the same policy outcome for communities with the same median opinion, it follows from our discussion that in comparison to politically homogeneous communities, more people in polarized communities will be dissatisfied with the resulting policy because more people are further from the median opinion. Thus, in communities that are polarized, more people may see government policy as unrepresentative of their interests, thus leading to lower levels of trust in government.

Political polarization may also affect confidence in government because governments may find it more difficult to function effectively in these settings, which in turn would be expected to have negative consequences for citizens' perceptions of government competence. Paul DiMaggio, John Evans, and Bethany Bryson (1996; see also King 1997) argue that polarization makes it more difficult to achieve compromise and reach political consensus, a hypothesis richly illustrated by Morris Fiorina's (1999) discussion of local politics in Concord, Massachusetts. In the dispute he describes, which involved some land to be used for the expansion of a private high school, the conflict between opponents and proponents of the expansion dragged on for more than four years, and was settled only because the contending parties went to mediation. On the flip side, Robert Putnam's (1993) study of regional governments in Italy indicates that as political elites became less polarized ideologically, it was easier for them to reach accommodation on issues. Sarah Binder (1999), in her study of legislative stalemate in the U.S. Congress, offers systematic evidence of polarization's deleterious impact on government's ability to reach decisions. Specifically, she finds that policy gridlock is a positive function of ideological heterogeneity in Congress. In our model, we measure political polarization as the standard deviation of the distribution of citizens' ideological preferences in a given community. To illustrate, both Rochester, New York, and Los Angeles have the same average opinion on the ideology scale, .44, slightly to the political right for a variable that ranges from 0, strongly conservative, to 1, strongly liberal. However, the standard deviation is .27 in Rochester and .30 in Los Angeles, indicating that even though these communities have about the same average opinion, the distribution of opinion is more polarized in Los Angeles.

Results

Table 13-5 displays the results from our multivariate model of trust in local government.[3] To facilitate interpretation, our dependent variable and several of our independent variables are coded on a 0 to 1 range. We have grouped the independent variables according to the different explanations we have outlined.

Consider first the individual-level determinants of trust in local government. Earlier we suggested that support for local government might be influenced by considerations of self-interest. Our results are partially consistent with that expectation. In the multivariate context, homeowners are, as expected, less trusting of local government. However, trust is positively associated with age, as older Americans voice greater confidence in local officials, contrary to expectations based on self-interest. Also contrary to expectations, people with school age children are not more supportive of local government.

Group identities and interests, particularly those associated with race, are often a key predictor of attitudes toward government and governmental policies (Kinder 1998). Apart from considerations of self-interest, our results show that indicators of group interest shape people's attitude toward local government. Compared with whites, Native Americans and blacks are less trustful of local government. In light of past discrimination against these two groups, sometimes sanctioned by local officials, it is perhaps not surprising that members of these groups would express less faith in local government. However, not all racial minorities are equally mistrustful of local government. Asians' attitudes toward local government are, statistically speaking, no different from those of whites. As indicated by its positive coefficient in Table 13-5, Hispanics are actually more supportive than whites of local government.

Trust in local government was also hypothesized to be a function of media use, as exposure to media was expected to drive trust downward. As Table 13-5 makes clear, though,

Table 13-5 Determinants of Trust in Local Government

Variables	OLS Coefficients	Standard Errors
Individual-level variable		
Self-interest		
Homeowner	−.014***	(.004)
Household income	−.001	(.007)
Number of children	−.001	(.001)
Age	.028**	(.012)
Group interest		
Black	−.044***	(.005)
Hispanic	.023***	(.007)
Asian	−.002	(.010)
Native American	−.026*	(.015)
Citizen	−.012	(.008)
Performance		
Quality of life in community	.126***	(.007)
Personal economic perceptions	.029***	(.005)
Integrity		
Local political efficacy	.087***	(.005)
Media		
Watch television	.001	(.001)
Read newspaper	.002***	(.001)
Controls		
Trust in national government	.551***	(.007)
Political ideology	−.052***	(.006)
Female	−.003	(.003)
Education	−.001	(.006)
Married	.001	(.004)
Constant	.347***	(.043)
Community-level variable		
Socioeconomic		
Income	−.042***	(.008)
Education	.041***	(.008)
Heterogeneity		
Racial and ethnic diversity	−.083***	(.013)
Political polarization	−.729***	(.167)
Adj. R^2	0.413	
Number of cases	14,746	

Source: Social Capital Community Benchmark Survey.

Note: Table entries are OLS coefficients with standard errors in parentheses.

*p < .10
**p < .05
***p < .01

our results provide no support for a media-based explanation of trust. The amount of time spent watching television has no impact on trust, and newspaper readership actually strengthens rather than weakens trust in local government. While media use appears to be relatively inconsequential, trust is powerfully influenced by people's beliefs about the integrity and responsiveness of local officials. As perceptions of local political efficacy increase, so, too, does trust in local government. Compared with the effects of the self- and group-interest variables noted above, the size of this effect is quite substantial. For example, being Native American or black decreases trust by about 2 and 4 percentage points, respectively. As perceptions of local political efficacy change from least to most favorable, trust increases by nearly 9 percentage points.

Our results also provide strong support for a performance-based explanation of trust. As expected, trust in local government is higher among those who report greater satisfaction with their personal financial situation. As ratings of personal economic satisfaction improve from "not at all satisfied" to "very satisfied," trust increases by 3 percentage points. An even stronger influence is exerted by the perceived quality of life in a community. Trust is substantially higher among those who rate their community as an "excellent" place to live. As the perceived quality of life in a community changes from "poor" to "excellent," trust in local government increases by almost 13 percentage points.

Despite controls for political ideology, trust in national government, and important demographic characteristics, the analysis thus far has identified several individual-level attributes that, to varying degrees, shape individuals' attitudes toward local government. But to fully understand the origins of people's views about their local government, we must consider contextual as well as individual-level factors.

As shown at the bottom of Table 13-5, our model also investigates several community-level predictors of trust in local government. At the individual level, we found that neither income nor education affected public attitudes toward local government. Such is not the case when we consider these variables at the community level. As hypothesized, communities with better-educated people have higher levels of trust. In contrast, our results show that wealthier communities have lower levels of trust, confirming our community income hypotheses.

Consistent with expectations, attitudes toward local government are strongly related to measures of community heterogeneity. In particular, trust is inversely related to a community's racial and ethnic diversity. To illustrate the magnitude of this effect, we compare the difference in trust levels between a community with relatively low racial and ethnic diversity such as Bismarck, North Dakota, and a community with relatively high levels of diversity like Los Angeles. Holding individual-level attributes and all other community-level factors constant, living in Los Angeles rather than in Bismarck decreases trust in local government by more than 5 percentage points.

Trust in local government is influenced by political as well as by racial and ethnic heterogeneity. As hypothesized, trust in local government is inversely related to a community's level of political polarization. Consider the difference in trust levels between York, Pennsylvania, a city with relatively little polarization, and Boston, a city with high levels of political polarization. All else being equal, the level of trust in local government among residents of Boston is more than 4 percentage points lower than that of people living in York.

Discussion

Our results support our contention that to understand why people view local governments differently, one needs to consider not only attributes of individuals, such as their self- and group interests, but also the characteristics of the communities in which local governments operate. Variation in these contexts help to explain why, on average, citizens in one place have more confidence in their political institutions than citizens living somewhere else. Unfortunately, the implication of our findings—that both political polarization and ethnic diversity contribute to more negative views of local government—is rather discouraging as local governments attempt to manage their new responsibilities. Even without more immigration, ethnic diversity in the United States will continue to grow because of differential birth rates across different racial and ethnic groups. And studies of mass opinion at the national (DiMaggio, Evans, and Bryson 1996; King 1997; Poole and Rosenthal 1984) and state (Wright et al. 2000) levels point to an increase in the polarization of American politics, especially among strong partisans. These are the people most likely to be active in politics, but whose opinions are much more extreme than the "average" citizen's (King 1997; Fiorina 1999). Elite polarization has reinvigorated partisan identification in the electorate (Bartels 2000), a development that many political scientists, used to thinking about American political parties as in decline, may well find surprising but also, perhaps, welcome. Our results suggest, however, that political polarization and trends in ethnic diversity will pose difficult challenges for local governments.

Notes

Preparation of this chapter was generously supported by a grant from the Northwest Area Foundation. A sabbatical leave from the University of Minnesota to the first author and fellowships to both authors from the National Election Studies and the Center for Political Studies at the University of Michigan made our collaboration possible and greatly facilitated the writing of the chapter. The authors alone are responsible for the results and interpretations discussed in this chapter.

1. Because our focus is on views of local government, we excluded community samples that were derived from entire state populations, regions within states that did not have a metropolitan focus, and samples drawn from areas within cities. By our logic, we deemed that thirty-two of the forty community samples approximated a local government jurisdiction.

2. Ethnic fractionalization is calculated as the $1 - \Sigma(\text{race}_i)^2$, where race_i = proportion non-Hispanic white, non-Hispanic black, Hispanic, Asian or Pacific Islander, or Native American.

3. We estimate our model using ordinary least squares (OLS) regression. In models such as ours, where variables are measured at different levels of analysis, OLS may produce inefficient estimates and biased standard errors (Steenbergen and Jones forthcoming). We reestimated a similar model using the more appropriate statistical technique, hierarchical linear modeling, and our substantive conclusions were not altered. For a discussion of the HLM results, see Rudolph and Rahn (2001).

14 The People's Craving for Unselfish Government

John R. Hibbing

The study of public opinion typically focuses on people's attitudes toward particular candidates, parties, ideologies, and issues, as is indicated by the subject matter of most chapters in this book. Such an orientation is perfectly appropriate since people's candidate, party, ideological, and issue preferences undoubtedly form the core of their political worldviews. As important as these topics are, they unfortunately obscure another central component of political public opinion: people's attitudes toward governing structures and processes. After all, if it is deemed important to understand what people think of the candidates and parties in government, is it not important to understand what people think about the government in which these candidates and parties serve?

Why Care About Public Attitudes Toward Government?

If the structure and operation of government were immutable—that is, if government were merely an unshakable arena in which candidates, parties, ideologies, and issue positions clashed—then determining people's attitudes toward government would be unnecessary. Government would simply operate in a neutral, deep-background fashion and people's attitudes toward it would be uninteresting and of little consequence. But perceptions of the structure and operation of government are anything but inconsequential. Public opinion of government affects its operation and, therefore, understanding why people view government as they do becomes a crucial task.

Until the late 1960s, little thought was given to the American public's views of its government. Indeed, what was there to say? Americans revered the Constitution, thought their government was the best in the world, harbored few desires for serious systemic reform, and were quite deferential to the people in government. A famous comparative study published in 1963 revealed that 82 percent of the people in the United States were proud of American governmental institutions, even as only 23 percent were proud of the American economic system and a minuscule 7 percent were proud of the American people. Of the other countries included in the survey, none came close to the pride in government possessed by Americans. To be specific, the highest percentage of residents outside of the United States taking pride in their government was in the United Kingdom, where only 46 percent did so. In Italy, only 3 percent of the people were proud of their government; Germany was not much better, at 7 percent (Almond and Verba 1963). To a great extent, it was Americans' pride in their form of government that helped to fuel the intense feelings of the cold war. The American way of government was best, people thought, and it was essential that it triumph over other ways.

But then came urban unrest, the Vietnam War, civil rights, rising crime rates, and Watergate. Government no longer had the solutions and sometimes appeared to cause the problems. Presidents lied to the American people about the status of the war in Southeast Asia and, while in the Oval Office, gave permission for hush money to be paid to criminals. Governors and members of Congress tried to block the pathways to real civil rights for African Americans and, more generally, were increasingly seen as grossly insensitive to the changes that were sweeping society. Starting around 1967, people's confidence in government began to drop. This drop was especially evident among liberals, traditionally the group most inclined to see government favorably (see Nie and Andersen 1974; Orren 1997, 91). But by the 1970s, as conservatives continued their usual lament that governmental collective decisions were inferior to individual decisions in a marketplace environment, liberals became convinced that government was little more than a cheerleader for the military-industrial complex. Government was left with few defenders anywhere on the ideological spectrum.

Scholarly research eventually noticed the decline in confidence. In a famous exchange in 1974, Arthur Miller and Jack Citrin agreed that major changes had occurred in the way people looked at government, but they disagreed on the exact meaning of these changes. Miller contended that "pervasive and enduring distrust of government ... [can] ... increase the potential for radical change" (1974, 971), but Citrin felt survey respondents were merely voicing frustration with incumbent officeholders and that they still supported (and even took pride in) the political system in a general sense. In other words, Miller implied that dissatisfaction could lead to serious systemic disruptions whereas Citrin believed it would probably result in nothing more than voting out the ins and voting in the outs.

It would appear that Citrin's position has better withstood the passage of time. Although the country has experienced occasional periods of increased satisfaction with government, mostly in the mid-1980s and late 1990s, governmental approval has generally been quite low ever since the decline of the 1970s; yet the American political system has never seemed seriously threatened by a lack of popular support. In academic jargon, people may not have approved of specific actions by the government but they mostly retained a "diffuse support" for the political system (Easton 1965a).

Since the revolution never came—indeed, the United States did not even experience a full-fledged party realignment—does this mean no systemic consequences flow from people's loss of confidence in government? This is where the original Miller–Citrin exchange may have done a disservice. If the issue is cast as one in which diffuse support is either present or absent, many of the possible consequences of unfavorable attitudes toward government are defined away. The truth of the matter is that the concept of diffuse support is not particularly useful beyond reminding us of the obvious point that it is possible for people to be upset with a particular action of government and still respect the existing governmental system at a more basic level. What is now apparent is that even if people do not want the current political system to go away, negative attitudes toward government have implications far beyond a desire to vote for the out party (a point made forcefully by Orren 1997; see also several of the contributors in Pharr and Putnam 2000).

For example, research has indicated that when the public has little confidence in institutions of government like Congress, prospective officeholders are less likely to be willing to serve (see Fowler and McClure 1989; Theriault 1998). Incumbents are more likely to quit and potential challengers are less likely to start when the public mood is palpably sour. One member of Congress who retired after serving just a few terms said: "People just presume we are dishonorable. . . . Imagine living under a cloud of suspicion all the time. If you can do that, you can understand why some of us think serving in Congress isn't enjoyable." Another said, "The vilification of the average politician in the eyes of the public is a very alarming trend. . . . Some people seem to think I should be ashamed to have served in the U.S. Congress" (both quoted in Hibbing 1982, 55–56). This last remark calls to mind former representative Pat Schroeder's favorite plea to reporters: "Please don't tell my mother I am in Congress; she thinks I am a prostitute and I would hate to disappoint her."

Other problems also accrue when people think ill of government. Sometimes, elected officials are so concerned about public attitudes toward their institution that they avoid tackling tough policy problems (Hess 1998). Usually the way for a political institution to preserve popularity is to avoid dealing with contentious issues (Durr, Gilmour, and Wolbrecht 1997), so the temptation is to leave the challenging problems for a later date. Another danger is that people who are unhappy with government may seek to change or reform various aspects of the political system without thoroughly considering whether those changes will in fact make people feel better about the government (Hibbing and Theiss-Morse forthcoming). Finally, research in psychology has indicated that people who lack confidence in an institution will be less likely to comply with the laws (or other outputs) of that institution (see Tyler 1990, 2001).

These are serious issues. If a decline in confidence in government leads to a lower quality of elected officials, to timidity rather than temerity in addressing serious problems, to counterproductive reforms, and to cavalier public attitudes toward compliance with government edicts, the health of our society will be affected. In short, the fact that a lack of confidence may not lead people to want to overthrow the existing governmental regime does not mean that a lack of confidence does not have deleterious consequences. People's attitudes toward government serve as important institutional constraints. If the attitudes are sufficiently negative, government will have more difficulty doing what it is supposed to do. But the extent to which public attitudes impinge upon the ability of the governmental system to do its job depends on the precise nature of the people's dissatisfaction. For that reason determining which aspect of government is responsible for the downturn in public approval becomes an important task.

Differences in Attitudes Toward Institutions and Officials

For quite some time now research has indicated that while most people are supportive of their own member of Congress they may at the same time think little of Congress itself (Fenno 1975). (In this respect, politics may be quite similar to the law and medicine since people tend to be fond of their own attorney and their own doctor but think less highly of the legal and medical professions generally.) Because a single representative is such a small part of the governmental system, a more fruitful distinction may be between the institutions (and overall institutional structure) of government and the collections of officials working within those institutions.

Americans are actually quite supportive of the governmental system when they are asked to focus on institutions in the abstract or, especially, on the constitutionally provided arrangement of institutions. It is only when people's attention turns to the elected officials and bureaucrats who labor within these institutions that opinion turns negative. This distinction is captured in Figure 14-1, which reports results from a national survey conducted in 1992.[1] In this survey, respondents were first presented with the following item: "Thinking about people in government, please tell me if you strongly approve, approve, disapprove, or strongly disapprove of the way the people in the Congress [in the Presidency; in the Supreme Court] are handling their jobs." Thus, in the case of Congress, for example, the referent was not just Congress generally but rather the people in Congress. Respondents were then told: "Now, sometimes when we talk about parts of the government, like the Supreme Court, the Presidency, and the Congress, we don't mean the people currently serving in office, we mean the institutions themselves, no matter who is in office. These institutions have their own buildings, historical traditions, and purposes." Then, they were asked whether they strongly approved, approved, disapproved, or strongly disapproved of each institution.

The results show a tremendous disparity between approval levels of the institutions on the one hand and of the people in those institutions on the other. The gap is especially large for Congress: three times as many respondents approved of the institution of Congress as of the members of Congress. (To simplify the figure, strongly approve and approve responses were collapsed, as were strongly disapprove and disapprove.) Well over twice as many people approved of the institution of the presidency as approved of President George H. W.

Figure 14-1 Contrasting Public Approval of Institutions and Members of Institutions

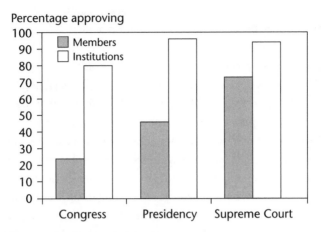

Percentage approving

Source: 1992 Public Attitudes Toward Political Institutions Survey in John R. Hibbing and Elizabeth Theiss-Morse, *Congress as Public Enemy: Public Attitudes Toward American Political Institutions* (New York: Cambridge University Press, 1995).

N = approximately 1,357.

Bush (remember, the survey was conducted in 1992). Even in the Supreme Court, which (predictably) had the smallest differential, it was still the case that the percent approving of the institution was 1.3 times the percent approving of the justices. Not surprisingly, then, when people are asked if they want "major change" in the structure of government, they say they do not. When in a 1998 national survey respondents were asked to agree or disagree with the statement that "our basic governmental structures are the best in the world and should not be changed in a major fashion," 65.7 agreed, leaving barely one-third supporting major change—and even at that many of the "major" changes the one-third had in mind turned out to be quite minor.[2] Surveys done in the early to mid-1970s (unfortunately, the item was not asked in the 1960s) show similar levels of public support for existing arrangements and opposition to major change.[3]

Attitudes That Have Not Become More Negative

To this point, the results suggest it is incorrect to leave the impression that people dislike everything about politics and government. They actually are remarkably approving of government (and government institutions) in the abstract. It is only when living, breathing human beings get involved that approval tends to dissipate. But what is it about the actions of government officials as a group that tends to upset modern Americans? In attempting to answer this question, it is useful to see how perceptions of those officials have changed over the years. To do so, I draw on data collected by the National Election Studies (NES) at the University of Michigan. The advantage of these data is that similar questions have been asked repeatedly, sometimes since the late 1950s. The repetition of identical items makes it possible to draw conclusions about the manner in which officials have lost much of the public trust.[4]

Perhaps the best way to proceed is to identify those potential sources of dissatisfaction that have not changed and therefore cannot be responsible for declining levels of trust. For example, some might suspect that the decline in public faith in government is explained by a growing perception that public officials waste a lot of taxpayers' money. This hypothesis does not withstand analytical scrutiny. In every election year since 1968, with the exception of 1986, NES's national sample has been asked whether "people in government waste tax money." It is true that a majority of respondents admit to believing that people in government waste "a lot" of money, but the percent responding in such a fashion did not change much from 1968 to 1998. As can be seen in Figure 14-2, after increasing in the second half of the 1970s, perceptions of the level of profligacy among people in government dropped back to levels present in the late 1960s. People tend to think governmental officials waste tax money, but this perception has not become more common over the past thirty years so would not seem to be at the core of people's decreased confidence in government.

Much the same thing can be said for the amount of attention people in government pay to ordinary people. Given the shrill populist tone of modern political rhetoric, it might reasonably be thought that the public has the perception that ordinary people are being ignored and that this perception is why many are upset with the political system. Once again, the sentiment is not supported by the data. The NES pollsters frequently ask respondents, "How much does the government listen to the people?" Permitted responses are "not much," "some," and "a good deal"; for simplicity's sake, Figure 14-3 presents the percent of respondents selecting the most negative answer—"not much." Unfortunately, this item has not been consistently posed in midterm elections so I present results only for presidential election years. The overall results speak surprisingly well for people's perception of government attentiveness, as only about one-fourth to one-third of those in the samples expressed the belief that government does not listen much. But with regard to the more telling matter of how perceptions have changed since the late 1960s, the pattern is similar to that appearing in Figure 14-2. After an increase in the late 1970s, perceptions that government officials do not listen much dropped and by the late 1990s were actually lower than they were in the late 1960s. People's frustration with governmental officials apparently cannot be traced to the perception that those officials are unwilling or unable to listen to the people.

These findings about "listening" are not an aberration. The people at NES compile something they call a government responsiveness index, which is computed by combining responses to two items: "How much attention do you feel the government pays to what the

Figure 14-2 How Much Taxpayer Money Do Public Officials Waste? 1968–1998

Percentage saying "a lot"

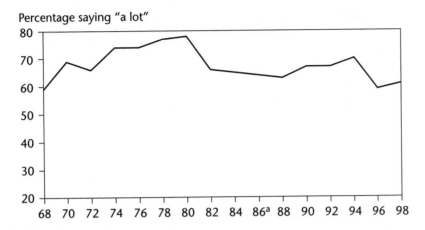

Source: National Election Studies.

[a]Data for 1986 are missing; the number reported here is the average of 1984 and 1988.

Figure 14-3 How Much Does the Government Listen to the People? 1968–1996

Percentage saying "not much"

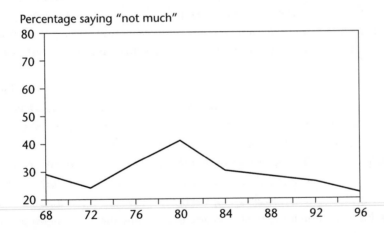

Source: National Election Studies.

Figure 14-4 Government Responsiveness Index,
1968–1996

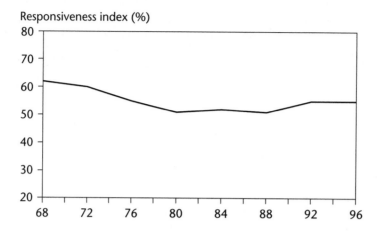

Responsiveness index (%)

Source: National Election Studies.

people think when it decides what to do," and "How much do you feel that having elections makes the government pay attention to what the people think?" As can be seen in Figure 14-4, this index was at 62 in 1968 and, while it is true that perceptions of governmental responsiveness have declined since then, the extent of this decline was minuscule over the thirty years covered, with the 1996 figure only a few points lower, at 55. To the extent people have become more hostile toward government it is not because they now perceive government to be much less responsive to the needs of the people than did those surveyed a few decades ago.

Finally, maybe people are upset with governmental officials because they have allowed politics to become too complicated. When officials exult in the nuances of issues and try to highlight their issue differences with other politicians, ordinary people might feel cut out of government. But, as it turns out, the people do not believe politics has become more complicated (see Figure 14-5). In fact, save for an unusual spike in 1998, the trend seems to be toward popular perceptions that politics is less complicated than it was in the past. No doubt, a majority of Americans has always agreed that politics was "too complicated," but no growth in this perception is apparent in Figure 14-5. To find the source of people's loss of confidence in governmental officials, our attention must be directed elsewhere.

People are not upset with the institutions of government and certainly not with the constitutional structure that holds these institutions together. They *are* upset with elected officials and other people in government, but what is the source of their displeasure? We have

Figure 14-5   Is Politics Too Complicated? 1968–1998

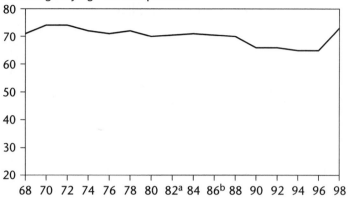

Percentage saying "too complicated"

Source: National Election Studies.

[a] Data for 1982 are missing; the number reported here is the average of 1980 and 1984.

[b] Data for 1986 are missing; the number reported here is the average of 1984 and 1988.

just seen that, compared with those of the late 1960s, people at the end of the millennium were not more likely to perceive government officials as greater spendthrifts, as less responsive, or as more likely to obfuscate and complicate issues. What, then, is it about these elected officials that has led to the alleged crisis of confidence in American government?

Attitudes That *Have* Become More Negative

The answer is surprisingly simple. People have become much more likely to believe that government officials are serving their own interests rather than the interests of the people. This simple change is at the core of any serious effort to come to terms with the decline in favorable public attitudes toward government. How are officials acting selfishly? By carrying water for special interests who then lavish benefits including campaign contributions, gifts, trips to warm countries, and lucrative postgovernment positions on those public officials. The people are convinced that government is now controlled by an unholy collusion of special interests and elected officials. Evidence for the prevalence of this perception is easy to muster.

Returning to the National Election Studies data, a useful and frequently asked item is this: "Is the government run for the benefit of all or is it run for the benefit of a few big in-

Figure 14-6 Is Government Run for the Benefit of a Few Big Interests? 1968–1998

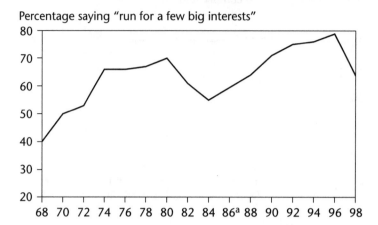

Percentage saying "run for a few big interests"

Source: National Election Studies.

[a] Data for 1986 are missing; the number reported here is the average of 1984 and 1988.

terests?" Unlike the other time-series findings reported to this point (which showed re-markable over-time stability), perceptions that the government is run for a few big interests have increased dramatically, as shown in Figure 14-6. In the 1960s, a clear minority of re-spondents said government was run by a few big interests. By 1975, over half believed that big interests ruled, and by the early to mid-1990s three out of four Americans believed gov-ernment was run by a few big interests. These figures dropped a little in the late 1990s but were still 25–30 percentage points above the levels present in the late 1960s.

Many people have even come to the conclusion that government officials commonly cross the line of legality in their self-serving actions. Survey respondents were asked how many "government officials are crooked." Believing officials to be crooked has serious im-plications for the state of democracy. In 1968 only one out of four people believed "quite a few" government officials were crooked (see Figure 14-7). By the time of Watergate, in the mid-1970s, the proportion of respondents who thought many officials were crooked had increased from 25 to 45 percent. While the data are not complete for the 1980s, it would ap-pear there was a modest drop in perceptions of the extent to which officials were crooked (many attitudes toward government improved in the mid-1980s in conjunction with what has been referred to as the era of Reagan "feel goodism") before the early 1990s witnessed a resumption of negative perceptions. In 1994 we even had the unprecedented situation

Figure 14-7 Are Government Officials Crooked?
1968–1998

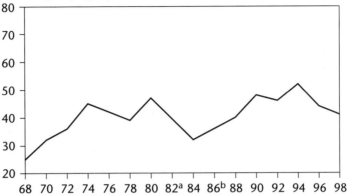

Percentage saying "quite a few"

Source: National Election Studies.

[a]Data for 1982 are missing; the number reported here is the average of 1980 and 1984.
[b]Data for 1986 are missing; the number reported here is the average of 1984 and 1988.

wherein a majority of the American people believed that "quite a few" of the people in government were crooked. Not only do the people believe that the government is being run for the sake of big interests, they believe that quite a few government officials are breaking the law in order to assist their special-interest friends.

In the light of these perceptions, is it any surprise that the people do not have much trust in government? How can government be trusted if those in it are trying only to help themselves and are willing even to break the law in order to achieve that goal? NES gives people the chance to say whether they trust the federal government only some of the time, most of the time, or just about always. In Figure 14-8, the percentage responding either "most of the time," or "just about always" is summed and presented for every election year survey since 1968. The pattern is similar to that evident in Figures 14-6 and 14-7. In 1968, the government was in good shape in the eyes of the people: 61 percent believed it could be trusted at least most of the time, a startling level of trust given all that was going on in 1968. But the salad days did not last long, and by the end of the 1970s trust was at just 25 percent, less than half the levels of just a decade before. The mid-1980s provided a modest resurgence in trust only to give way in the early to mid-1990s to the lowest levels ever. Trust, as with several

Figure 14-8   How Much Can Government Be Trusted?
                   1968–1998

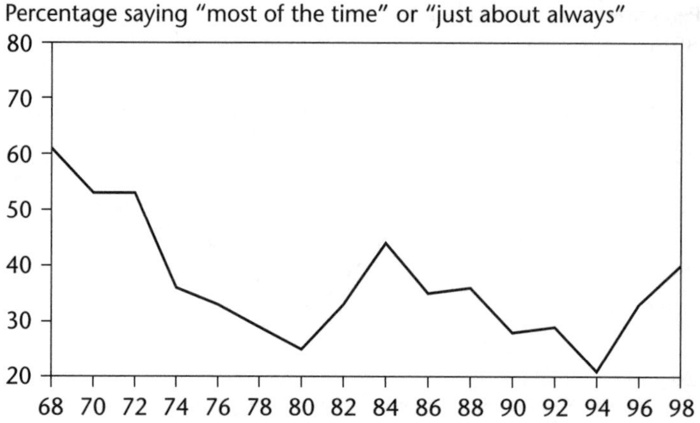

Percentage saying "most of the time" or "just about always"

Source: National Election Studies.

other indicators of public attitudes toward government, improved markedly from the early 1990s to the late 1990s, but even so, levels remained 20 to 25 percentage points lower than at the beginning of the time period.[5]

Focus Group Comments

Teasing people's attitudes from survey data is not always possible to do, particularly on matters such as the aspects of government they may like and dislike, and why they feel the way they do. Accordingly, some scholars have been turning to focus groups in order to allow people more liberties in explaining their true sentiments (see Conover, Crewe, and Searing 1991). Closed-ended survey questions are better suited to discerning cut-and-dried preferences regarding candidates and issues than to fleshing out people's sometimes sketchy thoughts about changes that might move the governing process closer to the kind they prefer. A well-known danger of using focus groups in public opinion research is the possibility that the group moderator could be in a position to lead participants toward certain statements, particularly when the topic is one the people have not thought much about (see Polsby 1993). Although the same is true of survey questions, the more structured format of survey instruments makes it easier at least to determine when question wording or question order has artificially influenced respondents. In focus groups, the best way to minimize the potential for external influence is for the moderator to play a minimalist role, to stick to a publicized script, and to make transcripts available so that interested researchers can check for possible moderator influence.

Focus groups that meet these criteria and that deal with the topic of public attitudes toward government were conducted in late 1997 at various places across the country.[6] In each of the eight sessions, groups of ten to thirteen previously unacquainted individuals were brought together for approximately two hours to discuss the aspects of government they liked and disliked. The following are some typical quotations from these focus group sessions, beginning with those highlighting people's dissatisfaction with the power of special interests over elected officials. Only first names are used since participants were promised anonymity.

(Robert) I think interest groups have too much control of what our elected officials say in our government. And congress people are basically just like, well this guy gave me ten million dollars so . . . I've got to vote this way. They're bought, you know, bought by the interest group.

(Lisa) [Politicians] seem so easily influenced by lobbyists. . . . Money and influential groups shouldn't be able to influence the decisions that the lawmakers make so easily.

(Maria) [Politicians] think about who's in power, who's the dominant group. And they do the laws according to who's going to benefit from it.

Although this antipathy toward special interests and selfish politicians will surprise few who have been listening to the American people of late, it is more surprising to learn that ordinary people are not eager to supplant special interests in the influence-peddling department. Though politicians and elite observers are forever striving to get the people more involved in politics, the people are at best ambivalent and at worst fearful of greater popular involvement. They are definitely averse to more direct forms of democracy that would require the public to spend more time on politics, such as town hall meetings, and they even prefer to avoid reforms in indirect democracy that attempt to heighten accountability and representation, thereby putting more of a burden on the people to communicate their preferences to, and then to monitor the actions of, elected officials, perhaps via the Internet or interactive cable television. Consider the following focus group comments.

(Alfredo) [Ordinary] people are not very intelligent relating to what's going on in politics [and] would be swayed by a couple of dollars.

(Eric) We have avenues to contact our representatives. I don't think that structurally we lack the ability to let our representatives know what we want; we just choose not to do so.

(Michelene) When I leave here, when I walk out this door, I'm not going to volunteer for anything. I'm not going to get involved in anything. I mean I know this. I'm not going to pretend I'm some political activist. I'm lazy. I'm not going to do it. I'm too busy obsessing on other things going on in my

life. . . . So somebody's got to do it and I don't care how much money they make, you know. . . . I don't want the job. I'm not interested in it.

(John) People are satisfied with their way of life and everything . . . and they're going to let someone else take care of [politics].

(Linda) Part of the problem is that [politicians] . . . have to have something that drives them to make them even run for office these days. And so sometimes you get the wrong kind of people in government. . . . He's got his own agenda. . . . He's not doing it for service to the people.

The composite picture is not one of a public champing at the bit to get into the political arena. Focus group participants lacked confidence in their own ability and the ability of people like them to play a more active role in government. They doubted people's political capabilities as well as their motivation. Eric remarks that people have plenty of opportunities to contact representatives but that they just "choose not to do so." Linda goes even further. She dislikes it when politicians offer an agenda that they believe would improve society. In Linda's mind, having an agenda prohibits politicians from being in a position to serve the people. But, of course, if politicians are not taking stances and offering ideas, people will not be able to choose officials on the basis of their positions or to hold them accountable for the successes and failures of those positions. If the people are not upset by a perceived lack of policy accountability, what has upset them?

Why People Dislike Officials

To the extent the focus group comments are accurate reflections of public sentiments, people do not seek more representation or greater systemic sensitivity to the policy preferences of ordinary people, even as people simultaneously plead for a reduction in the power of special interests. This combination of attitudes may seem puzzling but is actually a perfect parallel to the survey results indicating that respondents do not perceive that government officials fail to listen to the people (see Figure 14-3) but are convinced that government officials *are* listening to special interests. The explanation for this puzzling combination of views is that, contrary to much writing in the popular press and elsewhere, people are not eager for their own voices to be heard. People are not convinced they have much to say about most policy choices. Thus, negative views of government do not tend to sprout from perceptions of a lack of responsiveness. Many, many citizens do not want the government to be more responsive to them because this change would require them to follow issues and politics more carefully, and this is the last thing they want to do. But just because people do not want to play a bigger role in government themselves does not mean they cannot want special interests to play less of a role. In fact, this is precisely what the people do want.

More than anything, people dislike government when it is perceived to make suckers out of them, and people have become increasingly convinced that government can and does take advantage of the people.[7] Elected officials are believed to luxuriate in a pool of taxpayer-provided perquisites while they service the interests of the rich, the powerful, and the demanding, all the while growing increasingly out of touch with real people. This sentiment was apparent in the remarks of Robert, Lisa, and Maria. They believed that rich and loud groups are controlling members of Congress. Taxpayers pay for members' salaries and perquisites while special interests reap all the rewards. Oh, sure, elected officials may pay ritualistic attention to the regular people. They may hold town meetings and attend the occasional high school graduation and Kiwanis Club meeting, but they only engage in such activities because they want to be returned to office where they and their special interest chums can continue the cycle. This is why people do not like government.

Recognizing that people want to reduce the power of special interests but do not wish to increase their own power helps to solve several puzzles of public opinion. It explains why people sound so stridently populist in discussing the influence of special interests but are so reluctant to push out these interests if it means taking power in their own hands. It explains why people can support legislative term limits even though they recognize that limits reduce representation and accountability. (People's logic seems to be that, if we are unable to stop legislators from taking advantage of us, at least we can limit the length of time they are able to do so.) And it explains why people have so much more confidence in the Supreme Court than in Congress (justices may make stupid decisions but they are not enriching themselves in the process and so are much more likely to be forgiven than members of Congress).

Why did negativity toward government become so noticeable in the early 1970s and why did it moderate in the mid-1980s and the late-1990s even though aversion to being taken advantage of is likely to be relatively stable over time? Of course, societal conditions still have much to do with public attitudes toward government.[8] Society seemed to be coming apart in the late 1960s, and economic conditions were unsettled throughout much of the 1970s. By the mid-1980s and then again in the late 1990s conditions—especially economic conditions—were improved and attitudes toward government became more favorable. But societal conditions are only part of the explanation. The United States has never had a longer run of economic prosperity than from 1993 to 2000, yet public confidence in government in 2000 was still well beneath what it had been in the 1950s and 1960s. Why? Because government has become visibly a high-stakes endeavor. It was not until the end of the 1960s that big money began playing a consistent role in anything other than presidential elections. It was not until the end of the 1960s that the professionalization of politics, with its accompanying high salaries, pension plans, private banks, commissaries, health clubs, and oversized staffs, soaked into public awareness. It was not until the 1960s that government became involved in such a large number of issue areas that interest groups saw the advantage of setting up permanent residence in Washington. It was not until the 1960s that societal diversity really began to make itself felt, thus contributing to people's sense that somebody was out there on the other side of the issue ready to seek advantage through the political system. All these things make it possible for politicians to play the people for suckers and make it less likely that even a prosperous economy will return perceptions of government to the favorable levels of the 1950s and early 1960s. The change is not in people's sensitivity to being played for a sucker or in the perceived willingness of people to play others for suckers but rather in the perceived *ability* of those in and around government to play us for suckers, thanks largely to the growth and professionalization of government as well as to the increasingly evident diversity of society.

How to Improve Public Attitudes Toward Government

Traditionally, those who have studied public attitudes toward government have lumped together a variety of measures (several of these measures were presented in Figures 14-2 through 14-8) into an index of trust. By combining these diverse items, however, scholars are left unable to identify the real cause of dissatisfaction with government (for a critique of trust measures consistent with this observation, see Owen and Dennis 2001). More careful inspection indicates that the core source of popular dissatisfaction is not the policies government produces (for more on this point, see Hibbing and Theiss-Morse 2001), the lack of responsiveness to the people's wishes, erroneous decisions, or even the perception that government wastes taxpayer dollars. Instead, dissatisfaction springs mainly from the perception that governmental decisions—whatever those decisions may be—are being made for the wrong reasons. Self-serving politicians and greedy but politically astute and connected special interests play the people for suckers and this is the aspect of government that bothers people more than anything else.

The widely reported spike in Americans' support for government that followed the September 11, 2001, attacks on the World Trade Center in New York City and the Pentagon in the suburbs of Washington, D.C., although predictable, is also perfectly consistent with the interpretation of public attitudes offered here. (Levels of trust, for example, reached their highest levels since the mid-1960s.) It certainly was not the case that in the wake of the tragedy the American people had more input into government than usual; so that cannot be the reason they became so much more approving of government. Rather, what happened was that all public officials—Republicans and Democrats, the president, and members of Congress—for a time at least, refrained from arguing in public. Special interests were not visible, and it was hard for people to imagine how any particular actions of politicians could be designed for their own ends. Instead, officials' attention was focused on getting the country through those horrible days. That is how the public wanted those in government to behave.

Of course, the cost of this increase in public support for American government was far too high. Short of major threats to the security of the country and to the lives of its people, what can be done to lessen people's sense that government insiders are taking advantage of them? One solution would be to attempt to locate and empanel elected officials who are completely unselfish, but people are understandably dubious that such saints exist. When asked if the country has just been unlucky in ending up with greedy politicians or if it is instead the system that turns good people into self-serving public officials, a strong majority of survey respondents choose the latter. Focus group participants agree. Several even felt that if ordinary people were in Congress they would begin behaving just as current members of Congress do. For example, one said: "I really feel like it wouldn't matter if we were in Congress. I think we would more or less act just as they're acting" (quoted in Hibbing and Theiss-Morse 1995, 63). Rather than waiting for a group of saints to arrive, the public prefers the more proactive strategy of making it impossible, or at least much more difficult, for elected officials to benefit themselves. Thus, new campaign finance laws, gift-giving restrictions, salary cuts, staff reductions, perquisite eliminations, outside earnings bans, term limits, and restrictions on postgovernment employment are all extremely popular with citizens.

Making it more difficult for people in government to feather their own nests directly addresses the aspect of government that most troubles the people, but it is unlikely that even herculean reforms would convince the people that governmental decisions were largely devoid of self-interest on the part of the decision makers. People are just too cynical, the press is just too eager to connect every governmental action to a self-interested motive, and the Constitution would seem to stand in the way of several changes that would be needed, such as banning independent spending that helps (or hinders) a candidate's campaign or prohibiting certain types of employment once an individual leaves government service. As a result, a central part of improving public attitudes toward government would be to educate people to the hard reality that they cannot have it both ways. People need to be taught that if they want to bring special interests to heel, they will probably need to become more involved. As much as the people would like a system that both allows collective decisions to be made by unselfish officials *and* lets ordinary people stay relatively uninvolved, such a government is a logical impossibility, assuming the people also wish for the government to be somewhat democratic.

Notes

Funding for the collection of a portion of the data used in this chapter was provided by the National Science Foundation (SBR-97-09934). Other data were collected and provided by the National Election Studies. The author gratefully acknowledges the advice and assistance of Elizabeth Theiss-Morse and James T. Smith.

1. This survey was conducted by the Bureau of Sociological Research at the University of Nebraska for John Hibbing and Elizabeth Theiss-Morse from late July till early October of 1992 using standard random digit dialing techniques. There were 1,433 respondents. Full information is contained in Hibbing and Theiss-Morse 1995.

2. This survey was conducted by Gallup for John Hibbing and Elizabeth Theiss-Morse from mid-April till mid-May of 1998 using Gallup's standard three-call, "youngest male-oldest female" respondent selection procedure with 1,266 respondents. Full information is contained in Hibbing and Theiss-Morse forthcoming.

3. In 1972, the National Election Studies survey instrument included an item asking whether "a big change was needed in our form of government or should it be kept pretty much as is." Only 25 percent said that a big change was needed. In a 1976 NES item that speaks directly to the Miller-Citrin controversy, respondents were asked: "There has been some talk recently about how people have lost faith and confidence in the government in Washington. Do you think this lack of trust is just because of the individuals in office or is there something more seriously wrong with government in general and the way it operates?" Even right after Watergate, better than two-thirds of the respondents (68.1 percent) felt the lack of trust was due to the individuals in office. In the same survey, 80 percent claimed to be "proud of many things about our form of government." People may be dissatisfied with government but are skeptical of the need for major change.

4. The National Election Studies surveys are conducted every two years in conjunction with the federal elections, usually in a postelection survey. Interviews are conducted in person and the number of cases varies between 1,000 and 3,000. For further information, see <www.umich.edu/~nes>.

5. For excellent efforts to account for the decline in confidence and trust in government, see Lipset and Schneider 1987; Orren 1997; Alford 2001; Citrin and Luks 2001; and Chanley, Rahn, and Rudolph 2001.

6. Two sessions each were held in Omaha, Nebraska; Bangor, Maine; San Diego, California; and Atlanta, Georgia. Participants were recruited by advertisements, flyers, random telephone calls, and announcements at various civic and social meetings, and they were paid a small fee for their cooperation. Further details are available in Hibbing and Theiss-Morse forthcoming.

7. Experimental research even indicates that people are willing to sacrifice monetary gain to avoid being a sucker. In the ultimatum bargaining game, Player 1 divides $20 with another player, Player 2. Player 2 can accept or reject Player 1's proposed allocation, but if it is rejected neither player gets anything. The findings of this experiment consistently show that when Player 2 feels Player 1 was too self-serving, say by proposing to keep $18 while giving only $2 to Player 2, Player 2 typically rejects the allocation even though doing so costs $2. Better to not be played for a sucker than to reap a monetary gain (see, for example, Guth and Tietz 1990).

8. Evidence of the importance of economic conditions in explaining variations in approval of government is decidedly mixed. For an overview, see Lawrence 1997. When the focus is on individual institutions rather than government generally, it appears that approval of the president is quite sensitive to societal conditions, Congress somewhat, and the Supreme Court very little (see Hibbing and Theiss-Morse 1995, chap. 2, for a more thorough discussion). All in all, the message is that economic conditions are only one of many factors that explain governmental approval.

15 Public Support for Post-Communist Transitions in Central and Eastern Europe and the Former Soviet Union

William Mishler and Richard Rose

A defining characteristic of democratic governments is that their survival and effective functioning depend upon widespread public acquiescence and support (Easton 1965; Gamson 1968). Popular support not only confers legitimacy on democracies, it is vital to their effective performance. Public confidence enhances governments' abilities to make decisions and commit resources without resorting to coercion or the need to obtain citizens' approval for each and every decision. Governments that enjoy a measure of public approval and deference also are better able to withstand short-term political pressures or the blandishments of special interests while pursuing policies promoting longer-term societal interests or public good.

Widespread popular support for the regime is especially critical for the survival and development of new or democratizing regimes which typically confront greater stresses than older, more established democracies and also lack experienced leaders and institutions with which to cope with these stresses. Indeed, the term *democratization* is frequently a misnomer. Regime transformation is a better description, since the collapse of an old regime typically sets in motion a process of change the endpoint of which is difficult to predict. There is no certainty where the transition from an authoritarian regime will end—whether in some form of democracy, a different type of undemocratic regime, or the reemergence of something resembling the old undemocratic regime, as occurred in a number of the states created after World War II (see Linz and Stepan 1978). Importantly, whether the process of regime transformation ends in the establishment of a complete democracy, a broken-back democracy, or an undemocratic regime may depend less on popular support for democracy per se than on popular support for the incomplete regime that actually exists during the transition. For democratization to succeed, a new or transitional regime must enjoy sufficient support to survive and sustain a democratic course for the duration of the transition.

Although the importance of political support is widely acknowledged, it is impossible to specify an absolute level of support for democracy that is adequate for democracy to take root and flourish. This difficulty arises because popular support is a necessary but not a sufficient condition for democratic stability. The vitality of democracy depends, as well, on a variety of other considerations, including the severity of social cleavages and level of political stress, the extent of social capital, the nature of elite attitudes and behavior, and the existence of effective democratic institutions, to cite a few (see, among others, Eckstein 1971; Przeworski 1991; Rogowski 1974; Rose, Mishler, and Haerpfer 1998). Indeed, building support for the post-Communist regimes of Central and Eastern Europe (CEE) and the former Soviet Union (FSU) has been rendered more difficult because these political transitions are taking place in tandem with attempted transformations from centrally planned to market-oriented economies. In the long run, economic reforms and the discipline of the market may increase economic performance and enhance support for the political regime, but in the short run economic reforms have been responsible for widespread economic dislocations, which have undermined political support and greatly added to the stress placed on fledgling political institutions. These arguments suggest that the level of popular support necessary to establish and sustain democracy is contingent and context specific. The only generalization that can be confidently offered regarding levels of popular support for democracy is that stable or rising levels of support facilitate the maintenance of democracy, whereas declining levels of support undermine democracy and presage failure. It is the *trajectory* of political support that is critical.

This chapter examines the trajectories and dynamics of public support for post-Communist transitions in ten countries of Central and Eastern Europe and the former Soviet Union across the first decade since the collapse of communism. The regimes include seven CEE countries (Bulgaria, the Czech Republic, Hungary, Poland, Romania, Slovakia, and Slovenia) and three FSU regimes (Belarus, the Russian Federation, and Ukraine). Specifically, we use survey data from the New Democracies Barometer and the New Russia Barometer to trace patterns of popular approval for the new regimes in these countries beginning in 1991, shortly following the collapse of communism and the conduct of the first free elections, and ending in 1998, the most recent year for which comparable data are available.[1] We then compare the trajectories of support for the new regimes both with the public's evaluations of the old regimes and with their evaluations of potential undemocratic alternative regimes. Because the political and economic transitions in these countries are closely intertwined, we also examine trends in popular evaluations of the new market-oriented economies and of the former socialist regimes. To understand the dynamics underlying these trends, we proceed to develop and test a model of economic and political determinants of support, considering whether and to what extent underlying sources of support change over time as citizens acquire experience with the new political and economic regimes.

Political Support for Regimes in Transition

Although the idea of political support is venerable, systematic efforts at conceptualization (that is, developing precise definitions) and measurement usually begin with David Easton (1965) and his well-known distinction between specific and diffuse support. Easton defines *specific support* as the temporary and relatively ephemeral political approval that individuals feel as a result of the satisfaction of specific political demands; it is a quid pro quo for effective short-term political performance. In contrast, *diffuse support* is conceived as a deeper, more enduring, and more generalized political loyalty produced through political socialization; it is immune from short-term inducements, rewards, or performance (see, for example, Almond and Verba 1963; Eckstein 1966; Inglehart 1990). Easton's conception of support has endured despite substantial evidence that the specific–diffuse distinction is overdrawn (Craig 1993; Loewenberg 1971; Zimmerman 1979; Kornberg and Clarke 1992).

In contrast to the traditional Eastonian perspective, we conceptualize political support as all of a kind. What Easton identifies as different *types* of support are better conceived simply as different *levels*. Although the intensity of support may vary across individuals—some having deeper and others more superficial levels of commitment—we consider the nature of support to be fundamentally the same. Support is support; individuals either approve of their political system at some level and for whatever reason, or they do not.

Moreover, we believe that sources of support are fundamentally the same across different levels. The *socialization* and *performance* perspectives both assume that political support is learned; they differ principally in their time frames. The socialization perspective emphasizes childhood or early-life learning, frequently mediated through parents, school, or friends (Easton and Dennis 1969; Jennings and Niemi 1974; Hahn 1991). The performance perspective places greater emphasis on adult learning. Even this overstates the differences, however, since contemporary socialization research increasingly acknowledges that political learning continues throughout life and demonstrates, increasingly, the primacy of adult learning over childhood socialization in shaping most political attitudes (Conover and Searing 1994).

From our perspective, the socialization and performance perspectives are properly conceived as complementary parts of a single developmental or "lifetime learning" model in which political support is shaped initially by early-life agents and experiences but, then, evolves across life as initial beliefs are tempered, reinforced, or challenged by later-life experiences (Rose and McAllister 1990; Mishler and Rose 1997). Conceived in this way, the distinction between specific and diffuse support disappears; diffuse support becomes simply the residue of specific support that persists from the past (a similar formulation is advanced by Hibbing and Theiss-Morse 1995).[2]

In a new or transitional regime, political support not only is experiential, it also is likely to be indivisible; citizens are likely to evaluate new regimes holistically (on the concept of indivisibles, see Ragin 1987). Citizens of new democracies are not political scientists. They have little experience in the workings of democratic institutions and even less understanding of abstract democratic norms or principles. Even more than citizens of long-established democracies, whose knowledge of and commitment to democratic principles, institutions, and practices is limited, citizens of new democracies possess only vague and rudimentary ideas about what democracy means or how a democracy works (or should work) in practice. As a consequence, citizens of new or democratizing regimes are not well equipped to evaluate the democratic character of the new regime or assess its fidelity to democratic principles. Neither do they have the experience to pick and choose among different parts of the new political system, embracing some and rejecting others. What citizens of Central and Eastern Europe do possess is a lifetime of experience with a Communist regime whose totalitarian tendencies and ambitions discouraged citizens from distinguishing authorities from the regime or even one political institution from another. For most citizens, therefore, the experiential choice is between the Communist regime of the recent past and the democratizing regime of the present. Citizens may develop capacities for more abstract and nuanced evaluations later as they acquire experience with the new regime. At the start of the democratization process, however, the new regime must be judged as a whole, as fundamentally good or bad in comparison with past experience (for elaboration of this point and some empirical evidence, see Rose and Mishler 1994; Mishler and Rose 1994, 1996, 2001).

To measure support for new or transitional regimes, the New Democracies Barometer and the New Russia Barometer asked citizens in seven Central and Eastern European countries and in three of the former Soviet republics a very simple question:

Here is a scale for ranking systems of government; the top, $+100$, is the best, and the bottom, -100, is the worst. Where would you put:
a) the former Communist regime?
b) the present system with free elections and many parties?
c) our system of governing in five years' time?

A useful feature of this question is that it measures support for the current and past regime on a common metric. It also avoids normatively and emotionally laden words and concepts such as *democracy* that might bias responses, and it avoids country- and institution-specific references thereby facilitating cross-national comparisons.

Figure 15-1 Public Support for Current Communist Regimes, 1991–1998

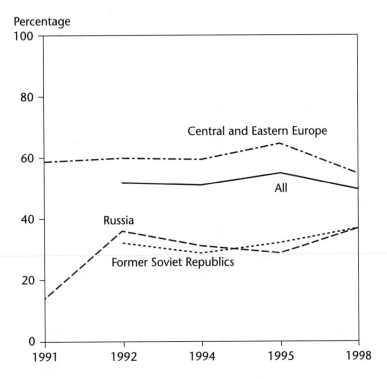

Percentage

Sources: Paul Lazersfeld Society, Vienna, New Democracies Barometer I–V, and Centre for the Study of Public Policy, New Russia Barometer I–VIII.

Note: Changes in the percentage of citizens in three Former Soviet Republics and seven former Communist countries of Central and Eastern Europe who express positive support for the current regime at different times during the transition.

Trajectories of Support for Regimes in Transition

Figure 15-1 sketches the trajectories of public support for ten post-Communist regimes in Eastern and Central Europe and the former Soviet Union from 1991 through 1998. It indicates that, while absolute levels of popular support for the new regimes across these countries are quite modest, the trajectory of support has been remarkably stable over time. Excluding 1991, when the absence of data from the Ukraine and Belarus inflates the overall level of regime support, an average of 52 percent of citizens across the ten countries and several years expresses positive support for the new regimes. Support ranges from a low of

50 percent in 1998 to a high of 55 percent three years earlier, and the standard deviation for the series over time is less than 2 percentage points. Significantly, there is little evidence of any trend over time. The pattern, such as it is, is sawtooth, though it is probably best described as flat. Rather than embracing or rejecting the new regimes, citizens of post-Communist societies have maintained an attitude of "wait and see"—an attitude that seems particularly appropriate to regimes in transition.

The experience of communism had powerful homogenizing effects on both individuals and regimes. Virtually all of the citizens in these ten societies were socialized into Communist principles and ideals, and the lessons of youth were reinforced by a lifetime of subjugation to Communist rule, state-controlled media, and a command economy. Uniformity was impressed upon regimes as well. The Soviet Union not only exhorted the other regimes to follow its example but enforced its leadership with sanctions backed by the Soviet Army. Nevertheless, there were and are differences among the regimes. One important difference is that, for a majority of these regimes, Communist rule was externally imposed and supported by a foreign (namely, Soviet) army. The specter of Soviet invasion was palpable right up to the end, and the collapse of communism was greeted enthusiastically in many quarters as national liberation. In contrast, Russia, Belarus, and Ukraine were integral parts of the Soviet Union for which the collapse of communism and the breakup of the Soviet Union created contradictory emotions and considerable ambivalence. Slovenia was different still, having experienced a largely indigenous brand of communism as a relatively wealthy but politically weak region of Yugoslavia.

Consistent with the more positive (less negative) legacy of communism, citizens of the former Soviet Union express significantly lower levels of support for the successor regimes throughout the transformation. On average only 32 percent of FSU respondents express positive support for the new regime across the transition to date, compared with an average of 60 percent for CEE respondents. Despite differences in the absolute level of support, however, the trajectories of support for the two sets of regimes are very similar; both are relatively flat and remarkably stable. For the three FSU regimes there is a modest, but generally steady, increase in the percentage of citizens who support the transitional regime over time. Among the CEE regimes, support increases slowly through 1995 before falling back to initial levels in 1998. Examination of the Russian case, for which more time points are available, shows a slightly different picture: there is a big increase in support from 1991 to 1994 and relatively steady support thereafter, except for a significant spike in 1997 in the immediate aftermath of the presidential elections.

Predictably, support for current regimes is inversely related to nostalgia for the old Communist regimes. Nostalgia is higher within the three FSU countries and lower in the CEE regimes (Figure 15-2). The trajectories of support for the old regimes also closely mirror (that is, reflect in reverse) those for the current regime. In most countries there is a moder-

Figure 15-2 Public Support for Former Communist Regimes, 1991–1998

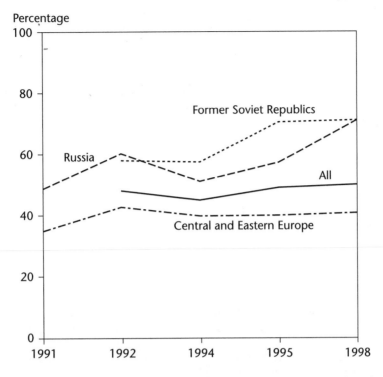

Sources: Paul Lazersfeld Society, Vienna, New Democracies Barometer I–V, and Centre for the Study of Public Policy, New Russia Barometer I–VIII.

Note: Changes in the percentage of citizens in three Former Soviet Republics and seven former Communist countries of Central and Eastern Europe who express positive support for the old regime at different times during the transition.

ate rise in nostalgia for the old regime at the start of the transition which levels out or slightly declines over the next several years before increasing modestly, again, between 1995 and 1998. The Soviet pattern is slightly different, with intermittently rising levels of nostalgia across the period, a pattern most pronounced in the Russian case.

Even citizens who are nostalgic toward the old regime and value it over the current regime may not want to risk the political and economic instability that would result from overthrowing the current regime to return either to communism or to a new and different type of undemocratic regime. Respondents were asked whether they would prefer various undemocratic regimes, including a return to communism, over their current regime. They

Figure 15-3 Public Support for Alternative Regimes, 1991–1998

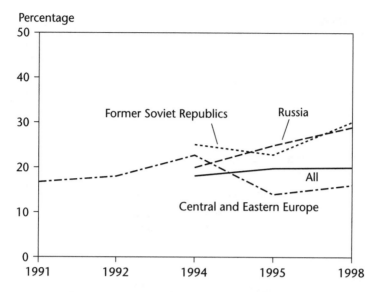

Sources: Paul Lazersfeld Society, Vienna, New Democracies Barometer I–V, and Centre for the Study of Public Policy, New Russia Barometer I–VIII.

Note: Changes in the percentage of citizens in three Former Soviet Republics and seven former Communist countries of Central and Eastern Europe who expressed preference for an alternative authoritarian regime over the current regime at different times during the transition.

also were asked whether they favored the suspension of parliament and abolition of competing parties regardless of the type of regime that might follow.[3]

Only a minority of citizens in any post-Communist society favors the suspension of parliament and parties, a return to Communist rule, or any other undemocratic alternative to the current regime (Figure 15-3). Overall, slightly less than 20 percent of citizens prefer any fundamental change in the current regime, a percentage that has remained unchanged across the transition. Citizens of FSU countries are more likely to favor a return to some form of authoritarian rule, but the differences are relatively small. Only a quarter of FSU citizens prefer a different regime; while the proportion has increased slightly since 1994, the more remarkable feature of the series is its stability. Among CEE countries, the percentage favoring any of the alternative authoritarian regimes has varied between 14 and 23 percent, but appears to have stabilized at about 15 percent.

Figure 15-4 Citizens Expecting to Support the Regime in Five Years, 1991–1998

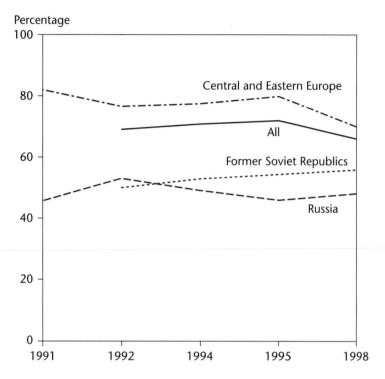

Percentage

Sources: Paul Lazersfeld Society, Vienna, New Democracies Barometer I–V, and Centre for the Study of Public Policy, New Russia Barometer I–VIII.

Note: Changes in the percentage of citizens in three Former Soviet Republics and seven former Communist countries of Central and Eastern Europe who expected to support their country's regime in the future.

Citizens skeptical about the current regime and unsure how much of an improvement it represents over the past may be patient with the regime to the extent that they believe it is developing in the right direction or that it is likely to become the sort of regime they favor in the near future. Despite deep reservations about current regimes, surprising optimism exists about the future of the regime in post-Communist societies (Figure 15-4). Overall, 65 to 70 percent of citizens in the ten post-Communist countries express positive support for the regime they think will exist within five years' time. In Central and Eastern Europe, support for the future regime ranges between 70 and 80 percent. Predictably, optimism is lower in Russia and the FSU. Nevertheless, small majorities of citizens in the three FSU republics expect to support the regime in five years' time, and the level of future support has risen modestly over time.

Public Support for Economic Regimes in Transition

As noted previously, post-Communist regimes in Central and Eastern Europe are doubly challenged, since the political transition from communism has occurred in tandem with the transformation from centrally planned to market-oriented economies. Although economic reforms and the discipline of the market should eventually improve economic efficiency, enhance performance, and generate wealth, their short-term effects have been largely negative and have exacerbated political stress and further threatened popular support for the new regimes. Indeed, the economic strains on the new regimes have been enormous from the start. In 1991, at the start of the transition, the mean level of inflation across the ten countries exceeded 135 percent, ranging from a low of 32 percent in Hungary to more than 300 percent in Bulgaria. In that same year, the economies of all ten countries experienced serious contraction. The decline in GDP ranged from 2 percent in Ukraine to 15 percent in Slovenia and averaged 10 percent overall (EBRD 1995). By 1998 the situation was significantly worse in the aggregate, although several countries had begun to improve. The median country suffered more than 80 percent inflation and a nearly 20 percent contraction in the official economy across the transition by 1998. In the former Soviet republics inflation levels exceeded a thousand percent across the period (EBRD 1998). In addition, crime and corruption increased dramatically in many of these countries, life expectancy declined slightly in several places, and social services disintegrated. The former Soviet republics suffered much more in all of these accounts, but Bulgaria and Romania suffered greatly as well, and even Poland, Slovenia, and the Czech Republic experienced significant economic and social distress.

Reacting to the economic chaos that accompanied the transition, few citizens at the outset expressed much support for the new economic regimes. When asked in 1991, only 35 percent gave the new economy positive ratings.[4] Predictably, support for the new economy was lowest in the FSU countries, especially Belarus and Ukraine, where economic conditions deteriorated most severely. By contrast, more than half of the respondents continued to hold positive views of the old centralized economy, including more than 70 percent of citizens in Russia and the former Soviet Union. On a more positive note, however, citizens of post-Communist regimes harbored considerable hope that economic reforms would produce better results in the near future; more than 60 percent of citizens held positive views of the new economic system as they expected it to perform within five years, although these economic hopes were much higher among the CEE nations than among the former Soviet republics.

Figure 15-5 Popular Support for the Economy: Past, Current, and Future, 1991–1998

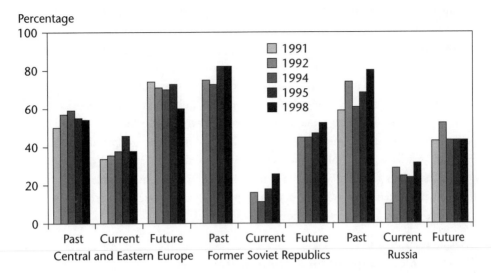

Percentage

Legend:
- 1991
- 1992
- 1994
- 1995
- 1998

Past Current Future
Central and Eastern Europe

Past Current Future
Former Soviet Republics

Past Current Future
Russia

Sources: Paul Lazersfeld Society, Vienna, New Democracies Barometer I–V, and Centre for the Study of Public Policy, New Russia Barometer I–VIII.

Note: Changes in the percentage of citizens in three Former Soviet Republics and seven former Communist countries of Central and Eastern Europe who expressed favorable evaluations of the current economy, the economy during the Communist era, and the economy they expect to exist in five years.

Figure 15-5 tracks public evaluations of the economy (past, present, and future) across the first decade of the transition. The patterns are generally encouraging. Although public evaluations of the new economic systems have remained quite low in absolute terms, the trajectory of approval has been gradually upward. Public recollections of the socialist economy continue to exceed current economic evaluations, but the gap, after widening slightly over the first several years, has been substantially reduced in recent years. Moreover, public expectations about future economic performance remain remarkably high. Economic hope not only has survived a decade of mostly miserable economic performance but has remained robust and even modestly increased in most post-Communist countries.

In summary, immediately following the collapse of communism in 1991, relatively small majorities of citizens held positive attitudes toward post-Communist regimes in Central and Eastern Europe. The situation was even worse in Russia and the former Soviet Union, where only small minorities endorsed the new regimes. Even less support existed for the new market-oriented economies, and nostalgia for the old regimes, both economic and political, was substantial. Despite this very limited initial support and the widespread economic and political stress that all of these countries have confronted in the interim, popular support for the new regimes has remained remarkably stable over the decade. At the end of the decade small increases in support for the new regimes have been balanced by similar increases in nostalgia for the past, but with no appreciable change in the minority supporting a major change in the direction of the transition or a return to a more authoritarian regime. While the gulf in support for the new regimes between former Soviet and CEE citizens remains effectively unchanged across the period, public opinion in post-Communist countries generally has been remarkably stable as citizens have exhibited a high degree of patience with the new regimes during the transitions. Given the widespread economic dislocations that have accompanied the transitions, the stability of political support appears curious, especially given the well-documented proclivity of citizens in Western democracies to vote their pocketbooks. Why has popular support for the new regimes proven so durable in the face of such problematic economic performance?

The Dynamics of Support for Regimes in Transition

A lifetime learning model provides a useful framework for understanding the development and persistence of support for incomplete democracies in the face of continuing unmet challenges. From a lifetime learning perspective, explanations of political support for a new and incomplete regime logically begin with the legacy of the old regime. Because these new regimes represent such a fundamental break from the past, post-Communist regimes cannot rely on the habitual support of citizens socialized from childhood. To the contrary, state-directed efforts to socialize citizens into communism mean that those citizens who were most effectively socialized by communism are the ones most likely to cling to the memory of the old regime and least likely to embrace the successor regime. By contrast, individuals whose personal experiences with the old regime taught them its failings and led them to reject communism may support the new regime, at least for a while, no matter what its initial shortcomings might be.

Although the legacy of communism provides a common frame of reference for citizens of Central and Eastern Europe, the experience of communism varied systematically according to individuals' positions in the social structure. In this regard, previous research emphasizes the importance of social characteristics such as education, generation, gender, urban vs. rural residence, and race or ethnicity (Finifter and Mickiewicz 1992 nicely summarize the rationale for each). In addition, Robert Putnam (1993, 2000) argues that the development of democratic attitudes depends substantially on a citizen's embeddedness in a civic community, defined as a "dense horizontal network" of association within a locality. The implication is that political support is likely to be greater among individuals who are more deeply involved in civic and political associations, including unions, churches, and political parties.

While the legacy of communism may be especially important early in the transition, a lifetime learning model implies that contemporary experiences and performance evaluations are likely to assume increasing importance as the transition progresses. Even if citizens initially regard emergent institutions as a mirror image of the past, eventually they will begin to make more subtle distinctions between past and present and to evaluate them independently, as well.

In established democracies regime performance typically is assessed in economic terms, as reflected both by individuals' economic well-being and by national, macroeconomic conditions (see, for example, Lewis-Beck 1988; Clarke et al. 1992). Economic considerations are likely to be at least equally important for evaluations of post-Communist regimes, not only because economic dislocation during the transition has been profound but also because one of the legacies of a state-run economy is that citizens are accustomed to holding government responsible for both macroeconomic conditions and individual welfare.

Although economic performance dominates discussions of the new regimes, political performance matters, too (Clarke, Dutt, and Kornberg 1993). Given the repressive legacy of the old regimes, the success of new regimes in securing individual liberty and promoting freedom can provide a potent source of political support. Moreover, creating liberty involves closing censorship offices, restraining state police, and allowing independent institutions to operate freely, actions that are more easily accomplished than creating the institutions of a free market, establishing property rights, and curtailing corruption (Rose 1995). Consistent with our argument that support for transitional regimes is relative and contingent, support also is likely to be influenced by public assessments of plausible alternative regimes (Rose and Mishler 1996). The most obvious alternative is communism, the immediate predecessor to the current regime. However, there are other alternatives as well, including military rule and rule by a dictator ("strong man"), both of which have precedents in Central and Eastern Europe in the period before communism.

The Basic Model

The logic of this discussion suggests an explanatory model of political support which is based on three broad classes of variables: (1) the legacy of Communist rule, (2) individual social background characteristics, and (3) performance evaluations of the economy, political freedoms, and alternative regimes. Using multiple measures from the New Democracies Barometer and New Russia Barometer (see Table 15-1 for details), we estimated separate models of political support at five different time periods across the decade. Because of the consistent evidence that aggregate levels of popular support for the new regimes are much lower in the former Soviet Union than elsewhere, we estimate separate but identical models

Table 15-1 Coding of Variables

Variable	Code
Current regime support	21-point scale (-10 to $+10$) registering satisfaction / dissatisfaction with the current political system
Communist regime support	21-point scale (-10 to $+10$) registering satisfaction / dissatisfaction with the old Communist political system
Communist living standards better	$2 =$ "much better than current"; $1 =$ "somewhat better"; $0 =$ "same"; $-1 =$ "somewhat worse"; $-2 =$ "much worse than current"
Former Communist Party member	$1 =$ self or family member previously member of Communist Party; $0 =$ never a Communist Party member
Education level	$1 =$ elementary; $2 =$ secondary; $3 =$ vocational; $4 =$ university
Age cohort: 18–25 years	$1 = 18$–25; $0 = 26+$ years
Age cohort: 65+ years	$1 = 65+$ years; $0 = 18$–64 years
Gender: female	$1 =$ female; $0 =$ male
Town size	$1 = 1$–$5,000$; $2 = 5001$–$20,000$; $3 = 20,001$–$100,000$; $4 = 100,001+$
Church attendance	$1 =$ never; $2 =$ seldom; $3 =$ several times / year; $4 =$ monthly; $5 =$ weekly
Evaluation of current economy	21-point scale (-10 to $+10$) registering satisfaction / dissatisfaction with current economic system
Evaluation of future economy	21-point scale (-10 to $+10$) registering satisfaction / dissatisfaction with economic system in five years
Future living standards better	$2 =$ "much better than current"; $1 =$ "somewhat better"; $0 =$ "same"; $-1 =$ "somewhat worse"; $-2 =$ "much worse than current"
Increased freedom since 1989	Calculated as the difference between the 7-point 1989 Freedom House index of civil and political liberties and the 7-point index in the years 1991–1998, respectively
Favor alternative regimes	Mean level of support for "return to Communist rule"; "return to monarch (tsar)"; "rule by army"; and suspension of parliament coded on 5-point (-2 to $+2$) scale

Sources: Paul Lazersfeld Society, Vienna, New Democracies Barometer I–V, and Centre for the Study of Public Policy, New Russia Barometer I–VIII.

Note: Variables used to explain variations in support of the regime in post-Communist societies.

for the seven CEE regimes (Table 15-2) and the three FSU regimes (Table 15-3). The dependent variable for both tables is respondents' evaluations of "the present system with free elections and many parties." The original -100 to $+100$ scale was collapsed to -10 to $+10$. The model performs fairly well for survey data, explaining approximately 25 percent of the variation in support for the current democratizing regimes (R^2 for all models varies from .129 to .393 with an average of .267).

In the tables we report unstandardized coefficients (b), their standard errors (se), and significance levels. Because of differences in the units of measure for different independent variables, unstandardized coefficients cannot easily be compared across variables within a single year. Standardized coefficients (betas) provide for easier within-year comparisons across variables, while unstandardized coefficients are used for across-year or across-country comparisons for the same variable. Given a pooled sample of nearly 7,000 cases in Table 15-2, virtually every relationship is statistically significant at the conventional .05 and .01 probability levels. Therefore, we use a more stringent probability level ($p < .0001$) to differentiate relationships more clearly. In Table 15-3, which has a much smaller, though still very large, pooled sample of nearly 3,000 cases, we use a .001 probability level. In addition to these standard indicators of the importance of each variable, we report bloc R^2 to indicate the importance of each of the three sets of variables (communist legacy, social structure, and performance evaluations). The sum of the three bloc R^2s is equal to the total R^2 for the entire model.

Consistent with a lifetime learning model, results in Tables 15-2 and 15-3 indicate that initial support for both sets of post-Communist regimes was substantially influenced by the legacy of the old regime (bloc 1) and especially by public evaluations of current economic and political performance (bloc 3). The effects of economic performance on regime support are especially and consistently powerful, while social structural influences (bloc 2) on support are virtually nil. Despite their very different *levels* of popular support for the new regimes, the salient *sources* of support in the former-Soviet and CEE regimes are very similar; indeed, they are virtually identical. This is to say that the same variables exert similar effects (similar b's) on regime support in both sets of countries over time. Although former Soviet and CEE citizens appear to have learned different lessons about their new regimes (in particular, CEE citizens embrace the new regimes with significantly greater enthusiasm), the learning *process* by which they acquired those different lessons is fundamentally the same.[5]

Communist Legacy

The legacy of communism has a modest influence on support for the current regimes, explaining on average 4 percent of the variation (bloc R^2 varies from .013 to .068) across individuals in levels of support for these governments. Among the legacy variables,

Table 15-2 OLS[a] Estimates of a Lifetime Learning Model of Popular Support for Seven Post-Communist Regimes, 1991–1998

	1991		1992		1994		1995		1998	
Variables	b (se)	beta	b (se)	beta	b (se)	beta	b (se)	beta	b (se)	beta
Communist Legacy										
Communist regime support	−.07** (.01)	−.08	−.12** (.01)	−.14	−.04** (.01)	−.04	−.04** (.01)	−.06	−.05** (.01)	−.05
Communist living standards better	−.14 (.05)	−.03	−.12 (.05)	−.03	−.03 (.04)	−.01	−.12 (.04)	−.03	−.11 (.04)	−.03
Former Communist Party member	na		.12 (.28)	.00	.04 (.11)	.00	.04 (.09)	.00	.52** (.11)	.05
Bloc R^2	.041		.068		.033		.044		.053	
Social Structure										
Education level	.03 (.04)	.01	.13 (.04)	.04	.02 (.04)	.01	.05 (.03)	.02	.04 (.04)	.01
Age cohort: 18–25 years	.05 (.14)	.00	.29 (.14)	.02	.11 (.15)	.01	.08 (.13)	.01	.22 (.15)	.01
Age cohort: 65+ years	−.09 (.13)	−.01	−.25 (.14)	−.02	−.04 (.15)	−.00	−.02 (.14)	−.00	−.16 (.15)	−.01
Gender: Female	−.07 (.09)	−.01	−.14 (.10)	−.01	−.04 (.10)	−.00	−.16 (.09)	−.02	.02 (.09)	.00
Town size	−.02 (.04)	−.00	.05 (.04)	.01	.02 (.04)	.00	.07 (.04)	.02	−.02 (.04)	−.00
Church attendance	.16** (.04)	.05	.10 (.04)	.03	.09 (.03)	.03	.07 (.03)	.02	.08 (.04)	.03
Bloc R^2	.006		.012		.007		.014		.015	
Performance										
Evaluation of current economy	.28** (.01)	.29	.26** (.01)	.26	.26** (.01)	.27	.25** (.01)	.26	.31** (.01)	.31
Evaluation of future economy	.21** (.01)	.20	.20** (.01)	.19	.18** (.01)	.18	.21** (.01)	.20	.21** (.01)	.21
Future living standards better	.30** (.05)	.06	.25** (.06)	.05	.03 (.06)	.01	.17 (.06)	.03	.20 (.06)	.04
Perceived increase in freedoms	na		na		.98** (.06)	.18	na		.67** (.06)	.11
Aggregate increase in freedom	.19** (.04)	.04	1.41** (.14)	.11	na		.69** (.06)	.11	na	

Table 15-2 *(Continued)*

Variables	1991 b (se)	1991 beta	1992 b (se)	1992 beta	1994 b (se)	1994 beta	1995 b (se)	1995 beta	1998 b (se)	1998 beta
Favor alternative regimes	−.25** (.03)	−.08	−.22** (.03)	−.07	−.42** (.07)	−.07	−.64** (.06)	−.12	−.58** (.07)	−.08
Bloc R^2	.242		.231		.244		.252		.327	
Total R^2	.254		.252		.249		.259		.333	
F	183.6		169.5		163.7		174.1		250.5	

Source: Paul Lazersfeld Society, Vienna, New Democracies Barometer I–V.

Note: Determinants of public support for the current regime in seven former Communist countries of Central and Eastern Europe at different times during the transition.

[a] Ordinary least squares.

N = approximately 7,000

** $p \leq .0001$

retrospective evaluations of the Communist regime exert a small but statistically significant impact on popular support for the current regime in both FSU and CEE countries. Given the radical break between the old and new regimes, the legacy of communism, predictably, is negative. Citizens who recall their experiences under the old regime approvingly are significantly less supportive of the new regime than those who harbor negative memories. Moreover, the size of these effects is virtually identical for both sets of regimes and over time. To see these similarities, note that the average unstandardized coefficient for Communist regime support across the five time periods in Table 15-2 (in CEE regimes) is just over −.06 and varies in a narrow range between −.04 and −.12, while the average unstandardized coefficient for the four time periods in Table 15-3 (in FSU regimes) is just over −.05 and varies between −.04 and −.07. Far from fading with time, memories of the old regimes continue to influence citizens' evaluations of the new regimes a decade after communism's collapse.

While memories of the old regime exert persistent, albeit modest effects, the socializing effects of former Communist Party membership are minimal. With one exception (1998 in Table 15-2), former Party members are no more likely to support or oppose the current regime in either FSU or CEE countries. Similarly, although large majorities of citizens in all of the countries believe that their personal financial situations were appreciably better under the old regime than at any time since its collapse, economic nostalgia ("Communist living standards better") has no impact on support for the current regime.

Table 15-3 OLS[a] Estimates of a Lifetime Learning Model of Popular Support for Three Post-Soviet Regimes, 1992–1998

Variables	1992 b (se)	beta	1994 b (se)	beta	1995 b (se)	beta	1998 b (se)	beta
Communist Legacy								
Communist regime support	−.06* (.01)	−.07	−.04 (.02)	− 04	−.07* (.01)	−.08	−.04* (.01)	−.04
Communist living standards better	.11 (.07)	.03	−.06 (.08)	−.01	.13 (.05)	.03	−.06 (.06)	−.01
Former Communist Party member	na		−.05 (.19)	−.00	−.05 (.15)	−.00	−.03 (.15)	−.00
Bloc R^2	.013		.021		.056		.032	
Social Structure								
Education level	.02 (.07)	.01	.13 (.09)	.03	.06 (.06)	.02	.01 (.06)	.00
Age cohort: 18–25 years	.08 (.21)	.01	.22 (.28)	.01	.01 (.28)	.00	−.07 (.21)	−.00
Age cohort: 65+ years	−.23 (.27)	−.01	.99 (.40)	.04	−.30 (.26)	−.02	−.32 (.22)	−.02
Gender: Female	−.11 (.16)	−.01	−.41 (.18)	−.03	.01 (.15)	.00	−.10 (.15)	−.01
Town size	−.27 (.07)	−.06	−.12 (.07)	−.02	.01 (.07)	.00	.01 (.06)	.00
Church attendance	.21 (.09)	.04	.26 (.10)	.04	.13 (.10)	.02	.17 (.07)	.04
Bloc R^2	.016		.013		.013		.010	
Performance								
Evaluation of current economy	.33* (.02)	.29	.24* (.02)	.19	.41* (.02)	.39	.54* (.02)	.51
Evaluation of future economy	.19* (.02)	.19	.14* (.02)	.14	.11* (.02)	.11	.11* (.02)	.11
Future living standards better	.42* (.09)	.08	.13 (.10)	.02	.19 (.08)	.04	.08 (.08)	.01
Perceived increase in freedoms	na		.92* (.12)	.14	na		.33* (.09)	.05
Aggregate increase in freedom	.93* (.20)	.08	na		.09 (.19)	.01	na	

Table 15-3 *(Continued)*

Variables	1992 b (se)	1992 beta	1994 b (se)	1994 beta	1995 b (se)	1995 beta	1998 b (se)	1998 beta
Favor alternative regimes	−.49* (.06)	−.13	−.47* (.12)	−.08	−.55* (.07)	−.13	−.49* (.09)	−.07
Bloc R^2	.234		.119		.279		.388	
Total R^2	.249		.129		.288		.393	
F	76.2		31.8		86.5		138.4	

Source: Centre for the Study of Public Policy, New Russia Barometer I–VIII.

Note: Determinants of public support for the current regime in three Former Soviet Republics at different times during the transition.

[a] Ordinary least squares.

N = approximately 3,000

* $p \leq .001$

Social Structure

To the extent that social background variables are proxies for early-life socialization experiences, the evidence suggests that early socialization effects on later-life differences in political support are minimal. This bloc of variables explains on average 1 percent of the variation (bloc R^2 varies from .006 to .016) in support for the current regime. None of the four social background and generational indicators has significant effects on regime support in either set of countries or in any year. The coefficients for education and gender are typically in the predicted direction; better-educated citizens and men express somewhat greater support for the new regimes. However, all of the differences are small. Moreover, generational differences in support are inconsistent. Sometimes younger generations appear more supportive of the new regime; other times older citizens appear more supportive. This is not to say that individual experiences, either of communism or of the new regime, are undifferentiated. Rather, it appears that individual differences in early-life socialization experiences are overwhelmed, at least during the early years of the transition, by more contemporaneous influences on support.[6]

Little evidence in these models lends credence to Putnam's hypothesis that support for democracy varies directly with the extent that citizens are embedded in communities of dense horizontal networks. Church attendance provides the best available measure in the surveys of individuals' associational activity, while community size serves as a rough indicator of a community's capacity for close, face-to-face relations. Both factors achieve statistical significance in only one of the nine models.

Performance Variables

In contrast to the modest effects of Communist legacy and the negligible effects of social structure, political and economic performance have substantial effects on regime support. This group of variables explains approximately one-fourth of the variation in evaluations of the current regime (bloc R^2 varies from .110 to .388). Consistent with research on voting behavior in the United States and Western Europe (MacKuen, Erikson, and Stimson 1992; Clarke et al. 1992), citizens appear to be affected more by the performance of the macroeconomy than by their personal financial situations. Indeed, popular evaluations of current and future macroeconomic conditions dwarf all else in the models, and they do so consistently for both sets of countries and over the whole of the transition. Personal prospective evaluations have much smaller effects, although they are in the predicted direction.

While current and future economic evaluations dominate the calculus of regime support, political performance considerations are highly salient as well. In those two years (1994, 1998) in which citizens were asked to assess the extent of individual freedom under the current regime as compared to the Communist past, their responses consistently have powerful effects on popular support (Rose, Mishler, and Haerpfer 1998; see also Gibson 1993). Related questions (not shown) asking about the perceived fairness of government compared with the past and whether individuals have more influence over government compared with Communist times have somewhat smaller but still positive and significant effects.

Since personal evaluations of perceived freedom were not available for all years, we substituted an aggregate measure of the level of freedom in each country. This measure comes from Freedom House (1998) and ranks the level of freedom in each country on a seven-point scale. We use the difference between a country's 1991 score and its 1998 score to measure the increase in level of freedom. This aggregate measure on the extent to which civil and political liberties have increased in these ten countries since the fall of communism is a far from perfect substitute for individual-level data on citizens' assessments of the new freedoms. Despite its limitations, however, the aggregate-level measure is the best available proxy measure for those years in which a survey question was not asked and provides strong evidence of the impact of increased freedom on support for current regimes.

A venerable thesis holds that citizens will support a new regime not only because of the good things the new regime has accomplished or is likely to accomplish, such as providing increased freedom, but also because of the negative things the new regime has not done that citizens have learned to expect from other types of regimes. Empirical support for this hypothesis was found in the first bloc of Communist legacy variables. Popular support for the post-Communist regimes increased in direct proportion to citizens' antipathy to the old regime. Additional support also is present in the performance bloc variables measuring support for alternative regimes. We noted previously that large majorities of citizens in all of the post-Communist societies oppose the suspension of parliament and the elimination of competitive parties and also oppose the replacement of the current regime with another communist regime, rule by the military, or rule by a dictator. Predictably, as indicated in Tables 15-2 and 15-3, those rejecting alternatives to democracy are substantially more likely to support the current regime. Although the relationship between support for authoritarian alternatives and current regime support is modest in comparison with the salience of macroeconomic evaluations, the relationship is consistently significant and properly signed, and it holds equally for both groups of post-Communist countries as well as over time.

Discussion

The years since the fall of communism in Central and Eastern Europe and the former Soviet Union have witnessed a series of severe political and economic challenges to successor regimes. The nature and extent of these challenges have varied widely, but virtually all of the regimes have been affected variously by high unemployment, rampant inflation, economic contraction, and political corruption. Nevertheless, public support for post-Communist regimes has remained remarkably stable and the transition from authoritarian to more pluralist regimes has continued, albeit at a very different pace in different contexts.

Although the level of support for the new regimes varies widely, especially between the new regimes in the former Soviet Union and those in Central and Eastern Europe, the dynamics underlying and driving political support are remarkably similar across countries. In this regard, political support everywhere is dominated by contemporary assessments of economic and political performance. Thus, the public's negative assessments of current economic performance remain the major impediment to greater citizen support of the regime, while the public's embrace of policies dismantling repressive institutions and expanding civil liberties provides the greatest impetus to increased support.

Although the process by which citizens evaluate the regime appears universal, the substance of those evaluations varies widely across contexts. Specifically, citizens of the former Soviet Union are much less supportive than those in Central and Eastern Europe of the new regimes. Three reasons stand out. First, although both FSU and CEE citizens were socialized under communism, former Soviet citizens remember the old regime with greater sympathy. For citizens in Central and Eastern Europe, communism was externally imposed; the

Soviet empire was something to be feared, not celebrated. Second, the break between old and new regimes was neither as abrupt nor as complete in the former Soviet Union as elsewhere in Central and Eastern Europe. Communists have continued to occupy prominent positions throughout the transition in the former Soviet Union. The Communist Party has continued to play a prominent role and has continued to advocate central economic planning and a return to something resembling the old regime. Third, while the economies of all of the post-Communist regimes contracted substantially in response to initial economic reforms, the magnitude of economic misery in the three post-Soviet regimes has been much greater and the countries have not yet shown significant signs of recovery.

No less than citizens of long-established democracies, citizens of new or transitional regimes are not fools; they base their support for the new regime on the extent to which its institutions and policies prove effective in providing prosperity and protecting freedom. From this perspective of the first decade of the transition, the prospects for the consolidation of democracy in Central and Eastern Europe are good and have strengthened considerably across the decade. The trajectory of support for the new regimes is stable, and the underlying dynamics of support are such as to encourage still higher levels of public support for the foreseeable future. In the former Soviet Union, by contrast, the prospects for the consolidation of democracy are mixed. While popular support for the new regime appears stable, the level of support is very low and the underlying dynamics are problematic. The failure to expedite market reforms or otherwise address economic misery, combined with the imposition of policies restricting civil liberties and political freedoms, threatens already tenuous levels of political support. This is not to say that the post-Soviet transitions are doomed or that a return to authoritarian rule is inevitable. It is to say, however, that, if political support declines, there is a very real prospect that the already faltering transitions in post-Soviet regimes will stall, leaving a broken-back democracy as a result.

Notes

1. The research reported in this chapter relies on data from the New Democracies Barometer (NDB I–IV) and the New Russia Barometer (I–VIII). The NDB was sponsored by the Austrian Federal Ministry for Science and Research and the Austrian National Bank and has been graciously made available to us by the Paul Lazarsfeld Society, Vienna. The New Russia Barometer was conducted by Richard Rose, as part of the Social Capital Initiative of the World Bank, supported by the Danish Development Fund. Additional support for this project was provided by grants from the National Science Foundation (SBR–09515079) and the University of Strathclyde. While appreciative of this support, we alone are responsible for all analyses and interpretations.

2. The idea inherent in this formulation is similar to Fiorina's (1981) conception of party identification as a "running tally of retrospective evaluations." Specifically, political support at any moment is effectively a weighted average of a lifetime's experiences, positive and negative, toward the regime. This means that support for the regime at any moment is a legacy of past support as modified by more recent or contemporary experiences (see Mishler and Rose 2001).

3. Specific questions included the following:

Our system of governing is not the only one this country has had. Some people think we would be better off if the country was governed differently today. What do you think? Do you strongly agree, somewhat agree, somewhat disagree or strongly disagree? a) We should return to communist rule; b) The army should govern the country; c) It would be best to get rid of parliament and have a strong leader who can decide things quickly; d) A return to the monarchy would be better.

The second question was: "If Parliament were suspended and parties abolished, would you approve or disapprove?" For this analysis, we created a simple binary variable based on these questions distinguishing individuals who either approved the suspension of parliament or supported any of the authoritarian alternatives from citizens who opposed both the suspension of parliament and all authoritarian alternatives.

4. Individual evaluations of macroeconomic performance, past, present, and future, were measured on thermometer scales on which respondents were asked to indicate their level of satisfaction or dissatisfaction with "the present economic system," "the socialist economic system before the revolution," and "the economic system in five years' time." The original scales ranged from -100 to $+100$ but have been collapsed into 21-point scales ($-10/+10$).

5. Separate regressions were conducted for each of the ten countries for each year. Predictably, there is somewhat more variation across individual countries, but the fundamental structure of the lifetime learning models that emerge is the same in every case. The lifetime learning model consistently explains about 25 percent of variance in support, and performance variables consistently dominate the models.

6. These findings are consistent with research on the sources of political trust in the United States, which finds few strong or consistent relationships between social background and trust. (See, for example, Citrin 1974, 973, and Abramson 1983, 232–237.)

Appendix
A Primer on Statistics and Public Opinion

The contributors to this book use survey and experimental data to test their hypotheses, and they rely on statistical techniques to determine whether these data support their ideas. All scientific disciplines develop standards of adequate evidence to support claims, and political science is no different. The statistics used in this book are all widely accepted in the discipline, but they may be unfamiliar to many readers. This appendix presents a short primer in statistics to help readers obtain a deeper understanding of the analyses presented in the chapters.

Statistics can be used to describe the attitudes of members of a sample or of various groups within the sample. For example, we might want to know how many Americans believe that President George W. Bush is doing a good job, or how men and women differ in their assessments of his presidency. Statistics can also help us untangle the multiple sources of attitudes. For example, statistics can tell us whether race, sex, income, or partisanship is more important in explaining evaluations of Bush's job performance.

Survey Sampling and Statistical Significance

Most of the chapters in this book report data from national surveys. Because it is impossible to interview every American in a survey, researchers must draw samples of citizens. There are many different ways to draw samples, but nearly all social scientists use some variation on random sampling. A truly random sample is one in which every element of the population has an equal chance of selection.

Using random samples allows social scientists to estimate how closely the sample represents the general public. Consider support for John McCain, who ran for the presidency in Republican primaries in 2000. Assume that if we could ask all Americans whether they think that McCain would make a good president, 50 percent would say yes. We cannot actually interview the entire population, but we can draw a sample of 1,500 or 2,000.

The Central Limit Theorem tells us that if we were to draw an infinite number of samples and calculate the average support for McCain in each sample, the average of those sample means would form a normal distribution (a symmetrical bell curve, as in Figure A-1)

Figure A-1 Normal Distribution and Percent of Cases Between Selected Points Under the Curve

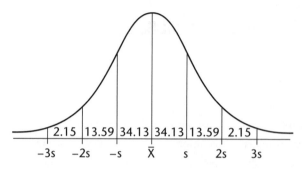

Note: $\overline{X}$ = population means; s = standard deviation

around 50 percent. Some samples would by chance have higher means because we selected a greater proportion of McCain supporters, and some would have lower means because we selected a greater proportion of his opponents' supporters. But if we draw samples that are sufficiently large, most of the samples will have close to 50 percent McCain supporters. For any given sample size, we can estimate just how close we are to the true population average if the sample is random.

Of course, there is always the random chance of drawing a truly unusual sample. We could select a sample that would be composed mostly of McCain voters, for example, or a sample of very conservative Republicans who detest McCain. The odds of drawing such a sample are very low. In general, we report the confidence interval with 95 percent certainty, meaning that for a given sample size, 95 percent of all samples drawn at random will have a sample mean that is within a certain distance from the true population mean (and 5 percent will not). A common confidence interval is ±3 percentage points. Thus if we draw a sample that has 47 percent McCain supporters, we can estimate that the true population figure would be between 44 percent and 50 percent.

If we are trying to determine whether a relationship can be generalized to the larger public, we consider two factors: the magnitude of the relationship and the size of the sample. Imagine, for example, that we are interested in gender differences in responses to John McCain. If we survey a random sample of 20 people and find that nearly all of the women dislike McCain and most of the men like him, we cannot be confident that this pattern could generalize to the larger public; our sample size is just too small. If we survey 2,000 individuals at random, however, and find that men are more favorable toward McCain than women are, we can be more confident that these differences are real. There are precise formulas for determining just how likely we would be to find any given relationship by chance, given the size of the sample.

By convention social scientists say that if they are 95 percent certain that a relationship can be generalized to the larger population, that relationship is statistically significant. Most of the tables in this book have notes indicating that a single asterisk next to a cell entry means statistical significance at the .01 level and two asterisks mean statistical significance at the .05 level. If a relationship is significant at the .05 level, there is about a 5 percent chance that the relationship is not valid in the general public.

Average Responses and Distributions:
Means, Medians, and Standard Deviations

If we want to know what Americans believe on a given issue, we can examine polling data, which are reported in percentages. For example, for many years Gallup and other pollsters have asked Americans whether they approve of the job the president is doing. Newspapers and television newscasts report the approval percentage and tell us whether that number is higher or lower than previous ratings.

Some poll questions are far more complex. Consider, for example, a question asking respondents to place themselves on a 7-point scale, where 1 indicates that they believe that the government should provide many fewer services and cut spending a lot, and 7 indicates that they believe the government should provide many more services and increase spending a lot.

Perhaps we would like to summarize the responses of all those who answered the survey. We can report an average position by calculating the mean response. In the 2000 National Election Study (NES), the government services question was asked; the frequencies for each response category are shown in Figure A-2. The mean response is simply obtained by adding together all the responses given (1s, 2s, 3s, and so on) and dividing by the number of people who answered the question. The mean response to this item is 4.41.

Means are appropriate with interval-level measures—when each unit of measurement is the same. But means are skewed when a few cases are far from the mean. Consider a question about the role of women, where a response of 1 indicates a strong view that women should be given an equal role in society, and a response of 7 indicates a strong view that a woman's place is in the home. The distribution of responses to this question in the 2000 NES is shown in Figure A-3. Here the mean is 2.04, even though most of the cases are in the 1 category. The small number of cases at 6 and 7 have a strong influence on the mean.

Sometimes a median, rather than a mean, response is reported for the average American's position. The median is the score for the middle-ranked person on the question. For

Figure A-2 Distribution of Responses on Government-
Services Question

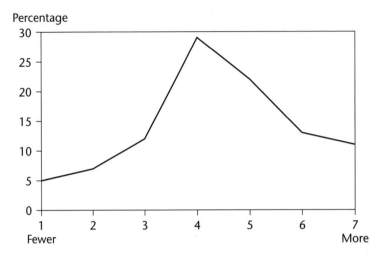

Percentage

Source: 2000 National Election Study.

Note: The question was worded as follows: "Some people think the government should provide fewer services even in areas such as health and education
in order to reduce spending. Suppose these people are at one end of a scale, at
point 1. Other people feel it is important for the government to provide many
more services even if it means an increase in spending. Suppose these people
are at the other end, at point 7. And, of course, some other people have opinions somewhere in between, at points 2, 3, 4, 5 or 6."

instance, assume that we ask five friends how much money they have in their wallets and we
get the following responses: $3, $5, $10, $20, $500. The median, or middle, response is $10;
the mean, or average, is $107.60. Medians are a more appropriate way to evaluate items that
are badly skewed, like income, and to describe ordinal data, where the values represent an
ordering but the intervals between the categories are not of the same size. In the case of the
government services question, the median is 4, while the median of the women's role question is 1. The median divides a sample into two groups of an equal number of cases. One
could divide cases into a larger number of equal-sized groups. In Chapter 10, Henry Brady,
Kay Schlozman, Sidney Verba, and Laurel Elms divide their samples into five equal-sized
groups called quintiles.

We can describe the distribution of issue positions by depicting the shape in a graph or
by using a statistic that measures the variation around the average response. When we describe the shape of a distribution, we often count the number of peaks. For example in Figure A-2, there is one peak in the middle of the distribution, and we refer to this as an

Figure A-3 Distribution of Responses on Role-of-Women Question

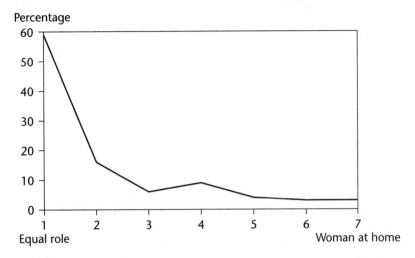

Percentage

Source: 2000 National Election Study.

Note: The question was worded as follows: "Recently there has been a lot of talk about women's rights. Some people feel that women should have an equal role with men in running business, industry, and government. Suppose these people are at one end of a scale, at point 1. Others feel that a woman's place is in the home. Suppose these people are at the other end, at point 7. And, of course, some other people have opinions somewhere in between, at points 2, 3, 4, 5 or 6."

unimodal distribution. In addition, the distribution is almost perfectly symmetrical, with more of the responses toward the center of the scale and few responses on the ends. Such a distribution is called a normal distribution or a bell-shaped distribution, as in Figure A-1. In contrast, Figure A-4 shows a bimodal distribution on a hypothetical attitude question, with large numbers of conservative responses on one side, a larger number of liberal responses on the other, and few moderate responses between.

If we wish to use a statistic to describe the distribution of cases, we most often use the standard deviation. The standard deviation is calculated by taking each case and subtracting the mean; this value is then squared (multiplied by itself). We make this calculation for each case, then add up the squared values. This sum is then divided by the total number of cases and the square root is taken. (The squaring process is used to eliminate negative values, since we do not care whether cases fall above or below the mean, just how far they are from the mean.) The standard deviation for the guaranteed services question is 1.58, and for the women's role scale it is 1.62. If the distribution of cases falls into a normal curve, we know that two-thirds of the cases fall between one standard deviation below and one stan-

Figure A-4 Distribution of Responses on Hypothetical Attitude Question

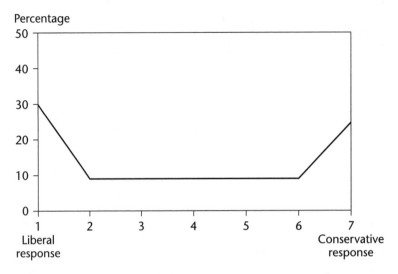

Note: The graph represents a bimodal distribution, with most respondents taking a liberal or conservative position and with few selecting a position in between.

dard deviation above the mean; 95 percent of the cases fall within two standard deviations of the mean.

Standard deviations are used to compare attitudes and respondents' qualities that are measured on different scales. For instance, we cannot directly compare the impact of age (measured in years) with the effects of ideology (measured on a 1–7 scale) on abortion attitudes. However, if we convert both items to standardized scales, measuring each as the distance from the mean for each question, then we can compare age to ideology. This is approximately what happens when we report standardized regression coefficients or calculate changes in probabilities in logistic regression, which are discussed in the following sections.

Experiments and Focus Groups

Although surveys are still the most common way for social scientists to study public opinion, scholars also use experiments and focus groups. These methodologies involve contact with fewer people, but they are better ways to help the researcher understand the underlying process by which people make up their minds about political entities. With surveys, researchers want to reach a large number of respondents who represent the general population. Having a representative sample ensures external validity, since the smaller group of people in the sample has the same characteristics as the population as a whole. Researchers can then generalize from the results of the survey to the whole population. With experiments the researcher hopes to achieve internal validity; the researcher controls the exposure of respondents to a specific stimulus to see the effects on some attitude. Focus group participants also do not accurately represent all groups of Americans, but the extended discussions and conversational settings that characterize focus groups allow researchers to understand how some Americans develop their political opinions. Experimental data are used by Shanto Iyengar and Markus Prior in Chapter 2 and by Kathleen McGraw in Chapter 12, while focus group responses are incorporated into John Hibbing's chapter (14).

In the simplest form of an experiment, participants are divided into two groups: the experimental group and the control group. The experimental group is exposed to some stimulus, such as a politician's commercial, while the control group does not receive this stimulus. Participants from both groups are subsequently asked several questions. Exposure to the stimulus should cause the experimental group to respond differently from the control group. These differences are most often tested through a statistical technique known as ANOVA, which stands for analysis of variance. The variation in participants' responses to each of the postexperiment questions is divided into two components: (1) differences between the mean responses of the two groups and (2) the remaining variation in responses within each group. The greater the differences between the mean responses across the two groups and the less variation remaining within each group, the more effect the experimental stimulus had on participants' attitudes. In other words, social scientists seek to see how different the responses are between the experimental and the control groups, compared with the average variation that naturally occurs within the groups.

The statistic in ANOVA that allows researchers to judge whether the amount of difference between the experimental and control groups exceeds random chance is the F-statistic. The F-statistic operates with the same principles as statistical significance for surveys. If the significance level of the F-statistic meets a certain criterion, often .05 or .10, then the researcher concludes that the experiment had an impact, with a 5 to 10 percent chance of being wrong in this conclusion. The magnitude of the effect of the experiment can be measured with the η^2 (eta squared) statistic, where a value of .25 would be interpreted to mean that the experiment explains 25 percent of the variation in the postexperiment attitude.

Focus groups are events in which a small number of respondents sit in the same room, usually around a table. A moderator asks questions and directs the discussion, but in many cases respondents reply directly to each other's comments as they might in an ordinary discussion. The focus group session is recorded and transcribed, and the transcripts then become the data from which the social scientist attempts to generalize. Sometimes focus group responses are coded for content—how often each respondent mentions leadership when they think of a candidate, or how often they talk of voting when they discuss citizenship. In other cases, focus group transcripts are the data for qualitative research, in which social scientists seek to find patterns in the things that respondents have said and in the responses they have to particular arguments. Focus groups are often used in conjunction with surveys, to help us better understand *why* citizens are responding in a particular way, or even to help researchers design better survey questions.

Measuring the Relationship Between Two Opinions

A variety of statistics can be used when we want to compare survey respondents' answers on one question to those on another question. These statistics are usually called correlations, and all of them tell us how closely aligned answers are between the two questions. If answers were to line up perfectly—such that, for example, all Democrats were liberals, all independents were moderates, and all Republicans were conservatives—then correlation statistics would take on the value of 1.0. If all answers were to line up perfectly, but in reverse order—say our result was that all Democrats were conservatives and all Republicans were liberals—then the correlation statistics would have a value of -1.0. The positive sign for a coefficient merely means that high scores on one variable are associated with high scores on the other; negative signs mean that a high score on the first is associated with a low score on the second.

In survey research, the patterns are never perfect. In fact, because of the wide variety of opinions and traits of Americans, most correlations in studies of public opinion fall in the range from 0, no pattern, to .3, a fairly strong pattern. Which statistic is used to report the opinions depends on the way the opinions are measured (interval, ordinal, or nominal levels of measurement) and the type of patterns the research is seeking. Wendy Rahn and Tom Rudolph in Chapter 13 use Pearson's r to measure the strength of the relationship, while Alan Abramowitz and Kyle Saunders in Chapter 9 use Kendall's tau-c. All of the correlation statistics can generally be interpreted in the same manner. The closer the statistic is to 1.0 or -1.0, the stronger the relationship is; the closer the statistic is to 0, the weaker the relationship is.

The statistical significance of a bivariate relationship is most often judged by the χ^2 (chi square) statistic. Once again, statistical significance indicates whether the pattern found in a sample is also true for the population as a whole. Thus, when the level of statistical significance for χ^2 is indicated as meeting the .05 criterion, there is only a 5 percent chance that a relationship between the two variables does not exist in the population. Carole Jean Uhlaner and F. Chris Garcia report χ^2 statistics in Chapter 4 to tell whether Mexican Americans, Cuban Americans, Puerto Ricans, and non-Hispanic whites differ in their political opinions.

Explaining Opinions Through Other Opinions and Personal Traits: OLS Regression and Logistic Regression

We often believe that many attitudes and personal traits, taken together, explain a person's opinions on a complex issue. Thus Clyde Wilcox and Barbara Norrander in Chapter 6 hypothesize that opinions on abortion are shaped by demographic factors such as education, religion, and other attitudes. These analysts are seeking to explain a single attitude, the attitude toward abortion, which in this case becomes the dependent variable because they believe that abortion attitudes will depend upon education and religion.

The traits and other opinions that are used to explain abortion attitudes are called the independent variables. Although we can correlate each of these variables with abortion attitudes, we cannot simply add up their effects because some of the explanatory power of one variable may be shared by another. For example, frequency of church attendance for Protestants correlates with abortion attitudes in the 2000 *Los Angeles Times* poll at −.26. (Protestants who attend church more often are less supportive of legal abortion for a wide variety of reasons; see Chapter 6.) Party identification correlates with abortion attitudes at −.32, with Republicans being more conservative. Yet church attendance and party identification also are correlated with each other, at .12. In other words, attendance is so highly correlated with abortion attitudes in part because those who attend church regularly are more likely than others to call themselves Republicans, and partisanship is so highly correlated with abortion attitudes in part because Republicans are more likely to be frequently attending Protestants than are Democrats. We need a way to sort out the impact of these two independent variables. In regression and logistic regression analyses we attempt to explain a dependent variable by using a variety of independent variables.

The basic form of regression is often called OLS (ordinary least squares) regression. In this form, regression predicts a straight linear relationship between the independent and dependent variables. If the regression analysis perfectly predicts the relationship between the two variables, all the data points will line up on the regression line. A perfect relationship, however, is extremely unlikely. Therefore, errors in prediction occur. For example, a regression model might predict that all Republicans who are also frequently attending Protestants will oppose abortion, but of course there will be exceptions to that rule. These errors, called residuals, are the differences between the predicted value and the actual value on the dependent variable for each value of the independent variable. Since we are concerned only with how large the prediction errors are, we square the errors to eliminate the direction of prediction error. The regression line represents the least amount of squared error over any other possible straight line, given the actual data.

A number of statistics are reported from a regression analysis. The explanatory power of all the independent variables together on the dependent variable is given by R^2 (R squared).

The R^2 can be interpreted as the amount of variation in the dependent variable explained by the independent variables. For example, in Chapter 8 William Jacoby describes the explanatory power of various sets of independent variables by referencing the R^2. In Table 8-6, about 40 percent ($R^2 = .39$) of the variation in opinions on government spending is explained by demographic variables and core values. Adding more independent variables will generally increase, and never decrease, the value of R^2. Thus, some authors report an adjusted R^2 which adjusts the value of R^2 for the number of independent variables—something especially important with small samples.

The impact of each independent variable is explained by two statistics. The first is the unstandardized regression coefficient, sometimes referred to as b. This tells how much change occurs in the dependent variable for a single unit change in the independent variable when all the other independent variables are held constant. In Table 15-1 William Mishler and Richard Rose attempt to explain support for the government in recently democratizing Eastern European countries. The value of the unstandardized coefficient for church attendance in the equation for 1991 is .16, and coefficient for support for the old Communist regime is −.07. Because church attendance is measured as a simple dichotomy (attend/not attend), the coefficient here represents the entire impact of church attendance, and those who attend church scored on average 0.16 points more support for the new governments on the 21-point scale. But support for the old Communist regime also is scored on a 21-point scale, which means that for each point of approval for the old Communist regime, respondents scored the new democratizing regimes 0.07 points lower.

The impact of different independent variables, however, cannot be directly compared if the variables are not measured on the same scale. To facilitate comparison, the regression coefficients are standardized (using the standard deviations of both the independent and dependent variables). These standardized regression coefficients can then be used to judge the relative impact of each of the independent variables. Notice in Table 15-1 that although the unstandardized coefficient for church attendance is larger than that for evaluation of the old Communist regime, the standardized coefficient (or beta) is higher for evaluations of the old regime. This is because once the entire 21-point range of evaluation of the old regime is considered, evaluations of the Communist regime have a greater impact on evaluations of the new regimes than does church attendance (2-point scale). Standardized regression coefficients have the virtue of allowing us to compare the importance of different variables within a given model. If we seek to compare across different models, however, we must use the unstandardized coefficients, because the standard deviations used to standardize the coefficients would not be the same in the different models.

Logistic regression is similar to OLS regression in that several independent variables are used to explain positions on one dependent variable. Logistic regression is appropriate when the dependent variable is measured at the ordinal level, and it is most often used when the dependent variable has only two categories. Alan Abramowitz and Kyle Saunders in Chapter 9 and Paul Brewer in Chapter 11 use logistic regression to predict vote choice between Democratic and Republican candidates. Logistic regression estimates the probability that a person will fall in one category versus the other of the dependent variable. The overall fit of the model is given by the percentage of cases classified correctly or by a pseudo-R^2. The equivalent of the unstandardized regression coefficient in logistic regression is maximum likelihood estimates (MLEs), sometimes simply referred to as logit coefficients. As with unstandardized regression coefficients, MLEs cannot be directly compared if the independent variables are measured on different scales. To compare the impact of a variety of independent variables, changes in the probabilities of falling into one category of the dependent variable are calculated. All the independent variables except one are held constant, usually at their mean values, while the remaining independent variable is changed by some value (often by one standard deviation). The change in probability of falling in the selected category of the dependent variable is then measured.

The statistical significance of an OLS regression coefficient or a logistic regression coefficient is derived by comparing it with the standard error of the coefficient, sometimes abbreviated as *s.e.* The standard error is the hypothetical variation in the regression coefficient that would occur if numerous samples were drawn and the regression analysis was repeated for each sample. A general rule of thumb for OLS regression coefficients is that if the unstandardized regression coefficient is two times the size of the standard error, the regression coefficient is statistically significant at the .05 level, or only a 5 percent chance exists that no relationship exists between the independent and the dependent variables in the population. Dividing a coefficient by its standard error produces a t-ratio. Many authors simply report statistical significance by attaching an asterisk to those regression or logit coefficients which have a probability at a specified level. This information is listed at the bottom of the table in a format similar to p < .05.

The statistical significance of an entire OLS regression equation is given by the same *F*-statistic as used in ANOVA. The overall significance of a logistic regression equation is given by chi square or a similar statistic reported as -2 log likelihood ratio. Both of these measures are comparing the amount of variation in the dependent variable explained by the regression or logistic regression equation to the amount of variation left unexplained.

Scaling: Factor Analysis and Cronbach's Alpha

Often a political science concept is too complex to be measured with a single survey question. In such cases, survey researchers ask many questions, and analysts seek ways to combine them into a single measure of a concept. Before combining questions, however, scholars must first determine whether all of the items measure the same attitude. The answer may depend on who is being surveyed. Consider the underlying concept of feminism. We might attempt to measure support for feminism by asking for respondents' evaluations of organizations such as the National Organization for Women (NOW); their attitudes toward general equality and rights for women; and their opinions about specific policies such as equal pay for equal work, access to child care for working mothers, parental leave to care for a baby or for a sick child, more stringent prosecution for sexual harassment, access to legal abortion, and legal protections for lesbians.

If we were conducting a survey of activists in feminist and antifeminist organizations, then all of these items would almost surely measure the central idea of feminism. But if we were conducting a survey of Catholic and fundamentalist working women, then the items on lesbian rights and abortion might tap into a different, religious, dimension of attitudes. We could see this by looking at the correlations. Among Catholic women employed outside the home, there might be a far lower correlation between attitudes on equal pay for equal work and parental leave on the one hand, and abortion and lesbian rights on the other, than we would find among feminist activists. If so, then we would need to create separate scales to measure these different attitudes among Catholic working women. Factor analysis and Cronbach's alpha are two statistical procedures that can be used to verify that the items chosen for a scale actually fit together.

Statistics and Replication

Many people are critical of statistics because there may be different ways to examine the same question, they may yield different answers. The old saying that there are "lies, damn lies, and statistics" conveys the thought that statistics can produce misleading portraits of reality, wrapped in scientific credibility. Although it is certainly possible to create misleading results using statistics, social science guards against this problem in a number of ways. Most important is the possibility of replication.

Most of the chapters in this book use data from large national surveys, such as the National Election Studies and the General Social Surveys, which are available to most social scientists. If, say, Roger Smith reports a result that is surprising, that contradicts other published results, or that is inconsistent with established theories, then it is likely that another scholar—call her Jane Jones—will use the same data to examine the same problem. If Professor Jones concludes that the previous study reached an erroneous result by using the wrong statistic or by considering the problem in the wrong way, then she will try to publish a rebuttal article in a scientific journal. Her article will be reviewed by "blind reviewers" who do not know that Jones is the author of the paper. If they accept the validity of her analysis, then the paper will probably be published. In this way, social science guards against the misuse of statistics.

Statistics are powerful tools that enable social scientists to test their hypotheses, refine their theories, and describe the world. They are used not only by scholars but by professional pollsters, consultants, and others who study public opinion.

References

Abramowitz, Alan I. 1980. "A Comparison of Voting for U.S. Senator and Representative." *American Political Science Review* 74: 633–640.

———. 1995. "It's Abortion, Stupid." *Journal of Politics* 57: 176–186.

———. 1997. "The Cultural Divide in American Politics: Moral Issues and Presidential Voting." In *Understanding Public Opinion,* ed. Barbara Norrander and Clyde Wilcox. Washington, D.C.: CQ Press.

Abramowitz, Alan I., and Kyle L. Saunders. 1998. "Ideological Realignment in the U.S. Electorate." *Journal of Politics* 60: 634–652.

Abramson, Paul R. 1983. *Political Attitudes in America.* San Francisco: W. H. Freeman.

Abramson, Paul R., John H. Aldrich, and David W. Rhode. 1985. *Change and Continuity in the 1984 Elections.* Washington, D.C.: CQ Press.

———. 1995. *Change and Continuity in the 1992 Elections.* Washington, D.C.: CQ Press.

Abramson, Paul R., and Ronald Inglehart. 1995. *Value Change in Global Perspective.* Ann Arbor: University of Michigan Press.

Adams, Greg D. 1997. "Abortion: Evidence of Issue Evolution." *American Journal of Political Science* 41: 718–737.

Adams, William C., and Michael Joblove. 1982. "The Unnewsworthy Holocaust: TV News and Terror in Cambodia." In *Television Coverage of International Affairs,* ed. William C. Adams. Norwood, N.J.: Ablex.

Advertising Age. 1991. "Political Ads Top Kroll's Agenda." April 29, 6.

———. 1996a. "Manning Attacks Political Ads." April 29, 50.

———. 1996b. "Transactions: Campaign Cloud; Battling the Threat Posed by Political Ads." June 24, 30.

Aldrich, John H. 1993. "Rational Choice and Turnout." *American Journal of Political Science* 37: 246–278.

Aldrich, John H., John L. Sullivan, and Eugene Borgida. 1989. "Foreign Affairs and Issue Voting: Do Presidential Candidates 'Waltz Before a Blind Audience'?" *American Political Science Review* 83: 123–141.

Alesina, Alberto, Reza Baqir, and William Easterly. 1997. "Public Goods and Ethnic Divisions." National Bureau of Economic Research Working Paper #6009, April.

Alesina, Alberto, and Romain Wacziarg. 2000. "The Economics of Civic Trust." In *Disaffected Democracies: What's Troubling the Trilateral Countries?* ed. Susan J. Pharr and Robert D. Putnam. Princeton: Princeton University Press.

Alford, John R. 2001. "We're All in This Together: The Decline in Trust in Government, 1958–1996." In *What Is It About Government That Americans Dislike?* ed. John R. Hibbing and Elizabeth Theiss-Morse. Cambridge: Cambridge University Press.

Allen, Richard L., Michael C. Dawson, and Ronald Brown. 1989. "A Schema-based Approach to Modeling an African-American Racial Belief System." *American Political Science Review* 83: 421–441.

Allport, Gordon W. 1935. "Attitudes." In *A Handbook of Social Psychology*, ed. C. Murchison. Worcester: Clark University Press.

Almond, Gabriel A. 1960. *The American People and Foreign Policy.* New York: Praeger.

Almond, Gabriel A., and Sidney Verba. 1963. *The Civic Culture.* Princeton: Princeton University Press.

Alvarez, R. Michael, and John Brehm. 1995. "American Ambivalence Towards Abortion Policy: Development of a Heteroskedastic Probit Model of Competing Values." *American Journal of Political Science* 39: 1055–1082.

———. 1997. "Are Americans Ambivalent Towards Racial Policies?" *American Journal of Political Science* 41: 345–374.

———. 1998. "Speaking in Two Voices: American Equivocation about the Internal Revenue Service." *American Journal of Political Science* 42: 418–452.

Alvarez, R. Michael, and Tara L. Butterfield. 1998. "Revolution Against Affirmative Action: Politics, Economics, and Proposition 209." Paper presented at the annual meeting of the Western Political Science Association, Los Angeles.

Alvarez, R. Michael, and Jonathan Nagler. 1995. "Economics, Issues, and the Perot Candidacy: Voter Choice in the 1992 Presidential Election." *American Journal of Political Science* 39: 714–744.

———. 1998. "Economics, Entitlements, and Social Issues: Voter Choice in the 1996 Presidential Election." *American Journal of Political Science* 42: 1349–1363.

Alwin, Duane F., and Jon A. Krosnick. 1985. "The Measurement of Values in Surveys: A Comparison of Ratings and Rankings." *Public Opinion Quarterly* 49: 535–552.

Andersen, Kristi. 1997. "Gender and Public Opinion." In *Understanding Public Opinion*, ed. Barbara Norrander and Clyde Wilcox. Washington, D.C.: CQ Press.

Andolina, Molly, and Clyde Wilcox. 2000. "The Paradoxes of Popularity: Public Support for Bill Clinton During the Lewinsky Scandal." In *The Clinton Scandal and the Future of American Government,* ed. Mark J. Rozell and Clyde Wilcox. Washington, D.C.: Georgetown University Press.

Ansolabehere, Stephen, Roy Behr, and Shanto Iyengar. 1993. *The Media Game: American Politics in the Television Age.* New York: Macmillan.

Ansolabehere, Stephen, and Shanto Iyengar. 1995. *Going Negative: How Attack Ads Shrink and Polarize the Electorate.* New York: Free Press.

Ansolabehere, Stephen, Shanto Iyengar, and Adam Simon. 1999. "Replicating Experiments Using Aggregate and Survey Data: The Case of Negative Advertising and Turnout." *American Political Science Review* 93: 901–910.

Antunes, George, and Charles M. Gaitz. 1975. "Ethnicity and Participation: A Study of Mexican Americans, Blacks and Whites." *American Journal of Sociology* 80: 1192–1211.

Arnold, R. Douglas. 1990. *The Logic of Congressional Action.* New Haven: Yale University Press.

Austen-Smith, David. 1992. "Explaining the Vote: Constituency Constraints on Sophisticated Voting." *American Journal of Political Science* 31: 68–95.

Austin, John L. 1961. "A Plea for Excuses." In *Philosophical Papers,* ed. J. D. Urmson and G. Warnock. Oxford: Clarendon Press.

Aylesworth, Andrew B., and Scott B. MacKenzie. 1998. "Context is the Key: The Effect of Program-Induced Mood on Thoughts About the Ad." *Journal of Advertising* 27: 17–31.

Bachrach, Peter. 1967. *The Theory of Democratic Elitism: A Critique.* Boston: Little, Brown.

Ball-Rokeach, Sandra J., Milton Rokeach, and Joel W. Grube. 1984. *The Great American Values Test: Influencing Behavior and Belief Through Television.* New York: Free Press.

Balz, Dan, and Terry M. Neal. 1999. "Gore Benefits, but Will War Issue Stay Hot?" *Washington Post,* June 6.

Bartels, Larry M. 2000. "Partisanship and Voting Behavior, 1952–1996." *American Journal of Political Science* 44: 35–50.

Bartels, Larry M., and Wendy M. Rahn. 2000. "Political Attitudes in the Post-Network Era." Paper presented at the annual meeting of the American Political Science Association, Washington, D.C.

Beck, Paul Allen, Hal G. Rainey, and Carol Traut. 1987. "Public Views of Taxes and Services: A Tale of Three Cities." *Social Science Quarterly* 68: 223–243.

———. 1990. "Disadvantage, Disaffection, and Race as Divergent Bases for Citizen Policy Preferences." *Journal of Politics* 52: 71–93.

Behr, Roy L., and Shanto Iyengar. 1985. "Television News, Real-World Cues, and Changes in the Public Agenda." *Public Opinion Quarterly* 49: 38–57.

Bell, Daniel. 2000. *The End of Ideology: On the Exhaustion of Political Ideas in the Fifties.* Cambridge: Harvard University Press.

Bennett, Stephen Earl, and Linda L. M. Bennett. 1986. "Political Participation." In *Annual Review of Political Science,* ed. Samuel Long. Norwood, N.J.: Ablex.

Bennett, W. Lance. 1980. "The Paradox of Public Discourse: A Framework for the Analysis of Political Accounts." *Journal of Politics* 42: 792–817.

———. 1989. "Marginalizing the Majority: Conditioning Public Opinion to Accept Managerial Democracy." In *Manipulating Public Opinion: Essays on Public Opinion as a Dependent Variable,* ed. Michael Margolis and Gary A. Mauser. Pacific Grove, Calif.: Brooks/Cole.

Berke, Richard L. 1996. "Politics: The Voters; Majority Give Clinton Credit On the Economy." *New York Times,* September 6.

Berlin, Isaiah. 1969. *Four Essays on Liberty.* Oxford: Oxford University Press.

Berman, Sheri. 1997. "Civil Society and Political Institutionalization." *American Behavioral Scientist* 40: 562–574.

Bianco, William T. 1994. *Trust: Representatives and Constituents.* Ann Arbor: University of Michigan Press.

Binder, Norman E., J. L. Polinard, and Robert D. Wrinkle. 1997. "Mexican American and Anglo Attitudes Toward Immigration Reform: A View from the Border." *Social Science Quarterly* 78: 324–337.

Binder, Sarah. 1999. "The Dynamics of Legislative Gridlock, 1947–96." *American Political Science Review* 93: 519–533.

Blair, Clay. 1987. *The Forgotten War: America in Korea, 1950–1953.* New York: Times Books.

Blair, Irene V., and Mahzarin R. Banaji. 1996. "Automatic and Controlled Processes in Stereotype Priming." *Journal of Personality and Social Psychology* 70: 1142–1145.

Blake, J., and K. Davis. 1964. "Norms, Values, and Sanctions." In *Handbook of Modern Sociology,* ed. R. E. L. Faris. Chicago: Rand McNally.

Blumer, Herbert. 1958. "Race Prejudice as a Sense of Group Position." *Pacific Sociological Review* 1: 3–7.

Bobo, Lawrence. 2000. "Race and Beliefs About Affirmative Action." In *Racialized Politics: The Debate About Racism in America,* ed. David O. Sears, Jim Sidanius, and Lawrence Bobo. Chicago: University of Chicago Press.

Bobo, Lawrence, James R. Kluegel, and Ryan A. Smith. 1997. "Laissez–Faire Racism: The Crystallization of a Kinder, Gentler, Antiblack Ideology." In *Racial Attitudes in the 1990s: Continuity and Change,* ed. Steven A. Tuch and Jack K. Martin. Westport, Conn.: Praeger.

Bobo, Lawrence, and Ryan A. Smith. 1998. "From Jim Crow Racism to Laissez-Faire Racism: The Transformation of Racial Attitudes." In *Beyond Pluralism: The Conception of Groups and Group Identity in America,* ed. Wendy F. Katkin, Ned Landsman, and Andrea Tyree. Urbana: University of Illinois Press.

Bok, Sissela. 1989. *Lying: Moral Choice in Public and Private Life.* New York: Vintage Books.

Boller, Paul F., Jr. 1996. *Presidential Campaigns.* New York: Oxford University Press.

Bosso, Christopher. 1989. "Setting the Agenda: Mass Media and the Discovery of Famine in Ethiopia." In *Manipulating Public Opinion: Essays on Public Opinion as a Dependent Variable,* ed. Michael Margolis and Gary A. Mauser. Pacific Grove, Calif.: Brooks/Cole.

Brace, Paul. 1993. *State Government and Economic Performance.* Baltimore: Johns Hopkins University Press.

Brace, Paul, and Barbara Hinckley. 1992. *Follow the Leader.* New York: Basic Books.

Brady, Henry E., Robert D. Putnam, Andrea L. Campbell, Laurel Elms, Steven Yonish, and Dorie Apollonio. 2001. *Roper Social and Political Trends Data, 1973–1994,* from Roper Starch Worldwide [Computer file]. Individual surveys conducted by the Roper Organization and Roper Starch Worldwide [producers], 1973–1994. Storrs, Conn.: Roper Center for Public Opinion Research, University of Connecticut [distributor], 2001.

Brady, Henry E., and Paul M. Sniderman. 1985. "Attitude Attribution: A Group Basis for Political Reasoning." *American Political Science Review* 79: 1061–1078.

Brehm, John, and Wendy Rahn. 1997. "Individual-Level Evidence for the Causes and Consequences of Social Capital." *American Journal of Political Science* 41: 999–1023.

Brewer, Paul. 1997. "When Words Collide: Values, Political Awareness, and Public Opinion Toward Gay Rights." Paper presented at the annual meeting of the Midwest Political Science Association.

Brody, Richard. 1991. *Assessing the President: The Media, Elite Opinion, and Public Support.* Stanford: Stanford University Press.

Brown, Clifford, Jr., Lynda Powell, and Clyde Wilcox. 1995. *Serious Money: Fundraising and Contributing in Presidential Nomination Campaigns.* New York: Cambridge University Press.

Brown, Ronald E., and Monica Wolford. 1994. "Religious Resources and African American Political Action." *National Political Science Review* 4: 30–48.

Brownstein, Ronald. 1992. "Economic Concerns Fueled Clinton's Drive to Victory." *Los Angeles Times,* November 4.

———. 1996. "Optimism, Moderation Power Clinton's Victory." *Los Angeles Times,* November 6.

Bruce, Steve. 1988. *The Rise and Fall of the New Christian Right.* New York: Oxford University Press.

Burk, James. 1999. "Public Support for Peacekeeping in Lebanon and Somalia: Assessing the Casualties Hypothesis." *Political Science Quarterly* 114: 53–78.

Buzan, Bert C. 1980. "Chicano Community Control, Political Cynicism, and the Validity of Political Trust Measures." *Western Political Quarterly* 33: 108–120.

Cain, Bruce E., and D. Roderick Kiewiet. 1984. "Ethnicity and Electoral Choice: Mexican American Voting Behavior in the California Thirtieth Congressional District." *Social Science Quarterly* 65: 315–327.

Calhoun-Brown, Allison. 1996. "African American Churches and Political Mobilization: The Psychological Impact of Organizational Resources." *Journal of Politics* 58: 935–953.

———. 1997. "Still Seeing in Black and White." In *Sojourners in the Wilderness: The Christian Right in Comparative Perspective,* ed. Corwin Smidt and James Penning. Lanham, Md.: Rowman and Littlefield.

———. 1998. "The Politics of Black Evangelicals: What Hinders Diversity in the Christian Right?" *American Politics Quarterly* 26: 81–109.

Campbell, Angus, Philip Converse, Warren Miller, and Donald Stokes. 1960. *The American Voter.* New York: Wiley.

Cantril, Hadley. 1967. *The Human Dimension: Experiences in Policy Research.* New Brunswick: Rutgers University Press.

Cantril, Hadley, and Associates. 1944. *Gauging Public Opinion.* Princeton: Princeton University Press.

Carmines, Edward G., and James A. Stimson. 1989. *Issue Evolution: Race and the Transformation of American Politics.* Princeton: Princeton University Press.

Center for Responsive Politics. 1997. "The Big Picture: Who Paid for the Last Election?" http://www.opensecrets.org/pubs/bigpicture/default.htm.

Chaney, Carole Kennedy, R. Michael Alvarez, and Jonathan Nagler. 1998. "Explaining the Gender Gap in U.S. Presidential Elections, 1980–1992." *Political Research Quarterly* 51: 311–339.

Chanley, Virginia, Wendy Rahn, and Thomas Rudolph. 2001. "The Origins and Consequences of Public Views about Government." In *What Is It About Government That Americans Dislike?* ed. John R. Hibbing and Elizabeth Theiss-Morse. Cambridge: Cambridge University Press.

Chanley, Virginia A., Thomas J. Rudolph, and Wendy M. Rahn. 2000. "The Origins and Consequences of Public Trust in Government." *Public Opinion Quarterly* 64: 239–256.

Chanley, Virginia, John L. Sullivan, Marti Hope Gonzales, and Margaret Bull Kovera. 1994. "Lust and Avarice in Politics: Damage Control by Four Politicians Accused of Wrongdoing (or, Politics as Usual)." *American Politics Quarterly* 22: 297–333.

Chong, Dennis. 2000. *Rational Lives: Norms and Values in Politics and Society.* Chicago: University of Chicago Press.

Citrin, Jack. 1974. "Comment: The Political Relevance of Trust in Government." *American Political Science Review* 68: 973–988.

Citrin, Jack, and Samantha Luks. 2001. "Political Trust Revisited: Deja Vu All Over Again?" In *What Is It About Government That Americans Dislike?* ed. John R. Hibbing and Elizabeth Theiss-Morse. Cambridge: Cambridge University Press.

Clarke, Harold, Nittish Dutt, and Allan Kornberg. 1993. "The Political Economy of Attitudes Toward Polity and Society in Western Europe." *Journal of Politics.* 55: 998–1021.

Clarke, Harold D., Euel W. Elliott, William Mishler, Marianne C. Stewart, Paul F. Whiteley, and Gary Zuk. 1992. *Controversies in Political Economy.* Boulder, Colo.: Westview Press.

Clinton, William J. 2001. "My Reasons for the Pardons." *New York Times,* February 18.

Cobas, Jose A. 1977. "Status Consciousness and Leftism: A Study of Mexican-American Adolescents." *Social Forces* 55: 1028–1042.

Cody, Michael J., and Margaret L. McLaughlin. 1990. "Interpersonal Accounting." In *Handbook of Language and Social Psychology,* ed. Howard Giles and Peter Robinson. New York: Wiley.

Cohen, Jeffrey E. 1995. "Presidential Rhetoric and the Public Agenda." *American Journal of Political Science* 39: 87–107.

Coleman, James S. 1988. "Social Capital in the Creation of Human Capital." *American Journal of Sociology* 94: 95–120.

Combs, Clyde H. 1964. *A Theory of Data.* New York: Wiley.

Comer, John C. 1978. "Street Level Bureaucracy and Political Support: Some Findings on Mexican Americans." *Urban Affairs Quarterly* 14: 207–228.

Connelly, Marjorie. 2000. "Who Voted: A Portrait of American Politics, 1976–2000." *New York Times,* November 12.

Conover, Pamela Johnston. 1988. "Feminists and the Gender Gap." *Journal of Politics* 50: 985–1010.

Conover, Pamela Johnston, Ivor M. Crewe, and Donald D. Searing. 1991. "The Nature of Citizenship in the United States and Great Britain: Empirical Comments on Theoretical Themes." *Journal of Politics* 53: 800–832.

Conover, Pamela Johnston, and Stanley Feldman. 1981. "The Origins and Meaning of Liberal/Conservative Self-Identification." *American Journal of Political Science* 25: 617–645.

Conover, Pamela Johnston, and Virginia Sapiro. 1992. "Gender Consciousness and Gender Politics in the 1991 Pilot Study: A Report to the ANES Board of Overseers." Ann Arbor: National Election Studies, http://www.umich.edu/~nes/resources/psreport/abs/91d.htm.

———. 1993. "Gender, Feminist Consciousness, and War." *American Journal of Political Science* 37: 1079–1099.

Conover, Pamela Johnson, and Donald D. Searing. 1994. "Democracy, Citizenship and the Study of Political Socialization." In *Democracy and Citizenship,* ed. Ian Budge and David McKay. London: Sage Publications.

Converse, Philip E. 1964. "The Nature of Belief Systems in Mass Publics." In *Ideology and Discontent,* ed. David Apter. New York: Free Press.

———. 1966. "The Concept of a Normal Vote." In *Elections and the Political Order,* ed. Angus Campbell, Philip E. Converse, Warren E. Miller, and Donald E. Stokes. New York: Wiley.

Conway, M. Margaret. 2000. *Political Participation in the United States,* 3d ed. Washington D.C.: CQ Press.

Cook, Elizabeth Adell. 1989. "Measuring Feminist Consciousness." *Women and Politics* 9: 71–88.

Cook, Elizabeth Adell, Ted G. Jelen, and Clyde Wilcox. 1992. *Between Two Absolutes: Public Opinion and the Politics of Abortion.* Boulder, Colo.: Westview Press.

———. 1995. "Issue Voting in U.S. Senate Elections: The Abortion Issue in 1990." *Congress and the Presidency* 21: 99–112.

Cook, Elizabeth Adell, and Clyde Wilcox. 1991. "Feminism and the Gender Gap: A Second Look." *Journal of Politics* 53: 1111–1122.

Cook, Timothy E. 1989. *Making Laws and Making News : Media Strategies in the U.S. House of Representatives.* Washington, D.C.: Brookings Institution.

Corrado, Anthony. 2000. *Campaign Finance Reform.* New York: Century Foundation Press.

Craig, Stephen C. 1993. *The Malevolent Leader: Popular Discontent in America.* Boulder, Colo.: Westview Press.

Cutler, David M., Edward J. Glaeser, and Jacob L. Vigdor. 1999. "The Rise and Decline of the American Ghetto." *Journal of Political Economy* 107: 455–506.

Dalton, Russell J. 1999. "Political Support in Advanced Industrial Democracies." In *Critical Citizens: Global Support for Democratic Governance,* ed. Pippa Norris. New York: Oxford University Press.

Davis, James A., and Tom W. Smith. 1995. *General Social Surveys, 1972–1994* [Cumulative File] [Computer file]. Chicago: National Opinion Research Center [producer], 1994. Ann Arbor, Mich.: Inter-university Consortium for Political and Social Research [distributor], 1995.

DeHoog, Ruth Hoogland, David Lowery, and William E. Lyons. 1990. "Citizen Satisfaction with Local Governance: A Test of Individual, Jurisdictional, and City-Specific Explanations." *Journal of Politics* 52: 807–837.

de la Garza, Rodolfo O., ed. 1987. *Ignored Voices: Public Opinion Polls and the Latino Community.* Austin: Center for Mexican American Studies, University of Texas at Austin Press.

de la Garza, Rodolfo O., and Robert O. Brischetto, with David Vaughn. 1983. "The Mexican American Electorate: Information Sources and Policy Orientations." Mexican American Electorate Series, Occasional Paper No. 2. Austin: Center for Mexican American Studies, University of Texas at Austin. San Antonio: Southwest Voter Registration Education Project.

de la Garza, Rodolfo O., Louis DeSipio, F. Chris Garcia, John Garcia, and Angelo Falcon. 1992. *Latino Voices: Mexican, Puerto Rican and Cuban Perspectives on American Politics.* Boulder, Colo.: Westview Press.

de la Garza, Rodolfo, Angelo Falcon, and F. Chris Garcia. 1996. "Will the Real Americans Please Stand Up: Anglo and Mexican-American Support of Core American Political Values." *American Journal of Political Science* 40: 335–351.

de la Garza, Rodolfo O., Jerry L. Polinard, Robert D. Wrinkle, and Tomas Longoria Jr. 1991. "Understanding Intra-Ethnic Attitude Variations: Mexican American Populations Views on Immigration." *Social Science Quarterly* 72: 379–387.

de la Garza, Rodolfo O., and David Vaughn. 1984. "The Political Socialization of Chicano Elites: A Generational Approach." *Social Science Quarterly* 65: 290–307.

de la Garza, Rodolfo O., and Janet Weaver. 1984. "Chicano and Anglo Public Policy Perspectives in San Antonio: Does Ethnicity Make a Difference?" *Social Science Quarterly* 66: 576–586.

della Porta, Donatella. 2000. "Social Capital, Beliefs in Government, and Political Corruption." In *Disaffected Democracies: What's Troubling the Trilateral Countries?* ed. Susan J. Pharr and Robert D. Putnam. Princeton: Princeton University Press.

DiMaggio, Paul, John Evans, and Bethany Bryson. 1996. "Have American's Social Attitudes Become More Polarized?" *American Journal of Sociology* 102: 690–755.

Dole, Bob. 1995. "Shaping America's Global Future." *Foreign Policy* (spring): 29–43.

Dowd, Maureen. 1997. "Leaders as Followers." *New York Times,* January 12.

Downs, Anthony. 1960. *An Economic Theory of Democracy.* New York: Harper and Row.

DuBois, W. E. B. 1903 [1965]. *The Souls of Black Folk.* New York: Avon.

Durr, Robert H., John B. Gilmour, and Christina Wolbrecht. 1997. "Explaining Congressional Approval." *American Journal of Political Science* 41: 175–207.

Eagly, Alice H., and Shelly Chaiken. 1993. *The Psychology of Attitudes.* New York: Harcourt, Brace, Jovanovich.

Easton, David. 1965a. *A Framework for Political Analysis.* Englewood Cliffs, N.J.: Prentice Hall.

———. 1965b. *A Systems Analysis of Political Life.* New York: Wiley.

Easton, David, and Jack Dennis. 1969. *Children in the Political System: Origins of Political Legitimacy.* New York: McGraw Hill.

EBRD (European Bank for Reconstruction and Development). 1995. *Transition Report Update.* London: EBRD.

———. 1998. *Transition Report Update.* London: EBRD.

Eckstein, Harry. 1966. *Division and Cohesion in Democracy.* Princeton: Princeton University Press.

———. 1971. *The Evaluation of Political Performance: Problems and Dimensions.* Beverly Hills, Calif.: Sage Publications.

Edelman, Murray. 1988. *Political Language: Words That Succeed and Policies That Fail.* New York: Academic Press.

Edwards, Bob, and Michael W. Foley. 1997. "Social Capital and the Political Economy of Our Discontent." *American Behavioral Scientist* 40: 669–678.

Edwards, George C. III. 1983. *The Public Presidency: The Pursuit of Popular Support.* New York: St. Martin's Press.

Eismeier, Theodore J. 1982. "Public Preferences About Government Spending." *Political Behavior* 4: 133–145.

Elazar, Daniel J. 1966. *American Federalism: A View from the States.* New York: Crowell.

Erikson, Robert S. 1971. "The Advantage of Incumbency in Congressional Elections." *Polity* 3: 395–405.

Erikson, Robert S., Gerald C. Wright Jr., and John P. McIver. 1989. "Political Parties, Public Opinion, and State Policy in the United States." *American Political Science Review* 83: 729–751.

———. 1993. *Statehouse Democracy: Public Opinion and Democracy in American States.* New York: Cambridge University Press.

Farah, Barbara G., and Ethel Klein. 1989. "Public Opinion Trends." In *The Election of 1988: Reports and Interpretations,* ed. Gerald M. Pomper. Chatham, N.J.: Chatham House.

Farley, Reynolds. 1996. *The New American Reality.* New York: Russell Sage Foundation.

Feaver, Peter D., and Christopher Gelpi. 1999. "Casualty Aversion: How Many Deaths Are Acceptable? A Surprising Answer." *Washington Post,* November 7.

Feldman, Stanley. 1988. "Structure and Consistency in Public Opinion: The Role of Core Beliefs and Values." *American Journal of Political Science* 32: 416–440.

Feldman, Stanley, and John Zaller. 1992. "The Political Culture of Ambivalence: Ideological Responses to the Welfare State." *American Journal of Political Science* 36: 268–307.

Fenno, Richard F., Jr. 1975. "If, as Ralph Nader Says, Congress Is 'The Broken Branch,' How Come We Love Our Congressmen So Much?" In *Congress in Change: Evolution and Reform,* ed. Norman J. Ornstein. New York: Praeger.

———. 1978. *Home Style: House Members in Their Districts.* Boston: Little, Brown.

Ferejohn, John A. 1977. "On the Decline of Competition in Congressional Elections." *American Political Science Review* 71: 166–176.

Festinger, Leon. 1957. *A Theory of Cognitive Dissonance.* Evanston, Ill.: Row, Peterson.

Finifter, Ada W., and Ellen Mickiewicz. 1992. "Redefining the Political System of the USSR: Mass Support for Political Change." *American Political Science Review.* 86: 857–874.

Finkel, Steven E., and John G. Geer. 1998. "Spot Checking: Casting Doubt on the Demobilizing Effect of Attack Advertising." *American Journal of Political Science* 42: 573–595.

Fiorina, Morris P. 1981. *Retrospective Voting in American Presidential Elections.* New Haven: Yale University Press.

———. 1994. "Divided Government in the American States: A Byproduct of Legislative Professionalism?" *American Political Science Review* 88: 304–316.

———. 1999. "Extreme Voices: The Dark Side of Civic Engagement." In *Civic Engagement in American Democracy,* ed. Theda Skocpol and Morris Fiorina. Washington, D.C.: Brookings Institution and Russell Sage Foundation.

Fireman, B., and W. A. Gamson. 1979. "Utilitarian Logic in the Resource Mobilization Perspective." In *The Dynamics of Social Movements,* ed. M. Zald and J. McCarthy. Cambridge, Mass.: Winthrop.

Fishbein, Martin, and Icek Ajzen. 1975. *Belief, Attitude, Intention, and Behavior.* Reading, Mass.: Addison-Wesley.

Fiske, Susan T., and Shelley E. Taylor. 1991. *Social Cognition,* 2d ed. New York: McGraw-Hill.

Flanigan, William, and Nancy Zingale. 1994. *Political Behavior of the American Electorate,* 8th ed. Washington, D.C.: CQ Press.

Foley, Michael W., and Bob Edwards. 1997. "Escape from Politics? Social Theory and the Social Capital Debate." *American Behavioral Scientist* 40: 550–561.

Forsyth, Elizabeth R., and Cesar M. Melgoza. 1987. "A Guide to Survey Research on Latino Public Opinion." In *Ignored Voices,* ed. Rodolfo de la Garza. Austin, Tex.: Center for Mexican American Studies, University of Texas at Austin Press.

Fowler, Linda L., and Robert D. McClure. 1989. *Political Ambition: Who Decides to Run for Congress.* New Haven: Yale University Press.

Franklin, Charles H., and Liane C. Kosaki. 1989. "Republican Schoolmaster: The U.S. Supreme Court, Public Opinion, and Abortion." *American Political Science Review* 83: 751–772.

Frazier, E. Franklin. 1976. *The Negro Church in America.* New York: Schocken.

Freedman, Paul, and Dale Lawton. 2000. "Campaign Advertising, Perceived Fairness, and Voter Turnout." Paper presented at the annual meeting of the Midwest Political Science Association.

Freedom House. 1998. http://www.freedomhouse.org.

Friedman, Howard S., and Joan S. Tucker. 1990. "Language and Deception." In *Handbook of Language and Social Psychology,* ed. Howard Giles and W. Peter Robinson. New York: Wiley.

Gaddis, John Lewis. 1974. "Was the Truman Doctrine a Real Turning Point?" *Foreign Affairs* 52: 386–401.

Gaertner, Samuel L., John F. Dovidio, Jason A. Nier, Christine M. Ward, and Brenda S. Banker. 1999. "Across Cultural Divides: The Value of a Superordinate Identity." In *Cul-*

tural Divides: Understanding and Overcoming Group Conflict, ed. Deborah A. Prentice and Dale T. Miller. New York: Russell Sage Foundation.

Gamson, William A. 1968. *Power and Discontent.* Homewood, Ill.: Dorsey Press.

Gant, Michael M., and Norman R. Luttbeg. 1991. *American Electoral Behavior.* Itasca, Ill.: F. E. Peacock.

Garcia, F. Chris. 1973. *Political Socialization of Chicano Children.* New York: Praeger.

———. 1997. "Latinos and the Affirmative Action Debate: Wedge or Coalition Issue?" In *Pursuing Power: Latinos and the Political System,* ed. F. Chris Garcia. Notre Dame: Notre Dame University Press.

Garcia, F. Chris, Rodolfo O. de la Garza, Angelo Falcon, and John A. Garcia. 1989. "Studying Latino Politics: The Development of the Latino National Political Survey." *PS: Political Science and Politics* 22: 848–852.

Garcia, F. Chris, John A. Garcia, Rodolfo de la Garza, Angelo Falcon, and Cara J. Abeyta. 1991. *Latinos and Politics: A Select Research Bibliography.* Austin: Center for Mexican American Studies, University of Texas.

Garcia, John A. 1982. "Ethnicity and Chicanos: Measurement of Ethnic Identification, Identity, and Consciousness." *Hispanic Journal of Behavioral Sciences* 4: 295–314.

———. 1987. "The Political Integration of Mexican Immigrants: Examining Some Political Orientations." *International Migration Review* 21: 372–389.

Gibson, James L. 1993. "Perceived Political Freedom in the Soviet Union." *Journal of Politics.* 55: 936–974.

Gilligan, Carol. 1982. *In a Different Voice: The Changing Political Attitudes of American Women.* Cambridge: Harvard University Press.

Glaser, Barney, and Anselm Strauss. 1967. *The Discovery of Grounded Theory.* Chicago: Aldine.

Goffman, Erving. 1959. *The Presentation of Self in Everyday Life.* Garden City, N.Y.: Doubleday Anchor.

———. 1971. *Relations in Public: Microstudies of the Public Order.* New York: Basic Books.

Goggin, Malcolm, and Christopher Wlezien. 1993. "The Courts, Interest Groups, and Public Opinion about Abortion." *Political Behavior* 15: 381–405.

Goldberg, M. E., and G. J. Gorn. 1987. "Happy and Sad TV Programs: How They Affect Reactions to Commercials." *Journal of Consumer Research* 12: 281–300.

Goldstein, Kenneth. 1998. "What Did They See and When Did They See It? Measuring the Volume, Tone, and Targeting of Television Advertising in the 1996 Presidential Election." Unpublished manuscript.

Gonzales, Marti Hope, Margaret Bull Kovera, John L. Sullivan, and Virginia Chanley. 1995. "Private Reactions to Public Transgressions: Predictors of Evaluative Responses to

Allegations of Political Misconduct." *Personality and Social Psychology Bulletin* 21: 136–148.

Goren, Paul. 2001. "Core Principles and Policy Reasoning in Mass Publics: A Test of Two Theories." *British Journal of Political Science* 31 (forthcoming).

Gourevitch, Philip. 1998. *We Wish to Inform You That Tomorrow We Will Be Killed with Our Families: Stories from Rwanda.* New York: Farrar Straus Giroux.

Graber, Doris A. 1976. *Verbal Behavior and Politics.* Urbana: University of Illinois Press.

———. 1984. *Processing the News: How People Tame the Information Tide.* White Plains, N.Y.: Longman.

———. 1994. "Why Voters Fail Information Tests: Can the Hurdles Be Overcome?" *Political Communication* 11: 331–346.

———. 1997. "Media as Opinion Resources: Are the 1990s a New Ball Game?" In *Understanding Public Opinion,* ed. Barbara Norrander and Clyde Wilcox. Washington, D.C.: CQ Press.

Gurin, Patricia, Shirley Hatchett, and James Jackson. 1989. *Hope and Independence.* New York: Russell Sage Foundation.

Guth, Werner, and Reihard Tietz. 1990. "Ultimatum Bargaining Behavior: A Survey and Comparison of Experimental Results." *Journal of Economic Psychology* 11: 417–449.

Gutierrez, Armando, and Herbert Hirsch. 1973. "The Militant Challenge to the American Ethos: 'Chicanos' and 'Mexican Americans.'" *Social Science Quarterly* 53: 830–845.

Guzman, Ralph C. 1976. *The Political Socialization of the Mexican American People.* Chicano Heritage Series. New York: Arno Press.

Hahn, Jeffrey. 1991. "Continuity and Change in Russian Political Culture." *British Journal of Political Science* 21: 393–421.

Hajnal, Zoltan, and Mark Baldassare. 2001. *Finding Common Ground: Racial and Ethnic Attitudes in California.* San Francisco: Public Policy Institute of California.

Hallin, Daniel C. 1986. *The "Uncensored War": The Media and Vietnam.* New York: Oxford University Press.

Hanson, Russell L. 1999. "Intergovernmental Relations." In *Politics in the American States: A Comparative Analysis,* 7th ed., ed. Virginia Gray, Russell L. Hanson, and Herbert Jacob. Washington, D.C.: CQ Press.

Hardle, Wolfgang. 1990. *Applied Nonparametric Regression.* Cambridge: Cambridge University Press.

Harris, Fredrick. 1994. "Something Within: Religion as a Mobilizer of African American Political Activism." *Journal of Politics* 56: 42–68.

———. 1999. *Something Within: Religion in African American Political Activism.* New York: Oxford University Press.

Harris, Louis. 1954. *Is There a Republican Majority? Political Trends, 1952–1956.* New York: Harper's.

Hedges, Chris. 1997. "On Bosnia's Ethnic Fault Lines, It's Still Tense, but World Is Silent." *New York Times,* February 28.

Hero, Rodney E. 1998. *Faces of Inequality: Social Diversity in American Politics.* New York: Oxford University Press.

Herrnson, Paul S., and Clyde Wilcox. 1997. "The 1996 Presidential Election: A Tale of a Campaign That Didn't Seem to Matter." In *Toward the Millennium: The Elections of 1996,* ed. Larry J. Sabato. Boston: Allyn and Bacon.

Hershey, Marjorie Randon. 1989. "The Campaign and the Media." In *The Election of 1988: Reports and Interpretations,* ed. Gerald M. Pomper. Chatham, N.J.: Chatham House.

Hess, David. 1998. "Congress Hibernating Till Fall." *Houston Chronicle,* March 19.

Hibbing, John R. 1982. *Choosing to Leave.* Washington, D.C.: University Press of America.

Hibbing, John R., and Elizabeth Theiss-Morse. 1995. *Congress as Public Enemy: Public Attitudes Toward American Political Institutions.* New York: Cambridge University Press.

———. 1997. "Public Opinion and Congressional Power." In *Understanding Public Opinion,* ed. Barbara Norrander and Clyde Wilcox. Washington, D.C.: CQ Press.

———. 2001. "Process Space and American Politics: What the People Want Government to Be." *American Political Science Review* 95: 145–154.

———. Forthcoming. *Stealth Democracy: Americans' Beliefs About How Government Should Work.* Cambridge: Cambridge University Press.

Hickey, Donald R. 1989. *The War of 1812: A Forgotten Conflict.* Urbana: University of Illinois Press.

Higgins, E. T., W. S. Rholes, and C. R. Jones. 1977. "Category Accessibility and Impression Formation." *Journal of Experimental Psychology* 13: 141–154.

Hinich, Melvin J., and Michael C. Munger. 1994. *Ideology and the Theory of Political Choice.* Ann Arbor: University of Michigan Press.

Hirsch, Herbert, and Armando Gutierrez. 1977. *Learning to be Militant: Ethnic Identity and the Development of Political Militance in a Chicano Community.* San Francisco: R & E Research Associates.

Hochschild, Jennifer L. 1981. *What's Fair? American Beliefs About Distributive Justice.* Cambridge: Harvard University Press.

———. 1995. *Facing Up to the American Dream: Race, Class, and the Soul of the Nation.* Princeton: Princeton University Press.

Holland, Barbara. 1989. *Hail to the Chiefs.* New York: Ballantine.

Holsti, Ole R. 1996. *Public Opinion and American Foreign Policy.* Ann Arbor: University of Michigan Press.

Houston D., K. Dean, and D. Roskos-Ewoldsen. 1999. "Negative Political Advertising and Choice Conflict." *Journal of Experimental Psychology: Applied* 5: 3–16.

Houston D., and D. Roskos-Ewoldsen. 1998. "Cancellation and Focus Model of Choice and Preferences for Political Candidates." *Basic and Applied Social Psychology* 20: 305–312.

Huckfeld, Robert, and Carol Kohfeld. 1989. *Race and the Decline of Class in American Politics.* Urbana: University of Illinois Press.

Huddy, Leonie, and Nayda Terkildsen. 1993. "Gender Stereotypes and the Perception of Male and Female Candidates." *American Journal of Political Science* 37: 119–147.

Hugick, Larry. 1992. "The 'Rubbergate' Scandal." *Gallup Poll Monthly,* March, 2–4.

Hunter, James Davison. 1991. *Culture Wars: The Struggle to Define America.* New York: Basic Books.

Inglehart, Ronald. 1971. "The Silent Revolution: Intergenerational Change in Post-Industrial Societies." *American Political Science Review* 65: 991–1017.

———. 1990. *Culture Shift in Advanced Industrial Society.* Princeton: Princeton University Press.

Institute for Puerto Rican Policy. 1984. *Puerto Ricans and the 1984 Presidential Race: A Report on the First National Puerto Rican Opinion Survey.* New York: Institute for Puerto Rican Policy.

Iyengar, Shanto. 1991. *Is Anyone Responsible? How Television Frames Political Issues.* Chicago: University of Chicago Press.

———. 1993. "Agenda Setting and Beyond: Television News and the Strength of Political Issues." In *Agenda Formation,* ed. William H. Riker. Ann Arbor: University of Michigan Press.

Iyengar, Shanto, and Donald R. Kinder. 1987. *News That Matters: Television and American Opinion.* Chicago: University of Chicago Press.

Jacobs, Lawrence R., and Robert Y. Shapiro. 2000. *Politicians Don't Pander: Political Manipulation and the Loss of Democratic Responsiveness.* Chicago: University of Chicago Press.

Jacobson, Gary C. 2001. *The Politics of Congressional Elections,* 5th ed. New York: Longman.

Jacoby, William G. 1994. "Public Attitudes Toward Government Spending." *American Journal of Political Science* 38: 336–361.

———. 1997. "Public Opinion and Economic Policy in 1992." In *Understanding Public Opinion,* ed. Barbara Norrander and Clyde Wilcox. Washington, D.C.: CQ Press.

———. 2000. "Issue Framing and Public Opinion on Government Spending." *American Journal of Political Science* 44: 750–767.

Jamieson, Kathleen Hall. 1992. *Dirty Politics: Deception, Distraction, and Democracy.* New York: Oxford University Press.

———. 2001. *Civility in the House of Representatives: The 106th Congress.* Annenberg Public Policy Center of the University of Pennsylvania.

Jamieson, Kathleen Hall, Paul Waldman, and Susan Sherr. 1998. "Eliminate the Negative? Defining and Refining Categories of Analysis for Political Advertisements." Paper presented at the Conference on Political Advertising in Election Campaigns, Washington, D.C.

Janda, Kenneth, Jeffrey M. Berry, and Jerry Goldman. 1995. *The Challenge of Democracy: Government in America,* 4th ed. Boston: Houghton Mifflin.

Jelen, Ted. 1991. *The Political Mobilization of Religious Beliefs.* New York: Praeger.

———. 1997. "Religion and Public Opinion in the 1990s: An Empirical Overview." In *Understanding Public Opinion,* ed. Barbara Norrander and Clyde Wilcox. Washington, D.C.: CQ Press.

Jelen, Ted G., and Clyde Wilcox. 1995. *Public Attitudes on Church and State.* Armonk, N.Y.: M. E. Sharpe.

Jenkins, J. Craig. 1983. "Resource Mobilization Theory and the Study of Social Movement." *Annual Review of Sociology* 9: 527–553.

Jennings, M. Kent. 1998. "Political Trust and the Roots of Devolution." In *Trust and Governance,* ed. Valerie Braithwaite and Margaret Levi. New York: Russell Sage Foundation.

Jennings, M. Kent, and Richard G. Niemi. 1971. "The Division of Political Labor Between Mothers and Fathers." *American Political Science Review* 32: 69–92.

———. 1974. *The Political Character of Adolescence.* Princeton: Princeton University Press.

———. 1981. *Generations and Politics.* Princeton: Princeton University Press.

Jentleson, Bruce W. 1992. "The Pretty Prudent Public: Post Post-Vietnam American Opinion on the Use of Military Force." *International Studies Quarterly* 36: 49–74.

Jervis, Robert. 1980. "The Impact of the Korean War on the Cold War." *Journal of Conflict Resolution* 24: 563–592.

Jewell, Malcolm E., and Sarah M. Morehouse. 2001. *Political Parties and Elections in American States,* 4th ed. Washington, D.C.: CQ Press.

Joffe, Josef. 1987. "Peace and Populism: Why the European Anti-Nuclear Movement Failed." *International Security* 11: 3–40.

Johnson, Glen. 2000. "Campaign 2000/The Vice President: Gore, at a Texas Pulpit, Talks of 'Cultural Pollution.'" *Boston Globe,* October 23.

Jones-Correa, Michael, and David L. Leal. 1996. "Becoming 'Hispanic': Secondary Panethnic Identification Among Latin American-Origin Populations in the United States." *Hispanic Journal of Behavioral Sciences* 18: 214–254.

Kabaker, Harvey M. 1969. "Estimating the Normal Vote in Congressional Elections." *Midwest Journal of Political Science* 13: 58–83.

Kaid, Lynda Lee, Mike Chanslor, and Mark Hovind. 1992. "The Influence of Program and Commercial Type on Political Advertising Effectiveness." *Journal of Broadcasting & Electronic Media* 36: 303–320.

Kamakura, Wagner A., and Jose Afonso Mazzon. 1991. "Value Segmentation: A Model for the Measurement of Values and Value Systems." *Journal of Consumer Research* 18: 208–218.

Kamins, Michael A., Lawrence J. Marks, and Deborah Skinner. 1991. "Television Commercial Evaluation in the Context of Program Induced Mood: Congruency Versus Consistency Effects." *Journal of Advertising* 20: 1–14.

Katz, Daniel. 1960. "The Functional Approach to the Study of Attitudes." *Public Opinion Quarterly* 24: 163–204.

Kaufmann, Karen M., and John R. Petrocik. 1999. "The Changing Politics of American Men: Understanding the Sources of the Gender Gap." *American Journal of Political Science* 43: 864–887.

Keeter, Scott. 1985. "Public Opinion in 1984." In *The Election of 1984: Reports and Interpretations,* ed. Gerald Pomper. Chatham, N.J.: Chatham House.

———. 1997. "Public Opinion and the Election." In *The Election of 1996: Reports and Interpretations,* ed. Gerald M. Pomper. Chatham, N.J.: Chatham House.

Kellstedt, Lyman, John Green, James Guth, and Corwin Smidt. 1994. "Religious Voting Blocs in the 1992 Election: The Year of the Evangelical?" *Sociology of Religion* 55: 307–326.

Kellstedt, Paul M. 2000. "Media Framing and the Dynamics of Racial Policy Preferences." *American Journal of Political Science* 44: 245–260.

Kernell, Samuel. 1997. *Going Public: New Strategies of Presidential Leadership,* 3d ed. Washington, D.C.: CQ Press.

Kettle, Martin. 1999. "Kosovo Holds the Key to Gore's Prospects." *Guardian Weekly,* June 6.

Key, V. O., Jr. 1959. "Secular Realignment and the Party System." *Journal of Politics* 21: 198–210.

———. 1961. *Public Opinion and American Democracy.* New York: Alfred A. Knopf.

———. 1964. *Politics, Parties, and Pressure Groups.* New York: Cromwell.

———. 1966. *The Responsible Electorate: Rationality in Presidential Voting, 1936–1960.* New York: Vintage.

Kimball, David C., and Samuel C. Patterson. 1997. "Living Up to Expectations: Public Attitudes Toward Congress." *Journal of Politics* 59: 701–728.

Kinder, Donald R. 1986. "Presidential Character Revisited." In *Political Cognition,* ed. Richard R. Lau and David O. Sears. Hillsdale, N.J.: Lawrence Erlbaum Associates.

———. 1998. "Opinion and Action in the Realm of Politics." In *Handbook of Social Psychology,* 4th ed., ed. Daniel L. Gilbert, Susan T. Fiske, and Garnder Lindzey. Boston: McGraw-Hill.

Kinder, Donald R., Cindy D. Kam, and Claudia Deane. 2000. "Ethnocentrism and the Golden Door." Manuscript, University of Michigan.

Kinder, Donald R., and D. Roderick Kiewet. 1979. "Economic Discontent and Political Behavior: The Role of Personal Grievances and Collective Economic Judgments in Congressional Voting." *American Journal of Political Science* 23: 495–527.

———. 1981. "Sociotropic Politics: The American Case." *British Journal of Political Science*
11: 129–161.

Kinder, Donald R., and Thomas R. Palfrey. 1992. "On Behalf of an Experimental Political
Science." In *Experimental Foundations of Political Science,* ed. Donald R. Kinder and
Thomas R. Palfrey. Ann Arbor: University of Michigan.

Kinder, Donald R., and Lynn M. Sanders. 1990. "Mimicking Political Debate with Survey
Questions: The Case of White Opinion on Affirmative Action for Blacks." *Social Cognition* 8: 73–103.

———. 1996. *Divided by Color: Racial Politics and Democratic Ideals.* Chicago: University
of Chicago Press.

Kinder, Donald R., and David O. Sears. 1981. "Prejudice and Politics: Symbolic Racism Versus Racial Threats to the Good Life." *Journal of Personality and Social Psychology* 40:
414–431.

———. 1985. "Public Opinion and Political Action." In *Handbook of Social Psychology,*
vol. 2, ed. Gardner Lindzey and Elliot Aronson. New York: Random House.

King, David C. 1997. "The Polarization of American Politics and Mistrust of Government."
In *Why People Don't Trust Government,* ed. Joseph S. Nye Jr., Philip Zelikow, and
David C. King. Cambridge: Harvard University Press.

Kingdon, John W. 1973. *Congressman's Voting Decisions.* New York: Harper and Row.

Klarevas, Louis J. 1999. "American Public Opinion on Peace Operations: The Cases of
Somalia, Rwanda, and Haiti." Unpublished Ph.D. dissertation, American University,
Washington, D.C.

Klein, Ethel. 1978. *Gender Politics.* Cambridge: Harvard University Press.

Klingmann, Hans-Dieter. 1999. "Mapping Political Support in the 1990s: A Global Analysis." In *Critical Citizens: Global Support for Democratic Government,* ed. Pippa Norris.
New York: Oxford University Press.

Knight, Kathleen, and Robert S. Erikson. 1997. "Ideology in the 1990s." In *Understanding
Public Opinion,* ed. Barbara Norrander and Clyde Wilcox. Washington, D.C.: CQ Press.

Koch, Jeffrey W. 2000. "Do Citizens Apply Gender Stereotypes to Infer Candidates' Ideological Orientations?" *Journal of Politics* 62: 414–429.

Kornberg, Allan, and Harold Clarke. 1992. *Citizens and Community: Political Support in
a Representative Democracy.* Cambridge: Cambridge University Press.

Kramer, Gerald H. 1983. "The Ecological Fallacy Revisited: Aggregate- versus Individual-
Level Findings on Economics and Elections and Sociotropic Voting." *American Political Science Review* 77: 92–111.

Kraus, Sidney. 1979. *The Great Debates: Carter vs. Ford, 1976.* Bloomington: Indiana University Press.

Kristiansen, Connie M., and Alan M. Hotte. 1996. "Morality and the Self: Implications for the When and How of Value-Attitude-Behavior Relations." In *The Psychology of Values: The Ontario Symposium,* vol. 8, ed. Clive Seligman, James M. Olson, and Mark P. Zanna. Mahwah, N.J.: Lawrence Erlbaum Associates.

Kritzer, Herbert. 1996. "The Data Puzzle: The Nature of Interpretation in Quantitative Research." *American Journal of Political Science* 40: 1–32.

Krosnick, Jon A., and Donald R. Kinder. 1990. "Altering the Foundations of Support for the President Through Priming." *American Political Science Review* 84: 497–512.

Kuklinski, James H., Paul M. Sniderman, Kathleen Knight, Thomas Piazza, Philip E. Tetlock, Gordon R. Lawrence, and Barbara Mellers. 1997. "Racial Prejudice and Attitudes Toward Affirmative Action." *American Journal of Political Science* 41: 402–419.

Kull, Steven, and I. M. Destler. 1999. *Misreading the Public: The Myth of a New Isolationism.* Washington, D.C.: Brookings Institution.

Ladd, Everett Carll. 1999. *The Ladd Report.* New York: Free Press.

LaMar, Lisa, and Mary Kite. 1998. "Sex Differences in Attitudes Toward Gay Men and Lesbians: A Multidimensional Perspective." *Journal of Sex Research* 35: 190–196.

Lamare, James W. 1982. "The Political Integration of Mexican American Children: A Generational Analysis." *International Migration Review* 16: 169–188.

Lane, Robert 1973. "Patterns of Political Beliefs." In *Handbook of Political Psychology,* ed. J. Knutson. San Francisco: Jossey-Bass.

Larson, Eric V. 1996. *Casualties and Consensus: The Historical Role of Casualties in Domestic Support for U.S. Military Operations.* Santa Monica, Calif.: RAND Corporation.

———. 1999. "Review of Kull and Destler, Misreading the Public." *Public Opinion Quarterly* 63: 624–627.

———. 2000. "Putting Theory to Work: Diagnosing Public Opinion on the U.S. Intervention in Bosnia." In *Being Useful: Policy Relevance and International Relations,* ed. Miroslav Nincic and Joseph Lepgold. Ann Arbor: University of Michigan Press.

Lawrence, Robert Z. 1997. "Is it Really the Economy, Stupid?" In *Why People Don't Trust Government,* ed. Joseph S. Nye Jr., Philip D. Zelikow, and David C. King. Cambridge: Harvard University Press.

Leege, David, and Lyman Kellstedt, eds. 1993. *Rediscovering the Impact of Religion on Political Behavior.* Armonk, N.Y.: M. E. Sharpe.

Levi, Margaret. 1997. *Consent, Dissent, and Patriotism.* New York: Cambridge University Press.

Levitin, Teresa E., and Warren E. Miller. 1979. "Ideological Interpretations of Presidential Elections." *American Political Science Review* 73: 751–771.

Lewis, I. A., and William Schneider. 1983. "Black Voting, Bloc Voting and Democrats." *Public Opinion* 6: 12–15, 59.

Lewis-Beck, Michael. 1988. *Economics and Elections: The Major Western Democracies.* Ann Arbor: University of Michigan Press.

Lien, Pei-Te. 1998. "Does the Gender Gap in Political Attitudes and Behavior Vary Across Racial Groups?" *Political Research Quarterly* 51: 869–894.

Lincoln, C. Eric. 1974. *The Black Church Since Frazier.* New York: Schocken.

Lincoln, C. Eric, and Lawrence Mamiya. 1990. *The Black Church in the African American Experience.* Durham, N.C.: Duke University.

Linderman, Gerald F. 1987. *Embattled Courage: The Experience of Combat in the Civil War.* New York: Free Press.

Link, Michael W., and Robert W. Oldendick. 1996. "Social Construction and White Attitudes Toward Equal Opportunity and Multiculturalism." *Journal of Politics* 58: 149–168.

Linz, Juan J., and Alfred C. Stepan. 1978. *The Breakdown of Democratic Regimes.* Baltimore: Johns Hopkins University Press.

Lippmann, Walter. 1922. *Public Opinion.* New York: Macmillan.

Lipset, Seymour Martin. 1967. *The First New Nation: The United States in Historical and Comparative Perspective.* Garden City, N.Y.: Doubleday Anchor.

Lipset, Seymour Martin, and William Schneider. 1987. *The Confidence Gap.* Baltimore: Johns Hopkins University Press.

Loewenberg, Gerhard. 1971. "The Influence of Parliamentary Behavior on Regime Stability." *Comparative Politics* 3: 177–200.

Lombardi, W. J., E. T. Higgins, and J. A. Bargh. 1987. "The Role of Consciousness in Priming Effects on Categorization: Assimilation Versus Contrast as a Function of Awareness of the Priming Task." *Personality and Social Psychology Bulletin* 13: 411–429.

Lovell, John P. 1985. *The Challenge of American Foreign Policy: Purpose and Adaptation.* New York: Macmillan.

———. 1992. "The Limits of 'Lessons Learned': From Vietnam to the Gulf War." *Peace & Change* 17: 379–401.

Lovrich, Nicholas P., and Otwin Marenin. 1976. "A Comparison of Black and Mexican American Voters in Denver: Assertive Versus Acquiescent Political Orientations and Voting Behavior in an American Electorate." *Western Political Quarterly* 29: 284–294.

Luker, Kristin. 1984. *Abortion and the Politics of Motherhood.* Berkeley: University of California Press.

MacAllister, Ian. 1999. "The Economic Performance of Governments." In *Critical Citizens: Global Support for Democratic Governance,* ed. Pippa Norris. New York: Oxford University Press.

Macintyre, Ben. 2000. "Blair's Adviser Gives Gore the Common Touch." *London Times*, August 29.

MacKenzie, Scott B., and Richard J. Lutz. 1989. "An Empirical Examination of the Structural Antecedents of Attitude Toward the Ad in an Advertising Pretesting Context." *Journal of Marketing* 53: 48–65.

MacKuen, Michael B. 1983. "Political Drama, Economic Conditions, and the Dynamics of Presidential Popularity." *American Journal of Political Science* 27: 165–192.

MacKuen, Michael B., Robert S. Erikson, and James A. Stimson. 1992. "Peasants or Bankers? The American Electorate and the U.S. Economy." *American Political Science Review* 86: 597–611.

MacManus, Susan, and Carol A. Cassel. 1982. "Mexican-Americans in City Politics: Participation, Representation, and Policy Preferences." *Urban Interest* 4: 57–69.

Maddox, William S., and Stuart A. Lilie. 1984. *Beyond Liberal and Conservative: Reassessing the Political Spectrum*. Washington, D.C.: Cato Institute.

Mandelbaum, Michael. 1981. "Vietnam: The Television War." *Daedalus* (fall): 157–169.

Mann, Thomas E. 1977. *Unsafe at Any Margin: Interpreting Congressional Elections*. Washington, D.C.: American Enterprise Institute.

Mann, Thomas E., and Raymond E. Wolfinger. 1980. "Candidates and Parties in Congressional Elections." *American Political Science Review* 74: 617–632.

Mansbridge, Jane. 1980. *Beyond Adversary Democracy*. New York: Basic Books.

———. 1997. "Social and Cultural Causes of Dissatisfaction with U.S. Government." In *Why People Don't Trust Government*, ed. Joseph S. Nye Jr., Philip D. Zelikow, and David C. King. Cambridge: Harvard University Press.

Margolis, Michael, and Gary A. Mauser. 1989. *Manipulating Public Opinion: Essays on Public Opinion as a Dependent Variable*. Pacific Grove, Calif.: Brooks/Cole.

Martin, Gary. 2000. "Pollsters See GOP Gains among Hispanic Voters." *San Antonio Express-News*, March 2.

Martinez, Andres. 2000. "Two Candidates, Seeking Votes with Salsa." *New York Times*, August 16.

Martinez, Anne. 2000. "Established Latinos More Likely to Support Curbing Immigration." *San Jose Mercury News*, October 15.

Marx, Gary. 1967. *Protest and Prejudice*. New York: Harper and Row.

Mattei, Laura R. Winsky, and Franco Mattei. 1998. "If Men Stayed Home . . . The Gender Gap in Recent Congressional Elections." *Political Research Quarterly* 5: 411–436.

Mattenklott, Axel. 1998. "Werbewirkung im Umfeld von Fernsehprogrammen: Programmvermittelte Aktivierung und Stimmung." [Commercial Effectiveness in the Context of TV Programs: Program-Induced Activation and Mood.] *Zeitschrift für Sozialpsychologie* 29: 175–193.

Maxwell, Carol J. C. 1994. "Meaning and Motivation in Pro-Life Direct Action." Unpublished Ph.D. dissertation, Washington University, St. Louis.

May, Ernest R. 1984. "The Cold War." In *The Making of America's Soviet Policy,* ed. Joseph S. Nye Jr. New Haven: Yale University Press.

Mayhew, David R. 1974. *Congress: The Electoral Connection.* New Haven: Yale University Press.

Mays, Benjamin Elijah, and Joseph William Nicholson. 1933. *The Negro's Church.* New York: Arno Press.

McAdam, Douglas. 1982. *Political Process and the Development of the Black Insurgency.* Chicago: University of Chicago Press.

McCann, James A. 1997. "Electoral Choices and Core Value Change: The 1992 Presidential Campaign." *American Journal of Political Science* 41: 564–583.

McCarty, John A., and L. J. Shrum. 2000. "Measurement of Personal Values in Research." *Public Opinion Quarterly* 64: 271–298.

McClosky, Herbert, and John Zaller. 1984. *The American Ethos: Public Attitudes Toward Capitalism and Democracy.* Cambridge: Harvard University Press.

McDonnell, Patrick J. 2001. "Latinos Recover Optimism Lost in 90s." *Los Angeles Times,* March 11.

McGraw, Kathleen M. 1991. "Managing Blame: An Experimental Investigation into the Effectiveness of Political Accounts." *American Political Science Review* 85: 1133–1158.

———. 1996. "Political Methodology: Research Design and Experimental Methods." In *A New Handbook of Political Science,* ed. Robert E. Goodin and Hans-Dieter Klingemann. New York: Oxford University Press.

———. 1998. "Manipulating Public Opinion with Moral Justification." *Annals, AAPSS* 560: 129–142.

———. 2001. "Political Accounts and Attribution Processes." In *Citizens and Politics: Perspectives from Political Psychology,* ed. James H. Kuklinski. New York: Cambridge University Press.

McGraw, Kathleen M., William Anderson, and Elaine Willey. 2000. "The E-Connection: House Members' Use of the Internet to Explain Impeachment Votes." Paper presented at the annual meeting of the Midwest Political Science Association, Chicago.

McGraw, Kathleen M., Samuel Best, and Richard Timpone. 1995. "'What They Say or What They Do?': The Impact of Elite Explanation and Policy Outcomes on Public Opinion." *American Journal of Political Science* 39: 53–74.

McGraw, Kathleen M., and Clark Hubbard. 1996. "Some of the People Some of the Time: Individual Differences in Acceptance of Political Accounts." In *Political Persuasion and Attitude Change,* ed. Diana C. Mutz, Paul M. Sniderman, and Richard Brody. Ann Arbor: University of Michigan Press.

McGraw, Kathleen M., Milton Lodge, and Jeffrey Jones. 2000. "The Pandering Politicians of Suspicious Minds." Unpublished manuscript.

McGraw, Kathleen M., Richard Timpone, and Gabor Bruck. 1993. "Justifying Controversial Political Decisions: Home Style in the Laboratory." *Political Behavior* 15: 289–308.

McGuire, William J. 1985. "Attitudes and Attitude Change." In *The Handbook of Social Psychology,* vol. 2, ed. Gardner Lindzey and Eliot Aronson. New York: Random House.

Meier, August, Elliot Rudwick, and Francis L. Broderick, eds. 1971. *Black Protest Thought in the Twentieth Century,* 2d ed. Indianapolis: Bobbs-Merrill.

Meier, Kenneth J., and Thomas M. Holbrook. 1992. "'I Seen My Opportunities and I Took 'Em': Political Corruption in the American States." *Journal of Politics* 54: 135–155.

Milbrath, Lester W., and Madan Lai Goel. 1977. *Political Participation,* 2d ed. Chicago: Rand McNally.

Miller, Arthur H. 1974. "Political Issues and Trust in Government, 1964–1970." *American Political Science Review* 68: 951–972.

———. 1979. "Normal Vote Analysis: Sensitivity to Change Over Time." *American Journal of Political Science* 23: 406–425.

Miller, Arthur, and Ola Listhaug. 1999. "Political Performance and Institutional Trust." In *Critical Citizens: Global Support for Democratic Governance,* ed. Pippa Norris. New York: Oxford University Press.

Miller, Arthur H., Martin P. Wattenberg, and Oksana Malanchuk. 1986. "Schematic Assessments of Presidential Candidates." *American Political Science Review* 80: 521–540.

Miller, L. W., Jerry Polinard, and Robert D. Wrinkle. 1984. "Attitudes Towards Undocumented Workers: The Mexican-American Perspective." *Social Sciences Quarterly* 65: 482–494.

Miller, Warren, and J. Merrill Shanks. 1996. *The New American Voter.* Cambridge: Harvard University Press.

Mills, C. Wright. 1959. *The Sociological Imagination.* New York: Oxford University Press.

Mishler, William, and Richard Rose. 1994. "Support for Parliaments and Regimes in the Transition Toward Democracy." *Legislative Studies Quarterly* 19: 5–32.

———. 1996. "Trajectories of Fear and Hope: Support for Democracy in Post-Communist Europe." *Comparative Political Studies* 28: 553–581.

———. 1997. "Trust, Distrust and Skepticism: Popular Evaluations of Civil and Political Institutions in Post-Communist Societies." *Journal of Politics* 50: 418–451.

———. 2001. "What are the Origins of Political Trust? Testing Institutional and Cultural Theories in Post-Communist Societies." *Comparative Political Studies* 34: 30–62.

Mitchell, Alison. 1996. "Clinton Honors Troops That Served in Haiti." *New York Times,* March 19.

Mondak, Jeffrey. 1993. "Source Cues and Policy Approval: The Cognitive Dynamics of Public Support for the Reagan Agenda." *American Journal of Political Science* 37: 186–212.

Moore, David W. 2000. "Booming Economy No Advantage for Gore." Princeton: The Gallup Organization, http://www.gallup.com/poll/release/pr000816.asp.

Moore, Solomon. 2001. "Survey Finds Optimism in State About Race Relations." *Los Angeles Times,* January 4.

Morris, Aldon. 1984. *The Origins of the Civil Rights Movement: Black Communities Organizing for Change.* New York: Free Press.

Morris, Dick. 1999. *The New Prince: Machiavelli Updated for the Twenty-First Century.* Los Angeles: Renaissance Books.

Mueller, John. 1973. *War, Presidents and Public Opinion.* New York: Wiley.

———. 1977. "Changes in American Public Attitudes Toward International Involvement." In *The Limits of Military Intervention,* ed. Ellen Stern. Beverly Hills, Calif.: Sage Publications.

———. 1979. "Public Expectations of War During the Cold War." *American Journal of Political Science* 23: 301–329.

———. 1984a. "Reflections on the Vietnam Protest Movement and on the Curious Calm at the War's End." In *Vietnam as History,* ed. Peter Braestrup. Lanham, Md.: University Press of America.

———. 1984b. "Lessons Learned Five Years After the Hostage Nightmare." *Wall Street Journal,* November 6.

———. 1987. "Presidents and Terrorists Should Not Mix." *Wall Street Journal,* March 31.

———. 1989. *Retreat from Doomsday: The Obsolescence of Major War.* New York: Basic Books.

———. 1994. *Policy and Opinion in the Gulf War.* Chicago: University of Chicago Press.

———. 1995a. *Quiet Cataclysm: Reflections on the Recent Transformation of World Politics.* New York: HarperCollins.

———. 1995b. "The Perfect Enemy: Assessing the Gulf War." *Security Studies* 5: 77–117.

———. 1996. "Policy Principles for Unthreatened Wealth-Seekers." *Foreign Policy* (spring): 22–33.

———. 1999. *Capitalism, Democracy, and Ralph's Pretty Good Grocery.* Princeton: Princeton University Press.

———. 2000a. "Public Opinion as a Constraint on U.S. Foreign Policy: Assessing the Perceived Value of American and Foreign Lives." Paper presented at the annual meeting of the International Studies Association, Los Angeles.

———. 2000b. "The Banality of 'Ethnic War.'" *International Security* 25: 42–70.

———. 2000c. "The Banality of 'Ethnic War': Yugoslavia and Rwanda." Paper presented at the annual meeting of the American Political Science Association, Washington, D.C.

Mueller, John, and Karl Mueller. 1999. "Sanctions of Mass Destruction." *Foreign Affairs* 78: 43–53.

———. 2000. "The Methodology of Mass Destruction: Assessing Threats in the New World Order." In *Preventing the Use of Weapons of Mass Destruction,* ed. Eric Herring. London: Frank Cass.

Murphy, Sheila T., and Robert B. Zajonc. 1993. "Affect, Cognition, and Awareness: Affective Priming with Optimal and Suboptimal Stimulus Exposures." *Journal of Personality and Social Psychology* 64: 723–739.

Murray, Sandra L., Geoffrey Haddock, and Mark P. Zanna. 1996. "On Creating Value-Expressive Attitudes: An Experimental Approach." In *The Psychology of Values: The Ontario Symposium,* vol. 8, ed. Clive Seligman, James M. Olson, and Mark P. Zanna. Mahwah, N.J.: Lawrence Erlbaum Associates.

Murray, Shoon Kathleen, Louis Klarevas, and Thomas Hartley. 1997. "Are Policymakers Misreading Public Views Toward the United Nations?" Paper presented at the annual meeting of the International Studies Association, Toronto.

Myrdal, Gunnar. 1944. *An American Dilemma.* New York: Harper and Row.

National Commission on Civic Renewal. 1998. *A Nation of Spectators: How Civic Disengagement Weakens America and What We Can Do About It.* College Park: University of Maryland.

National Opinion Research Center. 1944. *The Effect of Realistic War Pictures.* Report EW 20, March 13. Chicago: National Opinion Research Center.

National Safety Council (Chicago). 1997. *Accident Facts.*

Nelson, Thomas E., and Zoe M. Oxley. 1999. "Issue Framing Effects on Belief Importance and Opinion." *Journal of Politics* 61: 1040–1067.

Nelson, Thomas E., Zoe M. Oxley, and Rosalee A. Clawson. 1997. "Toward a Psychology of Framing Effects." *Political Behavior* 19: 221–246.

Nelson, William E. 1982. "Cleveland: The Rise and Fall of the New Black Politics." In *The New Black Politics: The Search for Political Power,* ed. Michael B. Preston, Lenneal J. Henderson, and Paul Lionel Puryear. New York: Longman.

Newton, Kenneth. 1997. "Social Capital and Democracy." *American Behavioral Scientist* 40: 575–586.

New York Times. 1996. "Advertising Agencies Make a Pitch to Politicians and Consultants, Urging Them to Clean Up Their Act." April 29.

Nie, Norman H., and Kristi Andersen. 1974. "Mass Belief Systems Revisited: Political Change and Attitude Structure." *Journal of Politics* 36: 541–591.

Nie, Norman H., Jane Junn, and Kenneth Stehlik-Barry. 1996. *Education and Democratic Citizenship in America.* Chicago: University of Chicago Press.

Niemi, Richard G., and M. Kent Jennings. 1991. "Issues and Inheritance in the Formation of Party Identification." *American Journal of Political Science* 35: 970–988.

Niemi, Richard G., John Mueller, and Tom W. Smith. 1989. *Trends in Public Opinion: A Compendium of Survey Data.* Westport, Conn.: Greenwood Press.

Niemi, Richard G., and Herbert F. Weisberg. 1993a. *Classics in Voting Behavior.* Washington, D.C.: CQ Press.

———. 1993b. *Controversies in Voting Behavior,* 3d ed. Washington, D.C.: CQ Press.

Nincic, Miroslav. 1992. *Democracy and Foreign Policy: The Fallacy of Political Realism.* New York: Columbia University Press.

Norpoth, Helmut. 1987a. "The Falklands War and Government Popularity in Britain: Rally Without Consequence or Surge Without Decline?" *Electoral Studies* 6: 3–16.

———. 1987b. "Guns and Butter and Government Popularity in Britain." *American Political Science Review* 81: 949–959.

———. 1996. "Presidents and the Prospective Voter." *Journal of Politics* 58: 776–792.

Norrander, Barbara. 1997. "The Independence Gap and the Gender Gap." *Public Opinion Quarterly* 61: 464–476.

———. 1999. "The Evolution of the Gender Gap." *Public Opinion Quarterly* 63: 566–576.

Norris, Pippa. 2000. "The Impact of Television on Civic Malaise." In *Disaffected Democracies: What's Troubling the Trilateral Democracies?* ed. Susan J. Pharr and Robert D. Putnam. Princeton: Princeton University Press.

Oliver, J. Eric. 2001. *Democracy in Suburbia.* Princeton, N.J.: Princeton University Press.

Oreskes, Michael. 1990. "American Fear of Soviets Declines, Survey Finds." *New York Times,* May 30.

Orren, Gary. 1997. "Fall from Grace: The Public's Loss of Faith in Government." In *Why People Don't Trust Government,* ed. Joseph S. Nye Jr., Philip D. Zelikow, and David C. King. Cambridge: Harvard University Press.

Orwin, Clifford. 1996. "Distant Comparison: CNN and Borrioboola-Gha." *National Interest* (spring): 42–49.

Ottati, Victor C., and Linda M. Isbell. 1996. "Effects of Mood During Exposure to Target Information on Subsequently Reported Judgments: An On-line Model of Misattribution and Correction." *Journal of Personality and Social Psychology* 71: 39–53.

Owen, Diana, and Jack Dennis. 2001. "Trust in Federal Government: The Phenomenon and Its Antecedents." In *What Is it About Government That Americans Dislike?* ed. John R. Hibbing and Elizabeth Theiss-Morse. Cambridge: Cambridge University Press.

Paarlberg, Rob. 1973. "Forgetting About the Unthinkable." *Foreign Policy* (spring): 132–140.

Page, Benjamin I. 1994. "Democratic Responsiveness? Untangling the Links between Public Opinion and Policy." *PS: Political Science and Politics* 27: 25–29.

———. 1996. *Who Deliberates? Mass Media in Modern Democracy.* Chicago: University of Chicago Press.

Page, Benjamin I., and Robert Y. Shapiro. 1983. "Effects of Public Opinion on Policy." *American Political Science Review* 77: 175–190.

———. 1984. "Presidents as Opinion Leaders: Some New Evidence." *Policy Studies Journal* 12: 649–661.

———. 1989. "Education and Manipulation of Public Opinion." In *Manipulating Public Opinion: Essays in Public Opinion as a Dependent Variable,* ed. Michael Margolis and Gary A. Mauser. Pacific Grove, Calif.: Brooks/Cole.

———. 1992. *The Rational Public: Fifty Years of Trends in Americans' Policy Preferences.* Chicago: University of Chicago Press.

Page, Susan. 1999. "Kosovo Can Help or Haunt Gore." *USA Today,* April 14.

Parry, Geraint. 1972. "The Idea of Political Participation." In *Participation in Politics,* ed. Geraint Parry. Totowa, N.J.: Rowman and Littlefield.

Parry, Geraint, George Moyser, and Neil Day. 1992. *Political Participation and Democracy in Britain.* Cambridge: Cambridge University Press.

Parsons, Talcott. 1951. *The Social System.* New York: Free Press.

———. 1966. *Societies.* Englewood Cliffs, N.J.: Prentice Hall.

Pateman, Carole. 1970. *Participation and Democratic Theory.* Cambridge: Cambridge University Press.

Patterson, Thomas E. 1994. *Out of Order.* New York: Alfred A. Knopf.

———. 2000. "Doing Well and Doing Good: How Soft News and Critical Journalism Are Shrinking the News Audience and Weakening Democracy—and What News Outlets Can Do About It." Joan Shorenstein Center, John F. Kennedy School of Government, Harvard University.

Payne, Thomas J., Jane M. Connor, and Gep Colletti. 1987. "Gender-Based Schematic Processing: An Empirical Investigation and Reevaluation." *Journal of Personality and Social Psychology* 52: 937–945.

Peffley, Mark A., and Jon Hurwitz. 1985. "A Hierarchical Model of Attitude Constraint." *American Journal of Political Science* 29: 871–890.

Petrocik, John R. 1989. "An Expected Party Vote: New Data for an Old Concept." *American Journal of Political Science* 33: 44–66.

Petty, Richard E., and John T. Cacioppo. 1986. *Communication and Persuasion: Central and Peripheral Routes to Attitude Change.* New York: Springer-Verlag.

Pew Commission. 1998. *Report of the Task Force on Campaign Reform: Insights and Evidence.* Princeton: Woodrow Wilson School of Public and International Affairs.

Pharr, Susan J. 2000. "Officials' Misconduct and Public Distrust: Japan and the Trilateral

Democracies." In *Disaffected Democracies: What's Troubling the Trilateral Democracies?* ed. Susan J. Pharr and Robert D. Putnam. Princeton: Princeton University Press.

Pharr, Susan J., and Robert D. Putnam, eds. 2000. *Disaffected Democracies: What's Troubling the Trilateral Democracies?* Princeton: Princeton University Press.

Piston, Walter. 1978. *Harmony,* 4th ed. New York: W. W. Norton.

Pitkin, Hanna F. 1967. *The Concept of Representation.* Berkeley: University of California Press.

Piven, France Fox, and Richard Cloward. 1977. *Poor People's Movement.* New York: Pantheon.

Plutzer, Eric, and John F. Zipp. 1996. "Identity Politics, Partisanship, and Voting for Women Candidates." *Public Opinion Quarterly* 60: 30 – 58.

Polinard, Jerry, Robert D. Wrinkle, and Rodolfo de la Garza. 1984. "Attitudes of Mexican Americans Toward Irregular Mexican Immigration." *International Migration Review* 18: 782 – 799.

Polsby, Nelson A. 1993. "Where Do Your Get Your Ideas?" *PS: Political Science and Politics* 26: 83 – 87.

Pomper, Gerald M. 1977. "The Presidential Election." In *The Election of 1976: Reports and Interpretations,* ed. Gerald M. Pomper. New York: David McKay.

———. 1981. "The Presidential Election." In *The Election of 1980: Reports and Interpretations,* ed. Gerald M. Pomper. Chatham, N.J.: Chatham House.

———. 1989. "The Presidential Election." In *The Election of 1988: Reports and Interpretations,* ed. Gerald M. Pomper. Chatham, N.J.: Chatham House.

———. 1997. "The Presidential Election." In *The Election of 1996: Reports and Interpretations,* ed. Gerald M. Pomper. Chatham, N.J.: Chatham House.

Poole, Keith T., and Howard Rosenthal. 1984. "The Polarization of American Politics." *Journal of Politics* 46: 1061 – 1079.

Popkin, Samuel L. 1991. *The Reasoning Voter: Communication and Persuasion in Presidential Campaigns.* Chicago: University of Chicago Press.

Portes, Alejandro. 1984. "The Rise of Ethnicity: Determinants of Ethnic Perceptions Among Cuban Exiles in Miami." *American Sociological Review* 3: 383 – 397.

Powdermaker, Hortense. 1939. *After Freedom: A Cultural History of the Deep South.* New York: Viking.

Powell, Colin L. 1992/93. "U.S. Forces: Challenges Ahead." *Foreign Affairs* 72: 32 – 45.

Preston, Michael, Lenneal Henderson, and Paul Puryear. 1982. *The New Black Politics: The Search for Political Power.* New York: Longman.

Price, Vincent, and John Zaller. 1993. "Who Gets the News? Alternative Measures of News Reception and Their Implications for Research." *Public Opinion Quarterly* 57: 133 – 164.

Prior, Markus. 2001. "Weighted Content Analysis of Political Advertisements." *Political Communications* 18: 335–345.

Przeworski, Adam. 1991. *Democracy and the Market.* New York: Cambridge University Press.

Purdum, Todd S. 2000. "Among Men, It's Bush the Maserati by a Mile." *New York Times,* October 8.

Putnam, Robert D. 1993. *Making Democracy Work: Civic Traditions in Modern Italy.* With Robert Leonardi and Raffaella Y. Nanetti. Princeton: Princeton University Press.

———. 1995. "Bowling Alone: America's Declining Social Capital." *Journal of Democracy* 6: 65–78.

———. 1996. "Robert Putnam Responds." *American Prospect* 25: 26–28.

———. 2000. *Bowling Alone: The Collapse and Revival of American Community.* New York: Simon and Schuster.

Putnam, Robert D., Susan J. Pharr, and Russell J. Dalton. 2000. "Introduction: What's Troubling the Trilateral Democracies?" In *Disaffected Democracies: What's Troubling the Trilateral Countries?* ed. Susan J. Pharr and Robert D. Putnam. Princeton: Princeton University Press.

Quirk, Paul J., and Joseph Hinchliffe. 1996. "Domestic Policy: The Trials of a Centrist Democrat." In *The Clinton Presidency: First Appraisals,* ed. Colin Campbell and Bert A. Rockman. Chatham, N.J.: Chatham House.

Raboteau, Albert. 1978. *Slave Religion.* New York: Orbis.

Ragin, Charles C. 1987. *The Comparative Method: Moving Beyond Qualitative and Quantitative Strategies.* Berkeley: University of California Press.

Ragsdale, Lyn. 1984. "The Politics of Presidential Speechmaking, 1949–1980." *American Political Science Review* 78: 971–984.

———. 1987. "Presidential Speechmaking and the Public Audience: Individual Presidents and Group Attitudes." *Journal of Politics* 49: 704–736.

Rainwater, Lee. 1974. *What Money Buys: Inequality and the Social Meanings of Money.* New York: Basic Books.

Reagan, Ronald. 1983. *Public Papers of the Presidents of the United States.* Washington, D.C.: U.S. Government Printing Office.

Reed, Adolph. 1986. *The Jesse Jackson Phenomenon.* New Haven: Yale University Press.

Reese, Laura A., and Ronald E. Brown. 1995. "The Effects of Religious Messages on Racial Identity and System Blame Among African Americans." *Journal of Politics* 57: 24–43.

Revkin, Andrew C. 1983. *Public Papers of the Presidents of the United States.* Washington, D.C.: U.S. Government Printing Office.

———. 1998. "Coming to the Suburbs: A Hit Squad for Deer." *New York Times,* November 30.

Riches, Julia, and Clyde Wilcox. 2001. "Pills in the Public's Mind: RU 486 and the Framing of the Abortion Issue." Paper presented at the annual meeting of the Western Political Science Association, Las Vegas.

Rielly, John E., ed. 1999. *American Public Opinion and U.S. Foreign Policy, 1999.* Chicago: Chicago Council on Foreign Relations.

Rimmerman, Craig A. 2002. *From Identity to Politics: The Lesbian and Gay Movements in the United States.* Philadelphia: Temple University Press.

Riordan, William L. 1995. *Plunkitt of Tammany Hall.* New York: Signet.

Robinson, W. Peter. 1993. "Lying in the Public Domain." *American Behavioral Scientist* 36: 359–382.

Rogowski, Ronald. 1974. *Rational Legitimacy: A Theory of Political Support.* Princeton: Princeton University Press.

Rohde, David W. 1991. *Parties and Leaders in the Postreform House.* Chicago: University of Chicago Press.

Rokeach, Milton. 1973. *The Nature of Human Values.* New York: Free Press.

———. 1979. *Understanding Human Values: Individual and Societal.* New York: Free Press.

Rose, Richard. 1995. "Freedom as a Fundamental Value." *International Social Science Journal* 145: 457–471.

Rose, Richard, and Ian McAllister. 1990. *The Loyalties of Voters.* London: Sage Publications.

Rose, Richard, and William Mishler. 1994. "Mass Reaction to Regime Change in Eastern Europe: Polarization or Leaders and Laggards?" *British Journal of Political Science* 24: 159–182.

———. 1996. "Testing the Churchill Hypothesis: Popular Support for Democracy and its Alternatives." *Journal of Public Policy* 16: 29–58.

Rose, Richard, William Mishler, and Christian Haerpfer. 1998. *Democracy and Its Alternatives.* Baltimore: Johns Hopkins University Press.

Rosenstone, Steven J., Roy Behr, and Edward Lazarus. 1984. *Third Parties in America.* Princeton: Princeton University Press.

Rosenstone, Steven J., and John Mark Hansen. 1993. *Mobilization, Participation, and Democracy in America.* New York: Macmillan.

Rossiter, Clinton. 1962. *Conservatism in America: The Thankless Persuasion.* New York: Vintage Books.

Rozell, Mark, and Clyde Wilcox. 1996. *Second Coming: The Christian Right in Virginia Politics.* Baltimore: Johns Hopkins University Press.

———, eds. 2000. *The Clinton Scandal and the Future of American Governance.* Washington, D.C.: Georgetown University Press.

Ruddick, Sara. 1980. "Maternal Thinking." *Feminist Studies* 6: 342–347.

Rudolph, Thomas J., and Wendy M. Rahn. 2001. "Community Heterogeneity and Trust in Local Government: Results of an HLM Model." Manuscript, University of Illinois-Urbana-Champaign and University of Minnesota.

Sabato, Larry J. 1997. "The November Vote: A Status Quo Election." In *Toward the Millenium: The Elections of 1996*, ed. Larry J. Sabato. Boston: Allyn and Bacon.

Sanbonmatsu, D. M., and R. H. Fazio. 1991. "Construct Accessibility: Determinants, Consequences, and Implications for the Media." In *Responding to the Screen: Reception and Reaction Processes*, ed. J. Bryant and D. Zillmann. Hillsdale, N.J.: Lawrence Erlbaum Associates.

Sanders, Arthur. 1988. "Rationality, Self-Interest, and Public Attitudes on Government Spending." *Social Science Quarterly* 69: 311–324.

Sapiro, Virginia. 1983. *The Political Integration of Women: Roles, Socialization and Politics.* Urbana: University of Illinois Press.

Sapiro, Virginia, and David Canon. 1999. "Race, Gender, and the Clinton Presidency." In *The Clinton Legacy*, ed. Colin Campbell and Bert Rockman. Chatham, N.J.: Chatham House.

Sapiro, Virginia, with Pamela Johnston Conover. 1997. "The Variable Gender Basis of Electoral Politics: Gender and Context in the 1992 U.S. Election." *British Journal of Political Science* 27: 497–523.

Sapiro, Virginia, and Joe Soss. 1999. "Spectacular Politics, Dramatic Interpretations: Multiple Meanings in the Thomas/Hill Hearings." *Political Communication* 16: 285–314.

Schlenker, Barry R. 1980. *Impression Management.* Monterey, Calif.: Brooks/Cole.

Schlozman, Kay Lehman, Nancy E. Burns, and Sidney Verba. 1999. "What Happened at Work Today? A Multi-Stage Model of Gender, Employment, and Political Participation." *Journal of Politics* 61: 29–54.

Schlozman, Kay Lehman, Sidney Verba, and Henry E. Brady. 1999. "Civic Participation and the Equality Problem." In *Civic Engagement in American Democracy*, ed. Theda Skocpol and Morris Fiorina. Washington, D.C.: Brookings Institution.

Scholz, John T., and Mark Lubell. 1998. "Trust and Taxpaying: Testing the Heuristic Approach to Collective Action." *American Journal of Political Science* 42: 398–417.

Schonbach, Peter. 1980. "A Category System for Account Phases." *European Journal of Social Psychology* 10: 195–200.

Schuman, Howard, and Stanley Presser. 1981. *Questions and Answers in Attitude Surveys: Experiments on Question Form, Wording, and Context.* New York: Academic Press.

Schuman, Howard, Charlotte Steeh, Lawrence Bobo, and Maria Krysan. 1997. *Racial Attitudes in America: Trends and Interpretations*, rev. ed. Cambridge: Harvard University Press.

Schwartz, Shalom H. 1992. "Universals in the Content and Structure of Values: Theoretical Advances and Empirical Tests in 20 Countries." In *Advances in Experimental Social Psychology*, ed. Mark P. Zanna. Orlando, Fla.: Academic Press.

————. 1996. "Value Priorities and Behavior: Applying a Theory of Integrated Value Systems." In *The Psychology of Values: The Ontario Symposium*, vol. 8, ed. Clive Seligman, James M. Olson, and Mark P. Zanna. Mahwah, N.J.: Lawrence Erlbaum Associates.

Schwartz, Shalom H., and Wolfgang Bilsky. 1987. "Toward a Universal Psychological Structure of Human Values." *Journal of Personality and Social Psychology* 53: 550–562.

Schwarz, Benjamin C. 1994. *Casualties, Public Opinion, U.S. Military Intervention: Implications for U.S. Regional Deterrence Strategies*. Santa Monica, Calif.: RAND Corporation.

Sciolino, Elaine. 1993. "Christopher Explains Conditions For Use of U.S. Force in Bosnia." *New York Times,* April 28.

Scott, Marvin B., and Stanford M. Lyman. 1968. "Accounts." *American Sociological Review* 33: 46–62.

Sears, David O. 1983. "The Person-Positivity Bias." *Journal of Personality and Social Psychology* 44: 233–240.

Sears, David O., and Jack Citrin. 1982. *Tax Revolt: Something for Nothing in California*. Cambridge: Cambridge University Press.

Sears, David O., and Carolyn L. Funk. 1990. "Self-Interest in Americans' Political Opinions." In *Beyond Self-Interest*, ed. Jane J. Mansbridge. Chicago: University of Chicago Press.

Seligman, Clive, and Albert N. Katz. 1996. "The Dynamics of Value Systems." In *The Psychology of Values: The Ontario Symposium*, vol. 8, ed. Clive Seligman, James M. Olson, and Mark P. Zanna. Mahwah, N.J.: Lawrence Erlbaum Associates.

Seligman, Clive, James M. Olson, and Mark P. Zanna, eds. 1996. *The Psychology of Values: The Ontario Symposium*, vol. 8. Mahwah, N.J.: Lawrence Erlbaum Associates.

Shanks, J. Merrill, and Warren E. Miller. 1990. "Policy Direction and Performance Evaluation: Complementary Explanations of the Reagan Election." *British Journal of Political Science* 20: 143–235.

————. 1991. "Policy and Performance: The Reagan Legacy in the 1988 Election." *British Journal of Political Science* 21: 129–197.

Shapiro, Robert Y., and Harpreet Mahajan. 1986. "Gender Differences in Policy Preferences: A Summary of Trends from the 1960s to the 1980s." *Public Opinion Quarterly* 50: 42–61.

Shavitt, Sharon, Pamela Lowrey, and James Haefner. 1998. "Public Attitudes Toward Advertising: More Favorable Than You Might Think." *Journal of Advertising Research* 38: 7–22.

Sherif, Muzafer, and Carl Iver Hovland. 1961. *Social Judgment: Assimilation and Contrast Effects in Communication and Attitude Change*. New Haven: Yale University Press.

Sigelman, Lee. 1980. "Gauging the Public Response to Presidential Leadership." *Presidential Studies Quarterly* 10:427–433.

Singh, Surendra N., and Jacqueline C. Hitchon. 1989. "The Intensifying Effects of Exciting

Television Programs on the Reception of Subsequent Commercials." *Psychology & Marketing* 6: 1–31.

Skocpol, Theda. 1996. "Unravelling from Above." *American Prospect* 25: 20–25.

Small, Melvin, and J. David Singer. 1982. *Resort to Arms: International Civil Wars, 1816–1980.* Beverly Hills, Calif.: Sage Publications.

Smith, Tom. 1990. "Ethnic Images." GSS Topical Report No. 19, December 1990. National Opinion Research Center, University of Chicago.

Smith, Tom W. 1985. "The Polls: America's Most Important Problems." *Public Opinion Quarterly* 49: 264–274.

Sniderman, Paul M. 1993. "The New Look in Public Opinion Research." In *Political Science: The State of the Discipline II,* ed. Ada W. Finifter. Washington, D.C.: American Political Science Association.

Sniderman, Paul M., Henry E. Brady, and Philip E. Tetlock. 1994. "The Multi-Investigator Study." *Public Opinion* 1: 10–11.

Sniderman, Paul M., and Richard Brody. 1977. "Coping: The Ethic of Self-Reliance." *American Journal of Political Science* 21: 501–522.

Sniderman, Paul M., and Edward G. Carmines. 1997. *Reaching Beyond Race.* Cambridge: Harvard University Press.

Sniderman, Paul M., Gretchen C. Crosby, and William G. Howell. 2000. "The Politics of Race." In *Racialized Politics: The Debate About Racism in America,* ed. David O. Sears, Jim Sidanius, and Lawrence Bobo. Chicago: University of Chicago Press.

Sniderman, Paul M., and Thomas Piazza. 1993. *The Scar of Race.* Cambridge: Belknap Press/Harvard University Press.

Sniderman, Paul M., Philip E. Tetlock, Edward G. Carmines, and Randall S. Peterson. 1993. "The Politics of the American Dilemma: Issue Pluralism." In *Prejudice, Politics, and the American Dilemma,* ed. Paul M. Sniderman, Philip E. Tetlock, and Edward G. Carmines. Stanford: Stanford University Press.

Sobel, Richard. 1998. "The Polls—Trends: United States Intervention in Bosnia." *Public Opinion Quarterly* 62: 250–278.

Spates, James L. 1983. "The Sociology of Values." *Annual Review of Sociology* 9: 27–49.

Stanley, Harold W., and Richard G. Niemi. 1992. *Vital Statistics on American Politics,* 3d ed. Washington, D.C.: CQ Press.

Steenbergen, Marco, and Bradford S. Jones. Forthcoming. "Modeling Multilevel Data Structures." *American Journal of Political Science.*

Sterngold, Arthur, Rex H. Warland, and Robert O. Herrmann. 1994. "Do Surveys Overstate Public Concerns?" *Public Opinion Quarterly* 58: 255–263.

Stimson, James A. 1984. "Pursuing Belief Structure: A Research Narrative." In *The Research Process in Political Science,* ed. W. Phillips Shively. Itasca, Ill.: F. E. Peacock.

————. 1999. *Public Opinion in America: Moods, Cycles, and Swings,* 2d ed. Boulder, Colo.: Westview Press.

Stimson, James A., Michael B. MacKuen, and Robert S. Erikson. 1995. "Dynamic Representation." *American Political Science Review* 89: 543–565.

Stone, Deborah. 1997. *Policy Paradox.* New York: W. W. Norton.

Stone, Walter J., Ronald B. Rapoport, and Alan I. Abramowitz. 1990. "The Reagan Revolution and Party Polarization in the 1980s." In *The Parties Respond,* ed. L. Sandy Maisel. Boulder, Colo.: Westview Press.

Stouffer, Samuel A. 1955. *Communism, Conformity, and Civil Liberties.* Garden City, N.Y.: Doubleday.

Strobel, Warren P. 1997. *Late-Breaking Foreign Policy: The News Media's Influence on Peace Operations.* Washington, D.C.: U.S. Institute of Peace Press.

Sundquist, James L. 1983. *Dynamics of the Party System: Alignment and Realignment of Political Parties in the United States.* Washington, D.C.: Brookings Institution.

Sykes, Gresham M., and David Matza. 1957. "Techniques of Neutralization: A Theory of Delinquency." *American Sociological Review* 22: 664–670.

Tarrow, Sidney. 1992. "Mentalities, Political Cultures and Collective Action Frames: Constituting Meaning Through Action." In *Frontiers in Social Movement Theory,* ed. Aldon D. Morris and Carol McClurg Mueller. New Haven: Yale University Press.

Tate, Katherine. 1991. "Black Political Participation in the 1984 and 1988 Presidential Elections." *American Political Science Review* 85: 1159–1176.

————. 1993. *From Protest to Politics.* New York: Russell Sage Foundation.

Tedeschi, James T., and Harry Reiss. 1980. "Predicaments and Verbal Tactics of Impression Management." In *Ordinary Language Explanations of Social Behavior,* ed. Charles Antaki. London: Academic Press.

Tetlock, Philip E. 1984. "Cognitive Style and Political Belief Systems in the British House of Commons." *Journal of Personality and Social Psychology* 46: 365–375.

————. 1985. "Towards an Intuitive Politician Model of Attribution Processes." In *The Self and Social Life,* ed. Barry R. Schlenker. New York: McGraw-Hill.

————. 1986. "A Value Pluralism Model of Ideological Reasoning." *Journal of Personality and Social Psychology* 50: 819–827.

————. 1992. "The Impact of Accountability on Judgment and Choice: Toward a Social Contingency Model." *Advances in Experimental Social Psychology* 25: 331–376.

Tetlock, Philip E., Randall S. Peterson, and Jennifer S. Lerner. 1996. "Revising the Value Pluralism Model: Incorporating Social Content and Context Postulates." In *The Psychology of Values: The Ontario Symposium,* vol. 8, ed. Clive Seligman, James M. Olson, and Mark P. Zanna. Mahwah, N.J.: Lawrence Erlbaum Associates.

Theriault, Sean. 1998. "Moving Up or Moving Out: Career Ceilings and Congressional Retirement." *Legislative Studies Quarterly* 23: 419–434.

Tilly, Charles. 1979. *From Mobilization to Revolution.* Reading, Mass.: Addison-Wesley.

———. 1981. *Introduction to Class Conflict and Collective Action,* ed. L. A. Tilly and C. Tilly. Beverly Hills, Calif.: Sage Publications.

Tinkham, Spencer F., and Ruth Ann Weaver-Lariscy. 1994. "Ethical Judgments of Political Television Commercials as Predictors of Attitude Toward the Ad." *Journal of Advertising* 23: 43–57.

Tolleson-Rinehart, Sue. 1992. *Gender Consciousness and Politics.* New York: Routledge.

Tribe, Laurence H. 1990. *Abortion: The Clash of Absolutes.* New York: W. W. Norton.

Tuch, Steven A., and Lee Sigelman. 1997. "Race, Class, and Black-White Differences in Social Policy Views." In *Understanding Public Opinion,* ed. Barbara Norrander and Clyde Wilcox. Washington, D.C.: CQ Press.

Tyler, Tom. 1990. *Why People Obey the Law.* New Haven: Yale University Press.

———. 2001. "The Psychology of Public Dissatisfaction with Government." In *What Is it About Government That Americans Dislike?* ed. John R. Hibbing and Elizabeth Theiss-Morse. Cambridge: Cambridge University Press.

Uhlaner, Carole Jean. 1991a. "Perceived Discrimination and Prejudice and the Coalition Prospects of Blacks, Latinos, and Asian Americans." In *Racial and Ethnic Politics in California,* ed. Byran O. Jackson and Michael B. Preston. Berkeley, Calif.: Institute for Governmental Studies.

———. 1991b. "Political Participation and Discrimination: A Comparative Analysis of Asians, Blacks, and Latinos." In *Political Participation and American Democracy,* ed. William Crotty. Westport Conn.: Greenwood Press.

Uhlaner, Carole J., Bruce E. Cain, and D. Roderick Kiewiet. 1989. "Political Participation of Ethnic Minorities in the 1980s." *Political Behavior* 11: 195–231.

Uhlaner, Carole Jean, and F. Chris Garcia. 1998. "Foundations of Latino Party Identification: Ethnicity and Other Demographic Foundations Among Mexicans, Puerto Ricans, Cubans and Anglos in the United States." Paper presented at the annual meeting of the Western Political Science Association, Los Angeles.

———. 2001. "Learning Which Party Fits: Experience, Ethnic Identity, and the Demographic Foundations of Latino Party Identification." Paper presented at the Conference on Minority Representation: Institutions, Behavior and Identity, Claremont Graduate University, Claremont, Calif.

Uhlaner, Carole Jean, Mark M. Gray, and F. Chris Garcia. 2000. "Ideology, Issues, and Partisanship Among Latinos." Paper presented at the annual meeting of the Western Political Science Association.

United States Department of State. 1998. *Patterns of Global Terrorism, 1997,* April.

U.S. Bureau of the Census. 1996. *Statistical Abstract of the United States: 1996,* 116th ed. Washington, D.C.

Valdez, Armando. 1987. "An Assessment of Data Resources on Latinos in the United States." In *Ignored Voices,* ed. Rodolfo de la Garza. Austin: Center for Mexican American Studies, University of Texas at Austin Press.

Verba, Sidney, Bashirrudin Ashmed, and Anil Bhatt. 1971. *Caste, Race and Politics.* Beverly Hills, Calif.: Sage Publications.

Verba, Sidney, and Norman Nie. 1972. *Participation in America.* New York: Harper.

Verba, Sidney, Kay Lehman Schlozman, and Henry E. Brady. 1995. *Voice and Equality: Civic Voluntarism in American Politics.* Cambridge: Harvard University Press.

Villareal, Roberto E. 1979. *Chicano Elites and Non-Elites: An Inquiry into Social and Political Change.* Palo Alto, Calif.: R & E Research Associates.

Wald, Kenneth. 1992. *Religion and Politics.* Washington, D.C.: CQ Press.

Wald, Kenneth, Dennis Owen, and Samuel Hill. 1988. "Churches as Political Communities." *American Political Science Review* 82: 531–548.

Walton, Hanes, Jr. 1985. *Invisible Politics.* Albany: State University of New York Press.

———. 1997. "African American Republican Partisanship." In *African American Power and Politics: The Political Context Variable,* ed. Hanes Walton Jr. New York: Columbia University Press.

Warren, Mark E. 1998. "Democracy and Associations: An Approach to the Contributions of Associations to Democracy." Paper presented at the annual meeting of the Western Political Science Association, Los Angeles.

Washington Post. 1996. "Cleaning Up the Mudslinging: Ad Executive Proposes Self-Regulating Body to Police Political Commercials," July 30.

Wattenberg, Martin. 1984. *The Decline of American Political Parties, 1952–1984.* Cambridge: Harvard University Press.

Wayne, Stephen J. 1996. *The Road to the White House 1996.* New York: St. Martin's Press.

Weaver, R. Kent. 1986. "The Politics of Blame Avoidance." *Journal of Public Policy* 6: 371–398.

———. 1988. *Automatic Government: The Politics of Indexation.* Washington, D.C.: Brookings Institution.

Weisberg, Herbert F. 1987. "The Demographics of a New Voting Gap: Marital Differences in American Voting." *Public Opinion Quarterly* 51: 335–343.

Weiss, Nancy. 1983. *Farewell to the Party of Lincoln.* Princeton: Princeton University Press.

Welch, Susan. 1977. "Identity in the Ethnic Political Community and Political Behavior." *Ethnicity* 4: 216–225.

Weller, Susan C., and A. Kimball Romney. 1988. *Systematic Data Collection.* Newbury Park, Calif.: Sage Publications.

West, Cornel. 1982. *Prophesy Deliverance! An Afro-American Revolutionary Christianity.* Philadelphia: Westminster.

West, Darrell, and Burdette Loomis. 1999. *The Sound of Money: How Political Interests Get What They Want.* New York: W. W. Norton.

Wilcox, Clyde. 1990. "Racial Differences in Abortion Attitudes." *Public Opinion Quarterly* 54: 248–255.

———. 1992. *God's Warriors.* Baltimore: Johns Hopkins University Press.

———. 1995. *The Latest American Revolution? The 1994 Elections and Their Implications for Governance.* New York: St. Martin's Press.

———. 1997. "Racial and Gender Consciousness Among African-American Women: Sources and Consequences." *Women and Politics* 17: 73–94.

———. 2001. *Onward Christian Soldiers: The Christian Right in American Politics,* 2d ed. Boulder, Colo.: Westview Press.

Wilcox, Clyde, Lee Sigelman, and Elizabeth Adell Cook. 1989. "Some Like It Hot: Individual Differences in Responses on Feeling Thermometers." *Public Opinion Quarterly* 53: 246–257.

Wilcox, Clyde, and Robin Wolpert. 2000. "Gay Rights in the Public Arena." In *The Politics of Gay Rights,* ed. Craig A. Rimmerman, Kenneth Wald, and Clyde Wilcox. Chicago: University of Chicago Press.

Willey, Elaine. 1998. "Explaining the Vote: Legislators' Styles of Interpersonal Influence." Paper presented at the annual meeting of the Midwest Political Science Association, Chicago.

Wilmore, Gayraud. 1983. *Black Religion and Black Radicalism.* Maryknoll, N.Y.: Orbis.

Wittkopf, Eugene R. 1990. *Faces of Internationalism: Public Opinion and American Foreign Policy.* Durham: Duke University Press.

Wright, Gerald C., John P. McIver, Robert S. Erikson, and David B. Holian. 2000. "Stability and Change in State Electorates, Carter through Clinton." Paper presented at the annual meerting of the Midwest Political Science Association, Chicago.

Wrinkle, Robert D. 1991. "Understanding Intra-Ethnic Attitude Variations: Mexican Origin Population Views of Immigration." *Social Science Quarterly* 72: 379–387.

Zaller, John R. 1992. *The Nature and Origins of Mass Opinion.* New York: Cambridge University Press.

Zaller, John, and Stanley Feldman. 1992. "A Simple Theory of the Survey Response: Answering Questions Versus Revealing Preferences." *American Journal of Political Science* 36: 579–617.

Zelnick, Bob. 1999. "Kosovo Crisis Carries Grave Risks for Gore." *USA Today,* April 8.

Zimmerman, E. 1979. "Crises and Crises Outcomes." *European Journal of Political Research* 7: 67–115.

Index

Abortion issue
  conflicting attitudes, 126–136
  gendered effects, 24, 30
  Hyde Amendment, 133
  public opinion, 14, 121–122, 126–128,
    133–135, 126–127, 136
  static nature, 126–136
Abortion pill, 146
Abramowitz, Alan I., 8, 175, 203, 350, 353
Academic surveys, 10, 12
Ad watch journalism, 46
Adams, Greg, 133
Advertising
  code of ethics, 43
  commercial, 43
  comparative, 43, 45
  electronic tools, 13
  influential, 18
  political explanations, 270
  strategic polling, 10
Advocacy polls, 10–11
Affirmative action
  African American opinion, 90–91, 105,
    111–114
  Latino opinion, 90–92
  Proposition 209 (California), 287
  whites' attitudes, 113, 114–115, 118
Afghanistan, 123, 152
African Americans
  abortion view, 14
  affirmative action, 90–91, 105
  bilingual education, 87
  church culture, 18–19, 61–74
  discrimination against, 92, 107–108
  education, 14, 105
  government spending, 195
  organizational membership, 67
  Proposition 187 (California), 288
  Proposition 209 (California), 287

  trust in government, 296, 297, 298
  values ratings, 191, 192
AIDS, 141
Ajzen, Icek, 3
Alesina, Alberto, 294–295
Allen, Richard, 64
Allport, Gordon, 3
Alvarez, R. Michael, 182, 287
American Association for Public Opinion
  Research, 1
American Association of Advertising Agencies
  (AAAA), 44
American Association of Political Consultants,
  45–46
American National Election Study (ANES),
  223
Analysis of variance (ANOVA), 52–53
Annenberg School of Communication, 45
Ansolabehere, Stephen, 244
Armey, Richard, 205
Arms control, 162
Asian Americans, 87, 296
Assimilation hypothesis, 44, 47, 48–50, 57–58
Attitude theory, 4
Attitudes. *See also* Public opinion
  acquired from parents, 17
  components, 3
  core values and, 177–200
  defined, 3, 179
  gender differences, 24–32
  toward government, 301–317
  issue, 191–199
  organization, 173
  political, 18–19, 46–47
  religion-based, 18–19

Baqir, Reza, 294–295
Bartels, Larry, 291
Basic values, 83–85, 123, 174

impeachment, 123, 205, 263, 271
Lewinsky affair, 121, 122, 263, 272, 273
media campaign, 18
nation building policy, 161
pardons, 270
priming, 268
reelection, 254–257
Republican-controlled Congress, 203, 205
viewed by voters, 66, 68–69, 71, 72–73
welfare reform bill, 68
Closed-ended survey, 312
CNN effect, 155–156, 161
Code of ethics, 43
Cold war, 150, 152, 155–157, 161, 169
College admissions criteria, 92, 113
Combs, Sean, 243
Commercial advertising, 43–57
Communism, 320, 324, 333–337
Community heterogeneity, 292–295, 298
Compassion issues, 22, 26
Complete democracy, 319
Concessions, 271–272
Congress, U.S.
    elections, 203–216
    public attitudes toward, 304–312, 315
Conover, Pamela Johnston, 25, 31
Conservatism
    of black churches, 74
    ideological realignment, 208–215
    public trust, 285–286
    values choices, 186, 187
    values ratings, 191, 192
Containment, 162
Contract with America, 11, 205
Contrast effect, 47, 48–50, 57–58
Contrast hypothesis, 44
Converse, Paul, 7, 207
Core values, 8, 174, 177–200
Corrective practices, 277
Correlations, 350
Corruption, 291, 310–311
Crafted talk, 268–269
Credit claiming, 270
Crime, 85–86, 290
Cronbach's alpha, 354
Cuban Americans
    foreign policy, 94
    ideology, 96–99

as Latinos, 79, 93
party identification, 94–96, 98
social issues, 86
trust in government, 85
Cultural issues
    affirmative action, 90–92
    bilingual education, 87–88
    discrimination, 92–94
    immigration, 88–90
    language policy, 87–88
    Latino and Hispanic, 86–94
Culture, 179, 181
Czech Republic, 320, 328

Damage control tactics, 277
Dawson, Michael, 64
Day care, 30
De la Garza, Rodolfo, 78, 79
Deane, Claudia, 294
Defense issues, 25, 123, 162
DeHoog, Ruth Hoogland, 283–284, 290–291
Democracy, 313–314
Democratic norms, 292
Democratic Party
    African Americans, 65–66, 68–69, 70
    gay rights, 144
    Latino populations, 94–99
    New Deal, 117
    prochoice forces, 134–135
    realignment, 175, 203–216
    support by women, 36, 37, 38–40
Democratic responsiveness, 265
Democratization, 319
Denials, 272
Détente, 150
Diffuse support, 321
DiMaggio, Paul, 295
Discrimination, 92–94, 107–110, 142–145
Distributions, 345–348
Dole, Robert, 68–69, 71, 254
Dowd, Maureen, 268
DuBois, W. E. B., 62
Dukakis, Michael, 247

Easterly, William, 294–295
Easton, David, 179, 321
Economic issues
    attitude gender differences, 26–28